Insurance Law in China

Insurance Law in China

Rui Zheng
Jinlei Zhang
Chenxuan Li

This book was originally published as a monograph in the International Encyclopaedia of Laws/Insurance Law.

Founding Editor: Roger Blanpain
General Editor: Frank Hendrickx
Volume Editor: Herman Cousy

Wolters Kluwer

Published by:
Kluwer Law International B.V.
PO Box 316
2400 AH Alphen aan den Rijn
The Netherlands
E-mail: international-sales@wolterskluwer.com
Website: lrus.wolterskluwer.com

Sold and distributed by:
Wolters Kluwer Legal & Regulatory U.S.
7201 McKinney Circle
Frederick, MD 21704
United States of America
Email: customer.service@wolterskluwer.com

ISBN 978-94-035-3323-0

e-Book: ISBN 978-94-035-3324-7
web-PDF: ISBN 978-94-035-3325-4

The Authors

Dr. Rui Zheng received his Ph.D. from Swansea University of United Kingdom (U.K.). He is currently an associate professor and Director of Maritime Law Division at the School of Law, Shanghai Maritime University of China. His principal teaching and research interests lie in contract law, maritime law, insurance law (IL), sales law and arbitration law in both China and U.K. He is a member of China Insurance Law Association and the Deputy Secretary-General of the Insurance and Legal Committee of China Shipowners Association. He is also a member of the working group entrusted by the Ministry of Transportation of China on the revision of China Maritime Code.

Dr. Jinlei Zhang was awarded Ph.D. from Swansea University of U.K. She is currently an associate professor at the School of Law and also serving as the Dean of College of International Collaboration at Dalian Maritime University of China. She is involved in the teaching of the following modules in DMU undergraduate and postgraduate programs: Maritime Law, Marine IL, International Maritime Private Law and Legal English. Her principal research interest is in the field of insurance, particularly marine insurance, but her interests extend broadly throughout maritime law. She published many articles in both domestic and international journals and presided over and participated in over ten research projects, supported by the National Social Science Fund of China, Social Science Fund of Liaoning Province and Ministry of Foreign Affairs, etc.

The Authors

Dr. Chenxuan Li is a lecturer at the School of Law, Shanghai Maritime University. She works in the areas of IL and maritime law. She studied law (L.L.B.) at Shanghai Maritime University, at Durham Law School (L.L.M.), and then at Exeter Law School (Ph.D.). Prior to coming to Shanghai, she was a senior research assistant at the Institute of Maritime Law, University of Southampton. Chenxuan has also worked at the People's Insurance Company of China (PICC) (Shanghai) and Thomas Miller (London), and gained substantial practical experience in insurance and reinsurance.

Table of Contents

Table of Contents

List of Abbreviations

AIR	Agricultural Insurance Regulations
AMHI	Administrative Measures on Health Insurance
AMILI	Actuarial Measures on Investment-Linked Insurance
APIC	Administrative Provisions on Insurance Companies
CBIRC	China Banking and Insurance Regulatory Commission
CC	China Civil Code
CIA	China Insurance Association
CIRC	China Insurance Regulatory Commission
CL	China Company Law
CPIC	China Pacific Insurance Co., Ltd.
CSRC	China Securities Regulatory Commission
FPA	Free from Particular Average
IL	Chinese Insurance Law
MC	China Maritime Code
NPC	National People's Congress of China
NPCSC	Standing Committee of National People's Congress of China
PBC	People's Bank of China
PICC	People's Insurance Company of China
PICC P&C	PICC Property and Casualty Company Limited
RMB	Renminbi (Chinese Currency)
SAR	Special Administrative Region
SIL	China Social Insurance Law
SINOSURE	China Export & Credit Insurance Corporation
SMPL	China Special Maritime Procedure Law
SPC	Supreme People's Court of China
UIR	Unemployment Insurance Regulations
VAT	Value-Added Tax
WTO	World Trade Organization
WA	With Average
WRIIR	Work-Related Injury Insurance Regulations

List of Abbreviations

Preface

As organized and encouraged by Prof. Dr. James Zhengliang Hu of the School of Law of Shanghai Maritime University who is the author of *China Transport Law of the International Encyclopedia of Transport Law* and who assisted us in determining the contents of this monograph on Chinese IL, we made great efforts in preparing this monograph.

The insurance industry and market have been developing rapidly and significantly in the past two decades in China, so do the laws, regulations, administrative measures and provisions on insurance, which are massive and scattered everywhere. We have tried our best to review them and put the things together systematically in this monograph. Hopefully, it will serve as a helpful access to those who are interested in knowing the basic format and structure of the fast-developing Chinese IL.

We acknowledge that only a few cases are cited in this monograph as China is not a country with case law traditions. However, the so-called judicial interpretations issued by the Supreme People's Court (SPC) of China may play a similar role, which are introduced in details in the relevant sections.

We appreciate the Schools of Law of both Shanghai Maritime University and Dalian Maritime University for providing us with the facilities and resources which assisted us in finishing this monograph. We also express our deepest gratitude to our respective families for their continuous support for our academic career.

The writing workload is divided as follows:

- Dr. Rui Zheng: Part I, Part II (Chapters 4–8), Part III, Part IV, Part VII, Part IX.
- Dr. Jinlei Zhang: Part II (Chapters 1–3), Part V, Part VI, Part VIII.
- Dr. Chenxuan Li: General Information.

The law is stated, to the best of our knowledge, as at the end of May 2020.

General Introduction

Chapter 1. General Background Information

§1. GEOGRAPHY AND DEMOGRAPHY

1. China, officially known as the People's Republic of China, is the third-largest country in the world by area after Russia and Canada. Lying in the eastern part of the Asian continent, it occupies approximately 9.6 million square kilometers of land and over 3 million square kilometers of offshore territory, including territorial waters, special economic areas and the continental shelf.[1] On the land, China shares borders with fourteen countries, that is North Korea to the east, Vietnam and Laos to the south, Myanmar, India, Bhutan and Nepal to the southwest, Pakistan, Afghanistan, Tajikistan, Kyrgyzstan and Kazakhstan to the west, and Mongolia and Russia to the north. By the sea, China is bounded by the Bohai, Yellow, East China, and South China Seas, sharing maritime boundaries with South Korea, Japan, Vietnam and the Philippines. Additionally, China possesses a land border of 20,000 kilometers and a coastline of 18,000 kilometers.

All regions of China except Hong Kong, Macao and Taiwan are collectively referred to as "mainland China." Those three regions, under the "one country, two systems" and the "One-China" principle, keep distinct political, legal and economic systems from that of mainland China. For the purpose of this monograph, discussions in this chapter pertain to mainland China, unless otherwise indicated.

§2. CLIMATE AND NATURAL HAZARDS

2. The climate in China varies significantly across its vast territory, which lies between latitudes 18°N and 54°N, and longitudes 73°E and 135°E. When northern China is wrapped by ice and snow, southern China is decorated with flowers and sunshine. In general, dry seasons and wet monsoons dominate the climate, resulting in marked temperature differences between winter and summer.

1. Unless otherwise indicated, the statistics in this section refer to the following websites: The State Council of the People's Republic of China http://www.gov.cn/guoqing/index.htm; National Data http://data.stats.gov.cn/tablequery.htm?code=AD03; World Bank Open Data https://data.worldbank.org/; WHO https://www.who.int/gho/countries/chn/ country_profiles/en/; China Banking and Insurance Regulatory Commission http://www.cbirc.gov.cn/en/view/pages/index/index.html, last accessed on 17 May 2020.

3. Although China has a very agriculturally friendly climate, it suffers from a variety of climate hazards, among which frequent typhoons (China's southern and eastern coasts suffer from about five typhoons per year), damaging floods, droughts and cold waves are the biggest threats to crops and economic growth. Floods and droughts affect huge parts of China, which have become more frequent and severe since the 1990s. This trend is likely to continue because of climate change. Devastating typhoons normally strike the southern and eastern regions of China, such as Guangdong, Fujian and Zhejiang provinces, causing millions or even billions of RMB in damage. The typhoon season lasts from the early summer to early autumn, reaching a peak between June and September.

Beyond climate disasters, another natural hazard—earthquake—also causes widespread financial and life losses, particularly in the western areas of China, such as Tibet, Yunnan, Xinjiang, Sichuan, Gansu and Qinghai provinces.

§3. Population

4. China is the most populated country in the world. By the end of 2019, the National Bureau of Statistics of China reported that the total population in mainland China was 1.4 billion, with a population growth rate of 0.34%. China officially recognizes fifty-six distinct ethnic groups. Among those, Han Chinese is the largest group and constitutes more than 90% of China's population. According to the 2010 census, there were 593,832 foreign nationals residing in mainland China, who mainly came from South Korea, United States (U.S.) and Japan.

§4. Aging and Health

5. Given decades of falling birth rates and steadily rising life expectancy, China now has the fastest aging population. By the end of 2019, about 16.77% of the population was 14 years old or younger, 70.66% were between 15 and 64 years old, and 12.57% were over 65 years old. The hotly debated "one-child policy" was implemented in 1979 for the purpose of controlling the rapid population growth in mainland China. It was abolished in late 2015 in order to improve the population balance. Since then, all couples are allowed to have two children. However, there still may not be a baby boom. In the coming decades, the aging population will pose considerable social and economic challenges for Chinese society.

6. Benefiting from the rapid economic development and the construction of advanced medical facilities, Chinese health conditions have improved significantly during the past half-century. As of 2018, China's life expectancy reached seventy-seven years. Still, many health conditions trouble China: for example, respiratory illnesses caused by widespread air pollution, smoking-related illnesses due to hundreds of millions of cigarette smokers, as well as an increase in obesity among urban youths. According to the World Health Organization, chronic diseases are currently the major cause of death and disability in China; most markedly, deaths from diabetes are rising at an alarming rate.

§5. URBANIZATION

7. China has urbanized at a stunning speed following the implementation of the "reform and opening-up" policy. As of 2019, 60.6% of the total population lived in urban areas, a dramatic increase from 17.92% in 1978. By 2018, 161 cities in China had a population of over one million. Rapid urbanization provides various benefits, such as the rapid growth of Gross domestic product (GDP), the improvement of transportation, education, and medical and health-care services. While on the negative side, Rapid urbanization poses considerable social, environmental and distributional challenges for China. For example, separating millions of young and middle-aged rural laborers from their children and elderly people, exhausting land and mineral resources, and introducing high levels of pollution.

Chapter 2. Political System

8. China is a unified multiethnic country with a unitary socialist political system. The supreme Constitution[2] provides that China "is a socialist state under the people's democratic dictatorship led by the working class and based on the alliance of workers and peasants," and that the state organs "apply the principle of democratic centralism."

§1. Government

9. All state power within China belongs to the people, which is excised through the National People's Congress (NPC) and the local people's congresses on four levels.[3] The primary organs of state power are the NPC, the president and the State Council.

The NPC is the supreme organ of state power and the national legislature. It meets in full session each year and votes on important pieces of legislation. While the NPC is not held, its power is mainly exercised by a permanent body—the Standing Committee of the National People's Congress (NPCSC). Under the Constitution, the NPC has the power to legislate; oversee the operations of the government, the Supreme People's Court (SPC), the National Commission of Supervision, the Supreme People's Procuratorate and the Central Military Commission; and elect the major officers of state. Delegates to the NPC are elected for a five-year term via a multitiered representative electoral system, and all ethnic groups are appropriately delegated.

10. The president and vice president are elected by the NPC. Since 2018, the latest amendment of the Constitution, there was no term limits attached to the presidency. As the head of state, the president, in pursuance of the NPC's and the NPCSC's decisions, has the power to promulgate laws, select and dismiss the premier (vice premiers) as well as the ministers of the State Council, confer state honors, grant presidential pardons, issue mobilization orders, and declare a state of emergency or war. On behalf of China, the president also engages in activities involving state affairs, receives foreign diplomatic representatives, appoints or recalls plenipotentiary representatives abroad, and ratifies or abrogates treaties and important agreements concluded with foreign states. Such appointments and ratifications shall be pursuant to the NPC's and the NPCSC's decisions.

11. The State Council, also known as the Central Government, is the chief administrative authority. It is chaired by the premier, and includes the state councilors, the ministers in charge of the ministries or commissions, the auditor general and the secretary-general. Under the Constitution, the State Council has the power to adopt administrative measures; enact administrative rules and regulations in

---

2. The Constitution of the People's Republic of China was enacted in 1982, with further revisions in 1988, 1993, 1999, 2004 and 2018.
3. Further information can be found on the NPC website www.npc.gov.cn.

accordance with *the Legislation Law*; issue decisions and orders in accordance with the Constitution and the law; direct and manage economic affairs, education, cultural affairs, social welfare, health, local government and so on; as well as perform other responsibilities assigned by the NPC and the NPCSC.

§2. Administrative Divisions

12. As of 2020, China centrally direct administers twenty-three provinces, five autonomous regions and four municipalities, as well as two special administrative regions (SARs). The twenty-three provinces are Heilongjiang, Jilin and Liaoning in the northeast; Hebei and Shanxi in the north; Shandong, Jiangsu, Anhui, Zhejiang, Jiangxi, Fujian and Taiwan in the east; Guangdong and Hainan in the south; Hunan, Hubei and Henan in the center; Yunnan, Sichuan and Guizhou in the southwest; Shanxi, Gansu and Qinghai in the west.

The five autonomous regions—which have a higher population of a particular minority ethnic group along with their local governments—are Inner Mongolia, Guangxi Zhuang, Tibet, Ningxia Hui and Xinjiang Uygur.

The four municipalities are Beijing, Tianjin, Shanghai and Chongqing. Beijing, the capital, is a megacity in North China with over 21 million residents. It serves as the nation's cultural, educational and political center. Shanghai, the largest Chinese city with a population of 24.28 million, is a global center for finance, innovation and transportation.

13. Hong Kong SAR and Macao SAR are highly autonomous under the "one country, two systems" principle, maintaining separate governing and economic systems from that of mainland China. Chinese law does not generally apply in SARs, with the exception of their regional constitutions—*the Basic Law of Hong Kong* and *the Basic Law of Macao*. As a result, Hong Kong SAR and Macao SAR are treated as separate jurisdictions, whose legal systems are based on common law and Portuguese civil law, respectively.

14. Taiwan, a special province of China, is currently administered by the "Taiwan authorities." China sets up the Taiwan Affairs Office of the State Council to coordinate Taiwan-related matters, but affairs including politics, economy and military are dominated by the Taiwan authorities, rather than the Central Government. Taiwan is also considered to be a separate jurisdiction, whose legal system is based on civil law with its origins in the Japanese law and German law.

Chapter 3. Economy

§1. General Information

15. China is the world's second-largest economy and biggest exporter. As of 2019, China's GDP reached USD 14.3 trillion. China also has the world's second-highest number of billionaires with a total wealth of USD 996 billion. By contrast, China's per capital income is only about a quarter of that of high-income countries, and about 373 million Chinese are earning less than USD 5.50 per day.

As the world's fastest-growing major economy, China largely relies on resource-intensive manufacturing, exports, and low-paid labor to keep its high growth; this has led to economic, social, and environmental imbalances. In order to reduce such imbalances, China attempts to shift its economic structure from low-end manufacturing to high-end manufacturing and services, and from investment to consumption.

16. The Renminbi (RMB), one of the world's reserve currencies, is the official currency of China. Since 2006, the RMB exchange rate has been allowed to float in a narrow margin around a fixed base rate determined with reference to a basket of world currencies. China seeks to internationalize RMB since the late 2000s; if it had been successful, the exchange risks of international trade and investment would be reduced, the transformation of economic growth model would be assisted, and the development of domestic financial markets would be boosted. RMB internationalization is in progress: as of August 2019, RMB's share (2.22%) as a global payment currency ranked 5th, after USD (42.52%), EUR (32.06%), GBP (6.21%) and JPY (3.61%).

§2. Insurance Industry

17. The insurance industry of China started its rapid modern development in 1980 when reform and opening-up policy was initiated in China. Initially, the People's Insurance Company of China (PICC) was the only insurance company, with limited insurance products and distribution channels. PICC was directly controlled by the Central Government, and the insurance industry was regulated by the People's Bank of China (PBC).

In 1985, the State Council of China adopted *the Interim Regulations on the Administration of Insurance Enterprises*, provided provisions with regard to the setting up of insurance companies. Accordingly, the Farming Insurance Company of Xinjiang Production and Construction Group was set up in 1986, which had ended the monopoly of PICC, followed by the establishment of Ping An and Pacific insurance companies as shareholding multiline insurers in 1988 and 1991, respectively.

Since the market-oriented reforms initiated in 1992, a rising concern for undertaking financial risks had boosted the insurance demand. At that time, Shanghai was appointed as an experimental city for opening Chinese insurance market. Under *the Temporary Measures for Administration of Foreign-Funded Insurance Institutions* in Shanghai, two foreign insurers had successfully established their affiliates, namely American International Assurance Company and American International Underwriters, Ltd. The number of insurers (domestic and foreign) kept rising since that time, and the average annual growth rate of gross premiums remained at over 30% between 1992 and 2003.

After China's entry into the World Trade Organization (WTO) in 2001, the State Council adopted *the Regulations on the Administration of Foreign Funded Insurance Companies*, which had relaxed many restrictions on foreign insurers with regard to business licenses in China. Accordingly, Munich Re., Swiss Re., and General Cologne Re. established their branches in China in 2003.

As the insurance market opens up further, the insurance industry in China is showing tremendous potential. As of 2019, there were 240 insurance companies. Based on the China Banking and Insurance Regulatory Commission (CBIRC) statistics for 2020 Q1:

- total assets of the insurance companies amounted to RMB 21.7 trillion, up by 5.6% from the beginning of the year;
- assets of property and casualty insurance companies registered RMB 2.4 trillion, up by 2.6% from the beginning of the year;
- assets of life insurance companies reached RMB 17.9 trillion, up by 5.8% from the beginning of the year;
- assets of reinsurance companies recorded RMB 471.4 billion, up by 10.6% from the beginning of the year;
- assets of insurance asset management companies were RMB 65.6 billion, up by 2.5% from the beginning of the year;
- the primary insurance premium income recorded RMB 1.7 trillion, up by 2.3% year on year;
- the claim and benefit payments reached RMB 303.1 billion, down by 8.7% year on year;
- the number of new insurance policies was 10.9 billion, up by 72.1% year on year.

Chapter 4. Sources of IL

18. China's legal system, officially the "socialist legal system," is primarily based on the model of civil law. Its primary sources include statutory law, judicial interpretation and treaties.

According to *the Legislation Law*, laws issued at different levels exist in a hierarchy, as follows:

- *the Constitution*;
- national laws which are issued by the NPC and the NPCSC;
- administrative regulations which are issued by the State Council;
- local regulations which are issued by local people's congresses and their standing committees;
- administrative rules, including: (a) local rules which are issued by the local government and (b) departmental rules which are issued by the ministries and commissions under the State Council, for example, by the CBIRC.

Accordingly, the sources of IL include:

- *the Civil Code* (CC), which was adopted on May 28, 2020 at the third session of the 13th NPC, and will take effect on January 1, 2021; in addition to general provisions and supplementary provisions, the CC, the world's latest modern-day civil law, has six parts on real rights, contracts, personality rights, marriage and family, succession, and tort liabilities; it is widely regarded as a milestone in developing the socialist legal system with Chinese characteristics, and will greatly boost the modernization of China's system and capacity for governance;
- *the IL*, and other relevant laws issued by the NPC and the NPCSC (e.g., *the Maritime Code*, MC);
- administrative regulations issued by the State Council;
- regulations, provisions, guidelines and administrative measures issued by the insurance regulatory authorities and other relevant government institutions;
- judicial interpretations issued by the SPC.

§1. Development of Insurance Legislation

19. Chinese insurance industries have been expanding rapidly since 1980; to regulate this fast-growing market, a comprehensive IL was adopted in 1995. Prior to the passing of IL, there were mainly four laws and regulations relating to insurance, namely *the Economic Contract Law*, *the Property Insurance Contracts Regulations*, *the Interim Regulations on the Administration of Insurance Enterprises* and *the MC*. In 1998, the China Insurance Regulatory Commission (CIRC) was established, and the Commission had broad regulatory authority over the insurance market of China. In order to become a member of the WTO, China made many specific commitments regarding access to its insurance market, such as to use prudential criteria for licensing. To fulfill those commitments, the IL was amended for the first time in 2002, with further amendments in 2009 and 2015.

§2. National Laws

20. The IL represents a basic legal framework for insurance operations in China, which consists of 185 articles in eight chapters. It provides provisions with regard to insurance contract as well as insurance regulation, and the following nine areas with regard to insurance contract are covered:

(1) formation of insurance contracts;
(2) the insured's precontractual duty;
(3) the insurer's precontractual duty;
(4) insurance clauses' constructions;
(5) claims handling and settlement;
(6) assignment of the subject matter insured;
(7) notification of the occurrence of the insured incident;
(8) double insurance; and
(9) liability insurance.

The MC applies specifically to maritime matters, including marine insurance (Chapter 12 of the MC), and the IL applies to insurance matters that are not covered by the MC.

§3. Administrative Regulations

21. Three administrative regulations have been enacted by the State Council, as follows:

(1) *the Compulsory Motor Vehicle Traffic Accident Liability Insurance Regulations*, which is the principal legislation governing the scheme of compulsory motor vehicle traffic accident liability insurance in China;
(2) *the Agriculture Insurance Regulations*, which is the principal legislation to regulate agricultural insurance activities;
(3) *the Administration of Foreign Funded Insurance Companies Regulations*, which provides provisions with regard to the setting up of foreign-funded insurance companies in China, as well as the supervision and administration of the companies.

§4. Departmental Rules

22. The CBIRC, as a ministerial-level agency of the State Council, is the principal regulator for insurance industries. It was established in April 2018 by a merger of the China Banking Regulatory Commission and the CIRC. The CBIRC's primary responsibilities include: (a) promoting uniform regulation and supervision for the banking and insurance industries; (b) maintaining the operation of the banking and insurance industries in a legal, stable and fair manner; (c) protecting financial consumers' legitimate rights; (d) forestalling and defusing financial risks and maintaining financial stability. The Rules and Regulations issued by the CBIRC can be checked on its website.[4]

The PBC, as a central bank, also formulates major draft laws and regulations, and basic prudential regulations for insurance industries. The Rules and Regulations issued by the PBC can be checked on its website.[5]

§5. Judicial Interpretations

23. Judicial precedents are not enforceable in China, and theoretically, each case stands as its own decision. However, the SPC has the authority to issue general interpretations of the law as guidelines to the trials, and such judicial interpretations are nationally enforceable.

There are currently four judicial interpretations that are directly concerned with the trials of insurance cases, three of which will be referred to in the following Chapters as *Interpretation II*, *Interpretation III* and *Interpretation IV*.

4. CBIRC http://www.cbirc.gov.cn/en/view/pages/index/index.html.
5. People's Bank of China http://www.pbc.gov.cn/en/3688006/index.html.

Chapter 5. Dispute Resolution

§1. Jurisdiction and Choice of Law

24. The People's Courts of China are the judicial organs of the state, which exercise judicial power at four levels. That is, with hierarchy, the primary, intermediate, high people's courts and the SPC. In addition, there are four special people's courts respectively which deal with cases involving military, maritime, railway and forestry matters.

The primary, intermediate, high people's courts and the SPC all have jurisdiction as courts of first instance over civil cases, including insurance litigation, in accordance with the amount of a dispute and the influence of the case. In general, the primary courts act as the first instance courts in most insurance cases. For cases involving marine insurance, the maritime courts act as the first instance courts, and the Special Maritime Procedure Law (SMPL) will be applied.

As regards territorial jurisdiction, a lawsuit brought on an insurance contract dispute will usually be under the jurisdiction of the court where the domicile of the defendant or the insured object is located. In the case of a dispute arising from a property insurance contract, if the subject-matter insured is a transport vehicle or goods that were in transit, the case may be under the jurisdiction of the court at the place where the transport vehicle is registered, the place of destination or the place where the insurance accident occurs. In the case of a personal insurance contract dispute, the case is under the jurisdiction of the court where the insured is domiciled.

25. In terms of choice of law, for an insurance contract concluded within mainland China, and where both the insurance applicant and insurer are Chinese entities or citizens, Chinese law will usually be applied compulsorily.

§2. Litigation

26. The litigation procedure for insurance disputes is no different from the other kinds of civil disputes, and *the Civil Procedure Law* and *Interpretation of the SPC on the Application of the Civil Procedure Law* will be applied. Cases are decided within two instances of trial in the people's courts. From a judgment or verdict of first instance, any party may appeal to the appellate court at the higher level. The judgment or verdict of the appellate court is binding. The remedy for a binding judgment and verdict is legal review, but this procedure is rarely initiated.

27. Pursuant to *Interpretation II*, for insurance disputes, the insurer shall bear the burden of proof under certain conditions. For example, if the parties concerned have any dispute over the scope and content of the inquiry at the time of concluding the insurance contracts, the insurer shall bear the burden of proof.

28. In terms of time limit, for life insurance, the time limit is five years which shall be counted from the day when the insured or beneficiary knew or should have known the occurrence of the insured accident; for non-life insurance (excludes marine insurance), the time limit is two years which shall be counted from the day when the insured or beneficiary knew or should have known the occurrence of the insured accident; for marine insurance, the time limit is two years, which shall be counted from the occurrence of the insured accident.

§3. Arbitration

29. Insurance companies often choose arbitration as their dispute resolution method, and the most popular arbitration institution in China is the China International Economic and Trade Arbitration Commission (CIETAC).

Article 7 of *the Interpretation of the SPC on Certain Issues Concerning the Application of the Arbitration Law* states that an arbitration agreement will be invalid if the parties thereto agree that disputes may be resolved either through submission to an arbitration institution for arbitration or by filing an action with a people's court, unless one of the parties applies to an arbitration institution for arbitration and the other party fails to raise an objection within the time limit specified in Article 20, paragraph 2 of *the Arbitration Law*. As a result, a dispute resolution clause which gives the parties the right to choose either arbitration or litigation may be deemed invalid if either party of the insurance contract refuses arbitration.

The arbitration procedure of insurance disputes is similar to that of other kinds of commercial disputes. The parties shall refer to the arbitration institution's arbitration rules and evidence guidelines in an arbitration procedure. The costs for arbitration are decided by each arbitration institution's rules.

§4. Mediation

30. Mediation is an efficient way of settling disputes, and costs much less than litigation and arbitration. The mediation agreement concluded by the parties to insurance disputes will take place under the mediation of a mediation organization or mediators. The parties may apply to the court with jurisdiction to confirm the validity of the mediation agreement, with the signatures and seals of the organization or mediators. A confirmed mediation agreement will have enforceability.

In 2012, the former CIRC and the SPC jointly issued the Notice of the SPC and the CIRC on Carrying Out Pilot Work of Establishing the Mechanism for Linking Insurance Dispute Litigation with Mediation in Some Regions of China to establish a mediation system for insurance litigation in some regions. The local courts and insurance association oversee this system.

In 2016, the former CIRC and the SPC jointly issued the Opinions on Comprehensively Advancing the Building of the Mechanism Linking Litigation with Mediation for Insurance Disputes, which expanded the scope of the regions carrying out the above mediation system to include all municipalities and all provincial capitals (capitals of autonomous regions).

Chapter 6. Consumer Protection

31. The principal legal framework for insurance consumer protection in China consists of: the CC, the IL and *the Protection of Consumer Rights and Interests Law*.

Pursuant to Article 17 of the IL, the insurer shall sufficiently warn the insured of any clause that excludes the insurer's liability under the insurance contract at the time of signing the contract, if the insurer fails to give such warnings, that exclusion clause will be invalid; and Article 30 provides that if there is a dispute between the insurer and the insured or beneficiary about a specific clause, that clause shall be interpreted in favor of the insured and beneficiary.

32. The CBIRC plays an important role in protecting the insurance consumer's rights. In 2019, the CBIRC released the Guidelines on Strengthening the Development of Consumer Rights and Interests Protection System and Mechanism in Banking and Insurance Institutions. The guidelines are designed to further enforce the responsibility of banking and insurance institutions to protect consumer rights and interests, and strengthen the consumer rights protection of the banking and insurance industry, which covers the following four aspects:

(1) *System.* Insurance institutions are required to integrate the protection of consumer rights and interests into all aspects of corporate governance.
(2) *Mechanism.* Insurance institutions should strengthen the decision-making, implementation and oversight mechanism of consumer rights and interests protection, effectively reinforce the management of business operations, and entrust the internal audit to function its role to rectify wrongdoings in consumer rights and interests protection and have the board of supervisors perform its duty in overseeing the performance of relevant duties at the governance level.
(3) *Supervision.* The supervisory authorities should strengthen the guidance and supervision on the development of consumer rights and interests protection system and mechanism in insurance institutions in their respective jurisdictions, incorporate the development of such system and mechanism into the supervisory assessment of consumer protection, and take the assessment results as an important reference for comprehensive supervisory rating, allocation of supervisory resources and adoption of supervisory measures.
(4) *Industry self-discipline.* The CIA is required to set up Consumer Rights and Interests Protection Committee to bring their professional advantages into full play, so as to enhance the self-governance capability of the insurance industry in consumer protection.

Part I. Insurance Company

Chapter 1. Insurance Companies: Their Forms

33. Insurance companies are companies which are established in accordance with the relevant laws and regulations, and specialized in insurance business. They collect the premiums, establish the insurance funds and provide the insurance protection to the society, while making profit.

Article 10 of the IL provides that an insurer refers to an insurance company which enters into an insurance contract with an applicant and is obliged to make indemnity or pay insurance benefits under the contract.

§1. Commercial Insurance Company

34. In China, unless otherwise indicated, insurance company normally refers to commercial insurance company. Article 3 of the Administrative Provisions on Insurance Companies (APIC) provides that insurance companies shall mean legally registered commercial insurance companies incorporated upon the approval of insurance regulatory authorities.

Unless otherwise provided in the IL, the China Company Law (CL) shall apply to insurance companies. In other words, the basic structure of a commercial insurance company in China could be either a limited liability company or a company limited by shares.

The establishment, alteration and termination of a commercial insurance company shall be examined in details below.

§2. Mutual Insurance Organization

I. Introduction

35. In accordance with Article 2 of *the Tentative Measures for the Supervision and Administration of Mutual Insurance Organizations*, "mutual insurance" refers to the insurance activities whereby entities or individuals with homogeneous risk protection needs enter into contracts to become members of an organization, and contribute insurance premiums to form a mutual assistance fund which shall be liable for compensating the losses caused by the occurrence of an accident agreed in the relevant contract, or be responsible for the payment of insurance benefits in the event that an insured dies; suffers injury, disability or illness; reaches the age or term agreed in the relevant contract; or satisfies other relevant conditions. "Mutual insurance organizations" refer to the organizations that, on the basis of equality, voluntariness and democratic management, are held by all members and provide insurance services for members in the form of mutual assistance and cooperation, including general mutual insurance organizations, professional or regional mutual insurance organizations, and organizations of other forms. Article 40 further provides that the *Measures* apply *mutatis mutandis* to the operation of the insurance business by mutual insurance companies and coinsurance organizations.

There are some general requirements as to the establishment of mutual insurance organizations. First, the name of a mutual insurance organization shall contain the word "mutual" or the words "mutual assistance"; second, mutual insurance organizations shall be established upon approval by the CBIRC, and be registered with the industrial and commercial administrative departments in accordance with the law; third, the procedures for the establishment of mutual insurance organizations shall be governed by the general provisions of the CBIRC on the establishment of insurance companies.

36. There are two typical examples of mutual insurance organization in China. The first is Sunshine Agricultural Mutual Insurance Company, which is the only mutual agricultural insurance company in China approved by the State Council in January 2005 and registered by the State Administration for Industry and Commerce. At present, the company provides more than hundred types of insurance products, including plantation insurance, farming insurance, other property/liability insurance. The total annual premium income is more than RMB 3 million.

The second is China Shipowners Mutual Assurance Association (also known as China P&I Club, CPI or the Association), which was founded in Beijing on 1 January 1984 under the approval of the State Council, and is a non-profit mutual marine insurance organization. The Association safeguards the prestige and interests of its members under the laws and regulations of China, as well as the applicable international laws and practices. The Association is registered as a social organization at the Ministry of Civil Affairs in accordance with regulations of the State Council, and under the supervision and operational guidance of the Ministry of Transport of China. China P&I Club provides its members with a package insurance solution, which includes one-stop claims handling service and a variety of insurance products such as P&I, Hull & Machinery, FD&D, Charterers Liability Covers and War Risks. Over the past thirty-five years, the Association has become an internationalized P&I Club with 188 members and over 65 million GT P&I Entered Tonnage.

II. Members

37. Members of a mutual insurance organization shall refer to the entities or individuals that acknowledge and abide by the articles of association of the mutual insurance organization and purchase insurance from the mutual insurance organization.

38. Members of a mutual insurance organization shall enjoy the following rights:

- attend the general meeting of members (representatives), and exercise the right to vote, to elect, to be elected and to participate in the democratic management of the mutual insurance organization;
- share surpluses in accordance with the articles of association of the mutual insurance organization and the relevant resolution of the general meeting of members (representatives);
- enjoy insurance and related services provided by the mutual insurance organization in accordance with the relevant contracts;
- criticize, put forward suggestions on, and supervise the work of the mutual insurance organization;
- inspect the articles of association, minutes of the general meeting of members (representatives), resolutions of the board of directors (council), resolutions of the board of supervisors, financial and accounting reports and account books of the mutual insurance organization; and
- exercise other rights under the articles of association of the mutual insurance organization.

39. Members of a mutual insurance organization shall perform the following obligations:

- abide by the articles of association of the mutual insurance organization;
- execute the resolutions of the general meeting of members (representatives) and the board of directors (council);
- pay insurance premiums in accordance with the relevant insurance contracts, and be responsible for the mutual insurance organization to the extent of their respective premium contribution, except as otherwise provided by the articles of association;
- refrain from abusing their rights as members to damage the interests of the mutual insurance organization or other members; and
- perform other obligations under the articles of association of the mutual insurance organization.

40. Under either of the following circumstances, the membership of a mutual insurance organization shall be automatically terminated:

- where the relevant insurance contract is terminated; and
- where any of the events prescribed by the articles of association of the mutual insurance organization occurs.

§3. Public-Policy-Oriented Insurance Company

41. A public-policy-oriented company is an insurance company that is established in accordance with relevant national policies to provide protection for certain specialized businesses. A public-policy-oriented insurance company is a company directly invested by the state finance or a commercial insurance agency commissioned exclusively by the state.

42. The risks insured by public-policy-oriented companies normally have a high degree of loss. For this reason, in practice, the premiums charged by them are relatively low. If the business operator incurs losses, the state will compensate them through state finances. Public-policy-oriented insurance mainly includes export credit insurance, investment insurance, agricultural insurance, etc.

For example, for the purpose of promoting Chinese exports of goods, technologies and services, especially high-tech and high-value-added capital products such as mechanical and electrical products, thus further supporting foreign trade and economic cooperation, economic growth, employment, and international balance of payments, the state has funded the establishment of the China Export & Credit Insurance Corporation (SINOSURE). With the independent legal person status, it was officially operated on December 18, 2001, and its service network covers the whole country.

§4. Captive Insurance Company

43. The captive insurance company refers to those insurance companies that are solely invested by a parent company or jointly invested by the parent company and its holding subsidiaries with the approval of the CBIRC to provide property insurance, short-term health insurance and short-term accident insurance only for the parent company and its holding subsidiaries.

44. Captive insurance companies may adopt either of two organization forms of company limited by shares and limited liability company, ensuring the use of words "Captive Insurance" in company names and defining the nature of property insurance. In addition to relevant requirements for insurance companies as specified in laws and regulations, the following requirements shall be met for the establishment of a captive insurance company:

- the registered capital shall match with risks to be undertaken by the company;
- the investor shall be a large-scale industrial and commercial enterprise with outstanding primary business, good profit status and total capital of not less than RMB 100 billion; and
- the investor's industry shall have such characteristics as higher risk concentration, broader distribution and harder risk transfer, and have steady insurance coverage demands and comparatively strong risk management and control abilities.

45. The progress of establishing a captive insurance company is divided into two phases: preparation and opening. Where a captive insurance company applies for an establishment, it shall provide explanation information on risk characteristics, demands, insured business scale, purpose of establishing the captive insurance company, operating mode, administration framework, outsourcing service and other relevant circumstances of the parent company and its holding subsidiaries in addition to the application material to be submitted as specified in relevant laws and provisions; where a parent company and its holding subsidiaries have already invested in the insurance industry, the existing insurance subsidiaries and the business division and functional orientation of the captive insurance companies proposed to be established shall be stated. The opening of a general commercial insurance company applies *mutatis mutandis* to that of a captive insurance company.

46. The business scope of a captive insurance company includes the property insurance and the short-term health insurance and short-term accident insurance for employee of a parent company and its holding subsidiaries. The captive insurance company may carry out insurance and reinsurance business in the place where the parent company and its holding subsidiaries locate; where there is no branch, a resolution for acceptance and claim in a different place and the like shall be submitted. The owners of subject matter of ceded business of reinsurance business of the captive insurance company are limited to the parent company and its holding subsidiaries. The parent company shall strictly abide by its commitments to undertake the risk responsibilities for the captive insurance companies it establishes without any arbitrary changes or cancelation.

47. A captive insurance company shall operate independently according to modern enterprise system, keeping it independent from its parent company in terms of personnel, capital and financial management. In addition to withdrawal of the liability reserve funds in accordance with relevant provisions of the CBIRC, the captive insurance company shall withdraw special reserve funds for disaster and damage prevention in accordance with relevant national provisions. The captive insurance company shall declare related-party transactions in relation to capital with the parent company and its holding subsidiaries in accordance with relevant provisions of the CBIRC. The business statistics of the captive insurance company shall comply with the statistical standard of the CBIRC. The captive insurance company shall neither pay insurance protection funds nor be included in the administration system of insurance protection funds. Where a captive insurance company is insolvent, while the CBIRC orders it to increase its capital funds, the parent company shall take some effective measures to cause the captive insurance company meet the requirements of insurance supervision in terms of capital funds.

Chapter 2. Access to Business-Authorization: Requirements and Procedures

§1. Basic Requirements of Establishment

48. The starting point is that insurance businesses shall be operated by insurance companies established subject to the IL and other insurance institutions specified in laws and administrative regulations. No other entity or individual may participate in insurance business or operate the same in a disguised form.

By Article 67 of the IL, establishment of insurance companies shall be subject to the approval of the CBIRC. When examining the application for the establishment of an insurance company, the CBIRC shall take into consideration the development of the insurance industry and the requirements of fair competition.

Till September 2019, the CBIRC has authorized the establishment of thirteen group (holding) insurance companies, eighty-six property insurance companies, eighty-nine life insurance companies and ten reinsurance companies in China.

49. The following conditions shall be fulfilled for the establishment of an insurance company:

- the main shareholders having the capacity for sustained profitability, a good reputation, not having a record of a major violation of laws or regulations during the more recent three years and having net assets of not less than RMB 20 million;
- having articles of association in compliance with the IL and CL;
- having the registered capital as specified therein;
- having directors, supervisors and senior management personnel with the professional knowledge of their positions and work experience in the business;
- having a sound organizational structure and management system;
- having a place of business that meets the requirements, and having other business-related facilities; and
- other conditions as specified by laws, administrative regulations or the State Council's insurance regulatory authority.

By Article 69 of the IL, the minimum registered capital required for the establishment of an insurance company shall be RMB 20 million. The CBIRC may, based on the scope of business and the size of the insurance companies, adjust the minimum registered capital provided that the same is not lower than the limit specified above. In addition, the registered capital must be paid-in monetary capital.

50. By Article 74 of the IL, subject to the approval of the CBIRC, an insurance company can apply for the establishment of a branch or subbranch in China. The branch or subbranch shall have no legal personality and its civil liability shall be borne by the insurance company.

In respect of establishment of a branch, an insurance company shall lodge an application and satisfy the following conditions:

- it has adequate solvency for the last year and for the consecutive two seasons prior to the application;
- its incorporation management structure is sound and internal control is complete and sound;
- the applicant possesses a perfect branch management system;
- it has conducted a full and thorough research on the feasibility of the branch establishment;
- if it intends to establish a branch other than a provincial branch, then a provincial branch must be established in the first place;
- the applicant has no material administrative penalties records imposed by any finance regulatory authority and no investigation by the CBIRC because of the suspicion of its serious violation of laws in the last two years;
- for applying for the establishment of a branch other than a provincial branch, the provincial branch shall have no material administrative penalties records imposed by any finance regulatory authority within the province, autonomous region or municipality directly under the Central Government where the proposed branch is to be established in the last two years and the other established branches therein shall have no records of insurance administrative penalties in the last six months;
- there is a person in charge of the preparation recognized by the applicant; and
- other conditions specified by the CBIRC.

By Articles 79 and 80 of the IL, an insurance company shall obtain the approval of the CBIRC for the establishment of a subsidiary, branch, subbranch or representative office outside China. If a foreign insurance institution wishes to establish a representative office in the PRC, it shall require the approval of the CBIRC. Such representative office may not engage in insurance business activities.

§2. Application for Establishment

51. By Article 70 of the IL, when applying to establish an insurance company, a written application and the following materials shall be submitted to the CBIRC:

- an application letter for establishment, specifying the name, registered capital and scope of business, etc. of the proposed insurance company;
- a feasibility study report;
- a plan for the preparation of establishment;
- the business licenses or other background information of the investors and their financial accounting reports for the previous year audited by an accounting firm;
- a list containing the names of the person in charge of the preparatory committee and the proposed chairman of the board and managers approved by the investors and those persons' proofs of acceptance; and
- other materials as specified by the CBIRC.

The CBIRC shall examine the application for the establishment of an insurance company, render its decision on whether to grant approval for the preparation of establishment and notify the applicant thereof in writing within six months from the date of acceptance of the application. If it decides to withhold approval, it shall give the reasons therefor in writing.

52. When an insurance company wishes to establish a branch or subbranch, it shall submit a written application and the following materials to the CBIRC:

- a written application for establishment;
- a three-year business development plan for the proposed institution and market analysis materials;
- the resumes of the proposed senior management personnel and the relevant supporting documentation; and
- other materials as specified by the CBIRC.

The CBIRC shall examine the application for the establishment of a branch or subbranch of an insurance company and render its decision on whether to grant approval within sixty days from the date of acceptance of the application. If it decides to grant approval, it shall issue a permit for the branch or subbranch to engage in insurance business. If it decides to withhold approval, it shall notify the applicant in writing and give the reason therefor.

§3. Preparation and Commencement of Business Operations

53. By Article 72 of the IL, the applicant shall complete the preparatory work within one year from the date of receipt of the notice of approval for preparation of establishment. It may not engage in insurance business activities during the preparatory period, and during the preparation period, an insurance company shall not change its major investors.

54. By Article 73 of the IL, if the application meets the conditions for establishment set forth in Article 68 after completion of the preparatory work, it may submit to the CBIRC an application to commence operations. The CBIRC shall render its decision on whether to grant approval for commencement of operations within sixty days from the date of acceptance of the application to commence operation. If it decides to grant approval, it shall issue a permit to engage in insurance business. If it decides to withhold approval, it shall notify the applicant in writing and give the reasons therefor.

For the purpose of commencement of operations, the following materials shall be submitted in triplicate:

- business commencement application;
- resolutions of the general founding meeting, or document or resolution of all shareholders on the consent of application for business start-up in the case of no general founding meeting;
- articles of association;

- names of shareholders and the proportion of shares or capitals they hold or contribute respectively, capital verification issued by an institution of sound credit standing, and a copy of the original bank receipt voucher evidencing payment of the registered capital;
- relevant materials that shareholders shall submit as required by the CBIRC;
- resumes and relevant evidential materials of the proposed directors, supervisors and senior managers;
- setting of company departments and composition of the staff;
- certificates on ownership of or the right of using the business site;
- firefighting certificates as required by authorities at the location of the business site;
- plan of insurance products to be provided; three-year business blueprint, reinsurance plan, medium and long-term asset allocation plan, and important systems of business, finance, legal compliance, risk control, asset management and anti-money laundering;
- report on information construction;
- notice of advance approval of company name; and
- other materials specified by the CBIRC.

55. By Articles 77-78 of the IL, the branch or subbranch of an insurance company that has been granted approval for establishment shall carry out registration procedures with and collect its business license from the administration for industry and commerce on the strength of its permit to engage in insurance business, failing which within six months from the date of obtaining the permit without a legitimate reason will render its permit null and void.

§4. Alteration, Dissolution and Cancelation

I. Alteration

56. In accordance with Article 26 of the APIC, an insurance company shall first obtain the approval of the CBIRC if it intends to alter in the following circumstances:

- change of an insurance company's name;
- change of its registered capital;
- expansion of its business scope;
- split-off and merger of an insurance company;
- amendment of an insurance company's articles of association;
- change of a shareholder who has made more than 5% capital contribution in a limited insurance company, or change of a shareholder who is holding more than 5% shares of an insurance company limited by shares;
- other circumstances specified by the CBIRC.

57. Where an insurance company is subject to any of the following circumstances, it shall report to the CBIRC within fifteen days after such circumstance happens:

- change of a shareholder who has made less than 5% capital contribution of a limited insurance company or change of a shareholder who is holding less than 5% of shares of an insurance company limited by shares, that of a publicly listed insurance company excluded;
- change of the names of its shareholders other than shareholders of listed companies;
- change of the name of a branch; or
- other circumstances specified by the CBIRC.

II. Dissolution and Cancelation

58. In accordance with Article 28 of the APIC, where an insurance company is legally dissolved, it shall obtain approval of the CBIRC in the first place and then submit the following documents in triplicate:

- application for dissolution;
- resolution of the general meeting of shareholders or meeting of shareholders;
- situations of the liquidation organization and its in-charge person;
- liquidation procedure;
- creditor's rights and liabilities arrangement scheme;
- asset distribution plan and asset disposition scheme; and
- other documents required by the CBIRC.

59. In accordance with Articles 29 and 30 of the APIC, in the case of legal dissolution, an insurance company shall set up a liquidation team. The liquidation team shall work under the supervision and guidance of the CBIRC. If the insurance company is canceled in accordance with law, the CBIRC shall form the liquidation team in time by organizing shareholders, relevant authorities and related professionals. The liquidation team shall notify the debtors within ten days and bulletin at least three times in newspapers designated by the CBIRC within sixty days after its formation. The liquidation team shall entrust an accounting firm and law firm of good credit standing to evaluate the assets and liabilities of the company.

60. As to the cancelation of the branches of an insurance company, Article 31 of the APIC provides that approval of the CBIRC shall be obtained and insurance business license of such branches shall become invalid automatically and be turned back within fifteen days from the date on which the cancelation is approved. In addition, where an insurance company consolidates or cancels a branch, it shall make announcement and inform the policyholders, the insured or beneficiaries of the details regarding payment of insurance premiums and drawing of insurance benefits in a written form.

61. Finally, the legally dissolved or canceled insurance company shall dispose of its assets via public auction, contractual transfer or other ways recognized by the CBIRC. The shareholders of a legally dissolved or canceled insurance company shall not distribute the assets of the company or obtain any benefits from the company until the liabilities of insurance contracts have been liquidated. Provided the circumstances trigger the application of Article 2 of *the Enterprise Bankruptcy Law*, an insurance company may apply for restructuring, settlement or bankruptcy liquidation in accordance with that law.

Chapter 3. Operation and Supervision

§1. Operation Rules

I. Scope of Business

62. Article 95 of the IL sets out the scope of business of insurance companies as follows:

- personal insurance business, including life insurance, health insurance and accidental injury insurance;
- property insurance business, including property loss insurance, liability insurance, credit insurance and guarantee insurance; and
- other business related to insurance as approved by the CBIRC.

It shall be noted that an insurance company may not concurrently engage in personal insurance business and property insurance business. However, an insurance company engaging in property insurance business may, with the approval of the CBIRC, engage in short-term health insurance business and accidental injury insurance business.

It goes without saying that an insurance company shall engage in insurance business activities within its scope of business approved by the CBIRC in accordance with the law.

Subject to the approval of the CBIRC, an insurance company may engage in the following reinsurance business for the insurance specified in Article 95 of the IL, namely:

- ceding reinsurance; and
- assuming reinsurance.

II. Rules of Conduct for the Insurance Companies and Their Staffs

63. Article 116 set out thirteen acts that are forbidden by insurance companies and their working personnel in the course of operation of insurance business:

- defrauding the insurance applicant, insured or beneficiary;
- concealing important circumstances pertinent to the insurance contract from the applicant;
- hindering the applicant from performing, or inducing the applicant not to perform the obligation of disclosure;
- offering or promising to offer rebates on insurance premiums or other benefits not specified in the insurance contract to the applicant;
- refusing to perform, in accordance with the law, the obligation to pay insurance indemnities or benefits as specified in the insurance contract;

- deliberately fabricating insured events or insurance contracts or overstating the extent of losses incurred by an insured event that has happened to lodge falsified claims, fraudulently obtain insurance proceeds or obtain other improper gains;
- diverting, retaining or misappropriating insurance premiums;
- engaging, for the purpose of conducting insurance sales activities, an organization or individual that lacks lawful qualifications;
- exploiting its or his/her engagement in the insurance business to seek improper gains for another organization or individual;
- using an insurance agent, insurance brokerage or insurance assessor to engage in illegal activities such as illicitly obtaining fees by engaging in fictitious insurance intermediary business or fabricating cancelation of insurance policies, etc.;
- damaging the goodwill of a competitor through means such as the fabrication and dissemination of false facts, or engaging in other acts of unfair competition to disturb the order of the insurance market;
- divulging the trade secrets of applicant or insured learnt in the course of business activities; or
- committing other acts that violate laws, administrative regulations or provisions of the CBIRC.

64. In addition, to be more specific, in accordance with the APIC, the operation of an insurance company and its branches shall also abide by the following basic rules:

- unless otherwise provided by the CBIRC, no branch of an insurance company may conduct insurance business in trans-administrative regions of provinces, autonomous regions and municipalities directly under the Central Government;
- where an insurance company participates in coinsurance, operates large-scale commercial insurance or master policy business or conducts insurance business in trans-administrative regions of provinces, autonomous regions and municipalities directly under the Central Government through internet or telephone marketing, it shall abide by relevant provisions of the CBIRC;
- an insurance company's business propaganda materials shall be objective, complete, and authentic, and shall state clear its name and address;
- an insurance company shall disclose relevant information as specified by the CBIRC;
- when carrying out business, an insurance company shall follow the principles of fair competition and shall not engage in unfair competition;
- an insurance company shall not fabricate or disperse false facts to damage the reputation of other insurance companies, and shall not squeeze out or obstruct other insurance companies' business operation by taking advantage of the government or its departments, monopoly enterprises or organizations;
- except for reinsurance companies, an insurance company shall establish a customer service department or consultation and complaint department and publicize the hotline number for consultation and complaint, and shall seriously deal with insurance complaints, and inform the complainant of the results in time;
- an insurance company shall establish and improve corporate governance, strengthen internal management, and set up a strict internal control system;

– an insurance company shall establish systems to control and manage its related transactions, and shall report their major related transactions to the CBIRC according to relevant provisions in a timely manner.

III. Rectification and Takeover of the Insurance Companies

65. Article 139 of the IL provides that if an insurance company fails to set aside or carry forward various liability reserves or to reinsure in breach of the IL, or seriously violates this law in the use of funds, the CBIRC may order it to rectify in a time limit and to adjust responsible persons and relevant management personnel. Failure of rectifying within the time limit will trigger the procedures for the rectification.

Articles 140-143 of the IL set out the basic procedures for the rectification:

> First, the CBIRC may decide to select insurance professionals or to designate relevant personnel of the insurance company to compose a group for the rectification of the company. The name of the company to be rectified, reason of rectification, members of the rectification group and the time limit for rectification shall be stated in the decision of rectification with an announcement.
> Second, the rectification group is entitled to monitor the routine business of the rectified insurance company, in which the responsible person and relevant management personnel shall perform their duties under the supervision of the rectification group.
> Third, the original business of the rectified insurance company shall be proceeded in the course of rectification. However, the CBIRC may order it to stop part of its original business, to stop accepting new business or to adjust the use of funds.
> Fourth, where the rectified insurance company has corrected its breach of the IL and resumed normal operation, the rectification group shall report the case to the CBIRC, which shall approve the termination of rectification with an announcement.

66. Article 144 of the IL provides that under any of the following two circumstances, the CBIRC shall take over an insurance company:

(1) a serious shortage of solvency; or
(2) damaging public interests in breach of the IL which may seriously jeopardize or have seriously jeopardized the company's solvency.

The credit-debt relationship of the company being taken over shall remain unchanged.

Articles 145-147 of the IL set out the basic procedures for the takeover:

– the specific measures for the composition of takeover group and the implementation of takeover shall be determined with an announcement by the CBIRC;

- at the expiration of takeover period, the CBIRC may decide to extend the takeover period, which shall not exceed two years;
- where an insurance company being taken over has resumed normal operating capacity at the expiration of takeover period, the CBIRC shall decide to terminate the takeover with an announcement.

67. Where an insurance company being rectified or being taken over is in the circumstance prescribed in Article 2 of *the Enterprise Bankruptcy Law*, the CBIRC may, in accordance with the law, apply to the people's court for the restructure or liquidation of the company.

§2. Solvency Control

68. Article 101 of the IL provides the basic requirement as to solvency control: an insurance company shall have the minimum solvency appropriate to the size of its business and its degree of risk. The difference derived by subtracting an insurance company's admissible liabilities from its admissible assets may not be lower than the figure specified by the CBIRC. If such difference falls below the specified figure, the insurance company shall, as required by the CBIRC, take appropriate measures to reach such figure.

69. In accordance with Articles 97-100 and Articles 102-105 of the IL, seven specific control methods are used:

> First, an insurance company shall deposit 20% of its registered capital as a security in the bank designated by the CBIRC, which shall not be used except for liquidation of the company.
> Second, an insurance company shall, in accordance with the principle of safeguarding the interests of the insured and guaranteeing the solvency, set aside various liability reserves.
> Third, an insurance company shall, in accordance with the CL, set aside provident funds.
> Fourth, an insurance company shall make contributions to an insurance protection fund. Such fund shall be managed centrally and use thereof shall be made in a coordinated manner in the following circumstances:
> - to provide relief to insurance applicants, insureds and beneficiaries when an insurance company is closed or is declared bankrupt;
> - to provide relief to the insurance company that accepts in accordance with the law its life insurance contracts when an insurance company is closed or declared bankrupt; or
> - other circumstances as specified by the State Council.
>
> Fifth, the self-retained insurance premiums of a year of an insurance company engaging in property insurance business may not exceed four times the sum of its paid-in capital and common reserve.
> Sixth, the liability borne by an insurance company for each risk unit, that is the maximum range of loss that may be caused by a single insured event,

may not be more than 10% of the sum of its paid-in capital and common reserve. The portion exceeding the sum shall be reinsured. The demarcation of risk units by an insurance company shall comply with the provisions of the CBIRC. An insurance company's methodology for demarcating risk units and its arrangement for catastrophic risks shall be submitted to the CBIRC for the record.
Seventh, an insurance company shall arrange for reinsurance in accordance with the provisions of the CBIRC and prudently select the reinsurer.

70. To be more specific, in accordance with *the Administrative Provisions on the Solvency of Insurance Companies*, the precise solvency control shall be conducted as follows:

As to the property insurance, the minimum capital of a property insurance company shall be the sum of the minimum capital for the non-life insurance business of the guarantee type and that for the non-life insurance business of the investment type:

- the minimum capital for the non-life insurance business of the guarantee type shall be the bigger one of the following two numbers: (a) of the net premiums of the company in the last accounting year after deducting the business tax and surtaxes, 18% of the amount below RMB 100 million and 16% of the amount above RMB 100 million; or (b) of the average amount of comprehensive indemnity in the last three years, 26% of the amount below RMB 70 million and 23% of the amount above RMB 70 million;
- the minimum capital for the non-life insurance business of the investment type shall be the summation of the minimum capital for risk-based insurance premiums and the minimum capital for investment capital. In particular, the assessment standards for the minimum capital of the non-life insurance business of the guarantee type are applicable to the calculation of the minimum capital for risk-based insurance premiums, while the minimum capital for investment capital shall be the summation of the following two: (a) 4% of the term-end liability reserves of the investment capital of non-life investment insurance products with assumed earnings; and (b) 1% of the term-end liability reserves of the investment capital of other non-life investment insurance products than those with assumed earnings.

As to the life insurance, the minimum capital of a life insurance company shall be the summation of the minimum capital for its long-term personal insurance business and that for its short-term personal insurance business. For this purpose, long-term personal insurance business refers to the personal insurance business with a duration of more than one year; while short-term personal insurance business refers to the personal insurance business with a duration of one year or less:

- the minimum capital for long-term personal insurance business shall be the summation of the following two: (1) 1% of the term-end liability reserves of

investment-linked life insurance products or 4% of the term-end liability reserves of other life insurance products; (2) 0.1% of the risk-based insurance premiums of term death insurance with a duration of less than three years, 0.15% of the risk-based insurance premiums of term death insurance with a duration of three to five years, or 0.3% of the risk-based insurance premiums of term death insurance with a duration of more than five years and other insurance categories.
- the assessment standards for the minimum capital for the non-life insurance business of the guarantee type are applicable to the calculation of the minimum capital for short-term personal insurance business.

As to the reinsurance, the minimum capital of a reinsurance company shall be the summation of the minimum capital for its property insurance business and that for its personal insurance business as calculated according to the abovementioned standards.

71. By Article 138 of the IL, for insurance companies insufficient of solvency, the CBIRC shall list it as the key regulatory target and take the following measures in accordance with the specific circumstance:

- ordering to increase capitals or to reinsurance;
- restriction on business scope;
- restriction on paying dividends to its shareholders;
- restriction on purchasing fixed assets or on operation cost scale;
- restriction on the form and proportion in using funds;
- restriction on the establishment of branch;
- ordering the company to auction bad assets and to transfer insurance business;
- restriction on the salary level of directors, supervisors and senior management personnel;
- restriction on commercial advertising; or
- ordering to stop accepting new business.

§3. Supervision of Tariffs and Insurance Conditions

72. By Article 114 of the IL, an insurance company shall draft its insurance terms and premium rates in a fair and reasonable manner in accordance with the provisions of the CBIRC and may not harm the lawful rights and interests of the insurance applicants, insureds and beneficiaries.

73. By Articles 135 and 136 of the IL, the insurance terms and premium rates of an insurance related to the public interests, of a compulsory insurance in accordance with the law or of a newly developed life insurance, shall be approved by the CBIRC, which shall follow the principles of protection of public interests and of prevention of unfair competition in the examination, and the terms and premium rates of other insurances shall be filed with the insurance supervision and control authority. Where an insurance company violates laws, administrative regulations or relevant provisions prescribed by the CBIRC in its terms and premium rates, the

CBIRC shall order the insurance company to stop use and rectify such terms and premium rates in a time limit, and in serious cases, may forbid the insurance company to file new insurance terms and premium rates in a specific term.

74. The CBIRC can conduct an on-site inspection of an insurance company as to whether the insurance clauses and premium rates it uses have been submitted for approval or filing in accordance with the laws and regulations. An insurance company shall cooperate with the CBIRC in the on-site inspection, and provide relevant documents and materials as required by the CBIRC.

Other basic requirements as the supervision of tariffs and insurance conditions are set out in the APIC as follows:

- an insurance company shall not utilize advertising or any other propaganda means to provide misleading information on their insurance clauses, service quality, etc.;
- an insurance institution shall clearly show policyholders such information as liability exemption, surrender, charge deduction, cash value, hesitation period, etc. in the insurance contract in accordance with the IL and provisions of the CBIRC;
- an insurance company shall not partially compare the insurance clauses and premium rates with those of similar insurance companies or with interest rates on deposits of financial institutions.

Chapter 4. Liability Reserves and Investments

§1. Liability Reserves

75. Article 98 of the IL provides that insurance companies shall make allocations to various liability reserves based on the principle of protecting the interests of the insured and guaranteeing solvency. Specific measures for the allocation and carryover of funds to liability reserves by insurance companies shall be formulated by the CBIRC.

If an insurance company that engages in life insurance business closes in accordance with the law or is declared bankrupt in accordance with the law, its liability reserve must be transferred to another insurance company that engages in life insurance business. If it fails to reach a transfer agreement with another insurance company, the CBIRC shall designate an insurance company that engages in life insurance business to accept the transfer. The transfer or the designated acceptance of the transfer by the CBIRC of the liability reserve shall safeguard the lawful rights and interests of the insureds and beneficiaries.

76. For non-life insurance business, in accordance with *the Administrative Measures for the Reserves for Non-life Insurance Business of Insurance Companies*, the reserves include undue liability reserve, reserve for outstanding losses and other liability reserves as provided for by the CBIRC, e.g. reserve for the pending cases and for the settlement expenses of claims:

- the "undue liability reserve" refers to the reserve that is drawn for the undue insurance liabilities that have not been terminated on the reserve evaluation date, including the reserve that is drawn by an insurance company for the undue insurance liabilities under the insurance contracts with an insurance term of one year or less, and the reserve that is drawn for the undue insurance liabilities under the insurance contracts with an insurance term of more than one year;
- the "reserve for outstanding losses" refers to the reserve that is drawn by an insurance company for the pending cases, including the reserve for the pending cases that already occurred and have been reported to the insurance company, the reserve for the pending cases that already occurred but have not been reported to the insurance company yet as well as the reserve for the expenses of settlement of claims;
- the reserve for the pending cases that already occurred and have been reported to the insurance company refers to the reserve that is drawn by the insurance company for the cases that insurance accidents already occurred, for which claims have been filed to the insurance company, but the claims are still unsettled;
- the reserve for the settlement expenses of claims refers to the reserve that is drawn for the possible settlement expenses of outstanding claims, of which the part drawn for the expertise fee, attorney's fee and loss inspection fee directly incurred in the concrete claim cases shall be the reserve for the direct expenses of settlement of claims; the other part drawn for the fees not directly incurred in the specific claim cases shall be the reserve for the indirect settlement expenses of claims.

77. For life insurance business, in accordance with the Administrative Measures on Health Insurance (AMHI), an insurance company that engages in health insurance business shall, in accordance with relevant provisions of the CBIRC, submit the actuarial report or reserve evaluation report of the previous year.

As for claim cases the insurance accidents of which have already occurred and claims have been made but have not been settled, the insurance company shall withdraw the reserve for the pending cases that have already occurred and have been reported to the insurance company. The reserve for the pending cases that have already occurred and have been reported to the insurance company shall be prudently drawn through the case-by-case estimation method, average compensation method or other reasonable methods. The insurance company that withdraws a reserve for the pending cases that have already occurred and have been reported through actuarial methods other than the case-by-case estimation method shall make a detailed statement of the basic data, parameter setting and estimation methods of the actuarial method, and specify the sources of the basic data, data quality and the reliability of the calculation results of the reserve. Where the chief actuary cannot determine the reliability of the estimation method, or the experience data of relevant businesses is less than three years, the reserve for the pending cases that have already occurred and have been reported shall be withdrawn in pursuance of the claimed amount.

As for the indemnity or benefit for which an insurance accident has occurred but no claim has been made, the insurance company shall withdraw a reserve for the pending cases that have already occurred but have not been reported to the insurance company. The insurance company shall, by considering the factors such as the nature of the risks, experience data of the insurance products, etc., adopt at least any two of such methods as the chain ladder method, the average compensation method, the method of progression of reserve, the B-F method and the loss ratio method to evaluate the reserve for the pending cases that have already occurred but have not been reported, and shall determine the optimal evaluation value according to the maximum value of the evaluation results. The insurance company shall make a detailed statement of the basic data, calculating methods and parameter setting of the reserve for the pending cases that have already occurred but have not been reported; and specify the sources of the basic data, data quality and the reliability of the calculation results of the reserve.

Where the chief actuary believes that the basic data cannot guarantee the reliability of the calculating results, or the experience data of the relevant business is less than three years, a reserve for the pending cases that have already occurred but have not been reported will be withdrawn at the rate of not less than 10% of the total sum of payment of actual indemnity for that accounting year.

As for short-term health insurance, an insurance company will withdraw an unearned premium reserve. The unearned premium reserve for short-term health insurance will be withdrawn through any of the following methods: (a) the 1/24 gross premium method (on a monthly basis); (b) the 1/365 gross premium method (on a daily basis); (c) the unearned premium reserve may be drawn through any other more prudent and reasonable method according to the distribution of risks, and the reserve withdrawn shall not be lower than that withdrawn through method 1 or 2, whichever is smaller.

The method for accruing the unearned liability reserve for long-term health insurance will be based on the relevant provisions of the CBIRC.

§2. Investment of Insurance Funds

78. Article 106 of the IL sets out the basic principle which must be followed by an insurance company when investing its fund. It provides that an insurance company shall apply its fund in a sound manner and comply with the principle of safety. The investment of an insurance company's capital shall be limited to the following:

- bank deposits;
- purchase and sale of negotiable securities, such as bonds, stocks and securities investment fund shares;
- investment in immovable property; and
- other means of capital investment as specified by the State Council.

79. The Administrative Measures for the Use of Insurance funds set out the specific measures as to the investment of insurance company's fund and summarized as follows.

> First, the "insurance funds" refer to the capital, provident funds, undistributed profits, various reserves and other funds of insurance group (holding) companies and insurance companies denominated in Renminbi and foreign currencies.
> Second, insurance funds shall mainly be used for serving the insurance industry. The use of insurance funds must be in compliance with the principle of prudence and safety and satisfy the regulatory requirements on solvency, and asset-liability management and full risk management shall be adopted subject to the nature of the insurance funds in order to realize such insurance funds are used in an intensified, specialized, standardized and market-oriented manner.
> Third, where insurance funds are used for bank deposits, the deposit bank shall be a commercial bank that meets the following conditions:
> - its capital adequacy ratio, net assets and provision coverage conform to the regulatory requirements;
> - it has a standardized governance structure, sound internal control system and good business performance;
> - it has committed no substantial act in violation of laws and regulations in the recent three years; and
> - it has a credit rating in accordance with the criteria as required by the CBIRC.
>
> Fourth, bonds invested with insurance funds shall reach the credit rating level assessed by a credit rating institution recognized by the CBIRC and be in compliance with the provisions, which mainly include government bonds, financial bonds, enterprise (corporate) bonds, non-financial enterprise debt financing instruments and other bonds that meet the requirements.

Fifth, stocks invested with insurance funds shall mainly include those publicly offered and listed for trade and those privately offered to specific targets by listed companies. Investment in stocks by insurance funds is divided into general stock investment, major stock investment, acquisition of listed companies and others, which are subject to differentiated regulation by the CBIRC according to different circumstances.

Sixth, where insurance funds invest in a securities investment fund, the fund manager shall meet the following conditions:

- has good corporate governance and sound risk control mechanism;
- performs the contract according to the law and protects the legitimate rights and interests of investors;
- has been established for more than one year (inclusive);
- has committed no major illegal act in the recent three years; if it has been established for less than three years, it has not committed major violations of laws and regulations since its establishment;
- has established an effective firewall system between the securities investment fund and the asset management business for specific customers; and
- has a stable investment team with good historical investment records, and a relatively stable asset management scale or fund shares.

Seventh, real estates invested in with insurance funds refer to land, buildings and other fixtures attached to the land. The specific measures shall otherwise be provided by the CBIRC.

Eighth, equity invested in with insurance funds shall be that of a company limited by shares and that of a limited liability company, which has been established and registered within the territory of China according to the law and not publicly listed on the stock exchanges.

Ninth, insurance funds may be invested in asset-backed securities, venture capital funds and other private funds, and the establishment of professional insurance asset management institutions such as real estate, infrastructure and pension.

Tenth, unless otherwise stipulated by the CBIRC, an insurance group (holding) company or insurance company engaging in the use of insurance funds may not commit the following acts:

- deposit into non-banking financial institutions;
- purchase of stocks subject to "special treatment" or "special treatment with a warning on delisting risk" by stock exchanges;
- investment in enterprise equities and immovable property, which are not in compliance with the state's industrial policies;
- direct involvement in real property development and construction;
- provision of a guarantee or release of loans (excluding individual insurance policy pledge loans) to other parties or individuals by means of investment assets from the use of investment funds; and
- other investment activities prohibited by the CBIRC.

80. With the approval of the CBIRC and China Securities Regulatory Commission (CSRC), an insurance company may establish an insurance asset management company. In engaging in securities investment activities, an insurance asset management company shall comply with laws and administrative regulations such as *the Securities Law*.

An insurance asset management company may use investment varieties within the scope of the use of insurance funds as fundamental assets to engage in the business of insurance asset management products in accordance with the relevant provisions of the CBIRC.

Where an insurance group (holding) company or insurance company makes entrusted investments or purchases insurance asset management products, the insurance asset management institution shall, in accordance with the contract, disclose to the parties concerned the information including the flow of funds, investment management, fund custody, risk management and major emergency incidents in a timely manner, and ensure the truthfulness, accuracy and completeness of the information disclosed.

The insurance asset management institution shall determine, based on the market, the standard for the provision of revenues from management fees and terms of payment under the contract with the custody or investment institutions in respect of the scale and category of assets under its custody, characteristics of product risks, investment performance and other factors.

Chapter 5. Accountancy

81. Articles 85-88 of the IL set out the basic rules as to the insurance companies' financial management as follows, for which accountancy is an important part:

- an insurance company shall employ professionals to set up the actuarial reporting system and the compliance reporting system;
- an insurance company shall, in accordance with the provisions stipulated by the CBIRC, submit the relevant reports, statements, documents and information. The solvency report, financial report, actuarial report, compliance report and other relevant reports, statements, documents and information must be truthful in recording insurance matters, and shall not have false records, misleading statements and material omissions;
- an insurance company shall, in accordance with the provisions stipulated by the CBIRC, properly keep complete books, original certificates and related information concerning business activities. The term to keep the books, original certificates and relevant information specified in the preceding paragraph shall be no less than five years for an insurance period of less than one year, and ten years for insurance period of more than one year starting from the date of termination of the insurance contract;
- an insurance company shall report the hire and dismissal of accountant firms, asset valuation agencies, credit rating agencies and other intermediary service agencies to the CBIRC and shall state the reason for the dismissal of accountant firms, asset valuation agencies, credit rating agencies and other intermediary service agencies.

82. In China, *the Accounting Law* is the fundamental law as to any accountancy activities. In addition to that, four specific rules apply to the accountancy of insurance activities, namely:

(1) the impairment of assets such as the post-loss goods produced by an original insurance contract issued by an insurer shall be subject to *the Accounting Standards for Enterprises No. 1—Inventories*;
(2) a contract issued by an insurer to the insured on a risk other than the insurance risks shall be subject to *the Accounting Standards for Enterprises No. 22—Recognition and Measurement of Financial Instruments* and *the Accounting Standards for Enterprises No. 37—Presentation of Financial Instruments*;
(3) a reinsurance contract issued or held by an insurer shall be subject to *the Accounting Standard for Enterprises—Reinsurance Contracts*;
(4) an original insurance contract issued or held by an insured shall be subject to *the Accounting Standard for Enterprises—Original Insurance Contracts*.

Chapter 6. Taxation

§1. Business Tax

83. In China, insurance companies are undoubtedly regarded as taxpayers and insurance business clearly falls within the taxation scope of the finance and insurance industries.

Business tax is the most important tax that needs to be paid by the insurance company. In addition to the *Tax Collection Administration Law and Its Implementing Rules, the Administrative Measures for Business Tax Returns for the Finance and Insurance Industries* are directly related to the issue.

84. In order to properly pay the business tax, first, the business turnover of the insurance company must be ascertained. There are two categories:

(1) premiums collected from clients when handling primary insurance; and
(2) saving business.

For the first one, the business turnover shall be all the payments collected from clients by a taxpayer undertaking insurance business, i.e. all the premiums collected from the insured.

For the second one, where an insurance company derives economic benefits by collecting savings (i.e., the insurance company collects interest of the funds paid by the insured as premium income and return the principal to the insured when the insurance period expires), the turnover of its savings business shall be the average balance of the savings within the period for taxpaying multiplied by the one-year monthly deposit interest published by the PBC. The average balance of savings shall be 50% of the sum of the savings balance at the beginning of the period and that at the end of the period.

85. The starting time of taxable period for an insurance business shall be the date when the premium income or the voucher of premium income collecting is obtained.

86. The insurance company shall file tax returns electronically with the competent tax authorities in accordance with the relevant provisions of *the Tax Collection Administration Law* and its Implementing Rules and submit the statements required by Article 23 of *the Administrative Measures for Business Tax Returns for the Finance and Insurance Industries*. All the statements shall be completed in accordance with the instructions and be submitted to the state and local taxation authorities in triplicate, respectively. After having signed for and accepted the statements from the insurance company, the tax authorities shall return one copy to the insurance company and preserve the other two.

§2. VALUED-ADDED TAX

87. According to Article 1 of *the Interim Value-Added Tax Regulations*, entities and individuals selling goods, providing labor services of processing, repairs or maintenance or selling services, intangible assets or real property in China, or importing goods to China, shall be identified as taxpayers of value-added tax (VAT), and shall pay VAT under these *Regulations*. Insurance companies are undoubtedly taxpayers for the purpose of these *Regulations*. The basic tax rate is 17% for the insurance business, unless otherwise stated.

88. Some of the insurance businesses may enjoy the following tax incentives:

– premium income from life insurance products run by insurance companies for more than one year may exempt from paying VAT. For this purpose, life insurance for more than one year refers to life insurance, pension annuity insurance and other annuities that return the principal and interest for one year or more and health insurance coverage for one year or more;
– agriculture insurance is exempt from paying VAT;
– export insurance and reinsurance are exempt from postal services, delivery services, insurance services for exported goods;
– reinsurance services provided by domestic insurance companies to overseas insurance companies that are completely consumed overseas are exempt from VAT.

Part II. Insurance Contract (General)

Chapter 1. Generalities

§1. CONCEPT

89. A contract is an agreement between natural persons, legal persons or other organizations with equal status, to establish, modify or terminate the relationship of civil rights and obligations. An insurance contract is such a kind of contract. Article 2 of the IL provides that in this law, the term "insurance" means the commercial insurance activities where an insurance applicant pays an insurance premium to an insurer under an insurance contract and the insurer pays indemnity for the property loss caused by the occurrence of a potential incident specified in the insurance contract or pays insurance benefits when the insured dies, becomes disabled or sick or reaches a specified age, time limit or any other condition specified in the contract.

The core contents of an insurance contract are as follows: the insurer shall assume the obligation to pay compensation or insurance benefits within the scope of insurance liability and shall have the right to collect insurance premiums as agreed in the contract; the insurance applicant shall assume the obligation to pay the insurance premium in accordance with the contract and enjoy the right to claim the insurance money.

§2. CATEGORIES

I. Valued & Unvalued Insurance Contract

90. According to whether the insurable value of the subject-matter insured is determined or not, the insurance contract can be divided into valued insurance contract and unvalued insurance contract.

91. Article 55 of the IL provides that where the insurance applicant and insurer agree upon the insurable value of the subject-matter insured and include it in the contract, when the subject-matter insured suffers any loss, the insurable value as agreed upon shall be the standard for calculation of indemnity. And where the insurance applicant and insurer fail to agree upon the insurable value of the subject-matter insured, when the subject-matter insured suffers any loss, the actual value of the subject matter insured at the time of occurrence of the insured incident shall be the standard for calculation of indemnity. Since human life and body cannot be measured by money, this classification applies only to property insurance and not to life insurance.

After the establishment of valued insurance contract, once an insurance accident occurs, the insured value determined by both parties in the insurance contract should be used as the basis for calculating the amount of indemnity paid by the insurer. If an insurance accident causes the total loss of the subject-matter insured, the insurer shall pay all the insurance premiums stipulated in the contract regardless of the actual losses of the subject-matter insured. In real life, valued policies are mostly applicable to property insurance contracts, the subject-matter insured of which is the property whose value is sometimes difficult to be determined.

92. The parties to an unvalued insurance contract do not agree on the value of the subject-matter insured at the attachment of the contract, and the estimation of the actual value of the subject-matter insured is left to be determined after the occurrence of an insurance accident. General property insurance, especially fire insurance, adopts the form of unvalued insurance contract. In the case of an unvalued insurance contract, if the loss of the subject-matter insured cannot be estimated by market price, the value of the subject matter of insurance can also be determined by replacement cost or other valuation methods.

II. Full-Insurance, Under-Insurance & Overinsurance Contract

93. According to the proportion between the insured amount and the insurable value, the insurance contract is divided into the full-insurance contract, the under-insurance contract and the overinsurance contract.

94. Full-insurance contract refers to the contract in which the insured amount agreed upon in the contract is equal to the actual value of the subject-matter insured. The insured amount is determined according to the value of the subject-matter insured. Therefore, the verification of the actual value of the subject-matter insured is very important for determining the insured amount and the rights and obligations of the parties to the insurance contract. In the case of full-insurance contract, when an insurance accident occurs, if there is a total loss, the insurer shall pay the full amount according to the insured amount. If the insurance subject is partially damaged, the insurer will pay the actual loss.

95. Under-insurance contract refers to the contract in which the insured amount is lower than the actual value of the subject-matter insured. In normal cases, the insured amount should be equal to the actual value of the subject-matter insured, but sometimes the insured may take the underinsurance in order to reduce part of the insurance premium considering his financial ability. Article 55 of the IL provides that if the insured amount is less than the insurable value, except as otherwise provided for by the contract, the insurer shall be liable to pay indemnity according to the proportion between the insured amount and the insurable value, which means the rest should be borne by the insured.

96. Overinsurance contract refers to the contract in which the insured amount is higher than the actual value of the subject-matter insured. There are many reasons for the overinsurance, some of which are due to the fact that the actual value of the subject-matter insured is overestimated; some of which are because the insurance period is long, the value of the subject-matter insured is reduced during the validity period of the insurance contract, so that its value is lower than the insured amount, and some of which are due to the repeated insurance. According to Article 55 of the IL, the insured amount shall not exceed the insurable value. In the case of excess, the excess shall be invalid, and the insurer shall refund the corresponding amount of insurance premium to the insurance applicant.

III. Property Insurance & Personal Insurance Contract

97. According to the different nature of the subject-matter insured, the insurance contract can be divided into property insurance contract and life insurance contract. This is the most common classification of insurance in the IL, and it is also the classification method adopted by the IL. Article 12(4) of the IL stipulates that property insurance shall be a type of insurance which takes property and interests related thereto as the subject-matter insured. In property insurance, the insurer assumes the liability of the loss of the property insured caused by natural disasters and accidents. The IL stipulates the following types of property insurance. First, the property loss insurance takes the tangible property as the subject-matter insured, including the enterprise property insurance, the family property insurance, the motor vehicle insurance, the cargo transportation insurance, and the construction engineering insurance, etc. Second, the liability insurance is the insurance which takes the insured's liability to the third party as the subject-matter insured, including the public liability insurance, the employer liability insurance, the product liability insurance, the professional liability insurance, the pollution liability insurance, etc. Third, the credit insurance is the insurance which takes the economic losses suffered by the creditor because the debtor cannot pay or refuse to pay the debt as the subject-matter insured, including the commercial credit insurance, the export credit insurance, the credit card insurance, etc. Lastly, the guarantee insurance is the insurance which takes the economic losses suffered by the right holder due to the behavior of the insured.

98. Article 12 of the IL provides that personal insurance shall be a type of insurance which takes the life and body of human beings as the subject-matter insured. In the personal insurance, the insurer pays the agreed insurance benefits to the insured when they die or become disabled due to accident, disaster, illness, aging, etc. or when they retire. According to Article 95 of the IL, personal insurance includes but not limited to life insurance, health insurance and accidental injury insurance. Life insurance contract is a kind of insurance contract which takes the insured's death or survival as the condition for payment of insurance money. It can be further divided into the term life insurance contract, the whole life insurance contract, the pure endowment insurance and the endowment insurance. Health insurance refers to the personal insurance in which the payment of insurance benefit is conditioned upon losses incurred for health reasons, including but not limited to disease insurance, medical insurance, disability income insurance, and health-care insurance. Accidental injury insurance refers to the personal insurance in which the payment of insurance benefit is conditioned upon the occurrence of an accident resulting in the death or disability of the insured or the occurrence of any other accident as agreed upon in the insurance contract.

IV. Indemnity Insurance & Contingency Insurance Contract

99. This classification is based on the different purpose of establishing the insurance contract. Indemnity insurance contracts are established to indemnify the insured for the economic losses incurred by the insurable accidents, which is, when the insurable accidents occur, the insurer evaluates the losses suffered by the insured and indemnifies them within the insured amount stipulated in the insurance contract. Property insurance contract generally belongs to indemnity insurance contract. In an unvalued insurance contract, as long as the actual loss of the insured is caused by the insurance accident, all indemnity can be obtained, but the amount of indemnity shall not exceed the insured amount. In a valued insurance contract, even if the insured value agreed upon in the contract is lower than the actual value at the time of total loss, the insured will still receive the corresponding indemnity, but his losses cannot be fully indemnified.

100. Contingency insurance contract belongs to the non-indemnity insurance contracts. Most life insurance contracts are contingency insurance contracts because the life or body of the insured as the subject matter of the life insurance contract cannot be measured by money, so when an insurance accident occurs, the personal injury suffered by the insured cannot objectively obtain real "indemnity." At the same time, in life insurance and other insurance contracts, as long as the insurer is still alive at the expiration of the insurance period, the insurer should pay the insurance benefit agreed upon in the contract to the insurer. In this case, there is neither accident nor loss. The payment of insurance benefit is only to meet the special needs of the insured. Therefore, in life insurance contracts, the amount of insurance is generally determined according to the needs of the insured and their ability to pay premiums. Once an insurance accident occurs or the insurance period expires, the insurer will fulfill the obligation to pay the benefit as agreed upon in the insurance contract. Because the insurer should pay a fixed amount in the life insurance contract, the life insurance contract is also known as the "valued policy."

V. Original Insurance & Reinsurance Contract

101. According to the order of the insurer's insurance liability, the insurance contract can be divided into the original insurance contract and the reinsurance contract. The original insurance contract refers to the original insurance contract concluded between the insurer and the insured. In order to distinguish them conveniently, the original insurance contract is generally called the first insurance contract, and the reinsurance contract is called the second insurance contract. According to the original insurance contract, the insurer is directly liable for the damage suffered by the insured due to the insurance accident. That is to say, the insurance liability assumed by the insurer arises from the insurance contract concluded between the insurer and the insured, and the liability assumed by the insurer has the nature of "beginning." In the original insurance contract, the parties are the insurer and the insured.

102. Reinsurance contract refers to the insurance contract in which after the direct insurer and the insured enter into an insurance contract, the direct insurer insures part of its insured liability to another insurer. In the case of reinsurance, the direct insurer will transfer part of the insurance premium to the reinsurer. When the insured event occurs, the reinsurer will bear part of the liability. In this sense, reinsurance is the insurance of insurance. The reinsurance method is conducive to diversifying risks, not only fully protecting the insured but also conducive to the stable operation of the insurance company, so that it will not suffer a huge loss due to huge claims.

103. The original insurance contract and reinsurance contract are two independent legal relationships. When the direct insurer takes part of his insurance liability as the subject matter to insure with the reinsurer, no matter how much the responsibility the reinsurer bears, the insured of the original insurance can only rely on the original insurance contract to be indemnified, and may not be reimbursed by the reinsurer.

VI. Non-compulsory Insurance & Compulsory Insurance Contract

104. In general, pursuant to Article 11 of the IL, the principle of voluntariness shall be followed in the conclusion of an insurance contract, except as otherwise provided by laws and administrative regulations. In other words, the conclusion of insurance contract in China is in general non-compulsory.

105. However, compulsory insurance is mandatory for individuals and businesses that want to engage in certain risky activities. In China, the following types of insurance are legally compulsory:

- motor vehicle third-party liability;
- nuclear liability;
- liability for marine oil pollution, injury to passengers and damage to their personal property;
- third-party liability for travel agents;
- professional indemnity for insolvency practitioners, insurance agencies and brokers, and accounting firms;
- environmental liability for the following industries: non-ferrous metal mining and smelting industry, lead battery manufacturing, leather and related products manufacturing, chemical and chemical products manufacturing;

– work-related personal accident insurance for miners working underground within the coal industry, and for workers engaged in dangerous operations within the construction industry.

§3. CHARACTERISTICS

I. Contract on Morality

106. The so-called contract on morality refers to the agreement between the parties based on the trust of the other party. For this reason, a contract of morality can also be called a contract to a person; that is, a contract is concluded based on the trust of someone. From a legal point of view, the trust must be the relying party doing something based on his inner belief. There are two reasons for emphasizing this: first, the relying party believes in the psychological state of the other party, but if he does not show it through certain behaviors, it cannot be known to the other party; second, although the relying party has the inner belief, if there is no external behavior, there will be no effect on the substantive interests, so the law cannot intervene. Based on this principle, the law raises the integrity of the two parties to an insurance contract to a statutory obligation. Anyone who fails to abide by the principle of good faith will fundamentally shake the foundation of the contract. For example, if the insured fails to fulfill the obligation of truthful disclosure, the insurer has the right to terminate the insurance contract; if the insurer fails to explain the clauses of the contract which exempt him from liability to the insured, the clauses are invalid. In fact, this characteristic of insurance contracts is rooted in the information asymmetry of the insurance market. It is precisely because of this asymmetry that it is more important to legally protect the trust relationship between the parties. As is known to all, in insurance practice, whether an insurer insures a subject matter and how the premium is determined depend mainly on the information provided by the insured and whether the insured applies for insurance or not depends mainly on the insurer's commitment to the insurance liability and interpretation of the insurance contract which determines the importance of the principle of good faith in insurance.

II. Contract of Mutual Obligation

107. According to the relationship between the rights and obligations of both parties in the contract, the contract is generally divided into two types: contract of mutual obligation and contract of single obligation. Contract of mutual obligation refers to a contract in which both parties have rights and obligations to each other, such as a sales contract. Contract of single obligation is a contract in which one party only undertakes obligations and the other party only holds rights, such as a loan contract.

Whether an insurance contract is a contract of single obligation or contract of mutual obligation has always been controversial in academic circles. In our opinion, insurance contract is a contract of mutual obligation. In the insurance contract, on the one hand, the insured has the obligation to pay the insurance premium; on the other hand, he has the right to be indemnified when the insurance accident occurs. Some scholars believe that when the insurance contract is established, only the insured has the obligation to pay the insurance premium unilaterally, and the insurer only assumes the obligation of indemnity only in the event of an insurance accident. In other words, if the insurance accident does not occur, the insurer does not have to bear this obligation; therefore, they believe that the insurance contract belongs to the contract of single obligation. Obviously, this kind of statement is to separate the rights and obligations of both parties completely. They make the mistake of seeing the trees without seeing the forest. The correct approach should be to take the insurance contract as a whole from the perspective of the contract law, instead of being partial. As a whole, if the insured wants to obtain indemnity from the insurer, he must pay the insurance premium; and if the insurer wants to collect the insurance premium, he must bear the indemnity obligation after the damage of the subject-matter insured, which is completely consistent with the characteristics of the contract of mutual obligation.

III. Contract of Indemnity

108. According to whether the parties need to pay the corresponding consideration while gaining certain benefits, the contract is generally divided into paid contract and unpaid contract. In the insurance contract, the insurer must bear the insurance liability while obtaining the insurance premium; while the insured obtains the insurance guarantee, the insured must also pay the corresponding insurance premium as the consideration. Therefore, the insurance contract should be a contract of indemnity. But the indemnity nature of insurance contract is different from other contracts, which is embodied in the following two aspects:

(1) the indemnity nature of insurance contract is ambiguous. As mentioned earlier, the insured must fulfill the obligation to pay premiums after the establishment of the insurance contract, while the equivalence of the insurer's payment is ambiguous, and his performance of the obligation to indemnify is conditional; that is, the occurrence of an insurance accident is the condition. If the insurance accident does not occur, the insurer in fact does not have to indemnify the insured equivalently at all; if an insurance accident occurs, the amount of indemnity paid by the insurer will sometimes exceed the premium paid by the insured;
(2) the indemnity nature of the insurance contract has integrity and relativity. The equivalence of the insurer's contribution to all insured is generally equivalent to that of all the insured.

It should be pointed out that the indemnity nature of insurance contract should comply with the mandatory provisions of law, which is determined by the nature of insurance contract and the purpose of insurance operation. The insurer, as a risk bearer, cannot indemnify the loss suffered by the insured due to the occurrence of the insurance accident without collecting the insurance premium.

IV. Contract upon Speculation

109. The insurance accident stipulated in the insurance contract is an uncertain event. Whether it happens, when it happens and how much damage it suffers after it happens are contingent. It is worth noting that insurance contracts are different from gambling. An insurance contract requires the insured to have an insurable interest in the subject-matter insured. When the subject-matter insured is damaged, the insurer shall indemnify for the insured's loss rather than increase the insured's benefit; otherwise it should be an unjust enrichment, while gambling is to make a few bets and agree on a particular one. When an accident occurs, the potential benefits of obtaining the agreed amount are not used to indemnify the damage suffered at the time of the accident.

V. Contract of Adhesion

110. A contract of adhesion is a contract in which one party can only express its consent or disagreement with the contract terms previously determined by the other party. That is to say, one party can only accept the clauses of the contract as a whole or refuses to conclude the contract. In the process of signing an insurance contract, due to the technical nature of the insurance act, the insurer usually provides the insurance contract terms that he has drawn up beforehand to the insured. For the standard clauses, the insured has only the freedom to accept or not, and has no right of negotiation on its contents.

111. This feature of insurance contracts is contrary to the value orientation of the principle of autonomy of will. Therefore, it is necessary to provide relief through certain channels and legislation is one of them. The IL has adopted a targeted regulatory approach to the accessibility of insurance contracts. Article 17 of the IL provides that where an insurance contract is concluded using the standard clauses of the insurer, the insurer shall provide an insurance policy with the standard clauses attached and explain the contents of the contract to the insurance applicant. For those clauses exempting the insurer from liability in the insurance contract, the insurer shall sufficiently warn the insurance applicant of those clauses in the insurance application form, the insurance policy or any other insurance certificate, and expressly explain those clauses to the insurance applicant in writing or verbally. If the insurer fails to make a warning or express explanation thereof, those clauses shall not be effective.

VI. Contract of Continuity

112. Contract of continuity refers to the contract that the content of the contract relationship cannot be completed by one payment, but by continuing to be realized. Interinsurance contract is a typical contract of continuity. The duration of the contract of continuity varies according to the types of insurance. Generally speaking, the life insurance contract has a longer period and the transportation insurance contract has a shorter period. Based on the continuity of insurance contracts, the principle of change of circumstances is generally applicable.

113. Article 5 of the IL provides that where the degree of peril of the subject-matter insured greatly increases during the term of validity of the contract, the insured shall notify the insurer in a timely manner as agreed upon in the contract, and the insurer may increase the insurance premium or rescind the contract as agreed upon in the contract. If the insurer rescinds the contract, it shall refund the insurance premium to the insurance applicant after deducting the receivable part from the day of commencement of insurance liability to the day of contract rescission as agreed upon in the contract. And if the relevant condition based on which the insurance premium rate is determined changes, and thus the degree of peril of the subject-matter insured evidently decreases or the insurable value of the subject-matter insured evidently decreases, the insurer shall reduce the insurance premium, and refund the corresponding amount of insurance premium calculated by day to the insurance applicant.

114. Because of the continuity of the insurance contract, the insurance contract pays special attention to the relationship of mutual trust between the parties. Once the trust between the parties is lost, or the basis of trust no longer exists due to objective reasons, it is difficult to maintain the original contract relationship. The law allows the parties to change or terminate the contract.

§4. Basic Principles of Insurance Contract Law

I. Principle of Good Faith

A. Definition

115. The principle of good faith, in the sense of contract law, is the basic requirement for the parties to the contract to be honest and trustworthy from the formation, performance to the termination of the contract. Specifically, it means that the parties should not induce the other party to enter into a contract by means of deception before the formation of the contract. They should actively fulfill their obligations under the contract according to the nature, purpose and trading habits of the contract and should fulfill their obligations of notification, assistance and confidentiality in accordance with the trading habits after the termination of the contract. The principle of good faith is of particular importance in the IL. Under this principle, parties to insurance activities are given more stringent obligations and responsibilities.

B. Reasons for the Existence of the Principle of Good Faith

1. Asymmetric Information of the Parties to the Insurance Contract

116. Asymmetric information in the commercial field refers to the inequality between the parties in transaction in terms of information mastery. Asymmetric information is a common phenomenon in commercial activities. For example, people who sell household appliances know more about the quality of the goods or the background of the manufacturer than the purchaser. The general manager of the listed company knows more about the actual performance of the company than ordinary investors. The greater the degree of information asymmetry is, the greater the likelihood of moral hazard, which will not only decrease the efficiency of economic activity but also may cause traders to lose some benefits. In the insurance market, this information asymmetry is more obvious. On the one hand, the insurer has less knowledge of the situation of the insured. It is impossible for the insurer to acquire a comprehensive knowledge of the insured's moral standards, assets and subject-matter insured when he faces a large number of insured. Whether the insurance company underwrites a subject-matter insured, to a large extent, is based on the insured's representation. This inevitably provides the possibility for some insured to conceal real information or even make up or provide false information to implement fraud. On the other hand, due to the limitations of the applicant's own condition and knowledge level, it is difficult for them to make a correct evaluation of the insurer's financial strength, credit rating, operating status, service quality and development prospects. Such information can only be obtained from the insurer's introduction. It is precisely because of this information asymmetry that the law requires the parties to the insurance contract to follow the principle of good faith and fulfill their obligations.

2. The Basis on Which the Insurance Contract Depends

117. An insurance contract is different from a general commercial contract. It is considered a contract of adhesion in the civil law system and a contract of credit in the Anglo-American legal system. However, no matter how it is identified, the formation and performance of such a contract are entirely dependent on the trust between the two parties. For the insurer, he needs to conduct a risk assessment of the subject-matter insured in order to determine whether or not to underwrite it and to determine the level of the insurance premium, which can only depend on the insured's representation of the subject-matter insured.

3. Differences in the Status of the Parties to the Insurance Contract

118. As a commercial contract, the legal status of the parties to the insurance contract should be equal. According to the principle of autonomy of will, the rights and obligations can be determined through mutual agreement. However, in reality, the status of the insurer and the insured are different in certain situations. In terms of the formation of the contract, since the formatted documents are adopted, for insured, the degree of understanding of the IL and the familiarity with the insurance business are certainly not as good as those of the insurer, and the complicated insurance clauses usually cannot be identified accurately by the insured. Therefore, he is insured on the condition of trusting the contractual conditions proposed by the insurer. In this sense, the insurer has a dominant or superior position in the process of entering into the insurance contract. Therefore, the law requires the insurer to follow the principle of good faith when interpreting the terms of the contract. However, from the perspective of the risk assessment of the subject-matter insured, the status of the insurer is slightly lower than that of the insured. In other words, the insurer becomes the weak, just as Mr. Parker stated in his book *Contract of Speculation*: "… the facts on which the risk is assessed are mostly only known to the insured. Therefore, the insurer has to rely on all necessary circumstances provided by the insured and believes that the insured has not concealed anything, so that they will not make a wrong assessment. If there is an error, even if the insured is not intentional, the contract is still invalid, because the risk faced by the subject-matter insured has been different from what the insurer expected. Therefore, the principle of good faith prohibits either party from concealing the information known by them privately and inducing the other party to close the transaction without knowing such information."

4. The Parties to the Insurance Contract Are Not Equal in the Level of Payment

119. Although the insurance contract has the attributes of a bilateral contract, it is different from the general civil contract in the payment method of the consideration. For example, in the contract for the sale of goods, the seller has the obligation to provide the agreed goods, and the buyer has the obligation to make the payment, in which the principle of compensation in equal value is fully reflected. However, in the insurance contract, although the applicant has the obligation to pay the insurance premium and the insurer has the obligation to pay indemnity or insurance money when the insured incident occurs, which also seems like a consideration theoretically, this kind of payment is a little uncertain because the occurrence of the insured event is uncertain. For the insurer, if the event insured does not occur, he will not be liable for the loss although the insurance premium is charged. For the insured, if the event insured occurs, he or she may receive the indemnity several times higher than the insurance premium. In this sense, no matter whether an insured event occurs or not, the payment received by both parties to the contract is not equal, which can easily induce the moral hazard, especially for the insured. It is for this reason that the law regards the principle of good faith as the basis for the existence of insurance contracts.

5. The Essential Requirement for Risk Management

120. As mentioned above, the risk refers to the uncertainty of the loss, and can also be called the difference in the probability of occurrence of a certain result in a specific environment. The risks referred to in the theory of insurance are divided into three types: one is the material risk, that is the danger that directly affects the substantive function of the subject-matter insured such as natural disasters. The second is the moral risk, which is the risk related to people's moral standards. For example, the applicant or the insured deliberately creates or makes up an insured event for the purpose of being indemnified. The third is the psychological risk which is associated with a person's mental state, such as a risk caused by an insured's mistake based on the misjudgment of the objective matter. For example, the subject-matter insured is under management due to the negligence of the insured, or the loss of the subject-matter insured is enlarged caused by the improper measures taken to reduce the loss. Therefore, the principle of good faith is implemented in insurance to clarify the obligations of risk management; for example, the insured is required to disclose the material circumstances before entering into the contract and notify the insurer in time when the danger increases, to strength the risk management for the subject-matter insured.

6. The Need to Reduce the Cost of Risk Management

121. Modern commercial legislation emphasizes the principle of economic efficiency. As an important part of commercial law, the IL also emphasizes this principle in legislation. With the development of science and technology, the complexity of subject-matter insured is getting higher and higher, especially in the case that some subject-matters insured are located abroad. Before the insurance contract is formed, if the insurer wants to conduct an on-the-spot investigation of the subject-matter insured, not only will it waste a large amount of time, but also it will cost a lot of money. In view of this, the implementation of the principle of good faith in insurance activities, which takes the applicant's duty of truthful disclosure as the bottom line of the formation of a contract, is the same as setting a barrier for the proper performance of the contract, which is beneficial to reduce the management costs and improve the economic efficiency.

7. Protecting the Interests of the Applicant

122. The insurer's ability for indemnity is based on the establishment of a solid insurance fund, which is formed by pooling the insurance premiums of a large number of applicants. Once an event insured occurs, the fund can be used for indemnity. Therefore, although the fund is owned by the insurer apparently, it is actually established for the benefit of all applicants. Any malicious act of the applicant or the insured (such as untruthful disclosure or defrauding the insurance money, etc.) not only directly harms the insurer's interests but also indirectly infringes upon the interests of other applicants. From this perspective, it is also necessary to implement the principle of good faith.

8. The Need to Interpret the Law Correctly

123. In judicial practice, it is natural to take the law as the criterion, but no law can be formulated flawlessly. For the omissions, it can be interpreted by the principle of law. The establishment of the principle of good faith in the IL gives the court a basis for interpreting the law. For example, the insured does not disclose a fact at the time of insurance, and the insurer does not make an inquiry either. At this time, if the law itself is solely relied on, it is impossible to determine whether the contract is valid. However, since the existence of the principle of good faith, the judge can determine whether the applicant has fulfilled the duty of disclosure according to the principle.

C. The Parities under the Principle of Good Faith

124. The basic principle in law is the common principle established for all the parties, not the one that is solely for one party. Since good faith is a basic principle of the IL, it should be observed by all parties. The reason why we emphasize the binding effect of the principle of good faith on the parties is to correct a wrong conclusion in the theoretical circle. In some books or essays published in the 1980s, a formula was formed. As long as the principle of good faith or the principle of utmost good faith is mentioned, it is naturally recognized that the principle refers to the insured's duty of disclosure and believes that the principle only binds the insured. For a long time, this interpretation can be seen everywhere, even in some dictionaries or other reference books. According to this interpretation, the insured's duty of disclosure seems to constitute the entire content of the principle of good faith. In recent years, with the improvement of insurance legislation and the deepening of theoretical research, although this misunderstanding has been corrected, it still affects people's thinking to a certain extent, so this must be reversed. In view of this, two points should be clarified about the principle of good faith in the IL. First, the content of the principle of good faith is not limited to the duty of disclosure which is only one of the basic obligations set for the insured under the principle of good faith. The warranty, notification of danger, disaster prevention and loss reduction, honest claim and so on, which are to be mentioned later, are also the specific requirements for the insured under the principle of good faith. Second, the principle of good faith not only binds the insured but also binds the insurer. For example, the insurer's obligation to explain the clauses of the contract and the special obligation to warn the applicant for those clauses exempting him from liability as stipulated in Article 17 of the IL and the provisions about the waiver and estoppel of the insurer as stipulated in Article 16(3), Article 49(3) and Article 58(1) of the IL are all the specific requirements for the insurer under the principle of good faith.

D. Basic Obligation of the Parties to the Contract under the Principle of Good Faith

125. Under the principle of good faith, the applicant or the insured and the insurer shall take some basic obligation, such as the obligation to pay the premium, the obligation to truthfully disclose, the obligation not to commit insurance fraud, the obligation to notify the insurer when the degree of risk to the subject matter of insurance increases substantially, the obligation to notify when the insured event occurs, the obligation to provide proofs and information as to the insured event, the obligation to notify the insurer in the situation of double insurance and the obligation to mitigate for the applicant or the insured, and the obligation to issue the insurance documents in a timely manner, the obligation to indemnify or pay insurance benefits in the case of insured event and the obligations to explain and draw attention for the insurer, which will be discussed in detail in relevant parts of Chapters 3–5 of Part II in this monograph.

II. Principle of the Insurable Interest

A. Definition of the Insurable Interest

126. Article 12 of the IL provides that an applicant for personal insurance shall, when entering into an insurance contract, have an insurable interest in the insured. The insured in property insurance shall have an insurable interest in the subject-matter insured when an insured incident occurs. The insurable interest is that the applicant or the insured has an economically beneficial interest in the subject-matter insured that is recognized by law. For example, in marine insurance, if the insured property arrives to the destination safely, the insured will benefit from it. If the insured property suffers loss, damage or detention, the insured will suffer losses or undertake corresponding liabilities. The reason for establishing the principle of insurable interest in the IL is to prevent someone from using insurance as a means of gambling.

B. Characteristics of Insurable Interests

127. By analyzing the definition of insurable interests, it can be seen that insurable interests have the following characteristics.:

> The first is legality which means that the applicant's insurable interests in the subject-matter insured must be recognized by law. In short, the insurable interests must be a legitimate interest, such as ownership right interests, usufructuary right interests, collateral right interests, and various interests arising from the sharing of property. Based on such a kind of characteristic of the insurable interests, properties which are stolen or smuggled, or property whose ownership cannot be proved obviously cannot be taken as the subject-matter insured.

The second is certainty; that is, the insurable interests must be interests that have been determined or could be determined. The determined interest refers to the vested interest or the existing interest. For example, in the international sale of goods, someone has acquired the ownership of the goods. If the goods are lost or damaged, the property owner will suffer economic losses. Thus, he has a vested interest in the property. However, if a company asks an insurance company to cover the risk of loss of profits or loss of the company, obviously the insurance company cannot accept it because these risks cannot be determined. As for the interests that could be determined, it refers to the expected profits, that is the profits that can be obtained in the future. For example, in the international maritime transportation, the obligation to pay the freight specified by the cargo owner in the contract of carriage is conditioned on the safe arrival of the goods. Therefore, the carrier has the expected profits in the freight.

The third is computability, which must be the benefit that can be calculated by money. For this reason, the insurer can only underwrite tangible risks. For example, if a company wants to participate in a major international engineering contract and is insured against the insurance company because it worries that it cannot win the bid, such interest cannot be calculated by money, so the insurer cannot accept the insurance.

The fourth is public welfare; that is, the insurable interests must be the interests accepted by the public and good morals. The purpose of insurance is to use the concentrated funds to disperse the losses suffered by a few people, thus maintaining the good functioning of the social and economic order. Therefore, those interests that violate good morals are naturally not allowed by the IL. In this sense, it circumvents the legal liability because the objective effect of doing so is equivalent to encourage the violation of laws and regulations, which is contrary to the aim of public interest.

The fifth is mandatory. The insurable interest is a basic principle established by the law. Therefore, it must be strictly followed by all parties. Any insurance that does not have the insurable interests is invalid. No one could stipulate the exclusion of the application of the principle of insurable interests in the contract.

C. Duration of Insurable Interests

128. In the IL enacted in 1995, there is no distinction between the insurable interests of life insurance and property insurance but a general provision that the applicant should have an insurable interest in the subject-matter insured and if there is no insurable interest, the insurance contract is invalid. It is naturally uncontroversial for personal insurance, but it is too mechanical for property insurance and is not conducive to the circulation and transfer of goods under the market economy. For this, we can take the international maritime transport as an example. It is all known that there are different price conditions in the international trade of goods. For example, under the CIF, the seller is responsible for chartering the ship, so the seller is the shipper and he has ownership of the goods before the ownership of the goods has been transferred to the buyer. Therefore, the insurable interests he owns when consigning the goods are unquestionable. However, due to the changing in the international trade market, even the goods insured by the applicant may be transferred several times in transit. If it is mandatory to require the applicant to have insurable interests when entering into an insurance contract, it would have no practical significance for the person who receives the insurance policy when the goods are transferred to the buyer or any other third party. As a consequence, in the formulation of the MC, the definition of marine insurance has been particularly defined as: "A contract of marine insurance is a contract whereby the insurer undertakes, as agreed, to indemnify the loss to the subject matter insured and the liability of the insured caused by perils covered by the insurance against the payment of an insurance money by the insured." This provision clearly tells that in marine insurance, the insured needs to have the insurable interests as long as the insurance accident occurs. In the new IL, the provisions on the principle of insurable interest have been revised. On the one hand, Article 12 of the IL provides that the insured in property insurance shall have an insurable interest in the subject-matter insured when an insured incident occurs. On the other hand, Article 48 provides that the insured who does not have an insurable interest in the subject-matter insured when an insured incident occurs shall not claim indemnity against the insurer. This provision achieves unity with international customs.

III. Principle of Indemnity

A. *Definition*

129. The principle of indemnity is that the loss of the subject-matter insured under the insurance contract is restored to the condition before the accident by way of money subsidy. This principle embodies the core function of the insurance system, which is to use the concentrated funds to indemnify the insured who has suffered economic losses in order to achieve the purpose of stabilizing the social life and economic order. According to this principle, no one can achieve profit by mean of insurance. In this sense, under the principle of indemnity, the "three noes" rule should be implemented, that is no less indemnity, no more indemnity, no twice indemnity.

B. *No Less Indemnity*

130. The so-called no less indemnity is to indemnify all losses within the coverage of the contract. In other words, as long as it is the loss caused by the insurance accident within the coverage, the insurer should fully indemnify the loss according to the insurance type. Some scholars believe that the principle of indemnity for all losses does not apply to the underinsurance and the insurance with the "deductible." However, it is not the case in fact. In the case of underinsurance, since the insurance indemnity is based on the insurable value rather than the actual value, it is also the full indemnity as for the part the insured is indemnified. Even in the case of a contract with a "deductible," it cannot be said that the insured has not received the full indemnity. It is known that the so-called deductible is a special agreement to strengthen the risk management and simplify the claims process to enhance the insured's awareness of risk prevention and reduce the cumbersomeness of the claim and settlement. The deductible is for each specific insurance accident during the insurance period, not for the entire subject-matter insured. In short, there is a deductible to be deducted in each case of the claim during the insurance period, but as far as the entire subject-matter insured is concerned, the accumulated insurance money paid by the insurer may not be offset by the deductible at the time of deduction. Therefore, it cannot be thought that the insured has not received full indemnity only because there is a deductible.

C. No More Indemnity

131. No more indemnity means that the indemnity made by the insurer cannot exceed the actual loss caused by the insurance accident; even in the case of over-insurance, the excess is invalid. In practice, the method of calculating the actual loss varies depending on the type of the subject-matter insured and the form of the loss. For example, the market price is used to determine the total loss; the repair cost is used to determine the partial loss; the cost of repurchasing the property deducted by the depreciation charge is used to calculate the loss of property without market price and so on.

D. No Twice Indemnity

132. No twice indemnity means that the insured may not claim the full loss against two or more insurers for the same loss of the same subject-matter insured for the same insured event. According to the provisions of the IL, no matter what kind of insurance the insured has applied and no matter how much insurance premium he has paid, the maximum indemnity he receives should not exceed the insured amount. Because of this, even in the case of overlapping insurance, the insured also cannot receive double indemnity. In the case of overlapping insurance, each insurer shall be liable to pay indemnity according to the proportion between its insured amount and the total insured amount. Any insurer who has paid an indemnification in an amount greater than that for which he is liable shall have the right of recourse against those who have not paid their indemnification in the amounts for which they are liable.

E. Scope of the Principle of Indemnity

133. Under the principle of indemnity, the insurer's indemnity for the loss of the subject-matter insured may include four parts.

(1) the first part is the actual loss suffered by the subject-matter insured itself, but it must not exceed the insurable value;

(2) the second part is the necessary and reasonable expenses incurred by the insured for avoiding or minimizing the loss recoverable under the contract after the occurrence of the insured event. According to the requirements of disaster prevention and loss reduction, after the insured event occurs, the insured is obliged to take measures to minimize the loss to the least. Therefore, the ILs of each country stipulate that the expenses paid for preventing or reducing the loss of the subject-matter insured shall be indemnified as long as they are necessary and reasonable. The IL also has similar provisions. The difference is that the indemnity in this respect in China cannot exceed the insured amount;

(3) the third part is the necessary and reasonable expenses incurred to determine the losses within the insurance coverage. After the event insured occurs, the insured cannot passively wait for the insurer's indemnity, but should take the initiative to verify the loss or actively assist the insurer in collecting the relevant evidence, and sometimes have to survey and assess the loss of the subject-matter insured. According to Article 64 of the IL, the assessment of the value shall be at the expense of the insurer;

(4) the fourth part is the necessary litigation and arbitration costs. Article 66 of the IL provides that where an arbitration or litigation is instituted against the insured in liability insurance for an insured incident which causes damage to a third party, the arbitration or litigation costs and other necessary and reasonable expenses paid by the insured shall be at the expense of the insurer, except as otherwise provided for by the insurance contract. After the occurrence of an insured event, the insured shall take the initiative to file a lawsuit or arbitration, the purpose of which is mainly to protect the interests of the insurer. Therefore, such expenses should be borne by the insurer. However, the IL only stipulates the arbitration and litigation costs in the case of liability insurance, and is only limited to the costs paid by the insured as the defendant in the lawsuit or the respondent in the arbitration. In the MC, even such expenses are not stipulated. This could be said to be a drawback because it will make the insured feel at a loss. Article 61 of the IL provides that where, after an insured incident occurs and before the insurer pays indemnity, the insured waives the right to claim indemnity against the third party, the insurer shall not be liable to pay indemnity. It can be seen that when an insured accident occurs due to the liability of a third party, the insured may not arbitrarily waive the right to claim against a third party. There are only two ways for the insured, directly file a lawsuit against the third party or directly claim against the insurer for indemnity. If the former approach is adopted, since the IL and the MC do not stipulate whether such litigation costs are borne by the insurer, the insured will worry a lot about it when they take action alone. If the insured takes the second approach and directly claim against the insurer for indemnity, and then the insurer exercises the right of subrogation, it may be the most ideal way for the insured. The fact whether the insurer agrees to pay the indemnity and how to pay the indemnity are still in an uncertain state. After the dispute between the insurer and the insured has been handled, no matter who will file the lawsuit

against the third party, the time limit may be surpassed. From this perspective, the provisions of the litigation and arbitration costs stipulated in the IL are not perfect.

IV. Principle of Proximate Cause

A. *Definition*

134. The proximate cause is the concept in the Anglo-American law, which plays a direct and decisive role in the occurrence of loss, and effectively causes the liability of indemnity. The principle of proximate cause means that there should be a direct causation between the occurrence of an insured accident and the loss result, so that the insurer will be liable to pay the indemnity; on the contrary, the insurer shall not be liable to pay the indemnity caused by incidents uncovered by the insurance. Article 55(1) of the Marine Insurance Act 1906 of United Kingdom (U.K.) provides that subject to the provisions of this Act, and unless the policy otherwise provides, the insurer is liable for any loss proximately caused by a peril insured against, but, subject as aforesaid, he is not liable for any loss which is not proximately caused by a peril insured against. The purpose of the principle of the proximate cause is to prevent the insurance liability undertaken by the insurer from expanding with no limitation on the one hand; on the other hand, it is to prevent the insurer from arbitrarily shirking the liability for indemnity. China's insurance practice usually follows this principle. The IL does not stipulate this principle explicitly, but it could be embodied in Articles 22–25 of the IL on insurance claims and in Article 251 of the MC on the insured's liability to provide evidence and materials related to the ascertainment of the nature of the peril and the extent of the loss.

B. *Identification Criteria of the Proximate Cause*

135. There are three kinds of theory on the identification criteria of the proximate cause, which are the theory of the closest cause, the theory of the last condition and the theory of the direct action. The theory of the closest cause takes the last cause before the result as a proximate cause. The theory of the last condition believes that the reasons that are indispensable for the results should be enumerated, and the last reason should be taken as a proximate cause. The theory of the direct action takes the most direct and decisive cause of the result as a proximate cause. If the peril insured against is the direct cause of the damage to the subject-matter insured, the insurer shall be liable for the loss; on the contrary, the insurer shall not be liable for the loss if the peril insured against is not the direct cause of the damage to the subject-matter insured. Now, the theory of the direct action is the identification criteria generally recognized in the insurance field.

C. Identification Method of the Proximate Cause

136. When the cause of the loss of the subject-matter insured is unique, the cause is just the proximate cause. The key to determining whether an insurer should assume the insurance liability is to determine whether the cause is an insured incident as agreed in the insurance contract. If the cause is covered by the insurance contract, the insurer shall be liable for the loss; otherwise, he shall not be liable for the loss.

137. When there are many causes for the loss of the subject-matter insured, it is the dominant and decisive cause that is the proximate cause. Specifically, if the subject-matter insured has suffered a loss caused by a variety of causes taking effects simultaneously, each cause is a proximate cause. If these causes are all the insured incidents agreed in the insurance contract, the insurer shall be liable for loss. If all of these causes are not covered by the insurance contract, the insurer shall not be liable for loss. If some of these causes are covered by the insurance contract and the scope of liability can be distinguished, the insurer shall pay the indemnity within that scope and if the scope cannot be distinguished, the indemnity shall be paid based on the negotiation between the two parties.

If the occurrence of the causes is continuous, and the latter cause is the inevitable result or the reasonable extension of the former cause, the former cause is the proximate cause. If the former cause and the latter cause are both insured, the insurer shall be liable for loss. If the former cause is an insured event but the latter is not, the insurer shall be liable for loss because the former cause constitutes a proximate cause. However, if the former cause is not an insured event but the latter is, the insurer is not liable for loss because the proximate cause is the former one.

If there are multiple causes for the loss of or damage to the subject-matter insured, the people's court has the discretion to determine the causative potency of each cause on the basis of the ascertained facts, and find out whether those causes are all covered. If the insured risks and exclusions are mixed, the people's court can still hold that the insurer is liable for part of the loss or damage in accordance with the contributing effect of the insured risks.

§5. PARTIES

138. The parties to an insurance contract are the persons who enjoy rights and assume obligations in an insurance contract and are the basic elements of an insurance contract. Generally speaking, the parties of an insurance contract can be divided into two types: one is the party to the insurance contract, that is the insurer and the applicant; the other is the parties concerned with an insurance contract, including the insured and the beneficiary who are directly related to the insurance contract.

I. Parties to an Insurance Contract

A. *Insurer*

139. The characteristics of the insurer, namely insurance company, are discussed in details in Part I *supra*.

B. *Applicant*

140. Article 10(2) of the IL provides that an insurance applicant means a person who enters into an insurance contract with an insurer and performs the obligation of paying an insurance premium under the insurance contract. The applicant is the other party to the insurance contract corresponding to the insurer, either the insured or other persons permitted by law. Article 7 of the IL provides that legal persons and other organizations within the territory of China which need domestic insurance shall take out insurance from insurance companies within the territory of China. It can be seen that the applicant can be a natural person, a legal person or an unincorporated organization. An applicant must meet the following two requirements.

1. The Applicant Shall Have the Corresponding Capacity for Civil Conduct

141. Insurance contract behavior is a civil legal act, and the establishment of civil legal acts requires the parties to be qualified. As a civil party, the applicant must have the corresponding capacity for civil conduct required by law, and can correctly foresee and distinguish the nature of the application and the legal consequences that may arise.

As far as the legal person is concerned, its capacity for civil conduct arises when the legal person is formed and ceases to exist when the legal person is terminated. However, the legal person's behavior must be conducted by its representative or its supreme organ and the rights and obligations established by the insurance contract are directly attributable to the legal person. For the unincorporated organizations, they must have the qualifications of the parties to civil legal relations, and they can exercise their rights and assume civil liability on their own.

2. The Applicant Shall Have an Insurable Interest in the Insured in the Life Insurance Contract

142. Article 12(1) of the IL stipulates that an applicant for personal insurance shall, when entering into an insurance contract, have an insurable interest in the insured. Therefore, this requirement is limited to the personal insurance contract. In the life insurance contract, the party who is the owner of insurable interests shall be the applicant, and the subject-matter insured shall be the life or health status of the insured. For example, the applicant shall apply for the insurance for his parents, and the health of the parents directly affects the economic status of the applicant, so the applicant has an insurable interest in his parents. The reason for this stipulation is to prevent moral hazard.

II. Parties Concerned with an Insurance Contract

143. The party concerned with an insurance contract refers to a person who has the right to claim independently for the benefits arising from the insurance contract due to the establishment of the insurance contract. In an ordinary civil contract, the legal effect of the contract can only bind the parties to the contract, but in some insurance contracts, the purpose of the establishment of the insurance contract is to bring benefits to a third party. In this case, the legal effect of the insurance contract will restrict not only the parties to the contract but also the interests of the third party, that is the parties concerned with an insurance contract, which includes the insured and the beneficiary.

A. *Insured*

144. Article 12(5) of the IL provides that an insured means a person whose property, life or body is covered by an insurance contract and who is entitled to claim the insurance money. An insurance applicant may be the insured. In a property insurance contract, the insured can be a natural person, a legal person or an unincorporated organization. In a life insurance contract, the insured can only be a natural person. In insurance practice, the insured can be both the applicant and an independent party. In a property insurance contract, if the applicant applies for insurance for his/her property, the applicant is the insured; if the insured applies for insurance for the interest of a third party about the property that is of interest to him, the insured is an independent party. In a life insurance contract, if the applicant is insured for his/her life or body, the applicant is also the insured. If the applicant applies for insurance for the life or body of another person, the insured is an independent party.

145. There are several requirements to be qualified as insured:

- The insured suffers loss as a result of an insured event. When an insurable accident occurs, the insured will inevitably suffer a loss. The form in which the insured suffers a loss varies in the property insurance and personal insurance. In property insurance, the insured must be the owner of the subject-matter insured or the person who has other rights to it, such as the right to use, mortgage, etc. Damage to the subject-matter insured will result in loss of the insured's interests economically. In life insurance, the insured is a person whose life or health is directly damaged by the occurrence of a dangerous accident. Since the subject-matter insured is the life or body of the insured, the occurrence of an insurable accident will inevitably cause damage to the life or health of the insured.

- The insured has the right to claim for the indemnity. The basic idea of the insurance legal relationship is "no cure no pay." The insured suffers loss due to the occurrence of an event insured, so he or she has the right to claim against the insurer. The insured's claim for insurance money also varies in property insurance and personal insurance. As far as property insurance is concerned, the insured can exercise the right to claim for indemnity on his own because it is the property rather than the life or body that is damaged. In personal insurance, if the insured still survives after the insured event, the insured still has the right to claim for indemnity. However, in the life insurance taking death as the payment condition, once the insured event occurs, the insured loses the capacity for civil rights and cannot exercise the claim for indemnity on his own. This right shall be obtained by the beneficiary designated by the insurance contract. If the insurance contract does not specify a beneficiary, it is obtained by the insured's heir.
- The insured's capacity for civil conduct is subject to certain restrictions under some special circumstances. Whether the insured must have the corresponding capacity for civil conduct depends on the nature of the insurance contract. In the property insurance contract, since the subject-matter insured is the property and its related interests, the protection from the insurance contract can be guaranteed regardless of the capacity for civil conduct of the natural person. In other words, a person with full capacity for civil conduct, a person with limited capacity for civil conduct, and a person without capacity for civil conduct can become the insured in the property insurance contract. In the life insurance contract, in order to respect the insured's right of personality and effectively prevent the occurrence of moral hazard, the law stipulates that the insured's capacity for civil conduct must be limited under certain special circumstances. Article 33 of the IL provides that no insurance applicant shall take out any personal insurance in which insurance money shall be paid conditioned upon the death of the insured for a person without the civil conduct capacity, and no insurer shall underwrite such insurance. Parents who take out personal insurance for their underage children shall not be subject to the preceding paragraph. However, the total insurance money paid for the death of the insured shall not exceed the limit as prescribed by the insurance regulatory body under the State Council. According to the provisions, in addition to parents can insure their underage children for personal insurance, no other person may take the person without capacity for civil conduct as the insured in insurance which takes the death as the condition for payment of insurance money; otherwise, the insurance contract is invalid.

B. Beneficiary

146. The beneficiary, also known as the recipient of insurance money, refers to the person who is designated by the applicant or the insured in the insurance contract and who has the right to claim for indemnity in the event of an insured event. Article 18(3) of the IL provides that a beneficiary means a person designated by the insured or the insurance applicant in a personal insurance contract to be entitled to claim the insurance money. An insurance applicant or insured may be a beneficiary. And the beneficiary may also be an independent third party.

Regarding the qualifications of beneficiaries, the IL does not impose any restrictions, and natural persons, legal persons or other unincorporated organizations can be designated as beneficiaries. If a natural person is designated as a beneficiary, a person without capacity for civil conduct and a person with limited capacity for civil conduct may also be designated as a beneficiary. The fetus can also be a beneficiary, but it is necessary to "live at birth." If the fetus is dead at birth, the beneficiary status is lost. In China's insurance practice, the beneficiaries are mostly family members, relatives or friends who have insurance interests or economic interests with the insured and the applicant. In addition, legal persons and other unincorporated organizations can also be beneficiaries.

147. The beneficiary has the following characteristics:

- The beneficiary only exists in the life insurance contract. As mentioned above, the subject-matter insured of the life insurance contract is the life or body of the insured. And when the insured dies, the question of who enjoys and exercises the right to claim the insurance money arises. Therefore, the beneficiary does have a necessity in the life insurance contract to clarify the party who enjoys and exercises the right to claim insurance money after the death of the insured, as the death of the insured is often the requirement of the insurance accident in life insurance. Therefore, in addition to the insured and the applicant, there must be a need for the beneficiary to receive the benefit of the insurance contract, that is the insurance money. As far as the property insurance contract is concerned, it is generally believed that when an event insured occurs, the insured can completely exercise the right to claim the insurance money; that is, the beneficiary is the insured itself and there is no need to agree on the beneficiary separately. However, some scholars have affirmed that the beneficiaries can also be designated in property insurance contracts. The IL adopts the general view, and does not stipulate that there is the need to be a beneficiary in the property insurance contract.
- The beneficiary has the right to claim insurance money. Since the beneficiary does not enter into an insurance contract with the insurer, it is not a party to the insurance contract and is not obliged to pay the premium. However, the beneficiary has the right to claim insurance money in the event of an event insured. The claim for insurance money is an inherent right, which is obtained from the original and is directly produced according to the agreement of the insurance contract. The insurance money received by the beneficiary shall not be taken as the inheritance of the insured.
- The beneficiary is designated by the applicant or the insured. Article 39 of the IL provides that the beneficiary in personal insurance shall be designated by the insured or insurance applicant. The insurance applicant shall obtain the consent of the insured when designating the beneficiary. Article 41(2) provides that to change a beneficiary, the insurance applicant must obtain the consent of the insured. It can be seen that both the applicant and the insured have the right to designate the beneficiary. However, the consent of the insured must be obtained when the applicant designates and changes the beneficiary. In this way, the beneficiary's final decision is attributed to the insured, which is helpful to prevent the moral hazard. At the same time, Article 40 of the IL also provides that the insured

or insurance applicant may designate one or more beneficiaries. If there are two or more beneficiaries, the insured or insurance applicant may determine the sequence and shares of the beneficiaries; if the shares of the beneficiaries are not determined, all beneficiaries shall equally enjoy the beneficiary right. According to this article, the insured and the applicant may specify a number of beneficiaries and determine the sequence and share of them.

- By Article 9 of *Interpretation III*, where the applicant names the beneficiary (or beneficiaries) without the consent of the insured, the court shall deem that the designation is not valid. Where the parties concerned have a dispute over the beneficiary (or beneficiaries) specified in the insurance contract, unless agreed otherwise by the applicant and the insured in the insurance contract, the dispute shall be handled as follows: (a) where it is agreed that the beneficiary or beneficiaries shall be "statutory" or the "statutory successor(s)," the statutory successor(s) stipulated in Article 1127 of the CC shall be the beneficiary or beneficiaries; (b) where the identity of the beneficiary or beneficiaries is specified, if the applicant and the insured are the same, the beneficiary or beneficiaries shall be determined in accordance with the relationship between the beneficiary or beneficiaries and the insured when the insurance accident occurs; if the applicant and the insured are not the same, the beneficiary or beneficiaries shall be determined in accordance with the relationship between the beneficiary or beneficiaries and the insured when the insurance contract is concluded; and (c) where both the name and identity of the beneficiary or beneficiaries are stated, if there is a change in the identity when the insurance accident occurs, it shall be deemed that the beneficiary or beneficiaries is/are not specified.
- By Article 41 of the IL, the insured or the applicant may change the beneficiary, and shall notify the insurer of the change in writing. The insurer shall endorse the change on the policy or other insurance certificates, or affix an endorsement slip thereto upon receipt of the notice. The change of a beneficiary by the policyholder shall be subject to the consent of the insured. By Article 10 of *Interpretation III*, where the beneficiary or beneficiaries is/are changed by the applicant or the insured, and a party concerned claims that the change has taken effect upon expression of intent for the change, the court shall support such claim. Where the beneficiary or beneficiaries is/are changed by the applicant or the insured without notifying the insurer, and the insurer claims that the change has no effect on the insurer, the court shall support such claim. Where the beneficiary or beneficiaries is/are changed by the applicant without the insured's consent, the court shall deem that the change is not valid.
- By Article 11 of *Interpretation III*, where the beneficiary or beneficiaries is/are changed by the applicant or the insured after an insurance accident occurs, and the new beneficiary or beneficiaries request(s) that the insurer makes insurance payout, the court shall not support such request.

148. The main right of the beneficiary is to claim insurance benefits. By Article 12 of *Interpretation III*, where more than one beneficiaries are specified by the applicant or the insured, if one of the beneficiaries died before the occurrence of the insurance accident, or relinquished or lost his beneficiary rights according to the law, the insurance benefits shall be distributed as agreed upon in the insurance contract; where there is no specific provision or the provision is not clear in the insurance contract, the benefits shall be distributed as follows:

- where there is no provision on the order of distribution and the proportions of the insurance benefits, the benefits shall be shared by the other beneficiaries on an equal basis;
- where there is no provision on the order of distribution but the proportions are specified, the benefits shall be distributed among the other beneficiaries pursuant to the contract provisions;
- where the order of distribution of the insurance benefits is specified but there is no provision on the proportions, the benefits shall be shared equally by the other beneficiaries of the same order;
- where there is no other beneficiary of the same order, the benefits shall be shared equally by the beneficiaries of the next order; and
- where the order of distribution and proportions are specified, they shall be shared by the other beneficiaries of the same order in accordance with the proportions; where there is no other beneficiary of the same order, they shall be shared equally by the beneficiaries of the next order.

As the entitlement of the beneficiary to the insurance benefits derives from the insurance contract, the insurance benefits received by the beneficiary shall not be regarded as the heritage of the deceased insured, and therefore shall not be used to repay the debt of the insured or be distributed as the heritage. However, by Article 42 of the IL, in the event of the death of the insured, the insurance benefits shall, in any of the following circumstances, be deemed to as the heritage of the deceased and the insurer shall be obliged to pay insurance benefits in accordance with the CC:

- where there is no designated beneficiary or the beneficiary is not clearly designated and cannot be determined;
- where the beneficiary dies before the insured another beneficiary being designated; or
- where the beneficiary forfeits or surrenders his/her beneficial interests in accordance with the law without any other beneficiary. Where both the beneficiary and the insured die in the same incident and it is impossible to determine the sequence of death, the beneficiary shall be presumed to have died first.

§6. Interpretation

149. As a commercial contract, an insurance contract shall follow the interpretation method of the general contract. Articles 142 and 466 of the CC provide that if any dispute arises between the parties over the understanding of any clause of the contract, the true meaning thereof shall be determined according to the words and sentences used in the contract, the relevant provisions in the contract, the nature and purpose of the contract, the transaction practices and the principle of good faith.

Where a contract is concluded in two or more languages and it is agreed that all versions are equally authentic, the words and sentences in each version are construed to have the same meaning. In case of any discrepancy in the words or sentences used in the different language versions, they shall be interpreted in light of the relevant provisions in the contract, the nature and purpose of the contract and the principle of good faith. If the method stipulated in this clause still cannot effectively solve the ambiguity arising from the clauses of the contract, that is if there are more than two interpretations of the clauses of the insurance contract, the "principle of unfavorable interpretation" of the format contract which is stipulated in Article 30 of the IL shall be applied.

I. Literary Interpretation

150. The literary interpretation is to clarify the clauses of the insurance contract by means of the words and sentences used in the contract and the unique, specific or general way of use of the clauses. The general reason for the interpretation of the insurance contract is that the meaning of the language of the insurance contract is unclear or discrepant. Therefore, literal interpretation is the basic method for interpreting the clauses of the insurance contract. All the clauses of the insurance contract are composed of words, and to accurately understand or master the meaning of the insurance clause, we must first understand the meaning of the words and phrases used. Therefore, the method of literary interpretation should be first used. When this method is applied, the literal meaning of the words used in the clauses of the insurance contract should be respected. If there is no discrepancy of the words and sentences used in the insurance contract, it is not allowed to expand or narrow the possible meaning of the words used in the insurance contract through interpretation.

The interpretation of the insurance contract should generally be interpreted according to the popular meaning of the sentence itself, and should not be limited to the philosophical or scientific meaning of the terms in the insurance contract, unless there are strong reasons for other interpretations of the insurance contract. However, for certain sentences with special meanings, a unified interpretation should be implemented with reference to relevant regulations and insurance customs. For example, the liability clause of an insurance contract stipulates the "storm," and the "storm" here is not what people usually call "a very heavy rain," but has a specific standard for measure, that is a rainfall of 16 mm per hour or more than 50 mm in twenty-four hours is called heavy rain. Below this standard, it cannot be interpreted as the storm.

II. Overall Explanation

151. The overall interpretation, also known as the contextual interpretation, refers to the meaning of the terms used in the insurance contract which is often bound by the context. In the event of a dispute, it should be properly interpreted through the relevant provisions in the insurance contract. Since the clauses in the insurance contract pay more attention to the logical connection and overall coordination of the clause than the general contract clause, the method of overall interpretation effectively prevents the contract clause from being misinterpreted unilaterally or out of context. This method of interpretation can be further divided into analogy interpretation and restrictive interpretation. When the items listed in the insurance contract belong to the same category, the items whose meanings indicated by the terms immediately after the enumeration refer to the items of the same type but not the other type, which is called the analogy interpretation. For example, Article 2 of the Commercial Property Insurance Clauses of the PICC stipulates that, unless agreed otherwise, gold and silver, jewelry, antiques, ancient books, ancient paintings, stamps, artworks, rare metals and other precious properties are not covered by the property insurance. The "other precious properties" should be interpreted as other items similar to the items listed in the previous. The restrictive interpretation refers to a method in which a restrictive term of an insurance contract is behind a general term; the preceding general term should not be interpreted according to its original meaning, but should be interpreted by the latter restrictive term.

III. Purposeful Interpretation

152. The purpose interpretation, also called the intent interpretation, means that when the clauses or contents of the insurance contract are vague and unclear, the interpretation should be made to facilitate the purpose and legitimacy of the contract. The purpose interpretation of the insurance contract should follow the principle of "five superiors":

(1) when the written agreement is inconsistent with the oral agreement, the written agreement is superior to the oral agreement;
(2) when the contents specified in the application form or other contract documents are inconsistent with the contents specified in the insurance policy, the contents specified in the insurance policy shall prevail;
(3) if the special clauses are inconsistent with other clauses in the insurance policy, the special clauses shall prevail;
(4) when the added insurance clauses are inconsistent with the original insurance clauses, the added is superior to the original ones;
(5) when the contents of the insurance contract are recorded in different ways and there is conflict, the handwritten insurance clauses are superior to the printed ones. The printed insurance clauses are superior to the posted ones. The posted clauses are superior to the preprinted ones on the insurance policy.

IV. Supplementary Interpretation

153. The supplementary interpretation refers to the interpretation of the lacked contents of the insurance contract that reflects the intention of the party by means of evaluating other than the words used in the insurance contract. When there is omission or incompletion of the insurance contract, and the intention of the party is also difficult to be determined, the interpretation of the insurance contract can be supplemented to find the true intention of the party according to the compulsory provisions of the law, the behavior of the insurer or his agent, the transaction process, commercial customs, international practice and the principle of fairness, etc. To explain the insurance contract by means of supplementary interpretation, it should be noted that:

- if there are compulsory provisions in the law, the insurance contract shall be interpreted in accordance with the law;
- if there is no compulsory provision in the law, the lacked contents of the insurance contract shall be supplemented according to the arbitrary provisions of the law, the behavior of the insurer or his agent, the transaction process, commercial customs, international practice and the principle of fairness and so on to make the contents of the contract clearer and more complete.

V. Principle of Unfavorable Interpretation

154. The principle of unfavorable interpretation means that when the clauses of the insurance contract are unclear, they should be interpreted as unfavorable to the insurer but in favor of the insured or the beneficiary. Article 30 of the IL clearly stipulates this principle that where there is any dispute between the insurer and the insurance applicant, insured or beneficiary over any clause of an insurance contract concluded using the standard clauses of the insurer, the clause shall be interpreted as commonly understood. If there are two or more different interpretations of the clause, the people's court or the arbitral institution shall interpret the clause in favor of the insured and beneficiary. The reason why the IL stipulates the principle of unfavorable interpretation is that the insurance contract is a format contract. When the insurer formulates the clauses of the insurance contract, it is inevitable for him to consider his own interests. The insured often cannot study the insurance clause carefully because of lack of professional knowledge. The principle of unfavorable interpretation effectively avoids the ambiguity of the contents when the insurer formulates the insurance contract, and avoids impairing the interests of the insured.

The principle of unfavorable interpretation can only be applied to the case where the terms of the insurance contract are ambiguous and the intention of the party is unclear, but this principle cannot be conflicted with the basic principles of interpreting the insurance contract; that is, the interpretation of the insurance contract should explore the true meaning of the parties. If the terms of the insurance policy are clear, express and unambiguous, it can be seen that the intention of the parties is clear and there is no room for interpreting the terms of the insurance contract; therefore, the literal interpretation that is unfavorable to the insured cannot be made and the principle of unfavorable interpretation cannot be used to misinterpret the terms of the insurance contract. Similarly, if the insurance contract has a clause that is unclear, but it is excluded by the interpretation of the parties, there is no room to apply the principle of unfavorable interpretation too. In addition, if the intention of the parties can be confirmed by other means, the unfavorable interpretation cannot be applied. Besides, if the terms of the insurance contract have been clarified by judicial interpretation, there is no ambiguity in the terms of the contract, and the principle of unfavorable interpretation cannot be applied either. However, if the terms of the insurance contract are interpreted by different courts, there are conflicting conclusions about the correct meaning of the term, the intention of the party expressed, and the effect produced accordingly, which indicate that the terms of the insurance contract are ambiguous; thus, the principle of unfavorable interpretation should be applied.

Chapter 2. Insurable Risk

§1. Definition of the Risk

155. The word "risk" seems simple at first sight, but actually it is not. Literally, there are many English expressions corresponding to or related to this word, such as "danger," "peril," "hazard" and so on. For a long time, the domestic insurance industry has been accustomed to using the term "danger" to explain the risks covered by insurance companies. Even the understanding of the word "danger" differs from person to person. For example, some explain from the perspective of objectivity that the danger is an objective existence in nature and people are always vigilant enough to cause a loss of social wealth, and a random phenomenon that affects the safety of human life. Some understand from the perspective of contingency that danger refers to the uncertainty that human beings cannot control and therefore cause loss, and some scholars directly define danger as the uncertainty of the loss.

In fact, what the insurance covers should be "risk" rather than "danger." For example, in marine cargo transportation insurance, "All Risks" is translated as all risks and not translated into all dangers or all perils. As we all know, the risk is likely to occur or not happen in the future, and once it happens, it will hurt people's lives or damage properties. As for "danger," it is a serious situation that has been detected and is imminent. Obviously, no insurer will cover the dangers that are already clearly felt. As for the meaning of peril and hazard, it mainly refers to the disaster that has already occurred. Based on the same principle as described above, it is impossible for the insurer to cover the losses caused by the peril and hazard that have already occurred.

§2. Features of the Risk

I. Contingency

156. The so-called contingency refers to the uncertainty of the accident. First, the uncertainty mentioned here is that whether the damage will happen or not can be uncertain. For example, although the applicant has taken fire insurance, it is uncertain whether the fire can occur. If the applicant has already confirmed that an accident is doomed to happen, this is not only inconsistent with the philosophy of the IL but also unfair to the insurer. For example, in the case of a serious fire risk near the factory building, the applicant apparently knows that there is a high possibility of a fire, but still insures against the fire. This kind of insurance is not recognized by law because such a behavior is equivalent to concentrate the scattered danger and then transfer them all to the insurer. Second, the time at which the damage occurred is uncertain. If the applicant has already predicted the happening time of an accident but still insures the subject, it constitutes a deception which fundamentally violates the principle of good faith. Third, the conditions for the occurrence of the risk are uncertain. If the applicant knows that an item must have an accident under certain condition, he or she should take measures to eliminate the hidden danger, and cannot wait for the insurer to provide protection without any action. Finally, the consequences of the damage are uncertain. If the applicant knows in advance that an accident is bound to happen and knows what kind of damage will occur after the accident, but preselects a type of insurance that is beneficial to him or her, for example the applicant is aware that an area is in a fierce war but still insure the war risk, it is apparent that the insurer is placed in a position that he is destined to bear the loss, which does not meet the characteristic of the contingent contract of the insurance contract. The uncertainty described in the above aspects can be attributed to the contingency of the insurable risk. If the insurer is allowed to cover a fait accompli or an inevitable fact, it is contrary to the original intention of insurance, and it is also contrary to the legislative purpose of the IL.

II. Objectivity

157. Objectivity refers to the natural property of the risk which means the risk is easy to occur due to the power of nature. It is this objectivity that is emphasized in the definition of insurance in Article 2 of the IL. The purpose of insurance is to minimize the losses when the risks occur. Therefore, risks that are envisaged from the standpoint of subjective idealism (such as those envisaged based on geomancy or fantasy reasons) cannot be covered by insurance companies because they are not objective.

III. Futurity

158. The so-called futurity refers to the fact that a risk does not occur in reality but may be transformed into objective facts in the future. As a kind of contingent contract, insurance covers the risk that may occur in the future. Therefore, if the applicant insures a risk that is already occurred by paying a low premium in exchange for the indemnities from the insurer, it violates the principle of fairness of the contract law, and its nature is the same as that of blaming others, and is therefore prohibited by law.

IV. Commonality

159. The risk covered by insurance is the risk that many subject-matter insured are generally exposed under the same or similar conditions. For example, crops are generally threatened by natural disasters such as drought, flood, wind, insect and so on; animals often encounter infectious diseases; goods in shipping are also often damaged by the occurrence of maritime accidents. These possibilities are summaries by people in long-term life and production practices. This commonality is emphasized in insurance with the aim to eliminate risks that are not universally representative.

§3. Classification of the Risk

160. Risks can be classified from different perspectives, which is of great significance for theoretical research.

First, according to the cause of the risk, it can be divided into subjective risk and objective risk. Subjective risks are the possibility of loss based on the individual's mental state. Due to the subjective reasons of the insured, the subject-matter insured may sometimes suffer a loss. For example, if the insured has no common sense of fire prevention and the measures taken to prevent the fire are improper, he or she cannot prevent the fire from happening, but instead causes a fire. Because the social experience, education level, cognitive degree of the objective matters, and capacity to deal with problems of each person are different, the probability and possibility of person or property being in danger are not exactly the same. Therefore, before the insurer makes the decision to underwrite a subject matter, he will conduct a risk assessment according to the actual situation of each insured person or property to achieve the purpose of controlling the risk. Objective risks refer to the possibility of an accident whose occurrence does not depend on the subjective consciousness of people. Although these risks are also uncertain, they are relatively regular, so they can be appropriately predicted. From this perspective, the objective risk is a kind of uncertainty of a measurable trait.

Second, according to the consequences of risk, it can be divided into pure risk and speculative risk. Pure risk refers to an objective circumstance that can only cause losses without any benefit. For example, a traffic accident can only result in property damage or personal injury without benefiting anyone. The speculative risk refers to a situation where there are both possibilities of suffering losses and opportunities for benefit. For example, in stock trading, the price of stocks may fall or rise; in international trade, as the international situation changes, traders may obtain huge profits and may also suffer major economic losses. When it comes to commercial insurance, the insurer only covers the pure risk with no consideration of the speculative risk. The principle of indemnity in the IL is also based on this philosophy.

Then, according to the happening condition of the risk, it can be divided into basic risks and specific risks. Basic risks are those that any person or property faces in general. For example, goods in maritime transportation are subject to the possibility of encountering natural disasters or navigational accidents at sea. Specific risks are those that a particular person or property may encounter under a certain circumstance; for example, a risk may occur only when a group is engaged in a particular industry or a property is under certain condition. For average people, there is no such problem. For this reason, in insurance practice, insurance companies distinguish the basic risks and the additional risks.

§4. Relationship Between Insurance and Risk

161. Citizens, legal persons or other organizations must manage the abovementioned objective risks, that is to recognize, estimate and analyze the risk, and to take measures to eliminate, reduce or transfer the risk. Insurance is one of the methods for people to deal with the risk, and it is also a sophisticated system designed to deal with risk. It has advantages that are unmatched by other methods. Though insurance itself cannot prevent the occurrence of risk, it can moderate the anxiety of risks and/or economic burdens. The purpose of the modern insurance legal system is to prevent risks and ensure safety. Everything on earth is nothing more than an issue of safety, and accurately, it is nothing more than an issue of insurance. Nowadays, with the accelerated development of science and technology, people are no longer at the mercy of fate as long as the manpower can make it. Insurance can pool risk of majority in a scientific way so as to build an insurance fund sufficient to meet the actual losses of such majority. As a result, the actual losses are spread.

Chapter 3. Formation of the Insurance Contract

§1. Precontractual Phase

I. Precontractual Duty of the Applicant and Insured: Duty of Disclosure

A. *Definition of the Duty of Disclosure*

162. The duty of disclosure means that when the insurance contract is concluded, the obligor is required to truthfully inform the insurer of all the relevant material circumstances of the subject-matter insured. Although the insurer clearly stipulates this duty in the contract, the duty of disclosure is a statutory duty and is not affected by the agreement. The performance of the duty of disclosure determines the quality of the insurance contract and influences the future development of the contract.

B. *Nature of the Duty of Disclosure*

163. The insurance liability of the insurer under the insurance contract is an uncertain risk liability. The reason why the insurer underwrites the uncertain risk is largely based on the measurement and estimation of the degree of the risk of the subject-matter insured, and the degree of risk determines the level of the insurance premium. Whether the assured truthfully discloses the material circumstances of the subject-matter insured directly affects the insurer's measurement and estimation of the risk and the determination of whether to underwrite or not, thereby affecting the insurer's choice of insurance rate. Therefore, the IL specifically stipulates the duty of disclosure.

The duty of disclosure is a statutory duty imposed on the assured under the IL. It is not a duty arising from the consent of the parties to the insurance contract. The breach of duty will not lead to liability for non-performance of the insurance contract.

C. *Parties of the Duty of Disclosure*

164. In theory, there are two main opinions on the parties of duty of disclosure. First, the applicant has the duty to disclose and the assured or the beneficiary has no such duty. Second, both the applicant and the assured have the duty of disclosure.

Article 16(1) of the IL provides that where the insurer inquiries about the subject-matter insured or about the insured when entering into an insurance contract, the insurance applicant shall tell the truth. Accordingly, the party of the duty of disclosure is the applicant, not the assured.

When the applicant and the assured are the same person, the objective result is the same regardless of who is the party of disclosure. If the applicant and the assured are not the same person, it is worth considering whether the assured is the party of disclosure. First of all, when an insured event occurs, the assured of the property insurance is the person who actually suffers loss. According to the principle of consistency of rights and obligations, the assured should also have the duty of disclosure. Then, the assured is the bearer of the risk and should be most concerned about the subject-matter insured. And he is also the person who actually holds and controls the subject-matter insured, so he should be most clear about the situation of the subject-matter insured. If he is the party of the disclosure, it is more convenient and easier to fulfill the duty than the case that the applicant is the party, and the purpose of the duty of disclosure is more likely to be achieved. What is more, if there is an intentional breach of the duty, the insurer will have the right to terminate the contract, which is in accordance with the purpose of insurance. Finally, life insurance takes the life or body of the assured as the subject-matter insured. Generally speaking, everyone should be most concerned about their own interests and everyone should also know the best about their own situation. Only the assured should be the most qualified to judge their own needs, and make corresponding choice based on their own needs. This will enable the insurer to better understand the circumstances of the subject-matter insured and, on this basis, make choices as to whether or not to underwrite. Therefore, the assured should also be the party of disclosure.

Accordingly, some people advocated an expansionary interpretation of the provisions of Article 16 of the IL, so that the party of disclosure is extended to the assured. This kind of treatment is a convenient way to solve the problem. However, the fundamental solution lies in the amendment of Article 16(1) of the IL, so that the applicant and the assured are both bound by the duty of disclosure.

D. *Time of Disclosure*

1. When the Insurance Contract Is Concluded

165. The obligor is required to truthfully inform the insurer of all the material circumstances of the subject-matter insured when the contract is concluded. The time when a contract is concluded generally refers to the period of time before the insurer underwrites; that is, the period starts from the time of the obligor proposing to the time when the insurance contract is established.

2. After the Insurance Contract Is Concluded

166. After the insurance contract is concluded, the performance of the duty of disclosure can be divided into two situations.

First, when renewing a contract, it is necessary to determine whether or not to perform the duty of disclosure according to different situations. The renewal of the insurance contract means that after the expiration of the insurance period, the parties agree to continue the validity of the original insurance contract. The renewal of an insurance contract is essentially two contracts; that is, the legal nature of the renewal is a recontract, so the assured should be obligated to inform the truth again. However, if the renewal of the contract is based on the fact that the parties agree upon an "automatic renewal clause" in the original contract, it means that both the parties intend to continue to maintain its validity without changing the contents of the original contract. The insurer underwrites on the condition of the contents disclosed by the assured at the conclusion of the original contract, so the assured does not have to perform the duty disclosure any more. If there is no "automatic renewal clause" in the contract, and the validity of the contract is extended by a new agreement at the expiration of the period or before the expiration of the period, the obligor should re-fulfill the duty of disclosure.

Second, when the insurance contract is reinstated, as to whether the obligor should perform the duty of disclosure, there are two opinions. It is said that the scholars who hold the affirmative opinion believe that the reinstatement of life insurance contract is intended to alleviate the difficulty of the assured to pay the subsequent insurance premium. It is difficult to avoid the circumstance that the assured asks for reinstatement when they find that they are sick, which can be prevented by the duty of disclosure of the obligor. Negating the duty of disclosure at the time of reinstatement will induce the obligor deliberately not to disclose the material circumstances when concluding the contract and try to make it in a state of cessation of validity after the contract is established, and then apply for reinstatement after the period of remission of the insurer's right of revocation, which disobeys the purpose of the insurance. This is reasonable logically, but the assumption that the assured applies for reinstatement when in danger lacks a statistical basis. Article 37 of the IL provides that the reinstatement of an insurance contract is subject to an agreement upon consultation between the insurer and the assured. So, at this time, the insurer can measure the danger of the subject-matter insured by the duty of disclosure.

The scholars who hold the negative opinion believe that the reinstatement aims to provide the assured with adequate insurance coverage. Reinstatement means that after the suspension of the validity of the contract, when the effect of the suspension ceases to exist, the validity of the contract will be resumed as it is never suspended. At the time of the conclusion of the contract, the insurer has measured the risk of underwriting through the truthful disclosure of the obligor and collects the corresponding insurance premium. When resuming, the obligor should not be required to fulfill the duty of disclosure again; otherwise, it would be contrary to the original intention of reinstatement. We believe that the negative opinion is more rational, but the implementation of this theory cannot eliminate the dangerous counterselection of the assured.

3. When the Insurance Contract Is Changed

167. If the insurance contract is changed, if it is a change of the contract element, the duty of disclosure should be fulfilled. The change in the contents of the insurance contract means that the insurance relationship is changed according to the agreement between the two parties. The changing of contract can be divided into the changing of the contract elements and the changing of the non-elements. The so-called changing of contract elements refers to the change of important parts of the payment, which leads to the loss of identity of the contractual relationship. A non-element change refers to a change in the non-significant portion of the payment that does not result in the loss of identity of the contractual relationship. When the insurance contract is changed, whether the obligor should fulfill the duty of disclosure shall be determined by whether or not the insurance contract is the same as the original contract. If there is an element changing, the duty of disclosure should be fulfilled due to the loss of identity of the contract and a new contract is concluded. If it is a non-element changing that does not affect the identity of the contract, the risk can be controlled by the notification obligation of the increased risk.

E. Methods of Disclosure

168. The insurer relies on the duty of disclosure to know the risk of underwriting, and the disclosure is not necessary to be restricted to a certain form. Obligors may take a written form, or an oral form. In practice, if there is an agreement, it shall be agreed upon; if there is no agreement, the obligor shall take the form in the manner mentioned above. If the obligor claims that he has fulfilled the duty, he must bear the burden of proof.

F. Scope of Duty of Disclosure

1. Matters to Be Disclosed

169. The matters that should be disclosed should be limited to material circumstances, not in details. There are two criteria for judging: first, the material circumstances have an influence on the insurer in deciding upon the premium or whether to agree to insure or not; second, the assured has knowledge of or ought to have knowledge of in his ordinary business practice before the conclusion of the contract. The matter known after the conclusion of the contract will not constitute a breach of the duty of disclosure even if it is not disclosed.

There are two legislative models for defining the matters to be disclosed. The first is the automatic declaration, which means that besides the contents inquired by the insurer in writing which should be disclosed truthfully, as for those the insurer has not inquired in writing but is sufficient to influence the risk assessment, the assured should also disclose truthfully if the matters are known to them. The countries adopting this kind of model mainly include Japan, Italy, the U.K., and the U.S. (most states). The second is the written inquiry, which means that the obligor only has to disclose the matters inquired by the insurer in writing. If the insurer does not inquire in writing, the obligor is not obliged to disclose whether or not the insurer inquires verbally. The countries adopting this kind of model include Germany, South Korea, Taiwan and so on. There are three advantages of written inquiry: first, it can limit the scope of duty of disclosure of the assured; second, it limits the contents that should be disclosed to matters that are known or ought to know, and the principle of fault liability is adopted; finally, the difficulty of the burden of proof can be avoided.

Article 16(1) of the IL provides that where the insurer inquiries about the subject-matter insured or about the insured when entering into an insurance contract, the insurance applicant shall tell the truth. Accordingly, the assured shall truthfully answer the insurer's inquiry about the subject-matter insured. As for the matters which are not inquired by the insurer, the obligor has no duty to make disclosure. The insurer's inquiry is usually in writing and the assured is required to truthfully fill out the application form. However, Article 222 of the MC provides that before the contract is concluded, the insured shall truthfully inform the insurer of the material circumstances which the insured had knowledge of or ought to have knowledge of in his ordinary business practice and which may have a bearing on the insurer in deciding the premium or whether he agrees to insure or not. The insured need not inform the insurer of the facts which the insurer has known of or the insurer ought to have knowledge of in his ordinary business practice if about which the insurer made no inquiry. This regulation is based on automatic declaration. According to the principle that the special law is superior to the common law, marine insurance should give priority to the provisions of the MC.

2. Matters Exempt from Disclosure

170. For certain matters, the obligor may not have to make the disclosure, generally including:

- facts known to the insurer;
- facts that the insurer should know but are unknown due to intentional or gross negligence.

G. Insurer's Waiver and the Loss of Right to Terminate

171. In order to protect the interests of the applicant and insured, the law provides that in certain circumstances, the insurer may waive the right to assert that the applicant or insured has breached the obligation to disclose:

- in marine insurance, Article 5 of *the Provisions of the SPC on Several Issues about the Trial of Cases Concerning Marine Insurance Disputes* provides that if the insurer knows that the insured has failed to truthfully disclose the material circumstance in accordance with Article 222(1) of the MC, nevertheless collects the premium or pays insurance indemnities, but still alleges to terminate the contract on the basis that the insured has failed to perform the obligation to disclose, the allegation will not be supported by the court;
- in other types of insurance, Article 7 of *Interpretation II* provides that after the formation of insurance contract, the insurer knows or ought to know that the applicant fails to perform the obligation to disclose, nevertheless collects the premium, but still alleges to terminate the contract based on Article 16(2) of the IL, the allegation will not be supported by the court;

– in life insurance, Article 5(2) of *Interpretation III* provides that if the insurer knows the result of the insured's medical examination, nevertheless alleges that the contract is terminable on the grounds that the insured has not truthfully disclosed the relevant circumstances, the allegation will not be supported by the court.

172. It should be noted that the right to terminate the contract in accordance with Article 16(2) of the IL shall be extinguished if it is not exercised within thirty days after the date on which the insurer learnt of the reason for termination. Once two years have lapsed from the date of formation of the contract, the insurer may not terminate the contract. If an insured event occurs, the insurer shall bear the obligation to pay indemnities or insurance benefits (Article 16(3) of the IL).

H. The Relationship Between Termination of Contract and Refusal of Paying Indemnities or Insurance Benefits

173. By Article 8 of *Interpretation II*, if the insurer does not exercise the right to terminate the contract, but refuses to pay indemnities or insurance benefits pursuant to Article 16(4) and (5) of the IL, the refusal will not be supported by the court, unless the parties reach the agreement otherwise regarding the payment issues and the validity of the contract. In short, the insurer must terminate the contract before it refuses to pay indemnities or insurance benefits.

II. Precontractual Duty of the Insurer: Obligation to Explain

A. Definition and Basis of the Obligation to Explain

174. The insurer's obligation to explain means that the insurer must make a definitive interpretation and clarification of the contents of the contract when entering into an insurance contract with the assured, so that the assured can understand the contents of the contract. The reasons why the insurer should explain to the assured are as follows:

– the contents of the insurance contract are professional and technical, which may be difficult for the general applicant to understand due to their lack of relevant professional knowledge;
– although the insurance contract is concluded by the two parties, the contents of the clauses are preprinted by the insurer; in other words, the applicant cannot actually negotiate with the insurer on an equal basis;
– because of the format contract nature of the insurance contract, the insurer is in a better position than that of the applicant when entering the insurance contract.

Thus, if the insurer does not clarify the clauses in particular exemption clause in advance, it is equivalent to actually impose the applicant to accept such clauses. As a consequence, the insurer should explain to the applicant the clauses of the insurance contract in detail when the contract is established, in particular the exemption clauses, and answer the applicant's questions about the clauses of the contract clearly.

B. Nature of the Obligation to Explain

175. Obligation to explain is a precontractual duty; that is, at the time of conclusion of the contract, the relationship between the parties to the contract changes from the general social relationship to a special social relationship, from ignorance to acquaintance, mutual understanding, and mutual dependence. Based on the trust, the insurer should explain the contents of the insurance contract to the counterpart, and equally, the applicant should inform the insurer of the material circumstances of the subject-matter insured.

C. Contents of the Explanation

176. Through the insurer's explanation, the applicants can know the contents of the insurance contract accurately and judge whether the contract conforms to their own situation and whether they can realize their aim to spread risk and obtain insurance protection. Therefore, the contents of the explanation mainly include the relevant information of the insurance contract clauses. The standard of insurer's explanation should be based on the understanding level of the average person, to the extent that the counterpart of the contract who is assumed to be the average person understands the contents of the insurance contract. The breadth of the scope of explanation depends on whether the counterpart can fully understand the insurance coverage provided by the insurance contract he will enter into. Article 17 of the IL stipulates that where an insurance contract is concluded using the standard clauses of the insurer, the insurer shall provide an insurance policy with the standard clauses attached and explain the contents of the contract to the insurance applicant. For those clauses exempting the insurer from liability in the insurance contract, the insurer shall sufficiently warn the insurance applicant of those clauses in the insurance application form, the insurance policy or any other insurance certificate, and expressly explain those clauses to the insurance applicant in writing or verbally. If the insurer fails to make a warning or express explanation thereof, those clauses shall not be effective.

D. Time and Method of the Explanation

177. The insurer shall explain the contents of the contract to the applicant before or at the time of the conclusion of the contract. When the contract is established, the rights and obligations of both parties have been determined. Therefore, there is no obligation to explain after the insurance contract has been established.

The method of explanation refers to the specific manners and steps of the explanation. The insurer may explain to the applicant in writing or verbally, or may explain to the applicant by the insurance agent. The insurer shall take the initiative to explain the contents, terms, purpose and scope of application of the clauses without the applicant's inquiry or request.

178. In practice, there are roughly three methods to make the explanation.

First, in written form; that is, the main clauses of the contract are printed on the back of the insurance policy, and the written explanation of the exemption clauses and related terminology is attached. The signature of the applicant on the insurance policy is the affirmation of the insurer to perform the obligation to explain.

Second, when the applicant goes through the formalities for insurance, the insurer verbally informs the applicant of the contents of the exemption clauses and its meanings.

Third, when the applicant applies for the insurance, the insurer will submit the written explanation about the exemption clauses which has been printed to the applicant. If there is any doubt for the applicant, the insurer will explain it to him or her in a timely manner and record the facts about reading and explaining accordingly.

§2. Actual Formation of the Contract

179. Article 11 of the IL provides that an insurance contract shall be concluded upon agreement between both parties after consultation, and the rights and obligations of both parties shall be determined according to the principle of fairness. An insurance contract shall be concluded voluntarily, unless the insurance is mandated by a law or administrative regulation. Accordingly, it is generally believed that the conclusion of an insurance contract is a legal act in which the insurer and the applicant agree upon the clauses of the insurance contract on an equal and voluntary basis according to the principle of fairness.

180. Article 471 of the CC provides that the parties shall conclude a contract in the form of an offer and an acceptance. This procedure applies to all types of civil contracts. An offer is an expression of an intent to enter into a contract with another person. An acceptance is the expression of an intention made by the offeree to assent to the offer. A contract is established when the acceptance becomes effective. As a civil contract, the formation of the insurance contract complies with the general formation procedures of the contract. Specifically, Article 13(1) of the IL clearly stipulates the procedure for the conclusion of an insurance contract; that is, an insurance contract shall be formed after the insurance applicant applies for insurance and the insurer agrees to underwrite the insurance. The insurer shall issue an insurance policy or any other insurance certificate to the insurance applicant in a timely manner. It can be seen that this article expresses the offer and acceptance in the CC as application and underwriting. At the same time, since the insurance contract is a consensual contract, the insurance contract is established when the insurer makes an acceptance to underwrite.

I. Application

181. The application is an offer which is an expression of an intent to apply for insurance expressly to the insurer, which is a prerequisite for entering into an insurance contract. Article 472 of the CC provides that an offer is an expression of an intent to enter into a contract with another person. Such expression of intent shall comply with the following:

- its contents shall be specific and definite;
- it indicates that the offeror will be bound by the expression of intent in case of acceptance by the offeree.

Such a rule also applies to the insurance application. The application is the unilateral expression of the applicant, and it is not effective unless it is accepted by the insurer.

182. Since the insurance contract is an informal contract, the applicant may apply for insurance using written form, and may also use the form of telephone, fax, email, interview or other non-written forms. However, in order to reduce the cost of entering into an insurance contract and prevent future disputes effectively, in practice, the application is often made in writing. In order to facilitate the development of insurance business, insurance companies have prepared and printed various insurance certificates in advance, unified the basic clauses of insurance contract, and actively carried out various businesses to attract customers. The abovementioned work done by an insurance company is an invitation for offer, which is an expression of an intent to invite other parties to make offers thereto.

183. When the applicant applies for insurance in a written form, the application form should first be filled out. An application form is a written offer sent by the applicant to express his/her intent to enter into an insurance contract with the insurer. The application form is usually printed by the insurer in advance, and its contents generally include the subject-matter insured, the type of insurance, the sum insured, the period of insurance, the insurance liability and so on. For the contents on the application form, the applicant must fill out in truth and determine the insurance type and coverage that meets his/her needs. After completing the application form, it should be returned to the insurer. The application form is mostly in the form of a format clause, so the applicant's filling out the form means that the clauses of the insurance contract have been confirmed. The act of filling out the application form reflects the intention of the applicant to enter into an insurance contract. The application form is binding on the applicant, and when the contents on the application form cannot fully meet the insurance needs, the applicant can also make a new offer to the insurer. The application is a legal act with the following components.

A. The Applicant Has the Capacity to Conclude the Contract

184. Not all the civil parties can apply for insurance independently. When the applicant makes an application, he or she shall have the corresponding capacity for civil conduct required by law. According to the difference of the capacity for civil conduct, the CC divides the natural person into three types, namely persons with full capacity for civil conduct, persons with limited capacity for civil conduct, and persons without capacity for civil conduct. A minor attaining the age of 16 and primarily relying on his/her own labor income for living is deemed a person with full capacity for civil conduct, so these persons can apply for the insurance independently. The persons with limited capacity for civil conduct are incapable of discerning their conduct so that their application will generally not produce the effect of the offer unless the application is consented to or ratified by his/her statutory agent. A person without civil capacity shall be represented in entering into the insurance contract by his/her statutory agent. Legal persons and other organizations can be the applicant to apply for insurance because they have the civil party qualification.

B. The Applicant's Expression of an Intent to Enter into a Contract Is True

185. The true expression of an intent to enter into an insurance contract is the embodiment of the effective conditions of the offer from the perspective of the IL. The applicant's application behavior should be based on his own true will. The subject-matter insured, the type of insurance, the time limit, etc. are all decided by the applicant independently, and the insurance company cannot use unfair means to force or induce the applicant to apply for insurance against his/her true will.

C. The Requirement of Insurable Interest in Personal Insurance

186. Article 12 of the IL provides that an applicant for personal insurance shall, when entering into an insurance contract, have an insurable interest in the insured. The insured in property insurance shall have an insurable interest in the subject-matter insured when an insured incident occurs. When an insurance contract is concluded, if the insurable interests are not stipulated, there will be a high risk of gambling by making use of the insurance, which is contrary to the original intention of the legislation of the IL. Therefore, in order to prevent the moral hazard of the applicant, the applicant of life insurance should have an interest in the relationship with the insured when the insurance contract is concluded.

II. Underwriting

187. Article 479 of the CC provides that an acceptance is the expression of an intention made by the offeree to assent to the offer. Article 13 of the IL provides that an insurance contract shall be formed after the insurance applicant applies for insurance and the insurer agrees to underwrite the insurance. The insurer shall issue an insurance policy or any other insurance certificate to the insurance applicant in a timely manner. According to the provisions of this article, the insurer's acceptance is made in the form of underwriting, and the underwriting is the expression of the insurer's intention to agree to accept the applicant's application.

188. The insurance contract is a consensual contract, and it is established when the expressions of the intent of both parties reach an agreement. Generally, the applicant fills in the items listed on the application form one by one according to the requirements thereon, and then submits it to the insurer for review. If the insurer believes that the contents of the application form meet the requirements of the insurance and accepts it, the insurance contract is established. The legal effect of underwriting is that it is the necessary and final stage in the establishment of an insurance contract, and the insurance contract becomes effective when the notice of agreeing to underwrite reaches the applicant. The form of the notice can be made in writing or orally via telephone, etc. Although the insurer does not expressly agree to underwrite, he has fulfilled the main obligations (such as issuing insurance certificates) and the conduct has been accepted by the applicant, which shall be deemed that the insurance contract is established. Underwriting can be made either by the insurer or by the insurer's agent. The insurer's acceptance to underwrite must be the complete acceptance of the contents of the offer, and the partial acceptance or modification of the offer does not constitute an acceptance but is regarded as a new offer. For example, because the applicant has special needs and added new requirements in addition to the original application form, the insurer requests to increase the insurance premium rate accordingly. In this case, the insurer's request to raise the insurance premium rate does not constitute the underwriting, but constitutes a counteroffer, that is a new offer. This new offer must be approved by the applicant so that the insurance contract can be established.

189. After the insurer agrees to underwrite, he shall promptly issue an insurance policy or other insurance certificates to the applicant. An insurance policy is an official certificate for entering into an insurance contract and the legal basis for the parties to the contract to perform their contractual obligations. Any party that violates the clauses of the insurance policy is liable for the breach of the contract. Other insurance certificates are simplified insurance policies with the same legal effect as the insurance policy. The "issuance of insurance policy or any other insurance certificates" as stipulated in Article 13 of the IL is not an essential requirement for the establishment of an insurance contract, but a necessary and independent stage after the completion of the insurance contract, and is the insurer's post-contractual duty. Insurance policies and other insurance certificates are only used as proof of insurance contract. Failure to issue insurance certificates does not affect the establishment of the insurance contract. In the insurance practice, the insurer usually does not send the underwriting notice separately when agreeing to underwrite, but issues the relevant insurance certificates directly, so that the insurance certificates not only serve as the evidence of underwriting but also fulfill the function of underwriting notice, which has a dual role.

§3. Validity Requirements

190. The insurance contract becomes effective when the established insurance contract meets the legal requirements and the effective requirements agreed by the parties; as a consequence, it is legally binding on both the parties. The establishment and validity of the insurance contract are two different legal concepts. The former manifests itself in the conclusion of an insurance contract between the insured and the applicant through an offer and an acceptance, emphasizing the actual existence of the insurance contract, and the latter manifests itself in the legal binding of the insurance contract as a result of compliance with the law and the conditions agreed by the parties, which is the result of value judgment. The establishment of an insurance contract is the logical premise of the validity of an insurance contract. The validity of an insurance contract is the ultimate destination of the establishment of an insurance contract. If there is no insurance contract, it is impossible to talk about whether it is effective. The established insurance contract must meet the validity requirements so that it can be recognized by the law and bind the parties.

The validity requirements of an insurance contract refer to the legal conditions based on which an established insurance contract may have legal effect in accordance with the contents expressed by the parties. Article 13(3) of the IL provides that a legally formed insurance contract shall become effective upon formation. The insurance applicant and insurer may attach a condition or time limit for the effectiveness of the contract. In other words, the validity requirements of the insurance contract in China include general validity requirements and special validity requirements.

I. General Validity Requirements

191. The general validity requirements of an insurance contract refer to the universal legal conditions that enable an established legal act to produce legal effects in accordance with the contents expressed by the parties. It is a common condition that all insurance contracts must have to produce the legal effects. According to the relevant laws and regulations of China, the general validity requirements include the following.

A. The Parties Have the Capacity to Enter into an Insurance Contract

192. The insurance contract is based on the expression of the intent of the parties who conclude the contract, and is the result of the parties' presupposition of the future life according to the law. Therefore, the parties who enter into the insurance contract should have the corresponding capacity for civil conduct and be able to rationally recognize and understand the legal meaning of their own behavior. In other words, only insurance contracts concluded by qualified parties can be legally valid.

B. The Expression of the Intent Is True

193. The true expression of the intent means that the inner will of the party is consistent with the external expression. If the expression of the intent of the parties to the contract is consistent with their true inner will, the legal consequences are that what the parties pursuing is bound by their expression. If the expression of the intent of the parties to the contract is made in the case of external force, such as fraud or coercion, the contents of the insurance contract do not meet the legal consequences expected by the parties, which will inevitably affect the binding effect of the contract. At the same time, Article 3 of *Interpretation II* also provides that where, when entering into an insurance contract, the insurance applicant or the agent thereof does not personally affix its signature or seal to the contract, and the insurer or the agent thereof affixes a signature or seal to the contract on behalf of the insurance applicant, the contract shall not be effective to the insurance applicant. However, if the insurance applicant has paid the insurance premium, the insurance applicant shall be deemed to have subsequently recognized the signature or seal affixed on its behalf. Where an insurer or the agent thereof fills out an insurance policy on behalf of an insurance applicant, which is then signed or sealed by the applicant for confirmation, the confirmation entered by the insurer or the agent thereof on behalf of the applicant shall be deemed to represent the true will of the applicant.

C. No Violation of the Compulsory Provisions of Laws and Damage of the Public Interests

194. The expression of intent of the parties is the core and basis of the insurance contract. However, the legal consequences expected by the parties can only be produced on the condition that the expression of intent of the parties does not violate the compulsory provisions of laws and damage the public interests. If the insurance contract violates the compulsory provisions of laws and damages the public interests, it is invalid. The situations that often appear in IL practice include:

- The applicant applies for personal insurance which takes the death of the insured as the condition for insurance benefit for a person without the civil conduct capacity. Article 33 of the IL provides that no insurance applicant shall take out any personal insurance in which insurance money shall be paid conditioned upon the death of the insured for a person without the civil conduct capacity, and no insurer shall underwrite such insurance. Therefore, unless prescribed by law, the applicant and the insurer cannot enter into an insurance contract in which the insurance money is paid conditioned upon the death of the insured for a person without the civil conduct capacity.
- The applicant insures for illegal subject-matter insured. The law protects the legitimate rights and interests of the parties but not their illegal interests. The insurance contract which is established to protect the illegal subject-matter insured by the applicant and the insurer is invalid.

II. Special Validity Requirements

195. Generally, the legal effect of the establishment, modification, termination of a relationship involving the civil rights and obligations can be produced if the general validity requirements are satisfied. However, in some special cases, although the general validity requirements are met, the insurance contract still cannot produce the legal effects. It must satisfy certain requirements to be effective. Article 13(3) of the IL provides that a legally formed insurance contract shall become effective upon formation. The insurance applicant and insurer may attach a condition or time limit for the effectiveness of the contract. An insurance contract attached with an effective condition is a contract attached with a cessation condition, and the contract is effective when the condition is fulfilled. The insurance contract attached with a time limit for effectiveness will take effect when the time limit is expired.

196. In addition, some insurance contracts also need to satisfy the statutory validity requirements. First, the situations where the insurance contract is null and void totally include the following:

- Article 31(3) of the IL provides that where the insurance applicant does not have an insurable interest in the insured when entering into a personal insurance contract, the contract shall be null and void. Article 48 of the IL stipulates that the insured who does not have an insurable interest in the subject-matter insured when an insured incident occurs shall not claim indemnity against the insurer.
- Article 34(1) of the IL provides that where an insurance contract takes death as the condition for payment of insurance money, and the insured has not consented thereto and recognized the insured amount, the contract shall be null and void.
- Article 33 of the IL provides that no insurance applicant shall take out any personal insurance in which insurance money shall be paid conditioned upon the death of the insured for a person without the civil conduct capacity, and no insurer shall underwrite such insurance. Otherwise, the insurance contract is null and void. But parents who take out personal insurance for their underage children shall not be subject to this.

And the situations where the insurance contract is null and void in part are as follows:

- Article 17(2) of the IL provides that for those clauses exempting the insurer from liability in the insurance contract, the insurer shall sufficiently warn the insurance applicant of those clauses in the insurance application form, the insurance policy or any other insurance certificate, and expressly explain those clauses to the insurance applicant in writing or orally. If the insurer fails to make a warning or express explanation thereof, those clauses shall not be effective.
- Article 55(3) of the IL provides that the insured amount shall not exceed the insurable value. In the case of excess, the excess shall be invalid.
- Article 33(2) of the IL provides that where the parents take out personal insurance for their underage children, the total insurance money paid for the death of

the insured shall not exceed the limit as prescribed by the insurance regulatory body under the State Council and the excess shall be invalid.

§4. PROOF OF THE CONTRACT

197. The form of the insurance contract is the carrier of the parties' consent and is the external expression of the contents of insurance contract. Historically, the form of contract has undergone a change from emphasizing its external form to emphasizing its internal meaning, which is a reflection of the law's pursuit of the value of trade convenience for economic relationship in the context of the rising of credit. Emphasizing on meaning is not equal to denying the form. It is difficult for the law to evaluate the pure inner meaning. It can only evaluate the meaning expressed in a certain form and can be understood and recognized by people. Therefore, the form of the contract is indispensable. Article 469 of the CC provides that the parties may use written, oral or other forms in entering into a contract. A contract shall be in written form if the laws or administrative regulations so provide. A contract shall be concluded in written form if the parties so agree. This regulation divides the contract form into a statutory form and an agreed form. Except for the statutory form, other contracts shall be concluded in any form based on the principle of freedom, and the law does not intervene. Article 13 of the IL stipulates that an insurance contract shall be formed after the insurance applicant applies for insurance and the insurer agrees to underwrite the insurance. The insurer shall issue an insurance policy or any other insurance certificate to the insurance applicant in a timely manner. The insurance policy or any other insurance certificate shall expressly state the provisions of the contract reached by both parties. Both parties may agree to state the provisions of the contract between them in any other written form. The insurance contract is not stipulated as a formal contract. When the parties reach an agreement, the contract is established and does not have to meet specific written requirements.

After the insurance contract is established and effective, the delivery of the written certificate is the performance of the contractual obligation. The written certificate of the insurance contract is roughly divided into two categories: the first is the insurance certificate, which is the most used form of insurance contract in practice, and the second is other written forms other than certificates.

I. Application Form

198. An application form refers to a written offer from the applicant to the insurer for the purpose of entering into an insurance contract. After the application form is accepted by the insurer, it becomes a part of the insurance contract. The application form is printed by the insurer in advance and is provided to the applicant. The applicant fills the form item by item and then submits it to the insurer. After the insurer seals the form, the insurance contract is established.

The legal significance of the application form is that, first, the contents contained in the application form are a written insurance offer issued by the applicant, and are binding on the applicant; second, the contents of the application form become part of the contract after being accepted by the insurer. Whether it is true or not it directly affects the effectiveness of the insurance contract.

II. Binding Slip

199. A binding slip, also known as a temporary insurance policy, refers to a temporary insurance certificate issued by the insurer before the issuance of a formal insurance policy. The contents of the binding slip are relatively simple, and generally only include the main contents of the insurance contract such as the name of the insured, the subject-matter insured, the insured amount, the rate of insurance premium, and the scope of insurance coverage. The legal effect of the binding slip is the same as that of the formal insurance policy. After the formal insurance policy is issued, it will become invalid automatically.

The binding slip is not a necessary certificate for an insurance contract, nor is it a necessary procedure for forming an insurance contract. It is only a temporary insurance certificate issued before the issuance of a formal insurance policy. It is generally used in the following situations:

- when the insurance agent competes for an insurance business but the formal insurance policy has not been completed by the insurer, the applicant shall be issued a binding slip by the agent;
- after the insurance company's branch accepts certain insurance business subject to approval by its parent company, it shall issue the binding slip to the applicant before the parent company has approved the business;
- when the applicant and the insurer have reached an agreement on the main terms of the insurance contract, but there are other specific issues yet to be negotiated, the insurer can issue a binding slip;
- when the export trade is settled, the insurer can issue a binding slip as one of the settlement documents to prove that the export goods are insured.

The legal significance of the binding slip is that before the formal insurance policy is issued, it is a written certificate to provide insurance protection for the insured. After the issuance of the binding slip, if an insurance accident occurs, the insurer shall bear the obligation to pay the insurance money accordingly.

III. Insurance Policy

200. An insurance policy refers to the formal written certificate issued by the insurer to the applicant after the insurance contract is established to specify the rights and obligations of the parties to the insurance contract. The insurance policy is made by the insurer and delivered to the applicant after signing. Article 13 of the IL provides that the insurer shall issue an insurance policy or any other insurance certificate to the insurance applicant in a timely manner after the formation of the insurance contract.

201. In practice, insurance contracts are generally reflected in written forms such as insurance policies. As the insurance contract develops from the formal contract to the informal contract, the effectiveness of the insurance policy has changed accordingly. Under the legislative mode in which the insurance contract is a formal contract, the insurance certificate is an essential requirement for the establishment of an insurance contract; that is, if the insurance contract is not concluded in accordance with the statutory form or procedure, the insurance contract is not established. In the history of IL legislation, Article 25 of the Economic Contract Law and the Property Insurance Contracts Regulations in China had adopted the doctrine of formal contract as the legislative guideline. The doctrine of informal insurance contract is also called the doctrine of evidence. The legislative model adopting this doctrine believes that the issuance of insurance policy or any other insurance certificate is not the establishment or validity requirement of the insurance contract. An insurance contract is formed when one party makes an offer and is accepted by the other party. The insurance policy or the binding slip is only the certificate of the insurance contract.

202. The requirements on the form of insurance contract of the insurance legislation in China have also undergone a transition from a formal contract to an informal one. In the legislative mode of the informal insurance contract, the insurance contract can be established before the insurance policy is issued. The legal effect of the insurance contract does not depend on the delivery of the insurance policy or any other certificate. Therefore, the nature and effectiveness of the insurance certificate are also changed from the establishment or validity requirement of the insurance contract to the evidence of the insurance contract; that is, if the insurance policy is not adopted by the insurance contract, the establishment and validity of the insurance contract are not affected, but it is only likely that the unfavorable consequences of the burden of proof due to lack of evidence shall be undertaken. Normally, when the two parties reach an agreement, the insurance contract will become effective. If the insurance accident occurs before the formal insurance policy is issued, the insurance contract is also binding. Article 13 of the IL just adopts the doctrine of evidence, that is the doctrine of informal contract. In insurance practice, insurance policies and insurance contracts can often be replaced by each other. Strictly speaking, the insurance policy is not a contract, but a formal written certificate of contracting.

203. The legal significance of the insurance policy is as follows.

First, the proof of the establishment of the insurance contract. According to Article 13 of the IL, the insurance contract is established before the issuance of the insurance certificate. The insurer's issuance of an insurance policy should be based on an existing insurance contract. The insurance certificate is a written certificate issued by the insurer based on the established insurance contract to prove the existence of it.

Second, the proof of the contents of the insurance contract. According to Article 13 of the IL, regardless of the form of the insurance contract, the insurer shall issue an insurance policy in a timely manner and the provisions of the contract should be expressly stated. When a dispute arises, the written insurance policy shall become the basis for the arbitration authority or the people's court to handle the case.

Third, specifying the rights and obligations of the parties to the contract. Both parties shall take the provisions stated in the insurance policy as the basis for the performance of the insurance contract and shall enjoy the rights and undertake the obligations accordingly. After the contract is established, the insurer is obliged to issue an insurance certificate to the other party. Article 17(1) of the IL stipulates that where an insurance contract is concluded using the standard clauses of the insurer, the insurer shall provide an insurance policy with the standard clauses attached. The right to hold an insurance policy is particularly important in a life insurance contract that can be transferred or pledged. The delivery of an insurance certificate is an obligation of the insurer and is not a validity requirement. The request for delivery of an insurance certificate is the applicant's right.

204. An insurance policy is not a security, and its effectiveness is similar to a "bank passbook." In loss indemnity insurance, the right owner of the insurance policy is still the owner of the insurable interest at the time of the insurance accident. If the order or bearer insurance policy is considered to be a marketable security, it may happen that the policyholder is not the owner of insurable interest (not a true victim) but the owner of the right in the insurance policy. For example, in the international trading practice, the seller applies for the maritime transport insurance based on the CIF price, and the insurer issues a bearer insurance policy to the seller after the contract is concluded. The seller sends it to the buyer together with the bill of lading after receipt. Unfortunately, the cargo was damaged at the factory terminal due to a dangerous accident covered by the insurance policy. At this time, the holder of the insurance policy is the buyer, but the risk burden is still borne by the seller because the goods have not been boarded; that is, if the damage is not caused by the seller's intention or negligence, the seller may be exempted from liability. But at the same time, the buyer is also exempt from paying. Therefore, if the insurance policy is regarded as a security, depending on the nature of the securities, the holder of the document is the owner of the rights in the document, and the buyer can still claim the insurance payment according to the insurance policy, and the insurer cannot refuse. Although the seller is the true victim, he is still unable to be protected by the insurance contract.

205. In property insurance, the purpose of insurance is to indemnify specific loss. Therefore, whether the insurance policy is a straight, bearer policy, or can be transferred in terms of endorsement, the right to claim should be vested in the actual owner of the insurable interest at the time of insurable incident. And the so-called order or bearer insurance policy only has the effect similar to prompting security; that is, the exercise of the right shall prompt the insurance policy, and the insurer's debt to the real right holder shall be extinguished after the payment to the policyholder. The right holder in the insurance policy can request the policyholder to deliver the insurance policy to him before the policyholder collects the insurance money. If the policyholder has already received the insurance money, the money will be unjust enrichment and should be returned. An insurance policy does not have the characteristics of a marketable security, but just has some similarity with marketable security. The transfer of the insurance policy is not the transfer of the insurable interest. The time for the transfer of insurable interest shall be based on the insurable interest, not the time when the insurance policy is transferred.

IV. Insurance Certificate

206. The insurance certificate is a written certificate issued by the insurer to the applicant to prove that the insurance contract has been established, and is a simplified insurance policy. Its legal effect is the same as the insurance policy, but the content is relatively simple. In practice, there is no listed content in the insurance certificate, and the formal insurance policy of the same insurance type shall prevail. If the insurance certificate conflicts with the content of the formal insurance policy, the special terms in the insurance certificate shall prevail. The insurance certificate is usually used in the following insurance business in China:

- to use the insurance certificate to simplify the document procedure; that is, the insurance certificate is used to replace the insurance policy;
- to issue an insurance certificate besides the insurance policy; e.g., in addition to the main insurance policy of the group insurance, the individual who participates in the group insurance is separately issued an insurance certificate.

The significance of the insurance certificate is that it not only has the legal effect same as the insurance policy but also simplifies the formality of the insurance document.

V. Other Forms

207. Other forms of insurance contracts refer to insurance contracts in writing other than insurance policies and other insurance certificates. According to the provisions of the IL, the applicant and the insurer may also agree to state the provisions of the contract between them in any other written form.

Chapter 4. Obligations of the Applicant and Insured

§1. Obligation to Pay the Premium

208. In Chinese law, insurance means the commercial insurance whereby the applicant pays insurance premiums to the insurer in accordance with the contract and the insurer is liable for payment of indemnities in connection with property losses arising due to the occurrence of an event the possibility of the occurrence of which is specified in the contract; or the insurer is liable to payment of insurance benefits due to the death, injury, disability or illness of the insured, or the conditions such as age and term specified in the contract being satisfied.

In the light of the above definition, it is well recognized that the consideration for the insurer to pay the indemnities or insurance benefits is the premiums paid by the applicant.

209. Article 10(2) of the IL provides that the applicant bears the obligation to pay insurance premiums in accordance with the contract. By Article 35 of the IL, an applicant may, in accordance with the contract, pay the entire insurance premium to the insurer in one lump sum or pay it in installments.

210. Depending upon the insured value, the insurance period and the rate, the amount of premium varies. The amount of the premium will usually be stated in the insurance contract or policy, and it will usually have to be sanctioned by the insurance regulatory authorities or calculated in accordance with the rate that is put on record to the insurance regulatory authorities.

211. In principle, the amount of premium charged cannot be changed after the contract is concluded. However, in the following situations stipulated in Article 52(1) and Article 53 of the IL, the insurer may increase or reduce the premium:

- if the degree of risk to the subject matter of insurance increases substantially during the term of the contract, the insured shall notify the insurer in accordance with the contract in a timely manner and the insurer may, in accordance with the contract, increase the insurance premium;
- unless the contract provides otherwise, the insurer shall reduce the premium and refund the appropriate amount of insurance premium calculated on a daily basis in any of the two circumstances: (1) a change occurs in the circumstance upon which the insurance premium rate was determined, resulting in a marked decrease of the risk to the subject matter of insurance; or (2) the insured value of the subject matter of insurance decreases markedly.

212. Although in principle the parties may agree when the premiums shall be paid, it should be noted that Article 14 of the IL provides that once the insurance contract has been concluded, the insurer shall pay the premiums in accordance therewith, and the insurer shall assume insurance liability starting from the time agreed thereto.

However, it is to be emphasized that pursuant to Article 13(3) of the IL, a lawfully concluded insurance contract shall come into effect once it is concluded, unless conditions are attached thereto. Thus, unless it is agreed otherwise, Article 14 does not make the payment of premium as a condition precedent to the liability of the insurer. The insurer may put a clause into the contract with the effect that the insurer does not assume liability unless the premium is paid, provided that such clause has been brought into the applicant's attention and expressly explained in accordance with Article 17 of the IL.

213. In marine insurance, by Article 5 of the Provisions of the SPC on Several Issues about the Trial of Cases Concerning Marine Insurance Disputes, the insured does not pay the agreed premium in accordance with Article 234 of the MC; before the attachment of insurance liability, the insurer has the right to terminate the contract, unless the insurer has already issued the insurance certificates. After the attachment of insurance liability, the insurer is not allowed to terminate the contract on the grounds that the insured has not paid the premium.

214. In life insurance contract, special provisions apply as regards the payment of premium in accordance with the IL and judicial interpretation:

- By Article 36, if the contract provides for the payment in installments of the premium, and the applicant, after payment of the initial installment of the insurance premium, fails to pay an installment within thirty days after the date of a reminder from the insurer or within sixty days after the specified time limit, the validity of the contract shall be suspended or the insurer shall reduce the insured amount in accordance with the conditions specified in the contract, unless otherwise provided in the contract. If an insured event occurs in respect of the insured during the period specified above, the insurer shall pay the insurance benefits in accordance with the contract, but may deduct the outstanding insurance premium therefrom.
- By Article 37, if the effect of a contract is suspended in accordance with Article 36, its validity shall be restored after the insurer and the applicant agree through consultations and the applicant pays the outstanding insurance premium. By Article 8 of *Interpretation III*, when the insurance is suspended pursuant to Article 36 stated above, if the applicant applies to restore the validity of insurance contract and agrees to pay the premium, unless the risk of the insured has increased substantially during the suspension, the insurer is not entitled to refuse to restore the validity of insurance contract. If the insurer receives the application for the restoration of the validity of insurance contract but does not expressly refuse within thirty days, the validity of insurance contract will be regarded as being restored. The insurer is entitled to the corresponding interests upon the restoration of the validity of insurance contract. However, if the parties fail to agree within two years from the date on which the effect of the contract is suspended, the insurer shall have the right to terminate the contract.
- By Article 38, an insurer may not resort to litigation to require payment from an applicant in respect of life insurance premium. Noticeably, this Article does not apply to health insurance and accident insurance.

- By Article 7 of *Interpretation III*, the parties are entitled to assert that the applicant's obligation to pay the premium has been fulfilled on the grounds that the insured, the beneficiary or others have paid the premium on behalf of the applicant.

§2. Obligation to Truthfully Disclose

215. The obligation to truthfully disclose is probably the most important obligation of the applicant, which has been fully discussed above. See Part I Chapter 3, §1 *supra*.

§3. Obligation Not to Commit Insurance Fraud

216. Insurance fraud is perhaps one of the most pressing problems challenging the insurance industry. Fraudulent claims account for a significant portion of all claims received by insurers, and cost billions annually. Types of insurance fraud are very diverse, and occur in all areas of insurance. Fraudulent activities also affect the lives of innocent people, both directly through accidental or purposeful injury or damage and indirectly as fraud causes insurance premiums to be higher. Therefore, the law must have played a significant role in tackling insurance fraud.

217. The insured is obliged not to commit insurance fraud. The types of fraudulent act and the legal consequences for submission are regulated by Article 27 of the IL:

- If an insured event has not occurred but the insured or beneficiary falsely claims that such an event has occurred, and submits a claim with the insurer for the payment of indemnities or insurance benefits, the insurer shall have the right to terminate the contract and not return the insurance premiums.
- If the applicant or the insured deliberately causes an insured event, the insurer shall have the right to terminate the contract and shall not be liable for the payment of indemnities or insurance benefits. Unless otherwise provided by Article 43 of the IL, it will not refund the insurance premiums.
- If the applicant, the insured or the beneficiary fabricates false causes for an event or overstates the extent of the losses by means of forged or altered relevant proofs, information or other evidence after the occurrence of such event, the insurer shall not be liable to pay indemnities or insurance benefits for the portion that is false.
- If the applicant, the insured or beneficiary commits any fraudulent act and causes the insurer to pay insurance proceeds or incur expenses, it shall return the insurance proceeds to or compensate the insurer.

218. Noticeably, the commitment of insurance fraud may also attract the administrative liability or even criminal liability.

As regards administrative liability, Article 176 of IL provides that:

- if an applicant, the insured or beneficiary commits insurance fraud act and the insurance fraud activity engaged in by it is not sufficient to constitute a criminal offense, it shall be subject to administrative penalties in accordance with the law;
- if an assessor, appraiser or attester of an insured event deliberately provides false supporting documents, thus creating the conditions for the applicant, the insured or the beneficiary to commit insurance fraud, it shall be too penalized.

As regards criminal liability, Article 198 of *the Criminal Law* provides that:

- if the amount involved is relatively large, the offender may be sentenced to fixed-term imprisonment of no more than five years or criminal detention and shall also be fined not less than RMB 10,000 but no more than RMB 100,000;
- if the amount involved is huge, or if there are other serious circumstances, the offender shall be sentenced to fixed-term imprisonment of no less than five years but no more than ten years and shall also be fined no less than RMB 20,000 but not more than RMB 200,000;
- if the amount involved is especially huge, or if there are other especially serious circumstances, the offender shall be sentenced to fixed-term imprisonment of no less than ten years or life imprisonment and shall also be fined not less than RMB 20,000 but not more than RMB 200,000 or be sentenced to confiscation of property;
- where a unit commits the claim, it shall be fined, and the persons who are directly in charge and the other persons who are directly responsible for the crime shall be sentenced to fixed-term imprisonment of no more than five years or criminal detention; if the amount involved is huge, or if there are other serious circumstances, they shall be sentenced to fixed-term imprisonment of no less than five years but not more than ten years; if the amount involved is especially huge, or if there are other especially serious circumstances, they shall be sentenced to fixed-term imprisonment of not less than ten years;
- any assessor, appraiser or attester of an insured event who deliberately provides false supporting documents, thus creating the conditions for another to practice fraud, shall be deemed an accomplice in insurance fraud and punished as such.

§4. Obligation to Maintain the Safety of Subject Matter of Insurance

219. The function of insurance is not just to indemnify after the occurrence of insured event but also to positively prevent and mitigate the possibility of insured event. Maintaining the safety of subject matter of insurance may help to reduce or even avoid insurance accidents.

220. Article 51(1) and (2) of the IL provides that the applicant and insured shall abide by relevant state provisions on fire prevention, safety, production operation, labor protection, etc. in order to protect the safety of the subject matter of insurance. The insurer may, in accordance with the contract, examine the circumstances of the safety of the subject matter of insurance, and issue to the applicant and/or insured written proposals for the elimination of unsafe factors and hidden dangers. Noticeably, this obligation of the insurer is stipulated in the part of "Property Insurance Contract" of the IL. Therefore, it seems that the obligation is only applicable to the applicant and insured of property insurance but not to the same of life insurance.

221. If either the applicant or insured fails to fulfill its due diligence requirements as regards the safety of the subject matter of insurance in accordance with the contract, by Article 51(3) and (4) of the IL, the insurer shall have the right to request an increase in the insurance premium or terminate the contract. Subject to the consent of the insured, the insurer may take precautionary measures to protect the safety of the subject matter of insurance.

§5. Obligation to Notify the Insurer When the Degree of Risk to the Subject Matter of Insurance Increases Substantially

222. The potential risk of the subject matter of insurance is a crucial factor for the insurer to determine whether or not to take the risk and the rate of premium. After the conclusion of the insurance contract, if the subject matter of insurance is not under the control of the insurer, it is possible that the degree of risk may alter in a constant state. If the degree of risk to the subject matter of insurance increases substantially during the term of the contract, the probabilities of insured event and the rate of premium may substantially exceed the same that could reasonably be anticipated and calculated by the insurer. Therefore, if the original agreement is maintained in such circumstances, the insurer may face disadvantageous and unconscionable result, and accordingly, the law imposes certain obligation to the insurer in order to protect the interests of the insurer.

223. Article 52(1) of the IL provides that if the degree of risks to the subject matter of insurance increases substantially during the term of the contract, the insured shall notify the insurer in accordance with the contract in a timely manner.

In Chinese law, this obligation only applies to the insured (not the applicant) of property insurance (not life insurance).

224. It is well recognized that substantial increase of the degree of risks has three characteristics: (a) materiality; (b) continuality; and (c) unpredictability. More specifically, the increase of the degree of risk should not be immaterial so that the balance of the relationship between the parties has not been shaken. The increase of the degree of risk must continue for a period and not just be temporary. The increase of the degree of risk should not be within the contemplation of parties when negotiating the contract.

225. By Article 4 of *Interpretation IV*, in determining whether the situation that the "degree of risks to the subject matter insured rises significantly" stipulated in Articles 49 and 52 of the IL arises, the people's court shall consider the following factors comprehensively:

- changes to the purpose of the subject-matter insured;
- changes to areas where the subject-matter insured is used;
- changes to conditions where the subject-matter insured is kept;
- changes arising as a result of refitting or other causes;
- changes to the user or the manager of the subject-matter insured;
- duration of increased degree of risks; and
- other factors that are likely to result in a significant increase in the degree of risks.

Where there is an increase in the degree of risks to the subject-matter insured, but increased risks are covered by the insurance contract that the insurer foresees or should foresee when the insurance contract is concluded, the situation does not constitute a significant increase in the degree of risks.

226. By Articles 52(1) and (2) of the IL, two consequences may follow if the insured does not perform the obligation in accordance with the law:

(1) The insurer may, in accordance with the contract, increase the insurance premium or terminate the contract. If the insurer terminates the contract, it shall refund to the applicant the insurance premium collected, minus, in accordance with the contract, the portion to which it is entitled for the period between the date of commencement of its insurance liability until the date of termination of the contract.
(2) If the insured fails to perform its notification obligation and an insured event occurs due to the substantial increase in the degree of risk to the subject matter of insurance, the insurer shall not be liable to pay indemnities.

§6. Obligation to Notify When the Insured Event Occurs

227. The purpose of the notification is to allow the insurer to get involved as practically as possible after the occurrence of insured event. On the one hand, the insured and insurer can work together and take the necessary measures to prevent further losses or damages; On the other, the insurer can promptly preserve the evidence, investigate the event, ascertain the nature, reason and extent of the losses or damages, so that the insurance claim could be handled properly and without delay.

228. Article 21 of IL provides that the applicant, the insured or the beneficiary shall notify the insurer in a timely manner once it has learnt of the occurrence of an insured event.

The insurance contract can provide more specific provisions as to the time of notification. For example, Article 18 of PICC's "Home Owned Vehicle Loss Insurance" states that the insured should notify the insurer within forty-eight hours after the occurrence of insured event.

229. The legal consequences for the failure of performance of obligation, by Article 21, are that if notification is deliberately not given or not given due to gross negligence, making the nature or cause of, or the extent of the losses due to, the insured event difficult to determine, the insurer shall not be liable to pay indemnities or insurance benefits for the portion that is impossible to ascertain, unless the insurer learnt or ought to have learnt in a timely manner of the occurrence of the insured event by other means.

§7. Obligation to Provide Proofs and Information as to the Insured Event

230. Article 22(1) of the IL provides that when submitting a claim to the insurer for payment of indemnities or insurance benefits in accordance with the insurance contract after the occurrence of an insured event, the applicant, insured or beneficiary shall provide to the insurer all proofs and information it can provide pertinent to determining the nature or cause of, the extent of the losses due to, and other circumstances of the insured event.

231. The proofs and information may include: (1) policy or other insurance certificates; (2) proof as to the payment of premium; (3) receipts, books, packing list and other original documents regarding the subject matter of insurance; (4) ID card, household registration and other documents regarding the name, age, occupation, etc. of the insured in life insurance; (5) proofs and documents that can be used to determine the nature, cause, extent of the insured event, such as investigation and inspection report, certificate of insured event, certificate of damage, death certificate, identification of the degree of incapacity, etc.; (6) claim lists, such as the list of damages property, the list of costs and expenses, etc. In practice, most of the insurance contracts will specify the types of proofs and information which the applicant, insured or beneficiary is required to provide.

232. Article 22(2) of the IL states that if the insurer, pursuant to the contract, believes that relevant supporting documentation and information is incomplete, it shall, in a timely manner, notify the applicant, insured or beneficiary one time to provide the missing documentation or information. The purpose of this article is to prevent the insurer from delaying the claim stage by repeatedly requiring the applicant, insured or beneficiary to provide the missing proofs.

233. The IL does not specify the legal consequence for the breach of obligation. However, considering Article 22 shares similar legislative purpose with Article 21, it is suggested that insured cannot terminate the contract or refuse to pay the indemnities or insurance benefits on the grounds that the applicant, insured or beneficiary has failed to provide the relevant proofs in accordance with the contract. However, if due to the failure of providing the relevant proofs, the nature, cause and extent of loss cannot be ascertained, the insurer may refuse to pay the indemnities or insurance benefits only to the extent of unascertainable portion.

234. If the applicant, insured or beneficiary provides false proofs, it may commit insurance fraud, and Article 27 of the IL and other corresponding legislations may apply accordingly.

§8. Obligation to Notify the Insurer in the Situation of Double Insurance

235. Double insurance means insurance where the applicant concludes insurance contract with two or more insurers in respect of the same subject matter of insurance, the same insurable interests and the same insured events, and the total of the insured amounts exceeds the insured value (Article 56(4) of the IL).

236. By Article 56(1) of the IL, information relevant to double insurance shall be notified by the applicant to all concerned insurers. The law does not specify the details of information, but it is generally recognized that the information may contain the name and residence of the insurer, subject matter of insurance, insured value, premium, insured amount, the scope of insurance liability, the duration of insurance contract, the payment condition of the insurance, etc.

The notification could be given in writing or otherwise, unless otherwise agreed, and should be given voluntarily.

In practice, it is suggested that the insurer should attach other insurance contracts with notification so that other insurers may fully comprehend the situation of double insurance.

§9. Obligation to Mitigate

237. Article 57(1) of the IL provides that when an insured event occurs, the insured shall, with due diligence, take necessary measures to prevent or mitigate the losses. In the context of marine insurance, this obligation is also referred to as the obligation to sue and labor.

As the measure to encourage the insured to mitigate, Article 57(2) further provides that the necessary and reasonable expenses incurred by the insured in the prevention or mitigation of losses of the subject matter of insurance after the occurrence of an insured event shall be borne by the insurer. The amount of such expenses shall be calculated separately from the amount of compensation for the losses of the subject matter of insurance, and the maximum shall not exceed the insured amount. In addition, the insured can claim the mitigation expense even if the measure took by him does not succeed. As it is provided by Article 6 of *Interpretation IV*, where the insured, after an insured accident occurs, requests the insurer to bear reasonable expenses necessary for preventing or reducing losses to the subject-matters insured, in accordance with provisions of Article 57 of the IL, but the insurer argues that measures taken by the insured do not create practical effects, the people's court shall not uphold such argument.

238. Article 57 of the IL does not provide the legal consequence for breach of the obligation. In the light of Article 591 of the CC, which provides that where a party breaches the contract, the other party shall take the appropriate measures to prevent the losses from increasing; where the other party's failure to take appropriate measures results in additional losses, it cannot demand compensation for the additional losses; it is probably to recognize that if the additional losses have occurred due to the insured's negligence in failing to mitigate, the insurer shall not be responsible for the additional losses.

Chapter 5. Obligations of the Insurer

§1. Obligation to Issue the Insurance Documents in a Timely Manner

239. Article 13(1) of IL provides that an insurance contract shall be concluded when an applicant makes a request for insurance and the insurer agrees to insure. The insurer shall issue the applicant an insurance policy or other insurance certificates in a timely manner.

For the purpose of this Article, insurance document means insurance policy and other insurance certificates, which are the written form or simple form of insurance contract. The insurance policy document or other insurance certificates shall specify the contractual terms agreed upon by the parties.

§2. Obligation to Indemnify or Pay Insurance Benefits on the Occurrence of Insured Event

240. As the consideration for the right to collect the premium from the insured, the fundamental obligation of the insurer is to pay insurance indemnities or insurance benefits when the subject matter of insurance suffers the loss or damage due to the insured event.

I. Scope of the Obligation

A. Property Insurance

241. In the light of the principle of indemnity, in property insurance, the insurer is obliged to pay the actual loss suffered by the subject matter of insurance, plus other expenses specified clearly by the law.

242. By Article 55(1) and (2) of the IL, if the applicant and the insurer agree upon the insured value of the subject matter of insurance and specify the same in the contract, the agreed insured value shall serve as the criterion for calculating the indemnities should the subject matter of insurance suffer a loss. If the applicant and the insurer have not agreed upon the insured value of the subject matter of insurance, the actual value of the subject matter shall serve as the criterion for calculating the indemnities should the subject matter of insurance suffer a loss.

Depending upon the circumstances, the actual value of the subject matter of insurance would usually be determined by the market value of the subject matter at the time and the place of insurance accident, or through the assessment by the qualified loss adjustment agencies.

243. If the insured amount is less than the insured value, the insurer shall, unless otherwise specified in the contract, be liable for payment of the indemnities in proportion to the percentage of the insured value accounted for by the insured amount.

244. There are three types of costs or expenses that should be borne by the insurer in accordance with the IL:

(1) By Article 57(2), the necessary and reasonable expenses incurred by the insured in the prevention or mitigation of losses of the subject matter of insurance after the occurrence of an insured event shall be borne by the insurer. The amount of such expenses shall be calculated separately from the amount of indemnities for the losses of the subject matter of insurance and the maximum shall not exceed the insured amount.
(2) By Article 64, the necessary and reasonable expenses incurred by the insurer and the insured in the investigation and determination of the nature or cause of an insured event and the extent of the losses incurred by the subject matter of insurance shall be borne by the insurer.
(3) By Article 66, if arbitration or litigation proceedings are instituted against the insured of a liability insurance policy due to an insured event that caused damage to a third party, the arbitration or litigation costs and other necessary and reasonable expenses paid by the insured shall be borne by the insurer, unless otherwise provided by the contract.

B. Life Insurance

245. Because the life of human being cannot be calculated by way of money, the principle of indemnity has no role to play in life insurance, and accordingly, the insurer's obligation to pay insurance benefits is not related or limited to the actual loss suffered by the insured. In addition, no issue as regards insured value will arise in life insurance.

In life insurance, the parties usually agree to certain conditions precedent to the payment of insurance benefits. If these conditions are satisfied, the insurer's obligation to pay is accordingly triggered.

II. Performance of the Obligation

246. Article 23 of the IL meticulously provides the procedure of performance of the obligation: once an insurer receives a claim form the insured or beneficiary for the payment of indemnities or insurance benefits, it shall render its determination in a timely manner. If the circumstances are complicated, it shall render its determination within thirty days, unless otherwise provided in the contract. The insurer shall notify the insured or beneficiary of the results of its determination. If the claim falls within the insured liability, the insurer shall perform its obligation to pay the indemnities or insurance benefits within ten days after reaching agreement on paying the indemnities or insurance benefits with the insured or beneficiary. If the insurance contract provides a time limit for payment, the insurer shall perform the obligation to pay in accordance with such provisions.

247. If the amount of indemnities or insurance benefits cannot be determined within sixty days after the insurer receives a claim and the relevant proofs and documents, by Article 25 of the IL, the insurer shall first pay the amount that can be determined based on the proofs and documents available. After determining the final amount of indemnities or insurance benefit, the insurer shall pay any differences thereof.

248. In life insurance, under certain circumstances, the insurer is not obliged to pay the insurance benefits in accordance with the IL:

- By Article 43, if the applicant deliberately causes the death, injury, disability or illness of the insured, the insurer shall not be liable for payment of insurance benefit. Where the applicant has already fully paid insurance premiums for two or more years, the insurer shall refund the cash value of the insurance policy to other entitled beneficiaries in accordance with the contract. If a beneficiary deliberately causes the death, injury, disability or illness of the insured or deliberately attempts to murder the insured, such beneficiary shall forfeit his/her beneficiary rights.
- By Article 44, if a contract stipulates the death of the insured as a condition for payment of insurance benefits and the insured commits suicide within two years from the date of formation of the contract or the restoration of its validity, the insurer shall not be liable to pay the insurance benefits, unless the insured, at the time of his/her suicide, was without civil capacity. However, the insurer, in accordance with the contract, shall refund the cash value of the policy. By Article 21 of *Interpretation III*, the insurer bears the burden of proof that the insured commits suicide and the beneficiary or the heir of the insured bears the burden of proof that the insured was without civil capacity.
- By Article 45, if the insured willfully commits a crime or resists lawfully applied criminal enforcement measures, resulting in his/her injury, disability or death, the insurer shall not be liable to pay insurance benefits. If the applicant has paid in full two or more years of insurance premiums, the insurer shall, in accordance with the contract, refund the cash value of the policy. By Article 22 of *Interpretation III*, the determination of the insured's willful commitment of crime shall be based upon the legal instruments or other concluding observations provided by the criminal investigation organ, the procuratorial organ and the judicial organ. By Article 23 of *Interpretation III*, the insurer bears the burden of proof that there is causal link between the insured's injury, disability or death and the insured's willful commitment of crime and resistance of lawfully applied criminal enforcement measures. The insurer is not entitled to refuse the payment of insurance benefits due to the insured's disability or death caused by accident or illness when the insured is in custody or serving his/her sentence.

249. In life insurance, if the insured dies, the insurance benefits shall become part of his/her estate and the insurer shall perform its obligation of paying the insurance benefits in accordance with the "Inheritance" part of the CC in any of the following circumstances:

– no beneficiary was designated or the designation of the beneficiary is unclear and determination thereof is impossible;
– the beneficiary dies before the insured, and there is no other beneficiary; or
– the beneficiary loses or waives his/her beneficiary rights in accordance with the law, and there is no other beneficiary.

If the beneficiary and the insured both die in the same event and the sequence of their deaths is impossible to ascertain, the beneficiary shall be assumed to have died first.

250. Where a life insurance contract stipulates the death of the insured as a condition for payment of insurance benefits, by Article 24 of *Interpretation III*, the insurer is obliged to pay the insurance benefits if the insured is declared as being dead. If the date of declaration of death is beyond the insurance period but the evidence shows that the insured was missing within the insurance period, the insurer is still obliged to pay the insurance benefits in accordance with the contract.

III. Legal Consequences for the Failure of Performance

251. The failure to pay the indemnities or insurance benefits in accordance with the law will trigger not only the civil liability but also the administrative liability on the part of the insurer.

252. By Article 23(2) of the IL, if the insurer fails to perform the obligations in a timely manner, in addition to paying the insurance proceeds, it shall also compensate the insured or the beneficiary for losses incurred therefrom.

If the insurer and its staffs refuse to pay the indemnities or insurance benefits in accordance with the law, by Article 116 and Article 162 of the IL, the insurance regulatory authority shall order it to correct the matter and impose a fine of no less than RMB 50,000 and no more than RMB 300,000. If the circumstances are serious, the insurance regulatory authority shall place restrictions on the insurer's scope of business, order it to cease accepting new business or revoke its business permit.

§3. Obligation to Explain

253. This obligation has been fully discussed above. See Part I Chapter 3, §2 *supra.*

§4. Obligation to Keep Confidentiality

254. Article 116 of the IL provides that the insurer and their working staffs should not divulge the trade secrets of the applicant or insured learnt in the course of business.

Chapter 6. Insurance Subrogation Right

§1. Definition and Function of Insurance Subrogation

I. Definition

255. Insurance subrogation is one of the core contents of insurance contract law, and is well recognized and regulated by the legislations of countries around the world, of which China has no exception. Article 60(1) of the IL provides: "where an insured event occurs due to damage to the subject matter of insurance caused by a third party, the insurer may, from the date of payment of indemnities to the insured, exercise the insured's right to claim compensation from the third party by subrogation within the amount of indemnities." It is well established under Chinese law that the nature of insurance subrogation is the statutory assignment of the insured's claim against the third party to the insurer.

II. Functions

256. It is well recognized that the insurance subrogation has twofold functions:

- to prevent the insured from unjust enrichment by double recovery from both the insurer and the third party.
- to avoid the third party getting away from its legal liabilities.

As a derivative function, the exercise of insurance subrogation right can bring down the burden of the insurer's liability to pay, which in turn will benefit the whole insurance industry and lower the overall rate of premium.

§2. Exercise of Insurance Subrogation Right

I. Conditions Precedent to the Exercise of Insurance Subrogation Right

257. By Article 60(1), there are three conditions precedent to the exercise of insurance subrogation right.

First, damage to the subject matter of insurance is caused by a third party. It does not matter whether the damage is caused by tort or breach of contract committed by a third party (Article 7 of *Interpretation IV*).

Second, subrogation has no role to play in life insurance, as Article 46 of the IL provides: "if the occurrence of an insured event such as death, injury, disability or illness of the insured is caused by the act of a third party, the insurer shall not be entitled to the right of recourse against the said third party after paying the insurance benefits to the insured or beneficiary. However, the insured or beneficiary shall still retain the right to claim compensation from the said third party."

Third, the insurer has fulfilled the obligation to pay.

The exercise of insurance subrogation does not depend upon the condition that all the damages of the insured have been fully paid. By Article 60(3) of the IL, the exercise by the insurer of its subrogation right in accordance with Article 60(1) shall not affect the insured's right to claim compensation from the third party for the portion that has not been compensated. In other words, where the insured has not been fully compensated, the insurer can still exercise the subrogation rights. In this circumstance, both the insurer and the insured can, in practice as joint plaintiffs, bring the claims against the third party.

258. In practice, in order to avoid the disputes, the insured will usually be required to issue the "Subrogation Form" to the insurer, the standard wording of which could be: "In consideration of having received this payment, we hereby agree to assign, transfer and subrogate to you, to the extent of your interest, all our rights and remedies in respect of the subject matter insured, and to grant you full power and give you any assistance you may reasonably require of us in our or your name and at your own expense."

Noticeably, the fact that the "Subrogation Form" is not issued will not prejudice the insurer's ability to obtain subrogation rights provided that all the condition precedents are fulfilled. As to subrogation rights exercisable under the marine insurance contract, Article 96 of the SMPL provides that when bringing an action or applying to participate in the proceedings, an insurer shall submit vouchers certifying the payment of insurance indemnity by the insurer, as well as other documents that ought to be submitted to the maritime court entertaining the case, but the subrogation form alone cannot be the vouchers mentioned above.

259. Although the "Subrogation Form" above states that the insurer could choose to exercise subrogation rights in the insured's name, by Article 16(1) of *Interpretation II*, the insurer claims against such a third person in its own name instead of the name of the insured in the exercise of the right of subrogation. As to marine insurance, Article 94 of SMPL and its Judicial Interpretation also provide that the insurer shall, in the name of itself, bring an action against the third party. If the insurer does not follow, the claim shall not be entertained or shall be rejected.

260. Where the insured has already obtained damages from the third party following the occurrence of an insured event, by Article 60(2) of the IL, the insurer may, when paying the indemnities, appropriately deduct the amount of compensation obtained by the insured from the third party.

In addition, by Article 10 of *Interpretation IV*, where an insured accident arises due to damage caused by a third party to the subject-matter insured, and the third party pays compensation again to the insured party within the range of insurance indemnity that the insured party has already received from the insurer, if such third party is not notified of the fact that the insurer obtains the subrogation right to seek compensation or the notice sent for this purpose has not yet been served on such third party, the people's court shall not uphold the claim of the insurer to exercise by subrogation the right of the insured party against the third party to demand compensation. However, where the insurer requests the insured party to return the corresponding insurance indemnity, the people's court shall uphold such request.

Where the third party compensates the insured party again even though it has learnt the fact that the insurer has gained the subrogation right to seek compensation, the people's court shall not uphold the argument of the third party that it has compensated the insured party, when the insurer claims to exercise by subrogation the right against the third party to seek compensation.

261. Last but not least, when hearing the case regarding the exercise of insurance subrogation right, the court is only required to examine the relationship between the third party causing the insurance accident and the insured. That is to say, the court is not obliged to conduct a substantive examination of the insurance contract, i.e. whether the insurance contract is valid, whether the payment made by the insurer is reasonable, etc.

II. Limits of the Exercise of Insurance Subrogation Right

A. *Time Limit*

262. By Article 16(2) of *Interpretation II*, the time limit starts to count from the insurer's procurement of the subrogation right.

However, one judicial interpretation of the SPC provides that the above stipulation does not apply to marine insurance. In marine insurance contract, the time starts to count in accordance with Chapter 13 of the MC.

B. *Agreed Limit*

263. Insurance contract can agree to limit or even exclude the exercise of insurance subrogation right. For example, pursuant to a measure implemented by the CIA from February 1, 2009, where two vehicles with compulsory liability insurance for traffic accidents of motor vehicles collide with each other, if the following four requirements are satisfied, parties to the accident can agree that the damages should be paid by each vehicle's insurer with no subrogation rights being exercised against the other:

(1) both parties are blameworthy;
(2) the damages to the vehicles are under RMB 2000;
(3) there are no personal death or injuries;
(4) there are no additional property damages other than the damages to the vehicles themselves.

C. *Statutory Limit*

264. By Article 62 of the IL, except where the family members or members of the household of the insured deliberately cause an insured event specified in Article

60(1) of the IL, the insurer may not exercise the insurance subrogation right against family members or members of the household of the insured.

Although it is not expressed by the legislation, it is well established that the insurer cannot exercise the insurance subrogation right against other coinsureds.

III. Procedure

265. First of all, the insurer must bring the subrogation claim in its own name (Article 16 of *Interpretation II*).

Second, where the insurer files litigation against the third party that causes the insured accident to seek the subrogation right, the court with jurisdiction shall be determined depending on the legal relationship between the insured party and the third party (Article 12 of *Interpretation IV*).

Third, where the insured has sued the third party when the insurer institutes litigation against the third party to seek subrogation right, the people's court may try both cases together according to the law. Where the insurer has already brought proceedings against the third party when the insurer exercises the subrogation right, and the insured consents to the application filed by the insurer for replacing the insured party as the litigant to exercise the right of the insured party to demand compensation from the third party, the people's court shall approve such application; however, if the insured does not consent to such application, the insurer may join the proceedings as the joint plaintiff (Article 13 of *Interpretation IV*).

Fourth, in the circumstances of coinsurance, the insurer is generally not allowed to exercise subrogation rights against any of the coinsured; otherwise, the insurance protection would be meaningless to the insured. However, Article 8 of *Interpretation IV* provides that where the applicant and the insured are two different parties, and an insured accident occurs due to damage caused by the insurance applicant to the subject-matter insured, and thus the insurer claims according to the law to exercise by subrogation the insured's right to demand compensation from the applicant, the people's court shall uphold such claim, unless otherwise stipulated by the law or agreed in the insurance contract.

§3. Insured's Obligation Regarding Subrogation

I. Insured's Obligation to Assist

266. By Article 63 of the IL, when the insurer exercises its subrogation rights, the insurer shall provide the insurer the necessary document and relevant circumstances within its knowledge.

Pursuant to Article 11 of *Interpretation IV*, where the insured fails to fulfill its obligations specified in Article 63 of the IL intentionally or due to culpable negligence, with the result that the insurer fails to exercise or fully exercise the subrogation right to demand compensation, the people's court shall uphold the claim of the insurer that a proportion of the insurance indemnity corresponding to its loss shall be deducted or returned.

II. Insured's Obligation Not to Prejudice the Subrogation Rights

267. By Article 61 of the IL, where the insured waives its right to claim compensation from the third party after the occurrence of an insurance event and before the insurer pays indemnities, the insurer shall not be liable for the payment. If, after the insurer has paid indemnities to the insured, the insured, without the consent of the insurer, waives the right to claim compensation from the third party, such waiver shall be deemed invalid. If, due to a deliberate act or gross negligence on the part of insured, the insurer cannot exercise the subrogation right, it may deduct, or demand reimbursement of, the corresponding portion of the indemnities.

In accordance with Article 9 of *Interpretation IV*, in the lawsuit brought by the insurer against the third party to seek subrogation right, if the third party argues that the insured has waived its right to seek compensation from this third party before the insurance contract is concluded, the people's court shall establish that such waiver is lawful and valid, and shall dismiss the claim of the insurer to exercise the subrogation right over the corresponding amount of indemnity. However, where the applicant fails to provide truthful answers to the question raised by the insurer that whether the applicant has waived its right as aforesaid, when the insurance contract is concluded, which results in the impossibility for the insurer to exercise by subrogation the right to demand compensation, the people's court shall uphold the claim of the insurer that the corresponding insurance indemnity shall be returned, unless the insurer still agrees to underwrite the insurance contract even when it knows or should know the waiver.

Chapter 7. Insurance and Third Parties

§1. Beneficiary

268. The legal issues as to beneficiary have been fully discussed in paragraphs 146-148 *supra*.

§2. Third Parties' Direct Action Against the Insurer

269. The issues of the third parties' direct action against the insurer are peculiar to liability insurance. In Chinese law, by Article 65(4) of the IL, the term "liability insurance" means insurance of which the subject matter is the liability borne by the insured to compensate a third party in accordance with the law.

270. Granting the third parties rights of bringing direct action against the insurer is the trend of the liability insurance for at least two reasons: (1) protecting the third parties injured by the insured, particularly when the insured goes bankrupt, closed or is lack of compensatory capacity; (2) avoiding the circularity of litigation.

271. By Articles 65(1) and (2) of the IL, for the damages to a third party caused by the insured of a liability insurance contract, the insurer may directly pay indemnities to the third party in accordance with the law or the contract. If the insured of a liability insurance policy causes damage to a third party and the compensation liability owed to the third party by the insured has been determined, the insurer shall, at the request of the insured, pay the indemnities directly to the third party. If the insured fails to make such request, the third party shall have the right to directly submit a claim with the insurer for payment of indemnities in respect of the portion of the compensation it is owed.

In addition to the IL, other legislations and judicial interpretations have also provided the third parties' direct action against the insurer:

– Article 76(1) of *the Road Traffic Safety Law* provides that where a motor vehicle meets with a traffic accident and causes personal injury or death or any property loss, the insurance company shall pay indemnity within the scope of limit of the compulsory third-party liability insurance liability for the motor vehicle. As a supplement, Article 21 of *the Compulsory Traffic Accident Liability Insurance for Motor Vehicles Regulations* makes it clear that the insurer is not liable for the damages caused by the intentional act of the third party. In addition, by Article 16 of *Interpretation of the SPC on Several Issues Concerning the Application of Law in the Trail of Cases on Compensation for Damage in Road Traffic Accidents*, if the vehicle insured by both compulsory third-party liability and commercial third-party liability insurance meets with a traffic accident and causes damages, the injured party has brought the claim against both the insurer and tortfeasor, the court shall determine the compensatory liability in accordance with the following rules: (a) the insurer providing compulsory third-party liability insurance shall compensate within the liability limit in the first place; (b) if the compensation is insufficient, the insurer providing commercial third-party liability insurance shall compensate in accordance with the contract; (c) if the compensation is still insufficient, the tortfeasor shall compensate in accordance with *the Road Traffic Safety Law* and the CC.

- Articles 166 and 168(1) of *the Civil Aviation Law* provide that the operator of a civil aircraft shall be covered by insurance against liability for third parties on the surface or obtain corresponding guarantee. Without prejudice to any right of direct action which the person suffering damage may have under the law governing the contract of insurance or guarantee, such person may bring a direct action against the insurer or guarantor only in the following cases: (a) where the insurance or guarantee is continued in force under the provisions of Articles 167(1) and (2) of this law and (b) the bankruptcy of the operator.
- Article 97 of the SMPL provides that with respect to a claim for indemnity against oil pollution damage caused by a ship, the person suffering by the damage may make the claim to the shipowner causing the oil pollution damage, or directly make the claim to the insurer bearing the liability for oil pollution damage of the shipowner or to other persons providing financial suretyship. Where the action filed is against the insurer bearing the liability for oil pollution damage of the shipowner or the other person providing financial suretyship, it is entitled to require the shipowner causing the oil pollution damage to participate in the proceedings.
- A judicial interpretation released by the SPC in 2000 regarding enforcement provides that if the insurance applicant does not fulfill the obligation of paying the debt, the court may upon the application of the creditor (or beneficiary) issue the notice of assistance in the enforcement to the insurer, who shall handle the claim in accordance with the relevant laws and regulations, and pay the creditor (or beneficiary) accordingly; the creditor (or beneficiary) may bring the claim against the insurer if it is doubtful as to the amount of claim settled by the insurer; if the insurer refuses to pay without legitimate cause, the court may enforce the claim in accordance with the law.

In practice, the insurance contract may contain the clause stipulating that unless the third party has brought the claim against the insured and implemented the enforcement on the property of the insured, it cannot require the insurer to undertake the insurance liability. It is suggested that if the law provides that the third party is entitled to bring direct action against the insurer, this kind of clause shall be null and void because it conflicts with the law.

Chapter 8. Termination of the Insurance Contract

§1. Agreed Termination

272. Although it is not stated in the IL, in accordance with Article 158 of the CC, the parties to insurance contract are naturally allowed to agree to the conditions in the contract, the fulfillment of which will trigger the termination. Alternatively, the insurance contract can be terminated by the agreement of the parties after the conclusion of it.

§2. Statutory Termination

I. Insurance Applicant's Statutory Right to Terminate

273. In order to balance the interests between the parties to the insurance contract, Article 15 of the IL enables the insurance applicant to terminate the contract at any time after the conclusion of the contract, unless otherwise provided by the law or agreed by the parties.

However, in certain types of insurance contract, the applicant's right to terminate is constrained. For example, by Article 50 of the IL, cargo insurance contracts or voyage insurance contracts may not be terminated by the contractual parties once the insurance liability has commenced.

II. Insurer's Statutory Right to Terminate

274. In principle, the insurer's right to terminate is constrained by the law, as Article 15 of the IL states that unless otherwise provided by the law or agreed in the insurance contract, the insurer may not terminate an insurance contract after it has been concluded.

Pursuant to the IL, the insurer is entitled to terminate the contract in the following circumstances:

- where the insurance applicant breaches the duty to disclose (Article 16(2));
- where an insured event has not occurred but the insured or beneficiary falsely claims that such an event has occurred, and submit a claim for the payment of indemnities or insurance benefits (Article 27(1));
- where the insurance applicant or insurer deliberately causes an insured event (Article 27(2));
- where the age of the insured reported by the insurance applicant is false and the insured's true age does not comply with the age restriction specified in the contract (Article 32(1));
- where the insured, by written notice to the insurer and applicant, withdraws his/her consent and approval of the insured amount in a contract stipulating death as a condition for payment of insurance benefits (Article 34(1));

- where the parties fail to reach an agreement within two years from the date on which the validity of the contract is suspended (Article 37(1));
- where the transfer of the subject matter of insurance substantially increases the degree of risk (Article 49(3));
- where either the insurance applicant or insured fails to fulfill due diligence requirements regarding the safety of the subject matter of insurance in accordance with the contract (Article 51(3));
- where the degree of risk to the subject matter of insurance increases substantially during the term of the contract (Article 52(1));
- where the subject matter of insurance suffers partial loss, unless otherwise provided by the contract, the insurer may terminate the contract but shall notify the insurance applicant fifteen days in advance (Article 58(1)).

§3. Time and Manner of the Termination of the Insurance Contract

I. Time of Termination of the Insurance Contract

275. In principle, the party who possesses the right to terminate shall exercise the right within the reasonable period.

The IL also has special provisions regulating the time of termination. For example:

- by Article 16(3), if the insurance applicant fails to fulfill the duty to disclose, the insurer's right to terminate shall be extinguished if it is not exercised within thirty days after the date on which the insurer is aware of the reason for termination; once two years have lapsed from the date of conclusion of the contract, the insurer may not terminate the contract;
- by Article 49(3), where the transfer of the subject matter of insurance substantially increases the degree of risk, the insurer may terminate the contract within thirty days of the date of receipt of the notice from the insured or transferee.

II. Manner of the Termination of the Insurance Contract

276. The IL does not specify the matter of the termination. In accordance with Articles 562 and 565 of the CC, in practice, the right to terminate is generally exercised by sending the notice of termination from one party to the other.

§4. Legal Consequences for Termination

277. As a general principle, when the insurance applicant exercises the right to terminate, by Article 54 of the IL:

- if the right is exercised before the commencement of the insurance liability, it shall, in accordance with the contract, pay the service charge to the insurer and the insurer shall refund the insurance premiums;
- if the right is exercised after commencement of the insurance liability, the insurer shall refund to the applicant the insurance premiums collected, minus, in accordance with the contract, the portion to which it is entitled for the period between the date of commencement of its insurance liability and the date of termination of the contract.

278. In life insurance, by Article 47 of the IL, if the insurance applicant terminates the contract, the insurer shall, in accordance with the contract, refund the cash value of the policy within thirty days from the date of receipt of the notice of termination of the contract.

By Article 15 of *Interpretation III*, when the insurance contract is terminated and the applicant is not the insured and beneficiary, unless otherwise agreed in the contract, the insured or beneficiary is not entitled to refund of cash value of the policy.

279. In special circumstances, the legal effect for termination will be retrospective. For example:

- by Article 16 of the IL, if the insurance applicant deliberately fails to perform the duty of disclosure, the insurer shall not be liable to pay indemnities or insurance benefits or refund the insurance premiums for insured events that occurred before the termination of the contract;
- by Article 27(2) of the IL, if the insurance applicant or the insured deliberately causes an insurance event, the insurer shall have the right to terminate the contract and shall not be liable for the payment of indemnities or insurance benefits. Unless otherwise provided in Article 43 of the IL thereof, it will not refund the insurance premiums.

Part III. Basic Property Insurance

280. To regulate the management of business scope of insurance companies, establish and improve the insurance market entry and exit mechanisms, and promote the professional and differentiated development of the insurance industry, in accordance with the IL, the Administration of Foreign-Funded Insurance Companies Regulations, the APIC and other relevant laws, administrative regulations and rules, the CBIRC has formulated the Measures for the Hierarchical Management of Business Scope of Insurance Companies.

For the purpose of these *Measures*, "business scope" refers to the original insurance businesses of insurance companies, excluding reinsurance business, the business of utilization of insurance funds, and agency sale of products of other insurance companies.

The business scope of insurance companies shall be divided into two levels in accordance with the insurance business attributes and risk features, namely basic businesses and extended businesses.

Article 5 of the *Measures* provides that the basic businesses of property insurance companies shall include the following five items: (1) motor vehicle insurance, including compulsory traffic accident liability insurance for motor vehicles and commercial insurance for motor vehicles; (2) commercial/family property insurance and construction insurance (excluding special risk insurance); (3) liability insurance; (4) hull insurance and cargo transportation insurance; and (5) short-term health/accidental insurance.

It should be noted that an insurer is forbidden to concurrently engage in the businesses of both life insurance and property insurance. However, upon approval of the insurance regulatory authority under the State Council, an insurance company which operates a property insurance business may operate a short-term health insurance business and accidental injury insurance business. Nevertheless, the short-term health/accidental insurance will be introduced in the part of life insurance.

Chapter 1. Motor Vehicle Insurance

§1. Commercial Motor Vehicle Insurance

281. As to the premium income, commercial motor vehicle insurance is the most important property insurance in Chinese insurance market.

The Model Clauses of Commercial Motor Vehicle Insurance of the IAC 2014 (hereinafter referred to "Model Clauses") are the most widely recognized and used clauses across the country. According to the Model Clauses, commercial motor vehicle insurance covers four separate main risks: vehicle damage insurance, third-party liability insurance, passenger liability insurance and robbery and theft insurance.

I. Vehicle Damage Insurance

A. *Scope of Coverage*

282. The coverage of vehicle damage insurance has two aspects: first, the loss of or damage to the insured vehicle caused by natural causes or accidents during its use by the insured or the driver allowed by the insured; second, the mitigation expenses incurred by the insured or the driver allowed by the insured for the purpose of preventing or reducing the loss or damage to the insured vehicle when the insured risks occur.

The driver allowed by the insured means the persons who are allowed by the insured to drive the insured vehicle, i.e. the spouse or the employee of the insured. In addition, those persons should have the qualification to drive the insured vehicle; i.e., they must possess the valid driver's license issued by the competent authority of China. If the loss of or damage to the vehicle occurs when it is used without explicit approval of the insured, the insurer is not responsible.

The natural disasters insured under the Model Clauses include lightning strike, storm, rainstorm, flood, tornado, hail, typhoon, tropical storm, subsidence, landslide, debris flow, avalanche, ice slush, ice trap, blizzard, sandstorm and cliff collapse. The natural disaster occurs to the ferry boat carrying the insured vehicle is also covered to the extent that the driver must be on board.

The accidents can be divided into two categories: collision accidents and non-collision accidents; the latter includes capsize, fall, fire, explosion of the insured vehicle.

B. *Exclusions*

1. The Incidents Not Covered by the Vehicle

283. No matter the reason for the loss and expense, if the following incidents occur, the insurer is not liable in any event:

(1) The insured or the driver allowed by the insured deliberately damages or destroys the evidence or forges the scene after the occurrence of the accidents.
(2) The driver has the following circumstances:
  - driving the insured vehicle or the abandoned insured vehicle and leaving the scene without taking the measures in accordance with the law after the occurrence of the accidents;
  - drinking, taking or injecting drugs, taking psychoactive drug or narcotic controlled by the state;
  - having no valid motor vehicle driving license, or the driving license being canceled, revoked or detained in accordance with the law;
  - driving the vehicle that is not in accordance with the permitted type clearly stated in the driving license;
  - driving the bus, commercial vehicle of passenger transport, the police vehicles carrying out a task, the vehicle carrying dangerous cargoes or the trailer during the internship;
  - driving the taxi or commercial vehicle without the permitting certificate or other necessary documents issued by the relevant authorities;
  - learning the driving without the qualified on-vehicle trainer;
  - being not the allowed driver by the insured.
(3) The insured vehicle has the following circumstances:
  - the registration and plate number being revoked, or the vehicle not being inspected or the inspection being failed when the accidents occur;
  - being detained, seized, confiscated by the government;
  - during the period of competing or testing, or being repaired, maintained or remodeled at a business site;
  - being used in committing the crime by the insured's or the driver allowed by the insured's deliberation or gross negligence;
  - the insured special vehicle being used to towing other vehicles or objects against the law.

2. The Cause Excluded

284. The loss or expense caused by the following reasons is not covered under the vehicle damage insurance:

- earthquake and related disasters;
- war, military conflict, terrorism, riot, contamination (including nuclear contamination), nuclear reaction, nuclear radiation;
- self-combustion, direct fuel supply by manpower, high-temperature heating, fire with unknown cause;
- in breach of the safe load regulations;
- where the insured vehicle being transferred, remodeled, installed or its nature of use being changed, the insured and the transferee do not disclose to the insurer in a timely manner, which result in the degree of risk encounter by the insured vehicle being substantially raised;
- the deliberate action of the insured and the driver allowed by the insured.

3. The Loss and Expense Excluded

285. The following loss and expense are not covered under the vehicle damage insurance:

- the devaluation caused by the fall of the market or the repair;
- the ordinary wear and tear, corrosion, rusty, breakdown and defect of the vehicle itself;
- the expanded loss due to the continuing use without the necessary repair and inspection after the suffering of the losses covered by the insured;
- where an insured accident is not notified in a timely manner intentionally or due to gross negligence, with the result that it is difficult for the insurer to determine the nature, cause and extent of the loss, etc. of the accident, the insurer shall not bear the obligation of indemnity or payment of insurance benefits for the part unable to be determined, except for the insured accident that the insurer has known its occurrence through other channels or should know its occurrence in a timely manner;
- due to the insured's reasons, the losses that cannot be determined as a result of the insurer being unable to examine the vehicle in order to determine the repair items, methods and costs;
- the insured vehicle being stolen, robbed, missing and the damages caused during this period; or the damages caused by the attempted theft, robbery;
- the damages caused to the wheels or the windows alone, or the scratches without obvious collision trace, or the damages of the new additional equipment;
- the damages to the main engine caused by water penetration.

C. Insured Amount

286. The insured amount is to be determined by the actual value of the insured vehicle (except the motorcycle and tractor) at the time of conclusion of insurance contract, which in turn is to be determined by the negotiation of the applicant and the insurer in accordance with the purchase price of new vehicle minus the depreciable amount of vehicle or other fair market value. The purchase price of new vehicle is determined by the price of new vehicle of the same type of insured vehicle at the place of conclusion of insurance contract, and the depreciable amount is calculated in accordance with the following formula: the depreciable amount=the purchase price of new vehicle × the used months of the insured vehicle × monthly depreciation factor.

D. Deductibles

287. The stipulations of deductibles provided by the Model Clauses can be summarized as follows:

- where the liability of insured vehicle is secondary, the excess ratio is 5%; where the liability is equal, the excess ratio is 10%; where the liability is primary, the excess ratio is 15%; where the insured is the only liable party, the excess ratio is 20%;
- where the loss of or damage to the insured vehicle is caused by the third party who cannot be located, the excess ratio is 30%;
- where the insured is in breach of the safe loading regulations which is not the direct reason of the accident, the excess ratio should be added 10%;
- the applicant and the insurer may negotiate the excess, and when calculating the insurance compensation, the insurer shall add the deductibles for each accident to the excess.

E. Premium

288. According to the Model Clauses, the formula for the premium is: premium=standard premium × adjustment rate factor.

$$\text{standard premium} = \frac{\text{standard pure risk premium}}{1-\text{additional rate}}$$

Adjustment rate factor=no claim discount factor × traffic violation factor × self-underwriting factor × self-channeling factor.

Standard pure risk premium, no claim discount factor and traffic violation factor are provided by the IAC. The insurer is allowed to adjust the additional rate (the preliminary figure is 35%), the self-underwriting factor (within the range of –15% to 15%) and self-channeling factor (within the range of –15% to 15%).

F. Insurance Compensation

289. Insurance compensation for total loss = (insured amount – the compensation received by the insured from the third party) × (1 – excess ratio) × (1 – the sum of deductible ratio) – deductibles;

Insurance compensation for partial loss = (actual repair expenses – the compensation received by the insured from the third party) × (1 – excess ratio) × (1 – the sum of deductible ratio) – deductibles.

Mitigation expenses are also recoverable up to the insured amount.

II. Third-Party Liability Insurance

A. Scope of Coverage

290. The insurer's liability corresponds with the insured vehicle's liability in the traffic accident. If the insured chooses to negotiate by himself or the proportion of the liability has not been determined by the traffic management department of public safety agency, then the proportion of liability is determined as follows: 70% if the insured vehicle bears primary liability; 50% if the insured vehicle bears equal liability; 30% if the insured vehicle bears secondary liability. If the determination involves the judicial or arbitrary process, the legal documentation issued by the court or arbitrary institution prevails.

B. The Definition of "Third Party"

291. Third party refers to the person who suffers personal injury or death or property loss due to the occurrence of the accident of insured vehicle, excluding on-vehicle person of the insured vehicle and the insured himself.

C. Exclusions

1. The Incidents Not Covered

292. They are the same as those of vehicle damage insurance.

2. The Cause Excluded

293. The insurer is not liable to the personal injury or death or property losses or expenses caused by the following reasons:

- earthquake and related disasters, war, military conflict, terrorism, riot, contamination (including nuclear contamination), nuclear reaction, nuclear radiation;
- where the insured vehicle being transferred, remodeled, installed or its nature of use being changed, the insured and the transferee does not disclose to the insurer in a timely manner, which resulting the degree of risk encounter by the insured vehicle being substantially raised;
- the intentional or the criminal action of the insured or the driver allowed by the insured, or the malicious collusion committed by the third party and the insured or other perpetrators.

3. The Loss and Expense Excluded

294. The insured is not liable for the following personal injury or death, property losses and expenses:

- the shutdown of business, the cutoff of electricity, water, gas, internet, production of any individual or unit, the voltage variation, the damages caused by the voltage variation and loss of data, and other indirect loss caused by the accidents of the insured vehicle;

- the devaluation of the third party's property caused by the fluctuation of the market, or the devaluation caused by the repair;
- the loss of property of the insured and his family or the driver allowed by the insured and his family, no matter whether the property is owned, rented, used, managed, transported or left with trust by them, and the loss of property on-vehicle;
- the personal injury or death of the insured and the driver allowed by the insured, or the persons on-vehicle;
- the parking fee, the custody charge, the impound charge, the fine or other punitive damages;
- the attorney fee, or other litigation or arbitration fee without the insurer's written consent in advance;
- the cost that exceeds the standard medical cost in accordance with the basic national medical insurance and the "Clinical Diagnosis Guide for the Victim of Traffic Accident";
- due to the insured's reasons, the losses that cannot be determined as a result of the insurer being unable to examine the vehicle in order to determine the repair items, methods and costs;
- where an insured accident is not notified in a timely manner intentionally or due to gross negligence, with the result that it is difficult for the insurer to determine the nature, cause and extent of the loss, etc. of the accident, the insurer shall not bear the obligation of indemnity or payment of insurance benefits for the part unable to be determined, except for the insured accidents that the insurer has known its occurrence through other channels or should know its occurrence in a timely manner;
- compensation for mental losses;
- the losses and expenses that should be covered by the compulsory liability insurance for the traffic accidents of motor vehicles.

D. Limit of Liability

295. The applicant and the insurer may agree to the limit of liability. In practice, it is usually for the insurer to set up the different limit for the applicant to choose, from RMB 50,000 to RMB 1 million.

E. Deductibles

296. The stipulations of deductibles of third-party liability insurance provided by the Model Clauses can be summarized as follows:

- where the liability of insured vehicle is secondary, the excess ratio is 5%; where the liability is equal, the excess ratio is 10%; where the liability is primary, the excess ratio is 15%; where the insured is the only liable party, the excess ratio is 20%;

– where the insured is in breach of the safe loading regulations which is not the direct reason of the accident, the excess ratio should be added 10%.

F. Insurance Compensation

1. The Handling of Compensation

297. Where the insured causes any damage to a third party and the liability of the insured for indemnity to the third party has been determined, the insurer shall directly pay insurance benefits to the third party according to the request of the insured. Where the insured is negligent in making such a request, the third party shall have the right to directly request the insurer to pay the insurance benefits for the damage to the third party. Where the insured has not indemnified the third party for the damage, the insurer shall not pay insurance benefits to the insured.

The damages to the third party's property shall be repaired to the greatest extent. The insured and insurer shall conduct the inspect jointly, negotiate the repair items, methods and costs. The insurer may recheck for the undetermined matters.

2. Calculation of Compensation

298. If (the approved losses of the third party – the respective compensation limit of compulsory liability insurance for traffic accident of motor vehicles) × proportion of accident liability ≥ the limit of liability per accident, then the compensation shall be on the basis of the limit of liability. The formula is: compensation=the limit of liability per accident × (1 – excess ratio) × (1 – the sum of deductible ratio).

If (the approved losses of the third party – the respective compensation limit of compulsory liability insurance for traffic accident of motor vehicles) × proportion of accident liability ≤ the limit of liability per accident, then the compensation shall be on the basis of the actual loss compensable by the insurer. The formula is: compensation = (the approved losses of the third party – the respective compensation limit of compulsory liability insurance for traffic accident of motor vehicles) × (1 – excess ratio) × (1 – the sum of deductible ratio).

III. Passenger Liability Insurance

A. Scope of Coverage

299. The passenger liability insurance covers the insured's or the driver allowed by the insured's liability to the personal injury or death of the passenger on-vehicle caused by the incidents when using the insured vehicle during the insurance period.

The passenger on-vehicle refers to the person or persons on-vehicle at the time of the incidents, including those getting on or off the vehicle.

B. Exclusions

300. The exclusions are basically the same as those of third-party liability insurance, except for the items of "the parking fee, the custody charge, the impound charge, the fine or other punitive damages" and "due to the insured's reasons, the losses that cannot be determined as a result of the insurer being unable to examine the vehicle in order to determine the repair items, methods and costs."

C. Limitation of Liability

301. The passenger liability insurance has two limits of liability: the limit of the driver or operator per incident and the limit of each seat per incident. The figure of limits shall be determined by the negotiation of the applicant and the insurer. The insured seat shall be determined by the authorized passenger-capacity of the insured vehicle (excluding the driver or the operator's seat).

D. Insurance Compensation

302. As to the victim per seat, if (the approved loss for the personal injury or death of each seat in accordance with the contract–the respective compensation limit of compulsory liability insurance for traffic accident of motor vehicles) × proportion of accident liability ≥ the limit of each seat per incident, then the compensation shall be on the basis of the limit of each seat per incident. The formula is: compensation = the limit of each seat per incident × (1 – deductible ratio).

If (the approved loss for the personal injury or death of each seat in accordance with the contract – the respective compensation limit of compulsory liability insurance for traffic accident of motor vehicles) × proportion of accident liability ≤ the limit of each seat per incident, then the compensation shall be on the basis of the actual loss compensable by the insurer. The formula is: (the approved loss for the personal injury or death of each seat in accordance with the contract – the respective compensation limit of compulsory liability insurance for traffic accident of motor vehicles) × proportion of accident liability × (1 – deductible ratio).

IV. Robbery and Theft Insurance

A. Scope of Coverage

303. The Robbery and Theft insurance (R&T insurance) covers the following loss or damage to the insured vehicle during the insurance period:

– after being stolen or robbed, the vehicle can still not be found after the expire of sixty days from the time when the criminal investigation department of the public security authority above the county level has started the investigation;

– after being stolen or robbed, the reasonable expenses or costs for repairing the damages of the vehicle, or the loss of the parts and accessories on-vehicle;
– the reasonable expenses or costs for repairing the damages of the vehicle during the process of robbery.

B. Exclusions

1. The Incidents Not Covered

304. Under the following circumstances, the insurer is not liable in any event for the loss of the insured vehicle or expenses:

– the insured does not provide the certificate of filing for investigation issued by the criminal investigation department of the public security authority above the county level when the incidents occur;
– the driver or operator, insured, applicant intentionally destroys or fabricates the scene or evidence;
– the insured vehicle being detained, seized, confiscated by the government;
– the insured vehicle is within the period of competing or testing, or being repaired, maintained or remodeled at a business site, or being transported.

2. The Loss and Expense Excluded

305. The insurer is not liable for the losses and expenses caused by the following reasons or under the following circumstances:

– earthquake and related disasters;
– war, military conflict, terrorism, riot, contamination (including nuclear contamination), nuclear reaction, nuclear radiation;
– the deliberate or criminal action of the insured and the driver allowed by the insured;
– being arising out of or in relation to fraud, or the civil or economic dispute between the applicant, insured and other people;
– the losses of the new apparatus;
– the damages or steal of the parts and accessories on-vehicle;
– the expanded loss due to the continuing use without the necessary repair and inspection after the suffering of the losses covered by the insured;
– where an insured accident is not notified in a timely manner intentionally or due to gross negligence, with the result that it is difficult for the insurer to determine the nature, cause and extent of the loss, etc. of the accident, the insurer shall not bear the obligation of indemnity or payment of insurance benefits for the part unable to be determined, except for the insured accidents that the insurer has known its occurrence through other channels or should know its occurrence in a timely manner;

- where the insured vehicle being transferred, remodeled, installed or its nature of use being changed, the insured and the transferee do not disclose to the insurer in a timely manner, which result in the degree of risk encounter by the insured vehicle being substantially raised;
- due to the insured's reasons, the losses that cannot be determined as a result of the insurer being unable to examine the vehicle in order to determine the repair items, methods and costs.

C. Deductibles

306. The R&T insurance has excess ratio. When the insured vehicle suffers total loss, the ratio is 20%; when the insured vehicle suffers total loss but the insured is unable to provide the vehicle registration, certificate as to the origin of vehicle and other necessary certificates, the ratio will be increased 1% for each certificate that cannot be provided.

D. Insurance Compensation

307. When the insured vehicle is robbed or stolen, the insured shall notify the local criminal department of public security authority within twenty-four hours when he should have known the incident, and shall notify the insurer too.

When the claim is submitted, the insured shall provide the policy, list of loss items, relevant lists of expenses and costs, vehicle registration, certificate as to origin of vehicle and the certificate of filing for investigation issued by the criminal investigation department of the public security authority above the county level. If the insurer confirms that the documents are all in order and effect, the insured shall issue the subrogation certificate and the insurer shall pay the insurance indemnity. If the insured vehicle suffers total loss, or the sum of the insurance indemnity and deductible equals to the insured amount, the insurer shall be discharged from all the liability thereafter when he pays the insurance indemnity, and he is allowed to keep the premium too.

When the whole vehicle is robbed or stolen, the insurance indemnity = insured amount × (1 – the sum of excess ratio). When the vehicle is damaged during the robbery and steal, or the parts and accessories on-vehicle are missing or need to be repaired, the insurer shall compensate the actual repair expense within the insured amount.

V. Additional Insurance

308. The Model Clauses contain eleven supplemental or additional clauses which cover the following special risks: the broken of windows alone, the self-combustion, the losses of the additional equipment, the scratches of the vehicle's body, the damages to the engines relating to water, the compensation of cost during the repair period, the liability for the cargo on-vehicle, the liability for the compensation of mental damages, the third party being unable to be located, the designated repair shops, the loss of or damage to the crane, reloader and excavator, and the loss of or damage to the fixed equipment and apparatus of special vehicles.

§2. Compulsory Liability Insurance for Traffic Accidents of Motor Vehicles

309. The Compulsory Motor Vehicle Traffic Accident Liability Insurance Regulations (Second Revision in 2012) is the current governing law which shall be applicable to the purchase of and compensation for the compulsory liability insurance for traffic accidents of motor vehicles, and the supervision and administration thereof.

I. Definition

310. The compulsory liability insurance for traffic accidents of motor vehicles refers to the compulsory liability insurance of an insurance company which compensates the victims other than the personnel in the motor vehicles and the insured for their personal injuries and death as well as property losses arising from the road traffic accidents caused by the insured motor vehicles within the scope of limit of liability for the compulsory liability insurance for traffic accidents of motor vehicles.

II. Supervision and Administration

311. The CBIRC shall conduct supervision and administration of insurance companies' business of the compulsory liability insurance for traffic accidents of motor vehicles in accordance with the law.

The traffic control departments of the public security organs and the competent departments of agriculture (farm machinery) (hereinafter uniformly referred to as the "competent departments of motor vehicles") shall conduct supervision and inspection of motor vehicles on their purchase of the compulsory liability insurance for traffic accidents of motor vehicles in accordance with the law. The competent department of motor vehicles will not register those motor vehicles not involved in the compulsory liability insurance for traffic accidents of motor vehicles, and the motor vehicle safety technical inspection organs shall not conduct inspection of them.

The traffic control departments of the public security organs and the traffic police shall, when investigating and handling acts against laws on road traffic safety and road traffic accidents, check the marks of the compulsory liability for traffic accidents of motor vehicles in accordance with the law.

312. Insurance companies may, upon the approval of the CBIRC, engage in the business of the compulsory liability insurance for traffic accidents of motor vehicles.

In order to ensure the implementation of the system of the compulsory liability insurance for traffic accidents of motor vehicles, the CBIRC shall be entitled to require insurance companies to engage in the business of the compulsory liability insurance for traffic accidents of motor vehicles. No unit or individual may engage in the compulsory liability insurance for traffic accidents of motor vehicles without the approval of the CBIRC.

313. The compulsory liability insurance for traffic accidents of motor vehicles shall apply the uniform insurance clauses and basic premium rates. The CBIRC shall examine and approve the premium rates under the principle of making no profit or loss in general for the business of the compulsory liability insurance for traffic accidents of motor vehicles.

314. An insurance company shall separate its business of the compulsory liability insurance for traffic accidents of motor vehicles from other insurance businesses for independent accounting. The CBIRC shall verify the business of the compulsory liability insurance for traffic accidents of motor vehicles of insurance companies and announce the results to the society on an annual basis. The CBIRC may require or allow insurance companies to adjust the premium rates accordingly on the basis of their overall profits or losses from the business of the compulsory liability insurance for traffic accidents of motor vehicles. Where there is any major adjustment on the premium rates, the CBIRC shall hold a hearing.

315. The CBIRC, the public security department under the State Council, the competent department of agriculture under the State Council, and other relevant departments shall establish, step by step, the mechanism for sharing the relevant information about the compulsory liability insurance for traffic accidents of motor vehicles, acts against laws on road traffic safety and road traffic accidents.

III. Purchase of Insurance

316. The owners or managers of the motor vehicles driving on the roads within China shall purchase the compulsory insurance for liability for traffic accidents of motor vehicles in accordance with the provisions of the Road Traffic Safety Law.

317. An applicant shall choose an insurance company qualified for engaging in the business of the compulsory liability insurance for traffic accidents of motor vehicles when purchasing the insurance, and the chosen insurance company shall not refuse to undertake or delay in undertaking the insurance.

An applicant shall, when purchasing the insurance, honestly disclose to the insurance company of the important matters, which shall include: type, model, identification number, plate number and nature of use of the motor vehicle, and name (title), gender, age, domicile, identity card or license number (organization code) of the owner or manager of the motor vehicle, information about the accidents of the motor vehicle before insurance renewal, and other matters prescribed by the CBIRC.

318. When an applicant signs a contract for the compulsory liability insurance for traffic accidents of motor vehicles, it shall pay the insurance premium in full; the insurance company shall issue an insurance policy and an insurance mark to the applicant. The insurance policy and the insurance mark shall indicate the insurance policy number, plate number, insurance period, as well as the insurance company's name, address and telephone number for compensation. The insured shall place the insurance mark on the insured motor vehicle. The patterns of insurance marks shall be uniformed nationwide. Insurance policies and insurance marks shall be made under the supervision of the CBIRC. No unit or individual may forge or alter insurance policies or insurance marks, or use forged or altered insurance policies or insurance marks.

When signing a contract for the compulsory liability insurance for traffic accidents of motor vehicles, an applicant may not request the insurance company to attach other conditions to the insurance clauses and the premium rate. When signing a contract for the compulsory liability insurance for traffic accidents of motor vehicles, an insurance company shall not force the applicant to sign a commercial insurance contract or make a request for adding other conditions.

319. An insurance company shall not terminate the contract for the compulsory liability insurance for traffic accidents of motor vehicles, unless the applicant fails to perform the obligation of truthfully disclosing to the insurance company of the important matters. If an applicant fails to perform the obligation of truthfully disclosing to the insurance company of the important matters, the insurance company shall inform the applicant in writing before terminating the contract, and the applicant shall perform the obligation of truthfully disclosing to the insurance company of the important matters within five days as of the date of receiving the notice; if the applicant has done so within the time limit, the insurance company shall not terminate the contract.

320. An insurance company shall, when terminating the contract for the compulsory liability insurance for traffic accidents of motor vehicles, withdraw the insurance policy and the insurance mark, and notify the competent department of motor vehicles in writing.

321. An applicant shall not terminate the contract for the compulsory liability insurance for traffic accidents of motor vehicles, except under any of the following circumstances: (1) the registration of the insured motor vehicle is canceled in accordance with the law; (2) formalities have been gone through for the drive stop of the insured motor vehicle; or (3) the insured motor vehicle is proved lost by the public security organ.

322. Before terminating a contract for the compulsory liability insurance for traffic accidents of motor vehicles, an insurance company shall assume the insurance liability in accordance with the contract. When the contract is terminated, the insurance company may collect the insurance premium from the day when the insurance liability attaches until the day when the contract is terminated, and the remaining amount of the premium shall be returned to the applicant.

323. Where the ownership of an insured motor vehicle is transferred, the owner of the motor vehicle shall go through the formalities for alteration of the contract for the compulsory liability insurance for traffic accidents of motor vehicles.

324. At the expiry of the contract for the compulsory liability for traffic accidents of motor vehicles, an applicant shall duly renew the insurance and provide the insurance policy of the previous year.

Where an insured motor vehicle has no act against laws on road traffic safety or has no road traffic accidents, the insurance company shall reduce its premium rate in the next year. Where the insured motor vehicle still has no act against laws on road traffic safety or has no road traffic accidents in the following years, the insurance company shall continue to reduce its premium rate till the minimum standards. Where the insured motor vehicle has any act against laws on road traffic safety or road traffic accident, the insurance company shall raise its premium rate in the next year. Where any act against laws on road traffic safety or any road traffic accident occurs frequently, or any serious road traffic accident occurs, the insurance company shall raise the range of increase in the premium rate. Where the insured is found faultless in road traffic accidents, the premium rate shall not be raised. The standards for reducing or raising the premium rate shall be formulated by the CBIRC in association with the public security department under the State Council.

325. The insurance period of the compulsory liability for traffic accidents of motor vehicles shall be one year, but an applicant may purchase the short-term compulsory liability insurance for traffic accidents of motor vehicles under any of the following circumstances: (1) a foreign motor vehicle enters the territory of China temporarily; (2) a motor vehicle drives on the road temporarily; (3) there is less than one year to the retirement of a motor vehicle; or (4) other circumstances prescribed by the CBIRC.

IV. Insurance Compensation

326. Where any road traffic accident occurring to an insured motor vehicle results in personal injury or death and property loss of any victim other than the personnel in the motor vehicle or the insured, the insurance company shall compensate within the scope of limit of liability for the compulsory liability insurance for traffic accidents of motor vehicles in accordance with the law. Where any loss from a road traffic accident is caused by a victim on purpose, the insurance company may not make any compensation.

327. Under any of the following circumstances, the insurance company shall make an advance payment of the rescue expenses within the scope of limit of liability for the compulsory liability insurance for traffic accidents of motor vehicles, and shall be entitled to recover the rescue expenses from the person causing the injury: (1) the driver has not obtained a qualification for driving or is drunk; (2) the insured motor vehicle causes an accident during the period when it is stolen or robbed; or

(3) the insured creates a road traffic accident on purpose. Under any of the circumstances as mentioned above, where any property loss of a victim is caused by a road traffic accident, the insurance company shall not be liable for compensation.

Rescue expenses refer to the medical expenses used by a medical institution to take necessary measures in reference to the relevant guide on clinical diagnosis and treatment formulated under the organization of the competent department of health under the State Council, for treating the injured in road traffic accidents caused by motor vehicles whose vital signs are unstable and who will be in grave danger, or be led to disabled or suffer from organ dysfunction, or whose course of disease will be prolonged evidently in spite of stable vital signs if no treatment measures are taken.

The compulsory liability insurance for traffic accidents of motor vehicles implements a uniform limit of liability nationwide. The limit of liability includes limit of compensation for death, injury and disability, limit of compensation for medical treatment, limit of compensation for property loss and limit of compensation for exemption of the insured from liability for road traffic accidents. The limit of liability for the compulsory liability insurance for traffic accidents of motor vehicles shall be prescribed by the CBIRC in association with the public security department, the competent department of health and the competent department of agriculture under the State Council.

328. The state has established the social relief fund for road traffic accidents (hereinafter referred to as the "relief fund"). Under any of the following circumstances, the relief fund shall be used as the advance for the funeral expenses and part or entire of the rescue expenses for dead and injured victims in road traffic accidents, and the relief fund administrative authority shall be entitled to recover the expenses from the persons that shall be liable for the road traffic accidents: (1) the rescue expenses exceed the limit of liability for the compulsory liability for traffic accidents of motor vehicles; (2) the motor vehicles causing road traffic accidents are not involved in the compulsory liability insurance for traffic accidents of motor vehicles; or (3) the motor vehicles flee after causing road traffic accidents.

The sources of the relief fund include: (1) a certain proportion of the premium on the compulsory liability insurance for traffic accidents of motor vehicles; (2) a fine on the owners or managers of the motor vehicles not involved in the compulsory liability insurance for traffic accidents of motor vehicles in accordance with the relevant regulations; (3) the fund recovered by the relief fund administrative authority from the persons that shall be liable for road traffic accidents in accordance with the law; (4) interests of the relief fund; and (5) other funds.

329. Where the insured or victim informs the insurance company of the road traffic accident of the insured motor vehicle, the insurance company shall immediately give a reply notifying the insured or victim of the relevant matters such as specific compensation procedures.

Where a motor vehicle is involved in a road traffic accident, the insured may apply to the insurance company for compensation. The insurance company shall, within one day as of the date of receiving the compensation application, notify the insured in writing of submitting the evidence and data related to the compensation.

330. The insurance company shall, within five days as of the date of receiving the evidence and data provided by the insured, verify whether it is an insurance liability and notify the insured of the result; where it is not an insurance liability, the insurance company shall explain the reason in writing; where it is an insurance liability, the insurance company shall, within ten days as of concluding an agreement on the payment of insurance indemnities with the insured, pay the insurance indemnities.

In case of any dispute between the insured and the insurance company as to compensation, either party may apply for arbitration or file a lawsuit to the people's court in accordance with the law.

An insurance company may pay the indemnities to the insured, or directly to the victim. Nevertheless, where a payment or advance payment from the insurance company is necessitated by rescuing the injured, the insurance company shall, upon receipt of the notice from the traffic control department of the public security organ and verification, duly make a payment or advance payment to the medical institution as the rescue expenses. Where an advance payment from the relief fund administrative authority is necessitated by rescuing the injured, the relief fund administrative authority shall, upon receipt of the notice from the traffic control department of the public security organ and verification, duly make an advance payment to the medical institution as the rescue expenses.

Where an insurance company or relief fund administrative authority needs to check with the relevant department and medical institution about the relevant information before making a payment or advance payment, the relevant department and medical institution shall give assistance.

331. The working staff of an insurance company or the relief fund administrative authority shall keep confidentiality with the privacy of the parties involved.

332. The owner of the trailer may not purchase the compulsory liability insurance for traffic accidents of motor vehicles. For the personal injuries and death as well as property losses arising from the road traffic accidents, the insurance company from which the owner purchased the compulsory liability insurance for traffic accidents of motor vehicles shall make compensation within the scope of limit of liability, and the insufficient part shall be compensated by the owner of the tractor and the owner of the trailer in accordance with the law.

Chapter 2. Commercial & Family Property Insurance and Construction Insurance

§1. Commercial Property Insurance

333. In current market practice, commercial property is covered by property insurance which could be divided into three types: property basic insurance, property composite insurance and property all risks insurance. In essence, the first two only cover the loss of or damage to the property insured caused by natural hazards or accidents named in the policy, while the third one's cover extends to loss or damage to the property insured caused by all the natural hazards or accidents save those caused by the exclusions listed in the policy.

PICC P&C Property All Risks Insurance Clauses 2009 are the typical and widely used clauses in the market, which will be introduced as follows.

I. Property Insured

334. The property insured shall include the following property contained in the premises specified in the policy:

- property belonging to the insured solely or jointly with others for which the insured is responsible;
- property under management, control, and/or in the custody of the insured;
- other property in which the insured has an economic interest legally admitted.

335. The following property shall not be insured by the policy, unless otherwise specifically agreed between the insurer and the insured and with insured value stated in the policy:

- gold, silver, pearls, diamonds, jades, jewelry, ancient coins, antiques, ancient books, ancient paintings, stamps, works of art, works of painting and calligraphy, rare metals and the like;
- embankments, water gates, railways, roads, culverts, tunnels, bridges, docks and piers;
- plants, equipment and materials in mines or mineral pits;
- mobile communication devices, portable computers, portable photographic apparatus, and other portable devices or equipment;
- construction or erection works not taken over or put into service.

336. The following items and articles are not insured by the policy:

- land, mineral resources, water and other natural resources;
- mines and mineral pits;
- banknotes, coupons, securities, magnetic and integrated circuit (IC) cards with cash value and the alike;

- files and documents, account books, drawings, technical data, computer software or data, and other properties of which the value could not be appraised;
- guns, ammunition or explosives;
- illegal or dilapidated buildings and structures, properties illegally occupied;
- vehicles licensed for general transport use;
- animals, plants, trees and growing crops.

II. Scope of Cover

337. Subject to the terms, exclusions, conditions and provisions contained in the policy or endorsed thereon, the insurer shall indemnify the insured for the following items:

- direct physical loss of or damage to the property insured (physical loss or damage being hereinafter termed "damage") caused by any natural hazard or accident which occurs during the period of insurance, other than those specifically excluded in the policy;
- physical loss of or damage to the property insured resulting from necessary and reasonable measures taken at the time of the happening of perils insured against by the policy for the purpose of preventing or diminishing imminent damage to property hereby insured and/or preventing the spread and/or aggravation of loss or damage;
- in respect of costs and expenses necessarily and reasonably incurred for the purpose of preventing or mitigating the loss of or damage to the property insured after the occurrence of an insured event.

III. Exclusions

338. The insurer shall not indemnify the insured in respect of any loss, damage, or expenses resulting from the following reasons:

- willful act or gross negligence of the applicant or the insured or its representative;
- governmental or judicial actions;
- war and warlike operation, hostilities, armed conflicts, strike, riot, civil commotion, coup d'état, conspiracy insurrection, terrorism;
- earthquake, tsunami and secondary disasters so caused;
- nuclear radiation, nuclear fission, nuclear fusion, nuclear pollution or contamination and other radioactive pollution or contamination;
- pollution of atmosphere, soil, water and other non-radioactive pollution, except non-radioactive pollution caused by perils hereby insured;
- inherent vice or latent defect of the property insured, wear and tear of the property insured, changes in atmospheric (climatic or temperature) conditions,

changes in normal water level or any other progressively operating causes; changes in substance, mold, humidity, mice, insects or vermin, birds, oxidation, rust, leakage, baking;
- theft, burglary or robbery.

The insurer shall also not be liable for:

- consequential loss of the property insured arising from an event insured;
- loss of or damage to the property insured itself arising from faulty design, defective material, or bad workmanship;
- loss of or damage to the outside ancillary devices of building such as advertising signs, antenna, neon lights, solar energy equipment and other property insured stored in the open or in the simple building and the loss of or damage to the simple building itself, caused by the lightning, rainstorm, flood, inundation, windstorm, tornado, hailstone, typhoon, hurricane, snowstorm, icicle, sandstorm;
- loss of or damage to the boilers or other pressure vessels themselves caused by their own explosion;
- loss of or damage to the mechanical or electrical devices themselves unless due to external forces;
- loss of or damage to electrical or mechanical equipment caused by faulty operation or lack of skills of the insured or any of his employee(s);
- shortage discovered at the time of taking an inventory;
- any loss or expenses caused by failure of public utilities, such as electricity, gas, water supply or other energy sources, due to any cause;
- the deductible(s) stated in the policy.

IV. Obligations of Insurer

339. The insurer has the following obligations to fulfill:

- In case of application of standard clauses, the insurer shall enclose them in the proposal form and explain the contents of the insurance contract to the applicant. For the clauses exempting the insurer's liability, the insurer shall make remarkable notice in the proposal form, policy or other certificates to draw the applicant's attention, and explain them clearly in written or oral form when entering into the contract. Otherwise, such clauses shall be void.
- The insurer shall issue the policy or other certificates in a timely manner after the establishment of an insurance contract.
- The insurer's right to terminate the policy as stated below is void if not exercised by the insurer within thirty days after his acknowledgement of any causes for termination of the policy. After two years from the establishment of the insurance contract, such right to cancel the policy is also void and the insurer shall be liable for damage insured by the policy.
- If before the establishment of the insurance contract the insurer is aware of the applicant's misrepresentation or non-disclosure, the insurer cannot terminate the policy, and still shall be liable for damage insured by the policy.

- If the insurer believes that the proofs and documents provided by the insured are not sufficient, the insurer shall request the applicant and/or the insured to provide additional materials in time and once for all.
- Upon receipt of a claim, the insurer shall confirm whether the damage is covered by the policy or not in a timely manner. For complicated cases, the insurer shall make decision within thirty days, unless otherwise stipulated in the insurance contract.
- The insurer shall notify the insured of the decision in a timely manner. If the damage is covered by the policy, the insurer shall make payment within ten days after reaching an agreement with the insured. If the time limit for indemnity is specifically stipulated in the insurance contact, the insurer shall make payment within such time limit. If the damage is not covered by the policy, within three days after the decision, the insurer shall issue a declination letter and explain the reasons to the insured.
- The insurer shall allow an advance payment that can be determined by the available proofs or documents if the final settlement amount cannot be determined within sixty days after receipt of such claim and relevant documents, and pay the balance to the insured after the final amount of indemnity is adjusted.

V. Obligations of the Applicant and/or Insured

340. The applicant and/or the insured has the following obligations to fulfill:

- Before entering into an insurance contract, the applicant shall make full and accurate representation and disclosure at the request and/or inquiry of the insurer in respect of the property insured and the insured itself and complete the proposal form faithfully. If the applicant fails to fulfill the obligation of making full and accurate representation and disclosure as aforementioned due to his willful act and/or gross negligence, which may affect the insurer's decision whether to write the risk of the insurance and, if so, whether to raise the premium rate, the insurer is entitled to terminate the policy. If the applicant willfully fails to comply with the obligation of making full and accurate representation and disclosure, the insurer shall not be liable for any loss or damage happening prior to the termination of the policy while no premium shall be refunded. If the applicant, due to gross negligence, fails to disclose in truth material particular(s) which has a significant contribution to the occurrence of the event insured hereby, the insurer shall not indemnify the insured for any loss or damage happening prior to the cancelation of the policy, but shall return premium collected.
- The applicant shall pay premium as agreed upon in the insurance contract. If the premium is agreed to be paid in a lump, the applicant shall pay the premium on or before the agreed due date. Otherwise, the insurer shall not be liable for any loss or damage which occurs prior to premium payment. If the premium is agreed to be paid in installments, the insurer shall undertake liability in proportion of the paid premium to the total premium payable before the occurrence of damage. The total premium payable refers to the total premium that the applicant shall pay as agreed prior to the occurrence.

- The insured shall observe and fulfill relevant laws, regulations and requirements on fire, safety, production operations and labor protection, improve management, take all reasonable precautions to protect the security of the property and prevent and/or minimize damage thereto. The insurer is entitled to inspect whether or not the insured has fulfilled the aforementioned obligation of reasonable precautions, and make recommendations in writing to the applicant or the insured on eliminating risks and dangers, which shall be implemented by the applicant and/or the insured in a serious manner accordingly. If the applicant or the insured fails to comply with due obligation of reasonable precautions, the insurer is entitled to charge additional premium or terminate the policy.
- Once any property insured is transferred, the insured or the assignee shall notify the insurer in time. If the risk increases materially due to that transfer, the insurer may charge additional premium or cancel the policy subject to the terms and conditions of the policy within thirty days after the insurer's receipt of such notice, in which case, the insurer shall retain the premium due for the period from the date of inception to the date of termination, and refund the remainder of the charged premium to the applicant. If the insured or assignee fails to comply with the aforementioned obligation of notification, the insurer shall not be liable for any damage due to the substantial increase of risks resulted from such transfer of the property insured.
- During the period of insurance, the insured shall give the insurer timely written notice of any alteration of the occupation and/or usage and/or location of the property insured and/or other material facts which may increase the risks materially and affect the insurer's decision whether to continue writing the risk of insurance and, if so, whether to increase the premium, and the insurer is entitled to charge additional premium or cancel the policy. If the insured fails to comply with the obligation of notification aforementioned, the insurer shall not be liable for any damage due to the material change of the risks.
- If any event giving rise to or likely to give rise to a claim under the policy comes to its knowledge, the insured shall: (1) take all necessary and reasonable measures to prevent or minimize the damage; otherwise, the insurer shall not be liable for any extended or aggravated loss or damage caused hereby; (2) give notice to the insurer immediately and submit a written report on the cause, course and extent of the loss or damage. If the applicant and/or insured fail to notify the insurer in time due to his willful act or gross negligence, which makes the insurer not able to ascertain the nature, cause and extent of the loss, the insurer shall not indemnify the insured in respect of such uncertain part of damage, except that the insurer is aware or ought to be aware of the occurrence timely by other means; (3) preserve the spot, permit and assist the insurer in the investigation of the damage. If the cause of the occurrence cannot be ascertained or the severity of the damage cannot be verified due to the refusal of or disturbance by the insured, the insurer shall not be liable for such uncertain part of damage.
- To lodge a claim, the insured shall submit the following proofs and documents:(1) the original policy, claims application, list of lost or damaged property, certificates of technical appraisal, report on the occurrence, invoices of rescue expenses, necessary accounting books, documents and certificates issued by relevant governmental departments or public authorities; (2) all other information

and available documents or proofs concerning the verification of the nature, cause and extent of the damage that can be provided by the applicant or insured. If the applicant or insured fails to comply with his/her obligation of providing the proofs and documents as aforementioned, which makes the insurer not able to verify the damage, the insurer shall not indemnify the insured in respect of the uncertain part of damage.

VI. Loss Settlement

341. The insurer may, at his option, indemnify the insured for loss of or damage to the property insured by either: (1) cash: the insurer makes cash payment as indemnity; or (2) replacement: the insurer replaces the lost or damaged property with that of the same type, structure, function and capacity as the nearest condition of the property immediately prior to loss; or (3) repair: the insurer repairs the damaged property. Nevertheless, the extra costs and/or expenses of any alterations, additions or improvements occurring in the course of repair or replacement carried out by the insured shall not be recoverable under the policy.

§2. Business Interruption Insurance

342. Provided that the applicant has purchased physical damage insurance for his/her property used in the insured's business operation in the premises, the applicant may further purchase a separate insurance to cover the business interruption risks caused by the losses or damages to his/her property.

PICC P&C Business Interruption Insurance Clauses 2009 are the typical and widely used clauses in the market, which will be introduced as follows.

I. Scope of Cover

343. If during the period of insurance the business carried out by the insured at the premises specified in the schedule of the policy is interrupted or interfered with in consequence of physical loss of or damage to the property used in business operation (physical damage) resulting from perils or hazards covered under the physical damage insurance (which herein refers to the standard clauses of the physical damage insurance, excluding the special provisions and conditions, extension clauses, endorsements and memorandum, etc.), the insurer shall indemnify the insured for the loss of gross profit resulting from such interruption or interference, subject to the terms, exclusions, conditions and provisions contained in the policy or endorsed thereon.

344. Indemnity period in this policy refers to the period beginning with the occurrence of the physical damage and ending no later than the maximum indemnity period stated in the policy thereafter during which the results of the business are affected in consequence of the damage.

Gross profit stated in this Policy is calculated as follows: gross profit = business profit + agreed standing charges; or gross profit = agreed standing charge – business deficit × agreed standing charges/total standing charges.

Standing charges stated in the policy refer to the costs or expenses incurred by the insured for the purpose of maintaining normal business operation and shall not be proportionately reduced in accordance with the reduction of the turnover. The agreed standing charges shall be determined by the insured subject to the confirmation of the insurer, and then specified in the policy.

Unless specifically agreed, the accounting terms used in aforementioned formulas shall have the same meaning usually attached to them in the books and accounts of the insured.

The sum insured of gross profit is determined by the applicant and stated in the policy.

The limit of indemnity for the auditor's fee is determined by the applicant and stated in the policy.

345. If any particulars or details contained in the insured's books of account or other business books or documents, which are required by the insurer for the purpose of investigating or verifying any claim hereunder, are produced by professional accountants if at the time they are regularly acting as such for the insured, the insurer shall indemnify the insured within the limit stated in this policy in respect of the necessary and reasonable charges payable by the insured to their professional accountants (auditor's fee) for producing such particulars or details or any other proofs, information or evidence as may be required by the insurer.

II. Exclusions

346. The insurer shall not be liable for:

- any loss or damage caused by or aggravated by willful act and/or gross negligence of the applicant and/or the insured; and/or
- any loss or damage caused by or aggravated by perils and/or hazards other than those covered by physical damage insurance, which refers to the standard clauses of the physical damage insurance, excluding the special provisions and conditions, extension clauses, endorsements and memorandum, etc.; and/or
- any loss or damage caused by or aggravated by earthquake or tsunami and secondary disasters so caused; and/or
- any loss or damage resulting from or aggravated by government's restrictions on recovery or repair of damaged property; and/or
- any loss or damage caused by or aggravated by terrorism activities; and/or
- the deductible or time excess set forth in the policy.

III. Loss Settlement

347. After an occurrence insured, it is a condition precedent to any liability on the part of the insurer that payment of indemnity has been made or liability has been admitted by the insurer under the physical damage insurance which refers to the standard clauses of the physical damage insurance, excluding the special provisions and conditions, extension clauses, endorsements and memorandum, etc., unless no such payment shall have been made or liability shall not have been admitted therefore solely owing to the operation of deductible proviso under the physical damage insurance.

348. The loss of the gross profit in the indemnity period is the sum of reduction in turnover and the increase in cost of working, deducting any sum saved during the indemnity period in respect of such charges and expenses of the business payable out of gross profit as may cease or be reduced in consequence of the incident covered hereby.

Loss of the gross profit resulting from reduction in turnover shall be the sum produced by applying the rate of gross profit to the amount by which the actual turnover during the indemnity period shall, in consequence of the incident, fall short of the standard turnover: rate of gross profit × (standard turnover – actual business turnover within the indemnity period).

Turnover stated in the policy refers to money paid or payable to the insured for goods sold and for services rendered and transferring assets in the course of the business.

Rate of gross profit stated in the policy refers to the rate of gross profit earned on the turnover during the financial year immediately before the date of the physical damage.

Standard turnover stated in the policy refers to the turnover during that period in the twelve months before the date of the physical damage which corresponds with the indemnity period.

Incomes, in connection with the insured's operation, brought into account elsewhere than at the stated premises in the policy, by either the insured or its representatives shall be included in the actual turnover.

Increase in cost of working refers to the additional expenditure necessarily and reasonably incurred for the sole purpose of avoiding or diminishing the reduction in turnover which but for that expenditure would have taken place during the indemnity period in consequence of the physical damage but not exceeding the sum produced by applying the rate of gross profit to the amount of the reduction thereby avoided.

If any standing charges of the business are not insured by the policy (having been deducted in arriving at the gross profit as defined herein), then in calculating the amount recoverable hereunder as increase in cost of working that proportion only of the additional expenditure shall be brought into account which the gross profit bears to the sum of the gross profit and the uninsured standing C = charges, as the following formula: increase in cost of working × gross profit / (gross profit + uninsured standing charges).

349. If the maximum indemnity period is shorter than or equivalent to twelve months, and the sum insured is less than the amount of rate of gross profit multiplying annual turnover, the amount of indemnity shall be determined on the basis of such proportion of the loss of gross profit as the sum insured bears to the abovementioned formula: amount of indemnity =loss of gross profit × sum insured / (rate of gross profit × annual turnover).

If the maximum indemnity period is longer than twelve months, and the sum insured is less than the amount that both rate of gross profit multiplying annual turnover and the maximum indemnity period multiplying 1/12, the amount of indemnity shall be determined on the basis of the abovementioned proportion of the actual loss of gross profit as the sum insured bears to the abovementioned formula: amount of indemnity =loss of gross profit × sum insured / (rate of gross profit × annual turnover × maximum indemnity period/12).

The annual turnover stated in the policy refers to the turnover during the twelve months immediately before the date of physical damage.

350. To which such adjustments shall be made as may be necessary to provide for the trend of business and for variations in or other circumstances affecting the business either before or after physical damage or which would have affected the business had the physical damage not occurred, so that the figures thus adjusted shall represent as nearly as may be reasonably practicable the results which but for the damage would have been obtained during the relative period after the physical property damage.

351. The insurer shall pay the actual auditor's fee incurred in consequence of a covered occurrence, subject to the limit of indemnity specified in the policy.

IV. Miscellaneous

352. If the insured declares at the latest six months after the expiry of any policy year that the gross profit earned by the insured during fiscal year most nearly concurrent with any period of this policy as certified by certified and/or chartered accountant appointed by the insured was less than the sum insured thereon, a pro rata return of premium not exceeding 50% of the premium paid on such sum insured for such period of this policy shall be made in respect of the difference.

If an insured accident has occurred giving rise to a claim, such return of premium shall be calculated as aforementioned after deducting the amount of indemnity hereby paid by the insurer from the sum insured.

§3. FAMILY PROPERTY INSURANCE

I. Subject-Matter Insured

A. The Insurable Property

353. The insurable property includes the house and indoor subsidiary facilities, and the indoor properties. The former includes the water/gas/electricity supply facilities, the heating facility and the sanitary fixture. The latter includes the indoor decorations, the household electrical appliances, the clothing and bedding, the furniture, the tools stored indoor, etc.

The facilities attached to the house are uninsurable, i.e. the swimming pool, the garage, the fence and the playing court.

B. The Insurable Property by Special Agreement

354. The insurable property by special agreement falls into three groups:

(1) the insurable property belonging to other people but in the custody of the insured, or in the co-ownership with the insured;
(2) uninhabited house and the property within;
(3) all other family property belonging to the insured and insurable by reason of the consent of insurer.

C. The Uninsurable Property

355. Usually, the following property is uninsurable under the ordinary family property insurance:

- the house being confiscated or possessed by the government authorities, the unauthorized construction, the dangerous construction, the property illegally owned, the property in the dangerous state;
- the house of which the structure is other than steel, reinforced concrete and half-timbered;
- the house and other property being used in production and business only;
- the simple and crude house or building using the straw, reed mat, bamboo, canvas, plastic cloth and paper, etc. as the outer wall, the shed for breeding fowl and livestock, the wall and toilet that are not parts of insured house;
- gold and silver, jewels and other precious stones, diamonds, calligraphy and painting, ancient coins and items, stamps, rare metals, artworks, watches and other precious properties;
- cash, notes and bills, securities, documents, books, software, electronic storage facilities and data;

– consumables for daily use, motor vehicles, the plants used for commercial purposes.

II. Scope of Coverage

A. *Basic Coverage*

356. The family property insurance usually covers the loss of or damage to the insured property caused by the fire, lightning, explosion, the fall of flying objects and other object running in the sky, the collapse of the buildings and other fixed objects that do not belong to or are not used by the insured. The costs and expenses incurred by the necessary and reasonable measures taken to prevent or minimize the loss of or damage to the insured property, and the mitigation expenses are also indemnifiable by the insurer.

B. *Extended Coverage*

357. The family property insurance can be extended to cover the loss of or damage to the insured property and the extra expenses by the following incidents: typhoon, tornado, storm, flood, blizzard, hailstone, ice slush, debris flow, collapse, sudden landslide and sudden earth subsidence.

C. *Additional Coverage*

358. The normal additional coverage of family property insurance includes:

– the safety of household electrical appliances insurance;
– the broken pipe and water damage insurance;
– the earthquake insurance;
– the third-party liability insurance;
– the robbery and theft insurance;
– the robbery and theft of cash and gold, silver and jewelry insurance.

III. Exclusions

359. The insurer is not liable for the loss of or damage to the insured property or the additional expense caused by the following reasons:

– the production and commercial activities within the insured house or its subsidiary buildings;
– the intentional or gross negligent act done by the insured and his/her family, employee, lodging guest or tenant;
– administrative or judicial activities;

- earthquake, tsunami and their secondary disasters;
- war, warlike operation, terrorism, military operation, armed conflicts, strike, riot and civil commotion;
- nuclear radiation, nuclear burst, nuclear contamination and other radioactive contamination.

Nor the insurer is liable for the following loss or damage or expense:

- the various indirect loss arising out of the loss of or damage to the insured property caused by insurable incidents;
- the loss of or damage to the insured property caused by inherent vice or careless storage;
- the deterioration, mildew and rot, damp, insect bite, ordinary wear and tear, self-combustion, roast of the insured property;
- the excessive use, overvoltage, short circuit, turnoff, electrical leakage, self-heating, roast of the household electrical appliances;
- being caused by flood and the property being located in the flood storage area or flood flowing area, or nearby river, low-lying land and places beyond flood protection embankment but below the water warning line all year round;
- the deductibles;
- other loss or damage or expense which is not covered by the insurance contract.

§4. Construction Insurance

360. Construction insurance is a type of property insurance. PICC officially started to provide this type of insurance in 1980, mainly undertaking foreign projects. The insured objects are civil projects of various industries, civil and public utilities. Coverage includes: (1) losses caused by certain natural disasters such as floods, lightning, and storms; (2) losses caused by certain man-made causes, such as theft, the fault of workers and technicians, and malicious behavior; (3)some unexpected accidents. The purpose of construction insurance is mainly to ensure that the economic losses suffered by the relevant units or individuals of the construction project during the implementation of the project plan can be promptly and reasonably compensated, so that the project plan can be carried out continuously and smoothly.

PICC P&C Construction All Risks Clauses 2009 are the typical and widely used clauses in the market, which will be introduced as follows.

I. Subject-Matter Insured

361. The property and costs which are related to the construction contract and situated in the specified worksite are insured hereby, provided being itemized and listed in the policy.

The following property or costs shall not be insured by this Policy, unless otherwise specifically agreed between the insurer and the insured and with sum insured stated in this Policy:

- construction plants, machinery and equipment;
- the property belonging to the insured which exists or is formed within or in the vicinity of the worksite before the commencement of the contract works insured;
- the property or any part of it which has been put into commercial use or taken over or actually occupied by the employer or the property or any part of it for which a certificate of completion has been issued or which has been accepted by the representative of the employer after the contractor formally proposes works acceptance before the expiry date of the policy;
- debris removal costs, which means necessary and reasonable costs and/or expenses incurred by the insured to remove and dispose of debris at the worksite for the purpose of repairing the insured property after an event giving rise to identifiable loss or damage under the policy.

362. The following items and articles are not insured by the policy:

- documents, books, drawings, technical data, computer software, computer data, and other property of which the value could not be appraised;
- portable communication devices, portable computer devices, portable photographic camera equipment and other portable devices or equipment;
- land, seabed, mineral, water, animals, plants, trees and growing crops;
- vehicles, ships or aircraft licensed for general transport use or covered by other insurance;
- illegal or dangerous buildings or structures, or illegally occupied property.

II. Scope of Cover

363. Subject to the terms, exclusions, conditions and provisions contained in the Policy or endorsed thereon, the insurer shall indemnify the insured for the physical loss of or damage to the property insured (physical loss or damage being hereinafter termed "damage") during the period of insurance within the specified worksite arising from any natural hazard or accident other than those specifically excluded in the policy.

Subject to the terms, exclusions, conditions and provisions contained in the policy or endorsed thereon, the insurer shall also indemnify the insured for the following costs and/or expenses incurred in consequence of the damage caused by event insured by the policy as stated above during the period of insurance: (1) costs and/or expenses necessarily and reasonably incurred by the insured for preventing or mitigating the damage of subject-matter insured after an event insured hereby; (2) other related costs and/or expenses specified in the policy in respect of the abovementioned loss or damage.

III. Exclusions

364. The insurer shall not be liable for:

- loss of or damage to property insured and/or any part thereof or any costs and/or expenses resulting from faulty design;
- loss of or damage to property insured itself and/or any costs and/or expenses resulting from wear and tear, inherent or latent defect, change in substance, spontaneous combustion, natural heating, oxidation, rust and corrosion, leakage, mice, insects or vermin, change in atmospheric (climatic or temperature) conditions, change in normal water level or any other progressively operating cause;
- loss of or damage to the property insured itself due to defective material or bad workmanship and expenses incurred to replace, repair or rectify such fault, defect, error, or omission;
- loss of or damage to the mechanical or electrical devices insured themselves unless due to external forces; loss of or damage to the construction plants machinery and equipment or mechanical devices themselves due to breakdown or derangement thereof;
- costs and/or expenses incurred for normal maintenance or overhaul;
- loss of or damage to files, documents, account books, bills, cash, securities, drawings, data and packing materials;
- shortage discovered at the time of taking an inventory;
- loss of or damage to vehicles, ships or aircraft licensed for general transport use or having been covered by any other insurance;
- unless otherwise agreed, loss of or damage to the property belonging to the insured which exists or is formed within or in the vicinity of the worksite before the commencement of the contract works;
- unless otherwise agreed, loss of or damage to the property insured or any part thereof for which a certificate of completion has been issued or which have been tested and accepted or actually occupied or put into service or taken over by the employer before the expiry date of the policy;
- war, warlike operation, hostilities, armed conflicts, terrorism, conspiracy insurrection, coup d'etat;
- governmental or judicial actions;
- strike, riot, civil commotion;
- willful act or gross negligence of the insured or his representative;
- nuclear fission, nuclear fusion, nuclear weapon, nuclear material, nuclear radiation, nuclear explosion, nuclear contamination and other radioactive contamination;
- pollution of any kind, including atmosphere, land and water pollutions;
- cessation of work whether total or partial;
- consequential loss of any kind or description whatsoever including penalties, losses due to delay or loss of contract;
- the deductibles stated in the policy to be borne by the insured;
- the deductibles calculated by the deductible ratio stated in the policy.

IV. Sum Insured

365. The sum insured of the policy shall not be less than:

- for contract works—the full value exposed at the completion of the contract works including costs and/ expenses of materials, equipment, construction and erection, freight and premium, customs duty, any other taxes and expenses, including any free issue material and equipment which are to be incorporated therein;
- for other items insured—the sums agreed upon between the insured and the insurer.

366. If the sum insured is based on the estimated value stated in the construction contract, the applicant and/or insured shall:

- notify the insurer in writing as soon as practical if the contract value, including all costs and expenses under the policy, exceeds the original insured contract value due to rise in price or appreciation, and the insurer shall then adjust the sum insured accordingly;
- keep a precise record in writing on the particulars of the contract works concerned during the period of insurance and allow the insurer to inspect and examine such record at any reasonable time;
- declare to the insurer the actual amount spent in the contract works by the time of declaration as well as updated estimate contract value at an interval of every twelve months from the inception date of the policy; if the construction period of the insured project is longer than thirty-six months, the insurer shall adjust the premium accordingly;
- provide the insurer with the actual final contract value within three months after the expiry date of the policy, and the premium shall be adjusted accordingly.

V. Loss Settlement

367. The insurer may, at his own option, indemnify the insured in respect of loss of or damage to the property insured either by way of payment in cash or by way of repair or replacement of the items lost or damaged. Nevertheless, the extra costs and/or expenses of any alterations, additions or improvements occurring in the course of repair or replacement carried out by the insured shall not be recoverable under this Policy.

368. In case of any loss or damage recoverable under the policy, the insurer shall ascertain the loss amount on the following basis:

- In cases where damage can be repaired, the insurer shall indemnify the costs incurred necessarily to repair or to restore the damaged property to its nearest condition immediately before the occurrence of loss or damage after deducting the salvage value. If, however, the costs of repair equal or exceed the actual value of the damaged property immediately before the occurrence of loss or damage, the settlement shall be made on the basis provided for below.

- In the event of a total or constructive total loss, the insurer shall pay the actual value of the insured property immediately before the occurrence of the loss or damage, after deducting the salvage value.

Salvage value after loss or damage shall be disposed upon agreement between the insured and insurer. If the salvage of the damaged property is retained by the insured, the salvage value shall be deducted from the actual amount of indemnity.

369. Any loss of or damage to the property insured arising during any one period of seventy-two consecutive hours, caused by storm, typhoon, flood or other continuous occurrences of natural hazards shall be deemed as a single event and constitute one loss occurrence, deducting the deductible (ratio) for one time in the settlement of any claim. The commencement of any such seventy-two-hour period can be decided at the discretion of the insured. However, there shall be no overlapping in any two or more such seventy-two-hour periods in the event of damage occurring over several continuous seventy-two-hour periods.

370. If the property insured specified in the policy has more than one item, the insurer shall calculate the amount of indemnity item by item and the liability of the insurer in respect of each item shall not exceed its insured amount specified in the policy nor the limit of indemnity as specified in the special provisions or endorsements where applicable. But in no case shall the maximum liability of the insurer in respect of material damage under this section exceed the total sum insured specified in the policy.

VI. Period of Insurance

371. The period of insurance of the policy shall follow the agreement stated below:

- The liability of the insurer shall begin notwithstanding any date to the contrary specified in the policy, directly upon commencement of the physical work or after the unloading of the insured materials or equipment on the worksite and shall expire immediately after a certificate of completion has been issued for part or whole of the insured project or part or whole of the insured project has been tested after completion or actually occupied or put into commercial use or taken over by the employer, whichever is the earlier. In no case shall the effective date be earlier or the expiry date be later than the period of insurance specified in the policy.
- Notwithstanding anything to the contrary stated in the contract concerned, the insurer shall be liable only for the loss, damage, expenses and/or liabilities caused by the testing or commissioning occurring during the testing or commissioning period stated in the policy. In the case of each used or second-hand item of property or equipment insured, the insurance to such items or equipment shall, however, terminate immediately on the commencement of the testing and commissioning.

– Any extensions of the period of insurance shall be subject to the prior written consent of the insurer. Otherwise, the insurer shall not be liable for any loss, damage, expense and/or liabilities after the expiry date of the construction period stated in the policy.

Chapter 3. Liability Insurance

§1. Introduction

372. By Article 65(4) of the IL, liability insurance refers to insurance where the subject matter of insured is the insured's liability to indemnify a third party in accordance with the law.

On the policy level, the Chinese government takes the development of liability insurance seriously. In the *Several Opinions of the State Council on Accelerating the Development of the Modern Insurance Service Industry* issued in 2014, it is clearly stated that the function and role of liability insurance in resolving conflicts and disputes must be exerted. Efforts shall be made to intensify the development mode of liability insurance which is guided by the government, operated by the market, and secured by the legislation, take the sectors that closely relate to the public interest, such as environmental protection, food safety, medical liability, medical accident, intern security and campus security, as the development priority in liability insurance, and explore and launch the pilot project for compulsory liability insurance; and accelerate the development of travel agencies, product quality and various professional liability insurance, product liability insurance and public liability insurance, fully play the function and role of liability insurance in prior risk prevention, interim risk control, *ex post* claim settlement service and other aspects, and resolve civil liability disputes through economic leverage and diversified liability insurance products.

373. Articles 65 and 66 of the IL set out the basic legal structure of indemnification under liability insurance:

- An insurer may, in accordance with the provisions of law or the terms of an insurance contract, directly indemnify a third party for loss or damage caused by the insured under liability insurance.
- Where the insured under liability insurance causes any damage to a third party and the liability of the insured for indemnity to the third party has been determined, the insurer shall directly pay insurance benefits to the third party according to the request of the insured. Where the insured is negligent in making such a request, the third party shall have the right to directly request the insurer to pay the insurance benefits for the damage to the third party.
- Where the insured under liability insurance causes any damage to a third party and the insured has not indemnified the third party for the damage, the insurer shall not pay insurance benefits to the insured.
- If the insured in a liability insurance contract is brought to arbitration or legal proceedings due to the occurrence of an incident covered by insurance which causes loss or damage to a third party, the insurer shall bear the cost of such arbitration or legal proceedings and other necessary and reasonable expenses paid by the insured, unless otherwise provided for in the insurance contract.

Articles 14-20 of *Interpretation IV* further provide several solutions regarding the common disputes as to liability insurance:

- The insured may request the insurer to directly provide a third party with the insurance indemnity, in accordance with provisions of the second paragraph of Article 65 of the IL, under any of the following circumstances: (1) where the compensation liability due by the insured against the third party is determined under an effective court judgment or an arbitral decision; (2) where the compensation liability due by the insured against the third party is determined under an agreement between the insured and the third party; or (3) any other circumstance where the compensation liability due by the insured against the third party can be determined. Where the insurer claims to determine the compensation liability as per the insurance contract, under any of the abovesaid circumstances, the people's court shall uphold such claim.
- Where the insured does not fulfill its compensation liability after its due compensation liability against a third party has been determined, and it has not requested the insurer to directly provide the third party with the insurance indemnity when the third party brings a lawsuit against the insurer as the defendant or against both the insurer and the insured as the joint defendants, the insured may be, under such circumstance, deemed to "have neglected to make a request," as provided in Article 65(2) of the IL.
- Where the insured under liability insurance is held jointly liable for contributory torturous act according to the law, and the insurer refuses to provide the insurance indemnity, arguing that such joint liability is greater than the share of liability due to be borne by the insured, the people's court shall not uphold such argument. Where the insurer, after fulfilling its insurance liability, claims recovery of the part greater than the share of liability due to be borne by the insured from any other liable party, the people's court shall uphold such claim.
- Where the compensation liability due by the insured under liability insurance against a third party has been determined by an effective ruling which has entered enforcement procedures, but the indemnity has not been paid or paid in full and the third party requests the insurer to pay out the insurance indemnity, the argument by the insurer that enforcement procedures for the said effective ruling have been initiated shall not be supported by the people's court.
- The limitation of action available for the insured under commercial liability insurance to demand insurance indemnity from the insurer shall commence from the date when the compensation liability due by the insured against a third party is determined.
- Where a settlement agreement is reached between the insured under liability insurance and a third party to specify the liability due by the insured against the third party and is recognized by the insurer, and the insured claims that the insurer shall fulfill the insurance liability as per the settlement agreement and to the extent specified in the insurance contract, the people's court shall uphold such claim. However, where a settlement agreement is reached between the insured and a third party to specify the compensation liability due by the insured against the third party but is not recognized by the insurer, the people's court shall uphold the claim by the insurer to have the extent of insurance liability and the amount of compensation reassessed.
- Where the insurer of liability insurance pays out insurance indemnity to the insured before the insured pays compensation due to the third party and therefore

refuses to pay out insurance indemnity again when the third party exercises its right to claim insurance indemnity according to of Article 65(2) of the IL, arguing that it has already paid out the indemnity to the insured, the people's court shall not uphold such argument. However, where the insurer requests to have the insured return the corresponding amount of insurance indemnity already paid out to the insured, after the insurer has compensated the third party, the people's court shall uphold such request.

§2. Public Liability Insurance

374. Public liability insurance mainly covers the economic compensation liability of the insured in accordance with law for the personal injury or death or property loss of others caused by accidents during the production, operation or other activities of the insured in public places. The insured may insure public liability insurance for various public activities such as factories, office buildings, hotels, residences, shops, hospitals, schools, theaters, exhibition halls and other public activities.

PICC P&C Public Liability Insurance Clauses 1999 are the typical and widely used clauses in the market, which will be introduced as follows.

I. Parties to Be Insured

375. Those to be insured under this policy can comprise enterprises, institutions, social groups, individual and private businesses, and other economic organizations legally established as well as natural persons.

II. Scope of Cover

376. The insurer agrees to indemnify the insured against such sums as the insured shall become legally liable to pay as damages in consequence of an accident occurring during the period of the insurance, on or about the premises and in the course of production, trade, or performance of duties in connection with the business or operations as specified in the schedule in respect of:

- bodily injury (including death and illness) or loss of/damage to property of the third party;
- legal costs incurred with prior consent of the insurer in writing; and
- necessary and reasonable expenses paid by the insured to reduce or minimize his liability for injury or damage after the occurrence of the accident.

The total sums payable for the first two items for each accident shall in no case exceed the limit of indemnity for each accident set forth in the schedule. The sum payable for the third items shall not exceed the limit of indemnity for each accident as specified in the schedule.

III. Exclusions

377. The insurer shall not be liable for any loss, expenses and liability caused by or arising from:

- intentional act or gross negligence of the insured or his representatives;
- war, hostilities, warlike operations, armed conflicts, strike, civil commotion, riot, theft, burglary or robbery;
- confiscation or requisition by the public authorities;
- nuclear reaction, nuclear radiation or radioactivity contamination;
- earthquake, lightning, storm, flood, volcanic eruption, subterranean fire, hurricane, typhoon, windstorm and other natural disasters;
- pollution of any kind, including fumes, air, soil or water pollution;
- explosion of boiler, drop of aerial devices;
- loss directly or indirectly arising from computer "Year 2000 Problems" bugs;
- bodily injury to the insured, its representatives, or its employees, and damage to the property owned by them or in their custody or control;
- fine, penalty or punitive indemnity;
- liability assumed by the insured in a contract or agreement except to the extent that such liability would have been implied by law.

The insurer shall also not be liable for the loss, expenses and liability, which should be covered by other insurances, arising from or caused by:

- professional advice or service provided by the insured or its employees acting as medical practitioners, lawyers, accountants, designers, architects and beauticians;
- being poisoned or affected by food or drink, unclean or poisonous or with foreign or deleterious matter therein, or injured by defective sanitary installations, or harmed by defective commodities, food or drink sold or supplied;
- loss arising from ownership or possession or use by or on behalf of the insured of any animal, vehicle, locomotive, vessel of any kind, aircraft, lift, elevator, escalator, crane, hoist or other lifting machinery unless specified in the schedule;
- damage to any land, property or building caused by vibration, removal or weakening of support, or injury or damage caused by alteration, maintenance, repair or decoration;
- indirect loss of any kind caused by suspension of business of the insured or any third party.

The insurer shall not be liable for bodily injury or damage to property caused by fire or explosion occurring on the insured's premises or to the equipment therein, which the public authorities have not checked and accepted, or have been considered disqualified for safety purpose after checking.

The insurer shall not pay for any liability incurred due to fire or explosion occurring in the neighboring building, spreading therefrom to the insured's premises and then further spreading therefrom to other places.

The insurer shall not be liable for any loss, expenses and liability caused by or arising from:

- accident occurring in the swimming pool located on the insured's premises as specified in the schedule of the policy, and owned or used or operated by the insured;
- accident occurring to the advertising signs, neon lights and lamps installed on the insured's premises;
- accident occurring in the parking lot on the insured's premises as specified in the schedule of the policy, and owned or used or operated by the insured;
- fire occurring in the house or building rented out by the insured.

The insurer shall not be liable for the excess or deductibles for each accident assumed by the insured as specified in the schedule, endorsement or other relevant clauses.

IV. Additional Clauses

378. The parties are entitled to incorporate the additional clauses attached to PICC P&C Public Liability Insurance Clauses 1999 into the contract, for example Guest's Property Clause, Swimming Pool Clause, Lessor's Liability Clause, Elevator or Escalator Clause, Billboards and Decorations Clause, Parking Lot Clause, Building Alteration Clause, Boiler's Explosion Clause, Cross Liability Insurance Clause, Loading and Unloading of Vehicle Clause, etc.

§3. Production Liability Insurance

379. Product liability insurance refers to a kind of liability insurance that takes product liability of product manufacturer, seller, repairer, etc. as the underwriting risk, and product liability is based on the product liability legal system of each country. The so-called product liability refers to the product supplier (including the manufacturer, seller, repairer, etc.) who should bear the civil liability in accordance with the relevant laws when the product causes defects or damages to the user, consumer or the public during the use of the product. If the user does not follow the product instructions to install, use or use the product in an abnormal state, the damage accident caused by the product does not belong to the product responsibility.

PICC P&C Products Liability Insurance Clauses 1995 are the typical and widely used clauses in the market, which will be introduced as follows.

I. Scope of Cover

380. The insurer will indemnify the insured in the manner and within the limit of liability specified in the schedule of the policy against such sums as the insured shall become legally liable to pay in respect of claims made against the insured arising from bodily injury to or illness or death of or loss of or damage to property of one or more persons using, consuming or handling the insured products or goods, or of any other persons consequent upon an occurrence taking place in the territory of coverage within the period of insurance caused by products or goods manufactured or sold by the insured stated in the schedule.

In respect of any claim covered under the policy, the insurer shall in addition indemnify the insured against the relevant legal costs payable by the insured and other expenses incurred in the abovementioned occurrence with the prior written consent of the insurer, but the total liability of the Company for the sums of compensation and the legal costs and expenses shall in no way exceed the limit of indemnity stated in the schedule of the policy.

II. Exclusions

381. The insurer shall not be liable for:

- liability assumed in accordance with any agreement between the insured and other parties, unless such liability would have been attached to the insured notwithstanding such agreement;
- liability assumed by the insured under any Labor Law or Workmen's Compensation Statute;
- liability of the insured to employees which is based on the relationship of master and servant;
- loss of or damage to the insured products;
- costs arising out of replacement or recall of the insured products;
- loss of or damage to property belonging to or held in care, custody or control of the insured;
- bodily injury, illness or death or damage to property sustained by any person caused by products or goods manufactured or sold by the insured in willful violation of any law;
- liability arising out of pollution of any kind or description whatsoever such as atmosphere, land and water caused by the insured products;
- liability for loss of or damage to the aircraft or ships caused by the insured products;
- liability for any consequence arising directly or indirectly from war, warlike operation, hostilities, armed conflicts, terrorism, conspiracy insurrection, coup d'etat;
- liability for any consequence arising directly or indirectly from strike, riot, civil commotion or malicious acts;
- liability arising directly or indirectly from nuclear fission, nuclear fusion, nuclear weapon, nuclear material, nuclear radiation and radioactive contamination;
- fines, penalties, punitive or exemplary indemnities;
- the deductibles stated in the schedule or stipulated in the policy to be borne by the insured.

III. Claims

382. In the event of any claim recoverable under the policy:

- no admission, rejection, offer, promise, payment or indemnity shall be made or given by or on behalf of the insured or its representative without the written consent of the insurer. And the insurer shall be entitled, if it so desires, to take over and conduct in the name of the insured the defense or settlement of any claim;
- the insurer shall be entitled, at its own expense and for its own benefit, to lodge in the name of the insured any claim for indemnity against any persons. Without the written consent of the insurer, the insured shall not accept the payment or arrangement of indemnity in respect of the loss or damage offered by any party held responsible for such loss or damage and shall not abandon the right of recovery from such party; otherwise, the insured shall be liable for any consequence arising therefrom;
- the insurer shall have full discretion to conduct any proceedings or settle any claim, and the insured shall give all such information and assistance as the insurer may require.

Bodily injury to or illness or death of or damage to property of more than one person arising from the same lot of products or goods manufactured sold due to the same cause shall be considered as resulting from one occurrence.

The time of validity of a claim under this insurance shall not exceed a period of two years counting from the date of loss.

IV. Additional Clauses

383. The parties are entitled to incorporate the additional clauses attached to PICC P&C Public Liability Insurance Clauses 1999 into the contract. For example, as to exclusions, there are War and Terrorism Exclusion; Absolute Pollution Exclusion; Absolute Asbestos Exclusion; Nuclear Energy Liability Exclusion; Lead Exclusion; Electromagnetic Radiation and Radiofrequency Waves Exclusion; Mold Exclusion; Genetic Modification Organization Exclusion; Allergy Exclusion; Infectious Disease Exclusion; Efficacy Exclusion; Silica or Silica-Related Dust Exclusion Clause; Fungus, Mildew and Mold Exclusion; Punitive/Exemplary Damage Exclusion; Employees' Bodily Injury Exclusion; Terrorism Exclusion; Cyber Risks Exclusion; Malpractice & Professional Services Exclusion; Terrorism for Contamination & Explosives Exclusion, etc.

§4. Employer Liability Insurance

384. Employer liability insurance is also known as labor compensation insurance. The insurer underwrites economic compensation liability that should be borne by the employer when the employee is injured or suffers from occupational disease during employment. This kind of insurance could be a compulsory insurance stipulated by law; the insured person is the employer, and the beneficiary is the employee or his family. Employer's liability insurance has the nature of social insurance.

Unlike commercial insurance, insurance premiums are mainly used to pay insurance premiums and operating expenses. There are few profits, and the rates are lower.

PICC P&C Employer's Liability Insurance Clause 1999 is the typical and widely used clause in the market, which will be introduced as follows.

I. Parties to Be Insured

385. For the purposes of the clause, enterprises including but not limited to foreign-invested enterprises, private enterprises, domestic stock companies, state-owned enterprises, non-profit enterprises, collective enterprises and collectively or privately contracted enterprises, and also public organizations, government institutions, schools, are all entitled to apply to the insurer to insure against their legal liability to their employees (regular workers, casual labor, temporary and seasonal workers and apprentices included) subject to the terms and conditions of the policy.

The aforesaid employees of the insured refer to those who are paid for a certain or uncertain period of employment by the insured and over the age of 16 or to those approved to be employed by statutes and other legal means.

II. Scope of Cover

386. The insurer will indemnify the insured against his liability under the contract of employment and at laws and regulations of China to pay medical expenses and other economic compensations within the agreed limit of indemnity in respect of death or bodily injury or disablement by accident or through occupational disease, to its employee(s) while, during the effective period of this insurance and in the course of employment (including to and off work) by the insured, being engaged in the insured's business as stated in the policy.

The insurer will also indemnify the insured within the agreed sublimit against defense costs payable by the insured to the claimant, and other legal costs and expenses incurred with the written consent of the insurer.

Within the period of insurance, the maximum amount of indemnity by the insurer for all and each item(s) mentioned above shall in no case exceed the aggregate limit of indemnity as stated in the policy schedule.

III. Exclusions

387. The insurer shall not be liable for:

- death, diseases, disability or bodily injury sustained by the insured's employee(s) named in the schedule in the course of employment by the insured, arising from war, military actions, strikes, riots, civil commotion or nuclear radiation;

- bodily injury and/or disability to, or death of the employee(s) in the course of employment by the insured, caused by or attributed to illness other than occupational diseases, infectious diseases, childbirth, abortion, medical treatment and surgical operations necessitated by such diseases;
- bodily injury and/or disability to, or death of the employee(s) in the course of employment by the insured, caused by or attributed to intentional self-injury, suicide and criminal act;
- bodily injury and/or disability to, or death of the employee(s) in the course of employment by the insured, caused by or attributed to alcohol or drug not necessitated by the aforesaid occupation;
- intentional act or gross negligence of the insured;
- the insured's liability to employees of contractors to the insured, unless otherwise stated;
- bodily injury and/or disability to, or death of the employee(s) in the course of employment by the insured, occurring outside the territorial limit of China, unless otherwise stated;
- other losses and expenses not included in the coverage of the policy.

IV. Claims

388. When lodging a claim against the insurer, the insured shall provide the original policy, the relevant proof of accident, medical report issued by medical organization(s) recognized by the insurer, original receipt of medical expenses and any other necessary and effective documents required by the insurer. The insurer shall as soon as possible examine all these documents, settling the claim and effect payment within ten days from the date when the amount of indemnity is mutually agreed upon.

389. In the event of occurrence falling within the coverage during the period of insurance, the insurer shall, in the manners as follows, indemnify the insured against his liability for the death of, bodily injury and disablement to the employee(s), specified in the name list provided by the insured:

- *In respect of death, permanent full disablement/permanent partial disablement*: the total amount of indemnity shall be calculated by multiplying the percentage set forth in the attached Indemnity Scale of the Policy by the limit of indemnity for death, bodily injury and disablement, respectively.
- *In respect of temporary disability for a period exceeding five days (the first five days not included)*: during this period, as certified by the hospital, the professional injury subsidy per person per day shall be in accordance with the minimum living expenses stipulated by the local government. Such subsidy shall be terminated once the medical treatment is completed or the extent of disablement is ascertained. But in no case shall the period of indemnity exceed one year. If permanent full or partial disablement is ascertained by medical organization(s), the indemnity shall be calculated according to the above section. The total

amount payable, including injury allowance/subsidy, shall not exceed the limit of indemnity for death or bodily injury stipulated in the schedule of the policy.
– *In respect of medical expenses*: the insurer shall pay the expenses for registration, treatment, operation, sickbed, examination (with a limit of RMB 300), and medicines as public expenses as stipulated by the government. But such expenses shall not include those for tending, food, nutrition, transportation, heating, air conditioning and artificial limb, tooth, eye and other supporting utensils for disabled persons. Except in the case of emergency, the injured employees should be treated in the hospitals at or above the county level or appointed by the government or the insurer.

The amount of indemnity payable to the insured for each of his employee under each section above shall not exceed his liability at law or under the contract of employment, and in no case exceed any sublimit of indemnity for any one person as indicated in the schedule of the policy.

The employees of the insured shall not have compensations for both death and bodily injury in respect of any one occurrence. The indemnity limit of medical expense payment and that to death or bodily injury payment shall be applied severally.

390. If a claim arises under the policy while there is in existence any other insurance covering the same liability, the insurer shall only be liable for its proportion of the claim for medical expenses, injury subsidy, and the defense costs, no matter whether any payment has been made under other insurance. If the actual number of the employees exceeds the number indicated in the schedule of the policy, the insurer shall only be liable to pay the claims for listed employees if the names of the employees insured are listed in the Policy, or to pay such proportion of the claim as the number of the employees indicated in the schedule bears to the actual number of the employees, unless otherwise agreed by the insurer if necessary.

V. Additional Clauses

391. The parties are entitled to incorporate the additional clauses attached to PICC P&C Employer's Liability Insurance Clauses 1999 into the contract, such as Additional Third-Party Liability Insurance Clause; Strike, Riot, Civil Commotion or Malicious Damage Extension Clause; Nuclear Radiation Liability Clause; and Overseas Business Trip Liability Clause.

Chapter 4. Hull Insurance and Cargo Insurance

§1. Hull Insurance

392. Hull clauses in China market were first published in January 1972 and were used by PICC. The clauses were amended several times afterwards and the current version used by the market is the 2009 Hull clauses.

I. Types of Insurance

A. *Voyage Insurance*

393. Under a voyage insurance policy, the vessel is covered for a particular and fixed voyage against the perils described in the insurance policy as agreed between the insurer and the insured, viz. the owners, operator or bareboat of the vessel, as the case may be.

The Chinese law does not define the voyage or the commencement and termination time of the voyage, but leaves the insurer and insured to agree. Under PICC P&C Hull Clauses 2009, the voyage in a voyage policy means the one described in the policy. Where the vessel is not loaded with cargo, the voyage shall commence when she casts off lines or weighs up anchor at the port of departure and end when she lets go anchor or ties up at the port of destination. Where the vessel is loaded with cargo, the voyage shall commence when loading operation starts and ends when discharge operation completes, but shall not exceed thirty days dating from the midnight of the day of her arrival at the port of destination.

B. *Time Insurance*

394. Under a time insurance policy, the vessel is covered for a fixed duration against the perils described in the insurance policy as agreed between the insurer and the insured.

Likewise, the Chinese law does not limit the duration of coverage, but leaves the insurer and the insured to agree. Under PICC P&C Hull Clauses 2009, the duration of coverage in the case of a time policy shall not exceed one year. The commencement and termination time shall be described in the policy.

C. *Combined Policy*

395. Combined voyage/time policy is not a statutory concept under the Chinese law, but is used in the hull insurance subject to agreement between the insurer and the insured. The purpose of a combined policy is to avoid the disadvantage of a time policy; i.e., when the agreed duration, normally twelve months, expires, the policy automatically comes to an end, while the insured vessel is often still at sea and has to complete a voyage. The combined policy enables the insured to have its vessel covered until her completion of voyage after the expiration of the agreed duration. The insured is normally required to pay extra premium for such extension.

Under PICC Hull Clause 2009, under a time policy, if the vessel is still on her voyage, in distress or at the port of refuge or port of call when the agreed duration expires, the coverage shall be extended until she arrives at the port of destination, provided that the insured notifies the insurer in advance thereof and pays additional daily premium in proportion. In such a case, if the vessel suffers a total loss during the time of extension, a premium for a period of six months shall be paid by the insured.

II. Scope of Cover

396. By virtue of Article 219(1) of MC, hull insurance covers the hull, machinery, equipment, bunkers, stores, gears, provisions and fresh water of the vessel insured. Under PICC P&C Hull Clauses of 2009, the insurance covers hull, lifeboats, machinery, equipment, instruments, gears, bunkers and stores.

A. *Total Loss Cover*

397. This insurance covers total loss of the vessel insured, including actual total loss and constructive total loss as mentioned *infra* caused by any of the following perils:

- earthquake, volcanic eruption, lighting or other natural calamities;
- grounding, collision, contacting with any fixed or floating object or other objects, or other peril of the sea;
- fire or explosion;
- violent theft by persons outside the vessel or piracy;
- jettison;
- breakdown of or accident to nuclear installation or reactor;
- accident in loading, discharging or shifting of cargo or fuel;
- latent defect in machinery or hull of the vessel;
- wrongful act willfully committed by the master or crew to the prejudice of the insured's interests;
- negligence of the master, crew or pilot, repairer or charterers;
- act of any governmental authority to prevent or minimize pollution resulting from damage to the vessel caused by peril insured against.

Noticeably, the coverage of the last five categories of perils listed *supra* is conditional upon that the total loss resulting therefrom has not caused by want of due diligence on the part of the insured, owners or managers of the vessel insured.

B. All Risks Cover

398. This insurance covers the total loss or partial loss of or damage to the insured vessel arising from the perils insured against under the Total Loss Cover and also the liabilities and expenses of collision, general average and salvage, and mitigation.

399. The provision of collision liability is called "Running Down Clause" (RDC). Under PICC P&C Hull Clauses of 2009, the insurance of collision liability covers legal liabilities of the insured as a consequence of the insured vessel coming into collision or contact with any other vessel or any object, fixed or floating or otherwise. Thus, this RDC covers 4/4 of the collision liability instead of 3/4 in some other countries and allision liability.

However, this RDC does not cover any liability resulting from collision or allision of the insured vessel in respect of:

- loss of life, personal injury or illness of any person whether on board or ashore;
- cargo or other property on, or engagement of, the insured vessel;
- removal or disposal of obstruction, wrecks, cargoes or any other things whatsoever;
- pollution or contamination of any property or thing whatsoever including the cost of preventive measures and cleaning operations, except pollution or contamination of the other vessel with which the insured vessel is in collision or property on such other vessel;
- indirect expenses arising from delay to or use of any object, fixed or floating or otherwise.

400. The insurance of general average and salvage covers the insured vessel's proportion of general average or salvage reward not in the nature of general average. Special compensation as provided for in Article 182 of MC is normally not covered under this clause, but is covered under the protection and indemnity insurance.

401. Noticeably, under PICC P&C Hull Clauses 2009, in the case of general average sacrifice of the insured vessel, the insured may recover such losses in full without first obtaining contribution from other parties. After the payment for such losses, the insurer has the right of subrogation to claim against other interests for contribution in general average.

Under these Clauses, the general average shall be adjusted in accordance with the relative contract of carriage and/or governing law or customs. Where the contract of carriage does not so provide, the general average shall be adjusted in accordance with Beijing Rules or other similar rules. In practice, where general average is adjusted in accordance with York-Antwerp Rules as in most cases, general average is covered under this insurance.

It is expressly provided for in PICC P&C Hull Clauses 2009 that, where all the contributing interests are owned by the insured, or when the insured vessel sails in ballast and there are no other contributing interests, the provisions of Beijing Rules except Rule 5, or similar adjustment rules, if expressly agreed upon, shall apply as if the interests were owned by different persons. The voyage for this purpose of adjustment shall be deemed to be from the port or place of departure until the arrival of the vessel at the first port thereafter other than a port of refuge or a port of call for bunkering. If, at any such intermediate port or place, there is an abandonment of the adventure originally contemplated, the voyage shall thereupon be deemed terminated.

402. Under the mitigation clause, where there is loss of or damage to the insured vessel from a peril insured against, or where she is in immediate danger of such a peril, and as a result, reasonable expenses are incurred by the insured in order to avert or minimize a loss that would be recoverable under this insurance, the insurer shall be liable for the expenses so incurred by the insured. However, this clause shall not apply to general average or salvage reward or other expenditures provided for in other clauses.

C. Mixed Cover

403. On some occasions in the practice of hull insurance in China, a mixed cover is agreed upon between the insurer and the insured. For example, especially in the past, as agreed in the hull insurance contract, the insurance covers total loss, partial loss arising from stranding or grounding, liability of collision or allision, salvage, general average and war and strike risks as discussed *infra*.

III. Exclusions

404. Under PICC P&C Hull Clauses 2009, losses, damages, liabilities and expenses resulting from the following causes shall be excluded under both the Total Loss Cover and All Risks Cover:

- unseaworthiness of the insured vessel, including not being properly manned, equipped or loaded, provided that the insured knew or should have known of such unseaworthiness when the vessel was sent to the sea;
- negligence or intentional act of the insured or its representative;
- ordinary wear and tear, rust, corrosion, rottenness or insufficient upkeep, or defect in material that the insured should have discovered with due diligence, or replacement of or repair to any part in unsound condition;
- war, civil war, revolution, rebellion or civil strife or hostile act arising therefrom;
- capture, seizure, arrest, detainment, confiscation or blockage;
- various war weapons including mines, torpedoes, bombs, atomic bombs, hydrogen bombs or nuclear weapons;
- strikes, lockouts or other similar events;
- civil commotions, riots or other similar events;
- malicious acts committed by any person with political intentions.

405. By Article 244 of MC, unless otherwise agreed upon in the insurance contract, the hull insurer shall not be liable for loss of or damage to the insured vessel arising from unseaworthiness of the vessel at the time of the commencement of the voyage, unless under a time policy the insured had no knowledge thereof, or from wear and tear or corrosion of the vessel.

Since the provisions of Article 244 of MC are not compulsorily applicable, the insurer and the insured are allowed to agree as to the exclusions of the insurer in a hull insurance contract. Thus, the exclusions contained in PICC P&C Hull Clauses of 2009 above have full effect, provided that they are agreed upon between the insurer and the insured.

In addition, by Article 242 of MC the insurer's liability for loss of or damage to the insured vessel caused by an intentional act of the insured shall be exempted.

IV. Hull War & Strike Clauses

A. *Scope of Cover*

406. Under PICC P&C War & Strike Clauses 2009, this insurance covers total or partial loss of the insured vessel, collision liability, contribution in general average and salvage as well as mitigation resulting from any of the following causes:

- war, civil war, revolution, rebellion or civil strife or hostile act arising therefrom;
- capture, seizure, arrest, detainment, confiscation or blockage, provided that such claims shall not be accepted before expiry of six months from the date of occurrence of such peril;
- various war weapons including mines, torpedoes, bombs;
- strikes, lockouts or other similar events;
- civil commotions, riots or other similar events;
- malicious acts committed by any person with political intentions.

B. *Exclusions*

407. Under the PICC P&C War & Strike Clauses 2009, this insurance does not cover loss of or damage to the insured vessel, liabilities or expenses resulting from:

- explosions of atomic bombs, hydrogen bombs or nuclear weapons;
- capture, seizure, arrest, detainment, confiscation of the insured vessel as taken or ordered by the government or local authorities of the state of the vessel's flag or registry;
- requisition, requisition for title or sale of the insured vessel;
- war broken between or among the permanent members of the Security Council of the United Nations, whether declared or not.

§2. Cargo Insurance

408. There are mainly five types of cargo insurance in China insurance market:

(1) domestic/international road cargo transport insurance;
(2) domestic railway cargo transport insurance;
(3) domestic waterway cargo transport insurance;
(4) domestic/international air cargo insurance; and
(5) ocean marine cargo insurance.

I. Domestic Road Cargo Transport Insurance

A. *Subject-Matter Insured*

409. Under PICC P&C Domestic Road Cargo Clauses 2009, any cargo carried by domestic road can be the subject matter of insurance, except fresh vegetables, fruits, live stocks, birds, fishes and other live animals. In addition, unless specially agreed upon between the insurer and the applicant and stated in the policy, valuables such as gold, silver, jewelry, diamond, jade, antique, ancient book, postage stamp, work of art and rare mental are not covered by the insurance.

B. *Scope of Cover*

410. Under PICC P&C Domestic Road Cargo Clauses 2009, the insurer shall be liable for the loss of or damage to the insured cargo or expenses resulting from:

- fire, explosion, lightning, hail, storm, rainstorm, flood, tsunami, subsidence of land, collapse of cliff, abrupt landslide, mud-rock flow;
- collision or capsize of vehicle, collapse of bridge, tunnel or wharf;
- accident occurred during loading, discharge or change of transport vehicles;
- loss or damage caused by accident during loading, discharge or transshipment of cargo;
- breakage, crook, concavity, split of cargo due to vibration, impact or extrusion;
- scatter and disappearance of cargo due to breakage of packing;
- leakage of liquid cargo due to damage to container including its seal thereof arising from vibration, impact or extrusion, or putrescence or deterioration of cargo preserved in liquid due to the leakage of liquid in which the cargo is preserved;
- rain on the condition that the safety transport provisions are conformed to;
- scatter and disappearance of cargo caused by disorder or direct and reasonable expenses arising from mitigation or protective measures taken on the occurrence of the above calamities and accidents.

C. Exclusions

411. Under PICC P&C Domestic Road Cargo Clauses 2009, the insurer shall not be liable for loss of or damage to the insured cargo arising from any of the following causes:

- war, hostility, military action, seizure, strike, riot or robbery;
- earthquake;
- theft or non-delivery of cargo in packages;
- defective quality or shortage in quantity of the insured cargo existing before the commencement of insurance liability;
- ordinary wear and tear, inherent vice or specific nature of the insured cargo;
- loss of market or delay in transport;
- responsibility of consignor;
- intentional or criminal act of the applicant or the insured;
- illegal cargo as recognized by relevant authorities.

D. Commencement and Termination of Insurance Liability

412. PICC P&C Domestic Road Cargo Clauses 2009 contain a "warehouse to warehouse" clause to the effect that the insurance liability shall commence from the time when the insured cargo is carried away from the last warehouse or other storage places of the consignor at the place of commencement of carriage after the issuance of the policy or other insurance certificate, and terminate at the time when the insured cargo arrives at the first warehouse or storage place of the consignee at destination stated in the insurance certificate, provided that the time limit of termination shall not exceed fifteen days from the time when the insured cargo was discharged from the vehicle in the case of failure of the consignee to take delivery of cargo in time.

E. Obligations of Insured

413. Under PICC P&C Domestic Road Cargo Clauses of 2009, the applicant or insured shall fulfill the following obligations:

- The applicant shall fulfill the obligation of disclosure according to the facts, answer to the inquiries of the insurer accurately concerning the subject-matter insured or the insured, failing which due to the applicant's intent or gross negligence sufficiently affecting the insurer in deciding whether to agree to cover or increase premium, the insurer is entitled to terminate the insurance contract; where non-disclosure is due to the applicant's intent, the insurer shall not be liable for insurance incident occurred before termination of insurance contract and shall not refund premium; where non-disclosure is due to the applicant's gross negligence and has material influence in the occurrence of the insurance incident, the insurer shall not be liable for incident occurred before termination of insurance contract, but shall refund premium.

- The applicant shall pay the insurance premium in one lump on the issuing of policy or other insurance certificates by the insurer or his agent, failing which the insurer shall not be liable for insurance incident that occurred before payment of premium.
- The insured shall strictly obey to the various provisions of the state and transport authorities concerning safety transport, maintain the safety of the subject-matter insured, make sure that the packing of cargo is in conformity with the standard provided for by the state and competent authorities, and implement written suggestions concerning eliminating the unsafe factors and hidden danger to the subject-matter insured put forward by the insurer to the applicant or insured, failing which the insurer shall not be liable for the insurance incident or the extended loss or damage arising therefrom.
- Where the extent of danger to the subject-matter insured increases remarkably during the period of validity of the insurance contract, the insured shall notify the insurer in time as agreed in the contract and the insurer is entitled to either increase the premium or terminate the contract; where the insured fails to notify, the insurer shall not be liable for insurance incident arising from any remarkable increase of the extent of danger to the subject-matter insured.
- Upon notice of the occurrence of loss of or damage to the insured cargo within the insurance coverage, the applicant or insured shall take reasonable mitigation or protective measures and notify the insurer's local branch thereof not later than ten days; where notification fails due to intent or gross negligence resulting in difficulty in determining the nature, causes or extent of loss or damage, etc., the insurer shall not be liable for the part which is unable to be determined, provided that the insurer has known or should have known the occurrence of the insurance incident through other means.

F. Settlement of Claim

414. In its claim for insurance indemnity against the insurer, the insured shall provide various documents in support of the claim including, *inter alia*: (1) the policy or other insurance certificates, waybill, delivery order, invoice or other evidence of cargo price; (2) accident record, receipt and delivery record made by carrier, and assessment report; (3) record of cargo entering warehouse made by consignee, survey report, breakdown of loss and vouchers of reasonable expenses incurred directly for the protection of cargo; (4) other documents concerning the determination of the nature, causes, extent of loss or damage, etc. which the insured is able to provide.

The insurer shall, after receipt of the above documents, immediately determine whether the loss or damage is within the insurance liability and notify the insured of the result. If agreement on settlement amount is reached between the insurer and the insured, the insurer shall make compensation within ten days.

Where the loss of or damage to the insured cargo is within the insurance liability, the insurer shall indemnify for the loss or damage in accordance with the actual loss, if the insured amount is determined by virtue of the insured value of cargo, but such indemnity shall be limited to the insured amount. Where the insured amount is less than the insured value, the amount of indemnity for the loss, damage or expenses of mitigation or protection shall be calculated in the proportion that the insured amount bears to the insured value. The indemnity for loss of or damage to the insured cargo and that for the reasonable expenses incurred directly for the mitigation and protection of cargo shall be calculated respectively and each shall not exceed the insured amount.

Where the carrier or other third party shall be liable wholly or partly for the loss of or damage to cargo insured within the insurance liability by virtue of law or relevant agreement, PICC P&C Domestic Road Cargo Clauses 2009 require the insured to claim against the third party first. However, strictly speaking, such a provision is illegal, as the insured may choose to make claim against either the insurer or the third party.

If the insured waives his claim against the third party, the insurer's liability shall be discharged. Where the insurer pays insurance indemnity as required by the insured, the insured is obliged to issue his letter of subrogation to the insurer, furnish the insurer with relevant documents and assist the insurer in pursuing recovery from the third person. If, due to the intent or gross negligence of the insured, the insurer is unable to exercise his right of subrogation, the insurer may deduct from the indemnity the corresponding amount.

II. International Road Cargo Transport Insurance

A. Scope of Cover

415. PICC P&C Land Cargo Clauses 2009 contain land risks cover and all land risks cover.

Under the land risks cover, the insurer shall be liable for the following loss of or damage to the insured cargo or expenses:

- total or partial loss of cargo arising from natural calamities of storm, lightning, flood or earthquake suffered by the insured cargo, or collision or capsize suffered by transport vehicle, or grounding, running on a reef, sinking, collision of transshipment means during transshipment, or arising from accident of collapse of tunnel or cliff, fire or explosion;
- reasonable expenses paid for the measures taken by the insured for the purpose of rescuing, preventing or mitigating loss of or damage to the cargo in danger within insurance coverage, provided that these expenses shall not exceed the insured amount of the insured cargo.

Under all land risks cover, the insured shall, besides his insurance liability under the land risks cover, also be liable for the total or partial loss of the insured cargo resulting from external causes during the carriage.

B. Exclusions

416. Under PICC P&C Land Cargo Clauses 2009, the insure shall not be liable for:

– loss or damage due to intentional act or negligence of the insured;
– loss or damage within the responsibility of the consignor of cargo;
– loss of or damage arising from defective quality or shortage in quantity of the insured cargo existing before the commencement of insurance liability;
– loss or damage or expenses arising from ordinary wear and tear, inherent vice or specific nature of the insured cargo as well as from loss of market or delay in transport;
– loss or damage or expenses within the scope of cover or exclusions under the war risks cover or strike risks cover of land cargo transport insurance.

C. Commencement and Termination of Insurance Liability

417. PICC P&C Land Cargo Clauses 2009 also contain a "warehouse to warehouse" clause to the effect that the insurance liability shall take effect from the time when the insured cargo is carried away from the warehouse or other storage places stated in insurance policy to the time when the insured cargo arrives at the last warehouse or storage place of the consignee at destination stated in the insurance policy or other places which are used for the distribution of cargo by the insured, including the period on land or of lightering on water during normal transport; where the cargo has not been carried to the above warehouse or other storage places, to the time of expiry of sixty days from the time when the cargo is carried to the land station where the cargo is finally discharged.

D. Obligations of Insured

418. Under PICC P&C Land Cargo Clauses 2009, the insured shall fulfill the following obligations:

– After the insured cargo has been carried to the destination stated in the insurance policy, the insured shall take delivery thereof in time; where loss of or damage to the cargo is found, the insured shall apply for survey to the insurer's agent authorized for survey or handling claims stated in the insurance policy; where there is shortage of packages of or apparent damage to the insured cargo, the insured shall try to obtain evidence of such damage or shortage from the carrier, his authorized party or relevant authority; where damage to or shortage of cargo is within the responsibility of the carrier, his authorized party or relevant authority, the insured shall file a formal claim in writing against them and obtain from them extension of time bar when necessary; otherwise, the insurer shall not be liable for the relevant loss or damage.

- Where there is danger to the insured cargo within the insurance liability, the insured shall immediately take reasonable rescue measures to avoid or mitigate loss of or damage to cargo; otherwise, the insurer shall not be liable for the extended loss or damage.
- The insured shall, in making claim against the insurer, provide documents including the original insurance policy, transport document, invoice, packing list, weight memo, evidence of damage to or shortage of cargo, survey report and breakdown of damages, correspondences for the purpose of making recourse claim against third party if the liability of third party is involved, as well as the other evidence or materials which the insured is able to provide relating to the determination of the nature, causes, extent of damage, etc.

III. Domestic Railway Cargo Transport Insurance

A. *Subject-Matter Insured*

419. Under PICC P&C Domestic Railway Cargo Clauses 2009, any cargo carried by domestic railway can be the subject matter of insurance, except fresh vegetables, fruits, live stocks, birds, fishes and other live animals. In addition, unless specially agreed upon between the insurer and the insured and stated in the policy, valuables such as gold, silver, jewelry, diamond, jade, antique, ancient book, postage stamp, work of art and rare mental are not covered by the insurance.

B. *Scope of Cover*

420. PICC P&C Domestic Railway Cargo Clauses 2009 contain basic risks cover and comprehensive risks cover.

Under the basic risks cover, the insurer shall be liable for the loss of or damage to the insured cargo or expenses resulting from:

- fire, explosion, lightning, hail, storm, rainstorm, flood, tsunami, subsidence of land, collapse of cliff, abrupt landslide, mud-rock flow;
- collision or going off the rails of the train, collapse of bridge, tunnel or wharf;
- loss or damage arising from accident occurred during loading, discharge or transshipment of transport vehicles;
- direct and reasonable expenses arising from mitigation or protective measures taken on the occurrence of the above calamities and accidents.

Under the comprehensive risks cover, the insurer shall also be liable for the loss of or damage to the insured cargo resulting from:

- breakage, crook, concavity, split of cargo due to vibration, impact or extrusion;
- scatter and disappearance of cargo due to breakage of packing;

– leakage of liquid cargo due to damage to container including its seal thereof arising from vibration, impact or extrusion, or putrescence or deterioration of cargo preserved in liquid due to the leakage of liquid in which the cargo is preserved;
– theft of cargo;
– non-delivery of cargo due to external causes;
– wetness by rain on the condition that the safety transport provisions are conformed to.

C. Exclusions

421. Under PICC P&C Railway Cargo Clauses 2009, the insurer shall not be liable for:

– loss of or damage to the cargo arising from war, military action, seizure, strike, robbery or riot;
– loss of or damage to the cargo arising from earthquake;
– loss of or damage to the cargo arising from nuclear reaction, nuclear radiation or radioactive pollution;
– loss of or damage to the cargo arising from ordinary wear and tear, pollution, putrescence or damage arising from inherent vice or specific nature of the insured cargo or improper packing of cargo;
– loss of or damage to the cargo arising from defective quality or shortage in quantity of the insured cargo existing before the commencement of insurance liability;
– loss of market due to the delay in transport;
– loss or damage due to the responsibility of the consignor of cargo;
– loss or damage due to the intentional or criminal act of the applicant or the insured;
– loss or damage arising from administrative act or enforcement of law.

D. Commencement and Termination of Insurance Liability

422. PICC P&C Domestic Railway Cargo Clauses 2009 contain a "warehouse to warehouse" clause to the effect that the insurance liability shall commence from the time the insured cargo is carried away from the last warehouse or other storage places of the consignor at the place of commencement of carriage and the issuance of the policy or other insurance certificates and terminate at the time when the insured cargo arrives at the first warehouse or storage place of the consignee at destination stated in the insurance certificate, provided that the time limit of termination shall not exceed fifteen days from the receipt of notice of arrival by the consignee in the case of failure of the consignee to take delivery of cargo in time.

E. Obligations of Insured

423. Under PICC P&C Domestic Railway Cargo Clauses 2009, the insured shall fulfill the following obligations:

- The applicant shall fulfill the obligation of disclosure according to the facts, answer to the inquiries of the insurer accurately concerning the subject-matter insured or the insured, failing which due to the applicant's intent or gross negligence sufficiently affecting the insurer in deciding whether to agree to cover or increase premium, the insurer is entitled to terminate the insurance contract; where non-disclosure is due to the applicant's intent, the insurer shall not be liable for insurance incident occurred before termination of insurance contract and shall not refund premium; where non-disclosure is due to the applicant's gross negligence and has material influence in the occurrence of the insurance incident, the insurer shall not be liable for incident occurred before termination of insurance contract, but shall refund premium.
- The applicant shall pay the insurance premium in one lump on the issuing of policy or other insurance certificates by the insurer or his agent, failing which the insurer shall not be liable for insurance incident occurred before payment of premium.
- The insured shall strictly obey to the various provisions of the state and transport authorities concerning safety transport, maintain the safety of the subject-matter insured, make sure that the packing of cargo is in conformity with the standard provided for by the state and competent authorities, and implement written suggestions concerning eliminating the unsafe factors and hidden danger to the subject-matter insured put forward by the insurer to the applicant or insured, failing which the insurer shall not be liable for the insurance incident or the extended loss or damage arising therefrom.
- Where the extent of danger to the subject-matter insured increases remarkably during the period of validity of the insurance contract, the insured shall notify the insurer in time as agreed in the contract and the insurer is entitled to either increase the premium or terminate the contract; where the insured fails to notify, the insurer shall not be liable for insurance incident arising from any remarkable increase of the extent of danger to the subject-matter insured.
- Upon notice of the occurrence of loss of or damage to the insured cargo within the insurance coverage, the applicant or insured shall take reasonable mitigation or protective measures and notify the insurer's local branch thereof not later than ten days; where notification fails due to intent or gross negligence resulting in difficulty in determining the nature, causes or extent of loss or damage, etc., the insurer shall not be liable for the part which is unable to be determined, provided that the insurer has known or should have known the occurrence of the insurance incident through other means.

F. Settlement of Claim

424. In his claim for insurance indemnity against the insurer, the insured shall provide various documents in support of the claim, including *inter alia*: (1) the policy or other insurance certificates, waybill, delivery order, invoice or other evidence of cargo price; (2) accident record, receipt and delivery record made by carrier, and assessment report; (3) record of cargo entering warehouse made by consignee, survey report, breakdown of loss and vouchers of reasonable expenses incurred directly for the protection of cargo; (4) other documents concerning determination of the nature, causes, extent of loss or damage, etc. which the insured is able to provide.

The insurer shall, after receipt of the above documents, immediately determine whether the loss or damage is within the insurance liability and notify the insured of the result. If agreement on settlement amount is reached between the insurer and the insured, the insurer shall make compensation within ten days.

Where the loss of or damage to the insured cargo is within the insurance liability, the insurer shall indemnify for the loss or damage in accordance with the actual loss, if the insured amount is determined by virtue of the insured value of cargo, but such indemnity shall be limited to the insured amount. Where the insured amount is less than the insured value, the amount of indemnity for the loss, damage or expenses of mitigation or protection shall be calculated in the proportion that the insured amount bears to the insured value. The indemnity for loss of or damage to the insured cargo and that for the reasonable expenses incurred directly for the mitigation and protection of cargo shall be calculated respectively and each shall not exceed the insured amount.

Where the carrier or other third party shall be liable wholly or partly for the loss of or damage to cargo insured within the insurance liability by virtue of law or relevant agreement, PICC P&C Domestic Railway Cargo Clauses 2009 require the insured to claim against the third party first. However, strictly speaking, such a provision is illegal, as the insured may choose to make claim against either the insurer or the third party.

If the insured waives his claim against the third party, the insurer's liability shall be discharged.

Where the insurer pays insurance indemnity as required by the insured, the insured is obliged to issue his letter of subrogation to the insurer, furnish the insurer with relevant documents and assist the insurer in pursuing recovery from the third person. If, due to the intent or gross negligence of the insured, the insurer is unable to exercise his right of subrogation, the insurer may deduct from the indemnity the corresponding amount.

IV. Waterway Cargo Transport Insurance

A. Subject-Matter Insured

425. By virtue of PICC P&C Waterway Cargo Clauses 2009, the subject-matter insured means the cargo carried by waterway in coastal waters, rivers and lakes excluding fresh vegetables, fruits, live stocks, birds, fishes and other live animals. In addition, unless specially agreed upon between the insurer and the insured and stated in the policy, valuables such as gold, silver, jewelry, diamond, jade, antique, ancient book, postage stamp, work of art and rare mental are not covered by this insurance.

B. Commencement and Termination of Insurance Liability

426. PICC P&C Waterway Cargo Clauses 2009 contain a "warehouse to warehouse" clause. The insurance liability shall, after the issuance of the policy or other insurance certificates, commence from the time when the insured cargo is carried away from the last warehouse or storage place of the consignor at the place of the commencement of transport and terminate at the time when the insured cargo arrives at the first warehouse or storage place of the consignee at destination stated in the insurance certificate, provided that the time limit of termination shall not exceed fifteen days from the time the insured cargo is discharged from the means of transport.

C. Scope of Cover

427. Under P&C PICC Waterway Cargo Clauses of 2009, the coverage includes basic cover and comprehensive cover.

Under the basic cover, the insurer shall be liable for the loss of or damage to the insured cargo or expenses caused by:

- fire, explosion, lightning, hail, storm, flood, tsunami, collapse of cliff, sudden landslide, mud-rock flow;
- collision, grounding or running on rocks of vessel, collapse of bridge or pier;
- sinking or missing of vessel resulting from the above causes;
- loss caused by accident in loading, discharging or transshipment;
- general average sacrifice, contribution in general average or salvage expenses to be borne in accordance with state's provisions or practice;
- scatter and disappearance of cargo due to disorder and reasonable costs paid directly for the mitigation or preservation of the cargo in the case of the above disasters.

Under the comprehensive cover, besides the liability under the basic cover, the insurer shall also be liable for loss or damage arising from:

- breakage, crook, concavity, split of cargo due to impact or extrusion;
- scatter and disappearance of cargo due to breakage of packing;
- damage to container including its seal of liquid cargo due to impact or extrusion, or putrescence or deterioration of cargo due to the leakage of liquid in which the cargo is preserved;
- theft;

- wet damage by rain under the condition of conformity with provisions of safety transport.

D. Exclusions

428. Under PICC P&C Waterway Cargo Clauses 2009, the insurer shall not be liable for the loss of or damage to the insured cargo or expenses caused by:

- war, military action, seizure, strike, robbery or riot;
- loss or damage arising from defective quality or shortage in quantity of the insured cargo existing before the commencement of insurance liability;
- ordinary wear and tear, pollution, putrescence or damage arising from vice or specific nature of the insured cargo;
- loss of market or loss or damage arising from delay in transport;
- loss or damage due to the responsibility of the consignor of cargo;
- intentional act or criminal act of the applicant or the insured;
- loss or damage arising from administrative act or enforcement of law.

E. Obligations of Insured

429. Under PICC P&C Waterway Cargo Clauses 2009, the insured shall fulfill the following obligations:

- The insured shall fulfill the obligation of disclosure truthfully, answer to the inquiries of the insurer truthfully concerning the subject-matter insured or the insured. Where the insured failed to perform the above obligation of truthful disclosure due to his intentional act or gross negligence which was sufficient to affect the insurer in deciding whether to agree to cover or to increase premium, the insurer has the right to terminate the contract. The insurance contract shall be terminated upon the arrival of the insurer's notice of termination at the applicant or insured. Where the insured failed to perform the obligation of truthful disclosure due to his intentional act, the insurer shall not be liable for any loss or damage arising from the insurance accident before the contract is terminated without refunding the premium. Where the insured failed to perform the obligation of truthful disclosure due to his gross negligence which has significant influence on the occurrence of the insurance accident, the insurer shall not compensate or pay insurance indemnity for any loss or damage arising from the insurance accident before the contract is terminated, but shall refund the premium.
- The applicant shall pay the insurance premium in one lump upon the issuance of policy or other insurance certificates by the insurer or his agent. Where the applicant fails to pay insurance premium as agreed, the insurer shall not be liable for insurance accident occurred before the payment of insurance premium.
- The applicant or insured shall choose with due diligence the carrier and urge him to strictly obey to the various provisions of the state and transport authorities concerning safety transport, accept and assist the insurer in the inspect and survey of

the cargo and in the taking of measures of preventing loss of the insured cargo, and shall make sure that the packing of cargo is in conformity with the standard provided for by the state and competent authorities. Where an insurance accident occurs due to failure of the insured in complying with the above agreement, the insurer shall not be liable. Where loss or damage is exaggerated due to such failure, the insurer shall not be liable for such exaggerated loss or damage.
- Where the extent of danger to the subject-matter insured increases during the period of insurance, the insured shall notify the insurer in time as agreed in the contract. The insurer is entitled to increase the premium or terminate the contract. Where the insured fails to perform the above obligation, the insurer shall not be liable for the insurance accident arising from the significant increase of extent of danger to the subject-matter insured.
- Upon notice of the occurrence of loss of or damage to the insured cargo within the insurance coverage, the insured shall notify the insurer or local branch or agent of the insurer on time and take reasonable measures to mitigate the loss or damage. In the case of failure of such notice due to the insured's intentional act or gross negligence causing difficulties in determining the nature, causes of the insurance accident or extent of loss or damage, etc., the insurer shall not be liable for the part of loss or damage which cannot be determined, unless the insurer has known or should have known in time of the occurrence of the insurance accident through other ways.

V. International Air Cargo Insurance

A. *Scope of Cover*

430. Under PICC P&C International Air Cargo Clauses 2009, the coverage includes air cargo risks cover and air cargo all risks cover.

Under the air cargo risks cover, the insurer shall be liable for:

- total or partial loss of cargo arising from lightning, fire, explosion, or abandonment of civil aircraft due to heavy weather or other accident of danger, or collision, capsize, falling down or accidental missing of the aircraft during transport;
- reasonable expenses arising from measures taken by the insured for the purpose of avoiding or mitigating loss of or damage to cargo in the case of danger covered, provided that these expenses shall not exceed the insured amount of the cargo concerned.

Under the air cargo all risks cover, the insurer shall, besides the liability under the air cargo risks cover, also be liable for the total or partial loss of the cargo insured arising from external causes.

B. Exclusions

431. Under PICC P&C International Air Cargo Clauses 2009, the insurer shall not be liable for the following loss of or damage to the insured cargo or expenses:

– loss or damage arising from intentional act or fault of the insured;
– loss or damage due to the responsibility of the consignor of cargo;
– loss or damage arising from defective quality or shortage in quantity of the insured cargo existing before the commencement of insurance liability;
– loss, damage or expenses arising from ordinary wear and tear, vice or specific nature of the insured cargo, drop of market or delay in transport thereof;
– loss, damage or expenses within the scope of cover or exclusions under the air cargo transport war risks clauses or strike risks clauses.

C. Commencement and Termination of Insurance Liability

432. PICC P&C International Air Cargo Clauses 2009 contain a "ware-house to warehouse" clause by which the insurance liability shall commence from the time when the insured cargo is carried away from the warehouse or storage place at the place of the commencement of transport stated in the insurance policy, and terminate at the time when the insured cargo arrives at the last warehouse or storage place of the consignee at destination stated in the insurance policy or at other storage places where cargo will be distributed by the insured or be further carried away not in normal process. However, if the insured cargo is not carried to the above warehouse or storage place, the insurance liability shall terminate thirty days after the insured cargo has been discharged from aircraft at the last place of discharge. Where the insured cargo will be transshipped to a place other than the destination stated in the insurance policy within thirty days, the insurance liability shall terminate at the time of transshipment.

433. Where, due to delay in carriage, deviation, enforced discharge, reloading or transshipment of cargo beyond the control of the insured, or change of flight or termination of contract of carriage arising from the exercise of right conferred on him by the contract of carriage, the insured cargo is carried to a place other than the destination stated in the insurance policy, the cargo shall be held covered on the condition that the insured notifies the insurer of the information the insured has known and that the insured has paid additional premium as necessary. Under such a circumstance, the insurance liability shall terminate as follows:

– Where the insured cargo is sold at a place other than the destination stated in the insurance policy, the insurance liability shall terminate at the time of delivery of the insured cargo, but in no case shall exceed thirty days after the cargo is discharged from the aircraft at the place of discharge.
– Where the insured cargo is still carried to the destination stated in the insurance policy or other destination within the above period of thirty days, the insurance

liability shall terminate as stated in the "warehouse to warehouse" clause contained in PICC P&C International Air Cargo Clauses 2009 as mentioned *supra*.

D. Obligations of Insured

434. Under PICC P&C International Air Cargo Clauses 2009, the insured shall fulfill the following obligations:

- After the insured cargo has been carried to the destination stated in the insurance policy, the insured shall take delivery thereof in time; where loss of or damage to the cargo is found, the insured shall apply for survey to the insurer's agent for survey or handling claims stated in the insurance policy; where there is shortage of packages of or apparent damage to the insured cargo, the insured shall try to obtain evidence of damage to or shortage of cargo from the carrier, his authorized party or relevant authority; where damage to or shortage of cargo is within the responsibility of the carrier, his authorized party or other relevant parties, the insured shall file a claim in writing against them and obtain from them extension of time bar when necessary; if the insured fails to fulfill the obligations, the insurer shall not be liable for the loss or damage concerned.
- Where there is danger to the insured cargo within the insurance liability, the insured shall immediately take reasonable measures to avoid or mitigate loss of or damage to cargo, failing which the insurer shall not be liable for the loss or damage exaggerated thereby.
- The insured shall, in making claim against the insurer, provide documents including the original insurance policy, waybill, invoice, packing list, weight memo, evidence of damage to or shortage of cargo, survey report and breakdown of damages, and correspondences in making claim against third party, if the liability of third party is involved, as well as documents and materials concerning determining the nature, causes of the insurance accident, extent of damage, etc. as the insured is able to provide, failing which the insurer is not liable for the part of damage which the insurer is unable to determine as a result of such failure.

VI. Domestic Air Cargo Insurance

A. Subject-Matter Insured

435. Under PICC P&C Domestic Air Cargo Clauses 2009, any cargo carried by domestic air can be the subject matter of insurance, except fresh vegetables, fruits, live stocks, birds, fishes and other live animals. In addition, unless specially agreed between the insurer and the insured and stated in the policy or other insurance certificates, valuables such as gold, silver, jewelry, diamond, jade, antique, ancient book, ancient painting, postage stamp, work of art and rare mental are not covered by the insurance.

B. Scope of Cover

436. Under PICC P&C Domestic Air Cargo Clauses 2009, the insurer shall be liable for the following losses of or damage to the insured cargo or expenses:

- loss or damage arising from fire, explosion, lightning, hail, storm, flood, tsunami, subsidence of land, collapse of cliff;
- loss or damage arising from collision, capsize, falling down of aircraft or missing of aircraft for a period of more than three months, discharge of cargo in case of danger and jettison of cargo in heavy weather or other accident of danger;
- loss or damage arising from breakage, crook, concavity, split of cargo due to vibration, impact or extrusion;
- loss or damage arising from scatter and disappearance of cargo due to breakage of packing;
- loss or damage arising from damage to container including its seal of liquid cargo, semiliquid cargo or other cargos to be preserved in liquid due to vibration, impact or extrusion, or arising from putrescence or deterioration of cargo due to the leakage of liquid in which the cargo is preserved;
- loss or damage arising from theft or non-delivery of cargo;
- loss or damage arising from force majeure or being wet by rain during loading or discharge or ground transport in airport;
- direct and reasonable expenses arising from mitigation or protection of cargo in the case of accident of calamity within insurance coverage.

C. Exclusions

437. Under PICC P&C Domestic Air Cargo Clauses 2009, the insurer shall not be liable for loss of or damage to the insured cargo arising from any of the following causes:

- war, military action, seizure, strike, robbery or riot;
- nuclear reaction, nuclear radiation and radioactive pollution;
- ordinary wear and tear, pollution, putrescence or damage arising from inherent vice or specific nature of the insured cargo;
- defective quality or shortage in quantity of the insured cargo existing before the commencement of insurance liability;
- loss of market or delay in transport;
- the responsibility of the consignor of cargo;
- intentional or criminal act of the insured or the applicant;
- administrative act or enforcement of law.

D. Commencement and Termination of Insurance Liability

438. PICC P&C Domestic Air Cargo Clauses 2009 also contain a "warehouse to warehouse" clause to the effect that the insurance liability shall commence from the time of receipt of cargo by the carrier and the issuance of the policy or other insurance certificates and terminate at the time when the insured cargo arrives at the first warehouse or storage place of the consignee at destination stated in the insurance certificate, provided that the time limit of termination shall not exceed fifteen days from the receipt of notice of arrival by the consignee in case the consignee fails to take delivery of cargo in time.

439. PICC P&C Domestic Air Cargo Clauses 2009 contain a "held covered" clause as in PICC P&C International Air Cargo Clauses 2009 as mentioned *supra.*

E. Obligations of Insured

440. Under PICC P&C Domestic Air Cargo Clauses 2009, the insured shall fulfill the following obligations:

- The insured shall fulfill the obligation of truthful disclosure, answer to the inquiries of the insurer truthfully concerning the subject-matter insured or the insured; if the insured fails to fulfill the above obligation of truthful disclosure due to his intentional act or gross negligence, which is sufficient to affect the insurer in deciding whether he agrees to insure or not or increasing the premium, the insurer has the right to terminate the contract; the contract of insurance shall be terminated upon arrival of the insurer's notice of termination of contract at the applicant or insured; if the insured intentionally did not fulfill the obligation of truthful disclosure, the insurer shall not be liable for any loss arising from the perils insured against before the contract is terminated without refunding the insurance premium; if the insured did not fulfill the obligation of truthful disclosure due to his gross negligence, which has significant impact on the occurrence of the insurance accident, the insurer shall not be liable for any loss arising from the perils insured against before the contract is terminated, but shall refund the insurance premium.
- The applicant shall pay the insurance premium in one lump upon the issuance of policy or other insurance certificates by the insurer or his agent; if the applicant fails to pay the insurance premium as agreed, the insurer shall not be liable for any insurance accident occurred before payment of insurance premium.
- The insured shall strictly obey to the various provisions of the state and transport authorities concerning safety transport, accept and assist the insurer in the inspection and survey of the cargo and the taking of measures of preventing loss of or damage to the insured cargo, and shall make sure that the packing of cargo is in conformity with the standards provided for by the state and competent authorities; if there is failure of the insured in complying with the above agreement, the insurer shall not be liable; if such failure results in exaggeration of loss or damage, the insurer shall not be liable for the exaggerated loss or damage.
- If the danger to the subject-matter insured increases significantly during the period of validity of contract, the insured shall notify the insurer timely, and the

insurer is entitled to demand increase of insurance premium or terminate the contract; if the insured fails to fulfill the obligation of such notification, the insurer shall not be liable for the insurance accident caused by the significant increase of danger to the subject-matter insured.
- Upon notice of the occurrence of loss of or damage to the insured cargo within the insurance coverage, the applicant or insured shall take mitigation and protective measures, and immediately notify the local branch of the insurer not later than ten days; in case of failure of timely notification due to intentional act or gross negligence which results in difficulty in determining the nature and causes of accident and extent of damage, etc., the insurer shall not be liable for the part which is unable to be determined, except where the insurer has known or should have known timely the occurrence of the insurance accident.

VII. Ocean Marine Cargo Insurance

A. *Scope of Cover*

441. The Chinese law does not contain any provision concerning the scope of cover in marine cargo insurance, but is up to the insurer and the insured to negotiate.

Marine cargo insurance coverage includes principal risks and additional risks.

Under PICC P&C Marine Cargo Clauses 2009, the principal risks include three conditions, viz. free from particular average (FPA), with average (WA) and all risks. Various additional risks are covered under various PICC P&C clauses 2009.

Additional risks cannot be insured against independently of the principal risks and include three types in the practice in China, viz. ordinary or general additional risks, special additional risks and peculiar additional risks which are mainly the war and strike risks. Ordinary additional risks are covered under the conditions of all risks and therefore can be insured against under the conditions of either FPA or WA upon agreement between the insurer and the insured.

1. FPA

442. This insurance covers:

- actual total loss or constructive total loss of the whole insured cargo caused in the course of carriage by natural calamities including heavy weather, lightning, tsunami, earthquake and flood; total or partial loss of the insured cargo caused by accidents of the carrying vessel being grounded, stranded, sunk, in collision with other vessel or floating ice or other objects, fire or explosion;
- partial loss of the insured cargo caused by natural calamities including heavy weather, lightning, tsunami, etc., where the carrying vessel has suffered accident of being grounded, stranded, sunk or burnt, irrespective of whether the event or events took place before or after such accidents;

- partial or total loss of the insured cargo consequent upon falling of entire package or packages into sea during loading, transshipment or discharge;
- reasonable costs incurred by the insured in salvaging the insured cargo, averting or minimizing a loss of the insured cargo recoverable under the insurance, i.e. the mitigation expenses, provided that such costs shall not exceed the insured amount of the cargo so saved;
- losses caused by discharge of the insured cargo at a port of refuge following a sea peril encountered by the means of transport as well as special charges arising from discharge, warehousing and forwarding of the cargo at an intermediate port of call or refuge;
- general average sacrifice and contribution in general average and salvage payment;
- such proportion of losses sustained by the shipowners/carrier as is to be reimbursed by the cargo owners under the "Both to Blame Collision" clause in the contract of carriage.

2. WA

443. Aside from the risks covered under FPA condition as introduced *supra*, this insurance also covers partial loss of the insured cargo caused by natural calamities, including heavy weather, lightning, tsunami, earthquake and/or flood.

3. All Risks

444. Aside from the risks covered under the FPA and WA conditions as introduced *supra*, this insurance also covers total or partial loss of the insured cargo arising from external causes in the course of carriage.

The "all risks" terms in insurance clauses have the following characteristics:

- "All risks" are not listed risks, but are non-listed risks. In insurance clauses involving carriage of goods by sea, FPA and WA are listed risks, whereas "all risks" cover FPA, WA, and non-listed losses of the insured subject which result from external causes when the insured subject is in transit.
- The losses of the insured subject must be caused by external causes. When the insured claims compensation from the insurer, the insured must prove that the losses of the insured subject resulted from external causes while in transit. External causes can be natural causes or accidents caused by human error. However, the risks covered by the all risks clause(s) must possess uncertainty in the sense that the insured risks cannot be certain risks, but rather are risks of accidental harm, and thus cannot be listed in advance. Those expected, certain, and normal hazards are not within the scope of liabilities that result from external causes.
- External causes should be limited to those that occur in transit, excluding events that occur before or after. As long as the insured proves that the losses are not

self-caused, but are caused by accidents that occurred while the insured subject was in transit, the insurer should bear the responsibility for paying insurance indemnities.

4. Ordinary Additional Risks

445. Upon agreement between the insurer and the insured, as the case may be, ordinary additional risks cover loss of the insured cargo, whether total or partial, arising from:

- theft, pilferage and non-delivery;
- fresh water and/or rain damage;
- shortage;
- intermixture and contamination;
- leakage;
- clash and breakage;
- taint of odor;
- sweat and heating;
- hook damage;
- breakage of packing;
- rust.

5. Special Additional Risks

446. Upon agreement between the insurer and the insured, as the case may be, loss of or damage to the insured cargo, expenses or liabilities is covered by the following clauses:

- Import Duty Clause which covers the insured's contingent interest on import customs duty arising from the insured goods arriving at the port of destination damaged by a peril insured against, but full import duty had been levied and paid thereon as if the goods had arrived sound, provided that claims payable hereunder shall not exceed an agreed percentage of the insured value on the damage portion of the insured goods.
- On Deck Clause which extends to cover the risks of jettison and/or washing overboard of the insured goods shipped on deck additional to the risks covered by the Marine Cargo Clauses.
- Rejection Clause which covers loss arising from rejection and/or condemnation at the port of entry by the government of the country of import or its relevant authorities on the basis of the insured value of the goods so rejected or condemned, or the cost of return freight to the country of export or the additional freight to other destination in the event of any embargo or prohibition being declared by the importing country after the insured goods left the port of shipment named in the policy not exceeding the insured value of the goods so rejected.

- Aflatoxin Clause which covers loss arising from rejection or confiscation of the insured goods or the original purpose the insured goods for which it is intended is compulsorily altered by reason of the existence of the aflatoxin to any extent exceeding the limit sanctioned by the importing country as evidenced by the inspection by the local Health Authorities at the port or place of import, to the extent of the insured value of the portion so rejected or confiscated or the loss arising from the alteration of the original purpose for which the cargo is intended.
- Failure to Deliver Clause which covers total loss of the insured goods in case the insured goods, once loaded onboard a seagoing vessel, fail to be delivered at destination within six months of scheduled arrived date from howsoever cause, excluding loss or damage recoverable under the Ocean Marine Cargo Clauses and Ocean Marine War Risks Clause.
- Perishable Goods Clause which covers loss of market or loss, damage or deterioration of the insured cargo arising from delay no matter whether it is caused by a peril insured against or otherwise.

6. Peculiar Additional Risks

447. Under PICC P&C Ocean Marine Cargo War Risks Clauses 2009, the insurance of war risks on cargo within the duration of insurance which is in principle limited to the period of the cargo being on board the carrying vessel, unless otherwise agreed upon to cover the war risks while the insured cargo is on land, covers the following loss of or damage to the insured cargo, expenses or liabilities:

- loss or damage directly caused by war, warlike operation, hostile act, armed conflict or piracy;
- loss or damage caused by capture, seizure, arrest, restraint or detainment consequently upon the above acts;
- loss or damage caused by various conventional weapons, including mines, torpedoes and bombs;
- general average sacrifice or contribution in general average and salvage occurred within the above scope of the cover.

448. Under this insurance, the insurer shall not be liable for loss, damage or expenses caused by nuclear or heat energy weapons used due to hostile act, or any claim caused by loss or frustration of the insured voyage due to seizure or detainment by rulers or armed group. The transshipment expenses and other losses caused by the loss or frustration of the insured voyage shall be covered under the conditions of "Additional Expenses—War Risks."

Under PICC P&C Strike Clauses 2009, the insurance of strike risks on cargo covers the losses directly caused by the acts of strikers, locked-out workmen or persons taking part in the labor disturbances, riots or civil commotions or malicious acts of any person, and general average sacrifice or contribution in general average or salvage arising from the above acts. The insurer shall not be liable for any loss or damage to the insured goods occurred in the strike due to insufficiency of labor or failure to perform duties in due course, including loss or damage to the insured refrigerated goods due to stoppage of work of refrigerator as a result of insufficiency of power or fuel.

Other peculiar additional risks are covered under PICC P&C Special Insurance Clauses of Carriage of Imported Containerized Goods 2009, PICC P&C Insurance Liability Extension Clauses of Imported Marine Cargo during Domestic Transshipment 2009, PICC P&C Customs Inspection Clauses 2009, PICC P&C Port Terminal Inspection Clauses 2009, PICC P&C Seller's Interest Insurance Clauses of 2009.

B. Exclusions

449. Under PICC P&C Marine Cargo Clauses 2009, the insurance of principal risks covered under the conditions of FPA, WA or all risks does not cover:

- loss or damage caused by intentional act or fault of the insured;
- loss or damage falling under the liability of the consignor;
- loss or damage arising from the interior quality or shortage of the insured cargo prior to the attachment of this insurance;
- loss or damage arising from normal loss, inherent vice or nature of the insured goods, loss of market and/or delay in carriage and any expenses arising therefrom;
- risks and liabilities covered and excluded by PICC P&C Ocean Marine Cargo War Risks Clauses and PICC P&C Strike Clauses.

450. Ordinary or special additional risks clauses may include their respective exclusions. Peculiar additional risks clauses include their respective exclusions.

By virtue of Articles 242 and 243 of the MC applicable to various marine insurance, the insurer shall not be liable for loss of or damage to the insured cargo caused by intentional act of the insured, delay in the voyage or in the delivery of cargo or change of market, fair wear and tear, inherent vice or nature of the cargo, or improper packing. However, these statutory exclusions are not compulsorily applicable. Instead, the insurer and the insured are allowed to agree as to the exclusions of the insurer in the marine cargo insurance contract.

C. Types of Insurance

1. Voyage Insurance

451. A voyage insurance of marine cargo covers the cargo in maritime transport on a particular voyage as agreed between the insurer and the insured and indicated in the policy. It is common that such an insurance contract contains a "warehouse to warehouse clause" to the effect that the insurance also covers risks on land at both ends of the voyage.

PICC P&C Marine Cargo Clauses 2009 contain a "warehouse to warehouse clause"; i.e., this insurance attaches from the time the cargo hereby insured leaves the warehouse or place of storage named in the Policy for the commencement of the transit and continues in force in the ordinary course of transit including sea, land and inland waterway transits and transit in the lighter until the insured cargo is delivered to the consignee's final warehouse or place of storage at the destination named in the Policy or to any other place used by the insured for allocation or distribution of the cargo or for storage other than in the ordinary course of transit. This insurance shall, however, be limited to sixty days after completion of discharge of the insured cargo from the seagoing vessel at the final port of discharge before it reaches the abovementioned warehouse or place of storage. If prior to the expiry of the abovementioned sixty days the insured cargo is to be forwarded to a destination other than that named in the Policy, this insurance shall terminate at the commencement of such transit.

452. The Chinese law does not contain provision concerning the time of commencement and termination of the voyage. Therefore, the parties are free to negotiate. PICC P&C Marine Cargo Clauses 2009 do not contain a separate "extended cover" clause. However, the "termination of contract of carriage" clause covers the situation where, owing to delay, deviation, forced discharge, reshipment or transshipment beyond the control of the insured or any change or termination of contract of carriage arising from the exercise of a liberty granted to the carrier under the contract of carriage, the insured cargo arrives at a port or place other than the destination named in the policy, subject to immediate notice being given to the insurer by the insured and an additional premium being paid; if required, this insurance shall remain in force. Under such circumstances, if the insured cargo is sold at port or place other than the destination named in the policy, the insurance shall terminate on delivery of the cargo sold, but in no event shall this insurance extend beyond sixty days after completion of discharge of the insured cargo from the seagoing vessel at the port of discharge; if the insured cargo is to be forwarded to the original destination named in the policy or any other destination, this insurance shall terminate in accordance with the "warehouse to warehouse" clause.

2. Open and Floating Insurance

453. By Article 231 of the MC, the insured may conclude an open cover with the insurer for the cargoes to be shipped or received in batches within a given period and the open cover shall be evidenced by an open policy to be issued by the insurer.

Thus, an open policy is a certificate of an open cover, under which, as agreed between the insurer and the insured, all the marine cargoes to be shipped or received in batches during a fixed period of time shall be automatically covered, whenever the cargoes are at risk during the fixed period of time, subject to possibly the agreed geographical limits. Besides the period of time, a floating marine cargo insurance contract or a floating policy of such insurance contains the description or types of cargoes insured, scope of cover, the maximum insured amount for each cargo or each place (locality clause) and payment of premiums.

Combining the advantages of voyage insurance and those of time insurance, this type of insurance has the benefit of saving expenses of both the insurer and the insured. Besides, it can effectively avoid any omission of cargo insurance by the insured. This type of insurance also benefits the insurer since it can bring out steady premium incomes during a long period of time. This is why it is common in China that professional traders conclude this type of marine cargo insurance contracts with insurers.

454. Under an open cover or policy of marine cargo, when any cargo covered is loaded on board a vessel, the insured shall notify the insurer immediately on learning that the cargo insured under open cover has been shipped or arrived of the name of the carrying vessel, voyage, value of the cargo and the insured amount (Article 233 of the MC). However, any omission of, delay in or mistakes of such notification by the insured shall not prejudice the effect of insurance, provided that it is not committed by the insured intentionally.

The insurer shall, upon request of the insured, issue policies or other insurance certificates separately for the cargoes shipped in batches in accordance with an open cover. Where the contents of such insurance certificates differ from those of the open cover, the former shall prevail (Article 232 of the MC).

455. Open policy was developed from floating policy and has replaced the latter on the whole in the practice of marine cargo insurance. Floating policies are now mainly used in the cargo warehousing insurance. The characteristics of a floating policy are that the subject-matters insured can be increased or decreased, and it contains no specific insured amount, but the maximum limit of the insurer's liability only.

Part IV. Extended Property Insurance

456. Article 6 of the Measures for the Hierarchical Management of Business Scope of Insurance Companies provides that the extended businesses of property insurance companies shall include the following four items: (1) agricultural insurance; (2) special risk insurance, including aviation and aerospace insurance, ocean exploitation insurance, petroleum and natural gas insurance and nuclear insurance; (3) credit guarantee insurance; and (4) investment-type insurance.

Chapter 1. Agricultural Insurance

§1. Introduction

457. With accelerating urbanization and industrialization since the 1980s, agriculture takes up lesser and lesser share in the GNP, but its role as the base and staunch pillar of the national economy has never changed. By using merely about 9% of the world's cultivated land, China has not only managed to meet the demand of nearly 1.4 billion people for grain and other agricultural products but also been able to provide raw materials, labors and a huge consumer market for industries, services and other sectors. Agriculture plays increasingly important roles in produce supply, food safety, and environment protection, as its multi-functionality fosters.

The development of modern agriculture needs the deep involvement of insurance, which plays an important role in distributing agricultural risks, reducing agricultural losses and enhancing the overall agricultural productive ability.

458. The Agricultural Insurance Regulations (AIR) promulgated in 2012 and revised in 2016 are currently the most important law regulating agricultural insurance in China, the purpose of which is to regulate agricultural insurance activities, protect lawful rights and interests of all parties to agricultural insurance activities, improve anti-risk capability of agricultural production and promote healthy development of the agricultural insurance business.

In case of no provision herein for agricultural insurance, relevant provisions specified in the IL may be referred to for application.

459. For the purposes of the AIR, "agricultural insurance" means the insurance activities whereby insurance institutions (insurance companies, legally established agricultural mutual insurance and other insurance organizations) assume responsibilities of insurance payment, in accordance with agricultural insurance contracts, for the insured's property loss in production of crop farming, forestry, stock raising and fishery as a result of the insurance objects' suffering from such contractual insured events as natural disasters, accidents, plagues and diseases, etc. By Article 32 of the AIR, if the insurer operates policy-supported agriculture-related insurance, such as insurance to provide guarantee for farmers' agricultural production and living other than agricultural insurance, including property insurance of farmers' houses, agricultural machines and tools and fishing ships, and short-term accident insurance covering farmers' life, body, etc. relevant provisions herein shall be referred for application.

§2. General Principles

460. In accordance with Articles 3–9 of the AIR, the general principles of agricultural insurance business could be summarized as follows.

The state supports the development of varying kinds of agricultural insurance and improves the policy-oriented agricultural insurance system. Agricultural insurance shall be conducted under the principle of guidance by government, market-oriented operation, independence and voluntariness and synergetic promotion. The people's governments of provinces, autonomous regions and municipalities directly under the Central Government may determine agricultural insurance operating modes applicable to local circumstances. No entity or individual may force or restrict farmers or agricultural production and operation organizations to participate in or from participating in agricultural insurance by advantage of administrative powers, positions or occupations or in other forms.

The insurance regulatory authority under the State Council shall be responsible for supervision and administration of agricultural insurance businesses. Authorities under the State Council as finance, agriculture, forestry, development and reform, taxation and civil affairs, etc. shall be responsible for affairs in connection with promotion and administration of agricultural insurance based on their respective duties. Authorities and institutions of finance, insurance supervision and administration, land and resources, agriculture, forestry and meteorology, etc. shall establish mechanisms for sharing information related to agricultural insurance.

Local people's governments above the county level shall uniformly guide, organize and coordinate local agricultural insurance affairs, and establish and improve working mechanisms for promoting the development of agricultural insurance. Competent departments of local people's governments above the county level shall be responsible for affairs in connection with promotion and administration of local agricultural insurance based on the duties assigned by the people's governments at the same level.

Relevant departments and institutions under the State Council and local people's governments at each level and their departments concerned shall adopt varying forms to strengthen the publicity of agricultural insurance, increase insurance awareness of farmers and agricultural production and operation organizations, organize and guide farmers and agricultural production and operation organizations to positively participate in agricultural insurance.

The state shall establish a finance-supported agricultural insurance major disaster risk dispersion mechanism, and the specific measures therefor shall be formulated by the finance authority under the State Council together with departments concerned under the State Council. The state supports local people's governments to establish local-finance-supported agricultural insurance major disaster risk dispersion mechanisms.

§3. Agricultural Insurance Contract

I. Formation of the Contract

461. Farmers and agricultural production and operation organizations may apply for agricultural insurance by themselves, or such entities as agricultural production and operation organizations or villagers' committees, etc. may organize farmers to apply for agricultural insurance. If such entities as agricultural production and operation organizations or villagers' committees, etc. organize farmers to apply for agricultural insurance, insurers shall, when entering into agricultural insurance contracts, prepare the detailed insurance information of the insured, and require signature of the insured for confirmation. The insurers shall publicize information on underwriting.

II. Performance of the Contract

462. In accordance with Articles 11–15 of the AIR, the rules regarding the performance of agricultural insurance contract could be summarized as follows.

During the valid term of an agricultural insurance contract, parties to the contract may not increase insurance premium or rescind the agricultural insurance contract due to change of the insurance object's degree of risk.

After receiving notice of insured event, the insurer shall promptly carry out on-site survey and assess injury of the subject-matter insured together with the insured. Where such entities as agricultural production and operation organizations or villagers' committees organize farmers to apply for agricultural insurance, the insurer shall publicize the result of survey and loss assessment. The insurer may adopt sampling approach or other manners as stipulated in the agricultural insurance contract to assess the loss degree of the subject-matter insured. If sampling approach is adopted to assess loss degree, technical specifications for sampling prescribed by the department concerned shall be followed.

If laws or administrative regulations set forth provisions on handling of injured subject matter of agricultural insurance, evidence or proving materials for the injured subject matter has been handled in accordance with law shall be obtained when settling claims. No insurer may claim residual value of the injured subject-matter insured, unless otherwise stipulated in the agricultural insurance contract.

463. The insurer shall pay insurance money to the insured within ten days upon reaching compensation agreement with the insured. If the agricultural insurance contract has any stipulation on the time limit of insurance money payment, the insurer shall fulfill obligations of insurance payment within the stipulated time limit.

The insurer shall pay insurance money in a full amount based on the assessed injury degree of subject-matter insured in accordance with the agricultural insurance contract. No entity or individual may illegally intervene in the insurer's fulfillment of insurance money payment obligation or restrict the insured from acquiring insurance money. If such entity organizations as agricultural production and operation organizations and villagers' committees organize farmers to apply for insurance, the list of claim settlement shall be signed by the insured for confirmation, and the insurer shall publicize the claim settlement result.

§4. Operational Rules

464. Article 7 and Articles 17-24 of the AIR provide the operational rules as to agricultural insurance business as follows.

For operating agricultural insurance business, an insurance institution shall meet the following requirements and be subject to law-based approval by the insurance regulatory organ under the State Council:

- possessing improved grass-rooted service networks;
- having departments special for operating agricultural insurance and staffed with corresponding professionals;
- having improved agricultural insurance internal control bylaws;
- having steady agricultural reinsurance and major disaster risk arrangement and risk response preplans;
- its solvency meets provisions specified by the insurance regulatory organ under the State Council; and
- other requirements specified by the insurance regulatory organ under the State Council.

No entity or individual may operate agricultural insurance business without law-based approval.

For operating agricultural insurance business, the insurer shall be in independent operation and assume sole responsibilities for its profits or losses. For operating agricultural insurance business, the insurer shall carry out management and profits or losses calculation separately from other insurance businesses.

465. The insurer shall fix agricultural insurance articles and rate of premium based on a fair and rational basis. For those insurance products entitled for premium finance subsidy, the insurance articles and rate of premium shall be fixed based on fully hearing opinions of the finance, agriculture and forestry departments under the people's governments of provinces, autonomous regions and municipalities directly under the Central Government and farmer representatives. Agricultural insurance terms and rate of premium shall be reported to the insurance regulatory authorities in accordance with law for approval or filing.

466. Reserves evaluation and solvency report for the insurer's operation of agricultural insurance business shall meet provisions formulated by the insurance regulatory authority under the State Council. If finance management and accounting of agricultural insurance business need extraordinary principles and methods, specific measures shall be formulated by the finance department under the State Council.

The insurer may entrust grass-rooted agricultural technology promotion institutions and other institutions to assist development of agricultural insurance business. The insurer shall conclude a written contract with the institution entrusted to assist development of agricultural insurance business, defining rights and obligations of each party and commission payment, and the insurer shall give business guidance to the institution assisting development of agricultural insurance business.

The insurer shall well keep original materials of agricultural insurance survey and loss assessment in accordance with provisions formulated by the insurance regulatory authority under the State Council. All entities and individuals are forbidden from altering, forging, concealing or destroying original materials of survey and loss assessment.

467. If the insured agricultural insurance object of any farmer or agricultural production and operation organization falls within the scope of premium subsidy granted by the finance authority under the State Council, the finance authority shall extend premium subsidy pursuant to provisions. And the specific measures shall be formulated by the finance authority under the State Council by consulting with the competent department of agriculture and forestry and insurance regulatory organ under the State Council. The state encourages local people's governments to adopt measures to support development of agricultural insurance, such as providing premium subsidy by use of local finance, etc.

468. It is forbidden to cheat premium subsidy for agricultural insurance in the following manners or any other manner: (1) fabricating or making false increase of subject-matter insured or making several applications for one subject-matter insured; or (2) writing off premiums payable by applicants or finance-granted premium subsidy in forms of false claim settlement, false disturbed expenses, false surrender or detaining or embezzling insurance money or embezzling operating costs, etc.

All entities and individuals are forbidden from embezzling, detaining or misappropriating insurance money the insurer shall pay to the insured.

Chapter 2. Special Risk Insurance

§1. Aircraft Insurance

469. Aircraft insurance is an insurance in which the aircraft and its related responsibilities and interests are the subject of insurance. It is an insurance field developed on the basis of marine insurance and personal accident insurance with the development of the aircraft manufacturing industry. It is a comprehensive insurance that combines property insurance and liability insurance.

China Pacific Insurance Co., Ltd. (CPIC) Property Aircraft Insurance Clauses are the widely recognized and used standard clauses in the Chinese market, which contains four sections:

(1) loss of or damage to aircraft;
(2) legal liability to third party (other than passengers);
(3) legal liability to passengers;
(4) clauses applicable to all sections.

I. Loss of or Damage to Aircraft

A. *Coverage*

470. The insurers will at their option pay for, replace or repair, accidental loss of or damage to the aircraft described in the policy arising from the risks covered, including disappearance if the aircraft is unreported for sixty days after the commencement of flight, but not exceeding the amount insured as specified in the policy or subject to the amounts to be deducted specified in the policy.

If the aircraft is insured hereby for the risks of flight, the insurers will, in addition, pay reasonable emergency expenses necessarily incurred by the insured for the immediate safety of the aircraft consequent upon damage or forced landing, up to 10% of the amount insured as specified in the policy.

B. *Exclusions to This Section Only*

471. The insurer shall not be liable for:

- wear and tear, deterioration, breakdown, defect or failure howsoever caused in any unit of the aircraft and the consequences thereof within such unit;
- damage to any unit by anything which has a progressive or cumulative effect but damage attributable to a single recorded incident is covered.

However, accidental loss of or damage to the aircraft consequent upon the above issues is covered under this section.

C. Conditions Applicable to This Section Only

472. The following conditions are only applied to the section of loss of or damage to the aircraft:

- Dismantling, Transport and Repairs: if the aircraft is damaged: (1) no dismantling or repairs shall be commenced without the consent of the insurers except whatever is necessary in the interests of safety, or to prevent further damage, or to comply with orders issued by the appropriate authority; (2) the insurers will pay only for repairs and transport of labor and materials by the most economical method unless the insurers agree otherwise with the insured.
- Payment or Replacement: if the insurers exercise their option to pay for or replace the aircraft: (1) the insurers may take the aircraft (together with all documents of record, registration and title thereto) as salvage; (2) the cover afforded by this Section is terminated in respect of the aircraft even if the aircraft is retained by the insured for valuable consideration or otherwise; (3) the replacement aircraft shall be of the same make and type and in reasonably like condition unless otherwise agreed with the insured.
- Amounts to be deducted from the claim: except where the insurers exercise their option to pay for or replace the aircraft, there shall be deducted from the claim under this section: (1) the amount specified in the schedule of the policy; (2) such proportion of the overhaul cost of any unit repaired or replaced as the used time bears to the overhaul life of the unit.
- No abandonment: unless the insurers elect to take the aircraft as salvage, the aircraft shall at all times remain the property of the insured who shall have no right of abandonment to the insurers.
- Other Insurance: no claim shall be payable under this section if other insurance which is payable in consequence of loss or damage covered under this section has been or shall be effected by or on behalf of the insured without the knowledge or consent of the insurers.

II. Legal Liability to Third Parties (Other Than Passengers)

A. Coverage

473. The insurers will indemnify the insured for all sums which the insured shall become legally liable to pay, and shall pay, as compensatory damages (including costs awarded against the insured) in respect of accidental bodily injury (fatal or otherwise) and accidental damage to property caused by the aircraft or by any person or object falling therefrom.

B. Exclusions to This Section Only

474. The insurers shall not be liable for:

- employees and others: injury (fatal or otherwise) or loss sustained by any director or employee of the insured or partner in the insured's business while acting in the course of his employment with or duties for the insured;
- operational crew: injury (fatal or otherwise) or loss sustained by any member of the flight, cabin or other crew while engaged in the operation of the aircraft;
- passengers: injury (fatal or otherwise) or loss sustained by any passenger while entering, on board, or alighting from the aircraft;
- property: loss of or damage to any property belonging to or in the care, custody or control of the insured;
- noise and pollution and other perils: claims excluded by the attached Noise and Pollution and Other Perils Exclusion Clause.

III. Legal Liability to Passengers

A. Coverage

475. The insurers will indemnify the insured in respect of all sums which the insured shall become legally liable to pay, and shall pay, as compensatory damages (including costs awarded against the insured) in respect of: (a) accidental bodily injury (fatal or otherwise) to passengers while entering, on board, or alighting from the aircraft and (b) loss of or damage to baggage and personal articles of passengers arising out of an occurrence involving the aircraft.

Provided always that: (1) before a passenger boards the aircraft the insured shall take such measures as are necessary to exclude or limit liability for claims under (a) and (b) above to the extent permitted by law; (2) if the measures referred to in proviso (1) above include the issue of a passenger ticket/baggage check, the same shall be delivered correctly to the passenger within a reasonable time before the passenger boards the aircraft.

In the event of failure to comply with proviso (1) or (2), the liability of the insurers under this Section shall not exceed the amount of the legal liability, if any, that would have existed had the proviso been complied with.

B. Exclusions to This Section Only

476. The insurers shall not be liable for injury (fatal or otherwise) or loss sustained by any:

- employees and others: director or employee of the insured or partner in the insured's business while acting in the course of his employment with or duties for the insured;
- operational crew: member of the flight, cabin or other crew while engaged in the operation of the aircraft.

IV. General Conditions Applicable to All Sections

A. General Exclusions Applicable to All Sections

477. The policy also does not cover:

- illegal uses: while the aircraft is being used for any illegal purpose or for any purpose other than those stated and as defined in the policy;
- geographical limits: while the aircraft is outside the geographical limits stated in the policy unless due to force majeure;
- pilots: while the aircraft is being piloted by any person other than as stated in policy except that the aircraft may be operated on the ground by any person competent for that purpose;
- transportation by other conveyance: while the aircraft is being transported by any means of conveyance except as the result of an accident giving rise to a claim under the policy;
- landing and take-off areas: while the aircraft is landing on or taking off or attempting to do so from a place which does not comply with the recommendations laid down by the manufacturer of the aircraft except as a result of force majeure;
- contractual liability: to liability assumed or rights waived by the insured under any agreement (other than a passenger ticket/baggage check issued under section III of the policy) except to the extent that such liability would have attached to the insured in the absence of such agreement;
- number of passengers: while the total number of passengers being carried in the aircraft exceeds the declared maximum number of passengers stated in the policy;
- non-contribution: to claims which are payable under any other policy or policies except in respect of any excess beyond the amount which would have been payable under such other policy or policies had this policy not been effected;
- war, hijacking, and other perils: to claims excluded by the attached War, Hi-Jacking and Other Perils Exclusion Clause;
- nuclear risks: to claims excluded by the attached Nuclear Risks Exclusion Clause;
- date recognition perils: to claims excluded by the attached Date Recognition Exclusion Clause;
- right of third parties' perils: to claims excluded by the attached Contracts (Right of Third Parties) Act 1999 Exclusion Clause;
- asbestos perils: to claims excluded by the attached Asbestos Exclusion Clause;
- non-aviation Risks: to claims excluded by the attached Non-Aviation Liability Clause.

B. Insured's Obligations

478. The insured shall observe and fulfill the following conditions before the insurers have any liability to make any payment under the policy:

- due diligence: the insured shall at all times use due diligence and do and concur in doing everything reasonably practicable to avoid accidents and to avoid or diminish any loss hereon;
- compliance with air navigation, orders, etc.: the insured shall comply with all air navigation and airworthiness orders and requirements issued by any competent authority affecting the safe operation of the aircraft and shall ensure that: (a) the aircraft is airworthy at the commencement of each flight; (b) all Log Books and other records in connection with the aircraft which are required by any official regulations in force from time to time shall be kept up to date and shall be produced to the insurers or their agents on request; (c) the employees and agents of the insured comply with such orders and requirements;
- claim procedure: immediate notice of any event likely to give rise to a claim under this policy shall be given. In all cases, the insured shall: (a) furnish full particulars in writing of such event and forward immediately notice of any claim with any letters or documents relating thereto; (b) give notice of any impending prosecution; (c) render such further information and assistance as the insurers may reasonably require; (d) not act in any way to the detriment or prejudice of the interest of the insurers. The insured shall not make any admission of liability or payment or offer or promise of payment without the written consent of the insurers. The insurers shall be entitled (if they so elect) at any time and for so long as they desire to take absolute control of all negotiations and proceedings and in the name of the insured to settle, defend or pursue any claim;
- variation in risk: should there be any change in the circumstances or nature of the risks which are the basis of this contract the insured shall give immediate notice thereof to the insurers and no claim arising subsequent to such change shall be recoverable hereunder unless such change has been accepted by the insurers;
- false and fraudulent claims: if the insured shall make any claim knowing the same to be false or fraudulent as regards amount, or otherwise this policy shall become void and all claims hereunder shall be forfeited.

§2. Nuclear Material Damage Insurance

479. Nuclear material damage insurance mainly covers property damage and damage to machinery and equipment caused by natural disasters, man-made accidents, nuclear radiation, etc. at nuclear power plants. CPIC Nuclear Material Damage Insurance Clause is the widely recognized and used standard clause in the Chinese market, which provides as follows.

I. Property Insured

480. The insureds covered by the policy are nuclear power company and/or their affiliates, subsidiaries and associated companies and/or their joint venture partners and/or corporations as now exist or may hereafter be constituted or acquired, including their interests as may appear in partnerships or joint ventures.

The property insured includes all property owned by or held in trust by the insured for which the insured has assumed or wishes to assume responsibility on the insured's nuclear power station including but not limited to:

- Item 1: (a) the buildings, machinery, plant, equipment and all other property comprising or contained in the nuclear steam plant; (b) nuclear fuel (and heavy water anywhere) on the site whether within the nuclear reactors or not and/or in transit by road, rail, air or inland or coastal waterways to or from the site all within the territorial boundaries of China.
- Item 2: the buildings, plant and all other property other than those in Item 1 on the site including but not limited to balance of plant, furniture, fixture, fittings, lands, roads, pathways, etc.

II. Scope of Cover

481. The insurer shall indemnify the insured in respect of accidental loss, destruction or damage by any cause to property insured described in the policy belonging to the insured or for which they are responsible or for which they may wish to accept responsibility on any licensed nuclear site anywhere in China and in transit hereto and therefrom but excluding as specified in the policy.

III. Exclusions

A. Excluded Perils

482. The policy excludes the cost necessary to replace, repair or rectify any defect in design, plan, specification, material or workmanship, but should unintended damage result from such defect, this exclusion shall be limited to the additional cost of improvement to the original design, plan or specification.

The policy does not cover loss, destruction or damage caused by:

- erosion, corrosion including stress corrosion, cracking, gradual deterioration or normal wear and tear over time including fatigue, whether or not thermal fatigue or high-cycle fatigue;
- embrittlement, including hydrogen embrittlement and neutron embrittlement within the calandria, due to prolonged neutron bombardment;
- slowly developing pitting, cracking, bulging, blistering, fretting, denting, deformation or distortion which accompanies or is directly associated with the perils specified above;
- shrinking, bulging, expansion, cracking, shifting, rising, settling, sinking, lateral or other movement of pavements, foundations, walls, floors, ceilings or roofs;
- machinery or plant being subject to experiments or overload or similar tests requiring the imposition of abnormal conditions (other than overload or similar tests carried out with the approval of the manufacturer or by normal rules of good operational practice);

- pressure waves caused by aircraft and other aerial devices traveling at sonic or supersonic speeds;
- disappearance, unexplained or inventory shortage, misfiling or misplacing of information, but this shall not include: (a) such loss, destruction or damage resulting from a cause which is not otherwise excluded; (b) subsequent loss, destruction or damage resulting from an ensuing cause which is not otherwise excluded.

The policy also excludes the cost necessary to replace, repair or rectify any defect in design, plan specification, material or workmanship, but should unintended damage not otherwise exclude result from such defect, this exclusion shall be limited to the additional cost of improvement to the original design, plan or specification.

B. Excluded Property

483. The policy does not cover loss, destruction or damage to:

- mechanically propelled motor vehicles or seagoing vessels or any aircraft owned by the insured and/or for which they are responsible or have assumed responsibility. This exclusion shall not however apply to loss, destruction or damage to mechanically propelled motor vehicles (including vehicles designed or adapted principally for use as a tool of trade) which at the time of the loss do not require compulsory insurance or security under any road traffic legislation;
- accounts, bills, currency, evidence of debt, money or securities.

C. General Exclusions

484. The policy does not cover:

- destruction or damage directly or indirectly occasioned by or happening through or in consequence of war, invasion, act of foreign enemy, hostilities (whether war be declared or not), civil war, rebellion, revolution, insurrection or military or usurped power;
- any consequential loss resulting from loss, destruction or damage to any property whatsoever due to the deliberate act of the government or any public authority of closure confiscation requisition seizure or destruction (this exclusion does not apply to destruction or damage at the time of fire for the purpose of preventing its spread);
- property insured that is insured under more specific insurances effected by or on behalf of the insured;
- consequential loss of any kind or description;
- any property whatsoever or any loss or expense arising therefrom or any consequential loss directly or indirectly caused by or contributed to or arising from: (a) the radioactive, toxic, explosive or other hazardous properties of any explosive nuclear assembly or nuclear component thereof; (b) except as provided in policy

and in respect of nuclear power station only irradiation or contamination by radioactivity from the normal operation of a nuclear reactor;
- unexplained or mysterious disappearance of property insured, or shortage disclosed upon taking inventory;
- any sums which the insured may be obligated to pay as damages because of third-party bodily injury or third-party property damage.

D. Terrorism Exclusion

485. Notwithstanding any provision to the contrary within this insurance or any endorsement thereto, it is agreed that this insurance excludes loss, damage, cost or expense of whatsoever nature directly or indirectly caused by, resulting from or in connection with any act of terrorism regardless of any other cause or event contributing concurrently or in any other sequence to the loss.

For the purpose of this clause an act of terrorism means an act, including but not limited to the use of force or violence and/or the threat thereof, of any person or group(s) of persons, whether acting alone or on behalf of or in connection with any organization(s) or government(s), committed for political, religious, ideological or similar purposes including the intention to influence any government and/or to put the public, or any section of the public, in fear.

This clause also excludes loss, damage, cost or expense of whatsoever nature directly or indirectly caused by, resulting from or in connection with any action taken in controlling, preventing, suppressing or in any way relating to any act of terrorism.

If the insurer alleges that by reason of this exclusion, any loss, damage, cost or expense is not covered by this insurance, the burden of proving the contrary shall be upon the insured.

In the event that any portion of this clause is found to be invalid or unenforceable, the remainder shall remain in full force and effect.

IV. Extensions

486. The policy contains a separate part named as “Extensions,” covering additional costs, expenses, fees and interests, subject to the limits of liability not being exceeded. Some of the extensions may be introduced as follows:

- Debris removal: all costs and expenses necessarily incurred by the insured with the consent of the insurer in removing the debris including dismantling demolishing and shoring or propping-up of the property insured which suffers damage and temporary repairs carried out for the purpose of preventing further loss destruction or damage or for the protection of life. However, this extension excludes all such costs and expenses arising from pollution or contamination elsewhere than at the nuclear power station insured by this policy.
- Making safe and decontamination: (aa) all costs and expenses necessarily incurred by the insured in making safe and/or decontaminating and/or isolating

any part of the property accidentally contaminated by radioactivity including the removal and disposal of contaminated materials, liquids or gases or of nuclear fuel; (b) this insurance will also include such costs and expenses incurred in making safe decontaminating or isolating property contaminated by the normal operation of the reactor as may be incurred solely in order to reinstate property which has been lost, destroyed or damaged by any accident insured hereby.

- Fees: (a) fees and related costs including but not limited to architects', surveyors' and consulting engineers' fees necessarily incurred in the reinstatement of the property insured consequent upon its destruction or damage or contamination by radioactivity; (b) reasonable charges payable by the insured for services and legal costs for producing such evidence as may be required by the insurer for the purpose of investigating or verifying any claim.
- Public authorities: as a result of accidental loss or damage indemnifiable under the policy, the additional cost of reinstatement (including undamaged property) incurred solely by reason of the necessity to comply with building or other regulations under or framed in pursuance of any Chinese government authority including municipal or local body or any Ministry or government department or any licensing authority in respect of: (a) the lost, destroyed or damaged property thereby insured; (b) undamaged portions thereof.

  However, this extension excludes: (a) the cost incurred in complying with any of the aforesaid regulations or bylaws: (i) in respect of damage occurring prior to the granting of this extension; (ii) in respect of loss destruction or damage not insured by the Policy; (iii) under which notice has been served upon the insured prior to the happening of the damage; (iv) in respect of undamaged property other than undamaged portions of property damaged by any cause hereby insured against; (b) the amount of any charge or assessment arising out of capital appreciation which may be payable in respect of the property or by the owner thereof by reason of compliance with any of the aforesaid regulations.
- Contractors and subcontractors: the policy extends to include the interest of the contractors and subcontractors providing services, materials, parts or equipment in connection with the construction, repair, maintenance, transportation of nuclear fuel, or operation of the nuclear power station insured by the policy.
- Emergency cold shutdown: the policy extends to include coverage against the reasonable extra shutdown cost incurred to effect an emergency cold shutdown of a nuclear power reactor that forms part of the property insured, provided the shutdown is necessary because of direct physical damage for which the insurer is liable to indemnify the insured.
- Fire brigade charges and extinguishing expenses: the policy extends to cover: (a) fire brigade charges and other extinguishing expenses for which the insured may be assessed; (b) loss of fire extinguishing materials expended.
- Immediate repairs: the insurer grants permission to the insured to carry out repairs in respect of any damage to the property insured hereby which conveniently and advantageously can be undertaken by them (subject to notification to the insurers as soon as practical). The insurer will reimburse the insured for the actual cost of such repairs and all expenses and fees incurred relative to any claims, including overtime and express freight or other rapid means of transportation, subject always to the policy terms and conditions.

Chapter 3. Credit and Guarantee Insurance

§1. Credit Insurance

I. Nature of Credit Insurance

487. The credit insurance's subject matter of insured is the credit risk of the obligor. It covers the economic loss suffered by the obligee caused by the act or omission of the obligor in the performance of obligations. After paying the insured, the insurer acquires the subrogation right against the obligor for indemnification.

II. Types of Credit Insurance

A. Short-Term Domestic Credit Insurance

1. Scope of Cover

488. The purpose of this insurance is to indemnify the insured, in accordance with the terms of the policy, up to the covered percentage of any loss the insured may sustain because of the occurrence of any of the following causes of loss:

- The insolvency of the buyer. Insolvency shall occur if a bankruptcy, winding-up or administration order is made against the buyer or the buyer is declared bankrupt by the court or in the course of execution of a judgment the levy of execution fails to satisfy the debt in full; or a valid assignment, composition or other arrangement is made for the benefit of the buyer's creditors generally according to a decision of the court; or an effective resolution is passed for the winding-up of the buyer; or a liquidation committee, an administrative or other receiver or manager of any of the buyer's property is appointed; or the insured shows, to the insurer's satisfaction, that the buyer's financial state is such that even partial payment is unlikely and that to enforce judgment or to apply for a bankruptcy or winding-up order would have no foreseeable result other than one disproportionate to the likely cost of the proceedings; such situations or events which, in the sole opinion of the insurer, in substance or effect are equivalent to the situations and events described above.
- The failure of a buyer to pay the insured the amount owing under the contract within six months of the original due date of payment.

2. Exclusions

489. The insured shall not be liable for any loss arising in connection with any of the following:

- any failure by the insured or by any person acting on his behalf to fulfill any of the terms and conditions of the contract or to comply with the provisions of any law (including any order, decree or regulation having the force of law);
- directly or indirectly caused by, contributed to contamination by or arising from the ionizing, radioactive, toxic, explosive or other hazardous or contaminating properties or effects of any explosive nuclear assembly or component thereto, nuclear fuel, combustion or waste;
- directly or indirectly from war (whether before or after the outbreak of hostilities) between any of the following countries: China, France, the U.K., the Russian Federation and the U.S.;
- where the buyer has failed or refused to accept good dispatched. However, if such failure or refusal is in breach of the contract, this exclusion shall not apply;
- any decision taken by a state or government department, local authority or any entity which cannot be declared insolvent that either hinders execution of the contract or prevents payment;
- directly or indirectly caused by, contributed to or arising from cyclone, flood, earthquake, volcanic eruption or tidal wave or other forms of natural disaster or force majeure.

B. Short-Term Export Credit Insurance

490. Short-term export credit insurance is mainly provided by SINOSURE in China. It is a state-funded policy-oriented insurance company with independent status of legal person, established for promoting China's foreign trade and economic cooperation. It began operations on December 18, 2001. Presently SINOSURE has formed a nationwide service network. Its business guideline is "by means of insurance service for foreign trade and investment, fully supporting the development of foreign trade and economic cooperation and promoting the economic growth, the employment and the equilibrium of international balance of payment." SINOSURE is mandated, in accordance with the Chinese government's diplomatic, international trade, industrial, fiscal and financial policies, to promote Chinese exports of goods, technologies and services, especially high-tech and high value-added capital goods like electromechanical products, and national enterprises' overseas investment, by means of export credit insurance against non-payment risks.

Since SINOSURE's foundation, the role of export credit insurance in supporting China's foreign trade and economic cooperation has become more and more evident. Especially in the time of financial crisis, it served as leverage in stabilizing foreign demands and driving export deals. SINOSURE's applicants were greatly helped in competing for orders and preserving their market share. By the end of 2015, SINOSURE has supported export, domestic trade and investment with a total value of USD 2.8 trillion, and claims paid has amounted to USD 9.5 billion. Its policies covered thousands of exporters and hundreds of medium- and long-term projects concerning high-technology export, large electro-machinery and complete-set equipment export, overseas engineering contracts, etc. In the meantime, SINOSURE has facilitated the lending of CNY 2.7 trillion by 233 banks.

In accordance with the SINOSURE's Short Term Export Credit Insurance Comprehensive Policy and the relevant laws, the main characteristics of the short-term export credit insurance can be summarized as follows.

1. Scope of Cover

491. Exports insurable under the policy are the exports conducted by the entities incorporated under the law and registered within the territory of China which are licensed to handle import-export business provided the following terms and conditions are satisfied:

– goods are exported from China;
– the sales contract, which specifies the transaction essentials including the name, quality standard, specification, quantity, price of the goods as well as the time limit for performance, is issued in written form and come into effect before the export;
– the payment term includes documents against payment, documents against acceptance and open account, etc. and the period of payment under which is not exceeding 180 days.

492. The insurer shall indemnify the insured against direct losses resulting from the following event occurring after the exports pursuant to the sales contracts:

– Commercial risk: (a) buyer's insolvency and/or inability to pay the debt due, namely the buyer is declared to be bankrupt or lose the capability of paying debt; (b) protracted default, which occurs when the buyer has received the goods while the debt remains unpaid in whole or in part after expiration of the due date due to the non-compliance of its contractual duty by the buyer; (c) buyer's refusal to take delivery of the goods, namely the buyer fails to observe its duties under the sales contract and refuses to take delivery of the arrived goods.
– Political risk: (a) the operation of any laws, regulations, orders, rules or administrative measures of the buyer's country or region which prevents or restricts the transfer of payments due in the currency designated in the invoice or in any other freely convertible currency; (b)the imposition of any laws, regulations, orders, rules or administrative measures by the buyer's country or region which restrains the import of the goods ordered by the buyer; (c) the imposition of any laws, regulations, orders, rules or administrative measures by the buyer's country or region which revokes the buyer's previous import license or prevents the extension of its validity; (d) a general moratorium decreed by the buyer's country or by a third country through which the payment must be effected; (e) the occurrence of war, civil commotion, insurrection, revolution or rebellion, which prevents the buyer from performing its contractual duty; (f) unless otherwise provided by the Policy, the occurrence of any other events deemed to be political risks by the insurer, which prevents the buyer from performing its contractual duties.

2. Exclusions

493. The insurer shall not be liable for any loss arising from the following events:

- wear and tear, damage, spoilage, loss or destruction of the goods occurred during the transportation and/or the storage period and/or the loss which has been insured or can be insured at the time of export in the customary way by cargo insurance or other similar class of insurance;
- exchange rate fluctuations;
- a breach of any duties under the sales contract or any competent law by the insured or its agent;
- insolvency, any breach of contract, fraud, violation of law and any similar acts on the part of the buyer's agent;
- commercial risks due from export to any affiliated company;
- frustration of the sales contract due to the failure of timely obtaining of any necessary import or export license, approval or authorizations by the insured or the buyer;
- the insured waives its rights to rescind or suspend the contract and carry on to release the goods despite the fact that risks listed in the policy and/or the material breach and/or anticipating breach to the sales contract by the defaulting buyers has occurred and the occurrence of which has come to the insured's knowledge before the export;
- when at the time of shipment, the buyer's Credit Limit is not approved by the insurer, or when the Credit Limit has been withdrawn or void, or when the Discretionary Credit Limit has no application;
- release of goods by any bank, freight forwarder or carrier without proper authority;
- loss occurred prior to the export;
- ionizing radiations or contamination directly or indirectly caused by radioactivity of nuclear waste or the combustion of nuclear fuel, and/or radioactive, toxic, explosive or other hazardous properties caused by any explosive nuclear assembly or nuclear components thereof;
- war(s) between any two or more of the permanent members of the Security Council of the United Nations;
- any other losses beyond the scope of coverage of the policy.

3. Applicable Law

494. The SPC's opinion on this issue is: the IL has no explicit provisions regarding the application of laws to export credit insurance contracts. Given the uniqueness of export credit insurance, the people's courts may refer to relevant provisions of the IL *mutatis mutandis* in trying cases of export credit insurance contract disputes. Where the export credit insurance contract otherwise provides for, such provisions shall prevail.

C. Investment Insurance

495. Investment insurance is a policy insurance that is intended to provide the insured with risk guarantee when it suffers economic losses because of war, currency exchange ban, requisition, or breach of contract by the government in countries where the insured have made investments. It is designed to support and promote Chinese companies and financial organizations in making overseas investments, and to encourage and advance overseas investors to make investments in mainland China. SINOSURE now operates two major kinds of insurance in this regard:

(1) Overseas investment insurance is designed to support and encourage Chinese enterprises and financial organizations to make investments overseas. It obligates the insurer to underwrite an investor's economic losses in overseas investment and profits caused by political risks of a host country. It consists of equity insurance and liability insurance.
(2) Inbound investment insurance is designed to encourage and promote investors from foreign countries and Hong Kong SAR, Macao SAR, and Taiwan to make investments in mainland China. It obligates the insurer to underwrite all economic losses of overseas investors incurred in their investments and profits because of political risks in China. It consists of equity insurance and liability insurance.

§2. Guarantee Insurance

I. Nature of Guarantee Insurance

496. The guarantee insurance is the insurance by which the obligor (applicant), in accordance with the requirements of obligee, applies to the insurer to insure (guarantee) its credit of performing the obligations. The insured of guarantee insurance is the obligee.

It is typical for the applicant (obligor) of guarantee insurance to provide counter-guarantee. Provided that the insurer pays the insurance benefits to the insured, the insurer may implement the counter-guarantee against the applicant.

The guarantee insurance may be classified as honesty guarantee insurance and surety guarantee insurance.

II. Types of Guarantee Insurance

A. Honesty Guarantee Insurance-Employee Fidelity Insurance

497. Employee fidelity insurance refers to the situations when an employee of an enterprise carries out activities that are unfaithful to the enterprise during employment, including fraudulent activities and other events that cause economic losses to the enterprise; the insurance company bears compensation for the losses suffered by the enterprise.

PICC P&C Fidelity Clauses are the widely recognized and used clauses in the Chinese market, which provide as follows.

1. Scope of Cover

498. Subject to the terms and conditions contained or endorsed or otherwise expressed in the policy and in consideration of the payment to the insurer of the premium, the insurer agrees to make good and reimburse to the employer all such direct pecuniary loss as the employer shall sustain by any act of fraud or dishonesty committed by any one or more of the employees as described in the schedule of the policy:

- during the period of indemnity;
- during the uninterrupted continuance of employment of the said employees; and
- in connection with the occupation and duties of the said employees.

2. Exclusions

499. The insurer shall not be liable:

- in respect of any act of fraud or dishonesty committed by the employee unless such act of fraud or dishonesty is discovered during the period of indemnity or within six months thereafter or within six months after the death dismissal or retirement of the employee whichever event shall first happen;
- if the nature of the business of the employer or the duties or conditions of employment be changed or the remuneration of the employee reduced without the sanction of the company or if the precautions and checks for securing accuracy of accounts shall not be duly observed;
- to pay more than the aggregate limit for the period of indemnity.

3. Conditions of the Policy

500. The employer shall duly observe and fulfill the following conditions of the policy:

- Every notice or communication to the insurer shall be in writing and sent to the PICC P&C, and notice or knowledge of anything relating to the policy or any claim hereunder shall not be deemed to be noticed to or within the knowledge of the insurer unless so given.

- Immediately the employer shall become aware of any circumstances giving rise or likely to give rise to a claim under the policy and the employer or its representative shall immediately give notice thereof to the insurer stating if known the whereabouts of the employee and particulars of the acts of defaults then discovered and shall within three months after such notice deliver to the insurer full details of the claim and shall furnish proof of the correctness of such claim.
- In the event or claim, all books of accounts of the employer and any accountant reports thereon shall be open to the inspection of the insurer and the employer shall give all information and assistance to enable the insurer to use for and obtain reimbursement by the employee or its estate of any money which the insurer shall have paid or become liable to pay under the policy.
- The employer should exercise right actively if and when required by the insurer but at the expense of the insurer.
- Any money of the employee in the hands of the employer and any money which but for any act of fraud or dishonesty that would have been due to the employee from the employer shall be deducted from the amount otherwise payable under the policy.
- If at the time of any claim arising under the policy there be any other subsisting guarantee or security in respect of the acts or defaults of the employee, the insurer shall not be liable to pay or contribute more than its ratable proportion of such claim.
- The policy may be canceled at any time by seven days' notice by registered letter from the company to the employer's last known address, and in such event the company will return a pro rata portion of the premium for the unexpired part of the period of indemnity. The policy may be canceled at any time by the employer on seven days' notice to the insurer and in such event the employer shall be entitled to a return of the premium at the company's short period rates for the time the policy has been in force during the then-current period of insurance.
- It is a condition precedent to any liability on the part of the insurer under the policy that the employer shall satisfy himself with the integrity of all employees prior to their engagement by taking up references with their former employers. Such references shall be retained by the employer and in the event of a claim shall be produced to the insurer.
- All disputes arising between the employer and the insurer under the policy shall be settled through friendly negotiations. Where both sides fail to reach a settlement after negotiations, such dispute shall be submitted to arbitration or to court for legal action.
- In no case whatever shall the insurer be liable for any loss after the expiration of twelve months from the occurrence of the loss unless the claim is the subject of pending court action or arbitration.

B. Surety Guarantee Insurance

501. The surety guarantee insurance in China mainly includes performance guarantee insurance and product quality guarantee insurance

502. Performance guarantee insurance means that the insurance company promises to the beneficiary of the performance guarantee insurance (i.e., the investor) that if the policyholder (i.e., the debtor, here usually specifically refers to the borrower) does not perform its obligations according to the contract or the law, the insurance company will bear the liability for compensation.

503. Product quality guarantee insurance covers the economic losses caused to consumers by manufacturers, sellers, or repairers because of the inherent defects in the quality of the products they manufacture, sell, or repair, which usually includes: the loss and cost caused by the replacement and repair of products with quality problems; the loss and cost caused by the use of other methods to achieve the purpose because the product is unusable; the losses and expenses caused by the recovery, replacement or repairment of products in accordance with the court decision or the order of the relevant government department. The insurable amount is generally determined by the amount of the purchase invoice or the receipt of the repair charge for the insurance subject; the insurance period varies according to the performance and use of the product, and is generally determined by the quality assurance period confirmed by the product quality certification agency.

Chapter 4. Investment-Type Insurance

§1. Definition of Investment-Type Insurance

504. The investment-type insurance refers to the insurance combining the functions of insurance and capital utilization, through which the insurers use the investments made by insurance applicants into investment-typed insurance in capital operations, calculate and collect insurance premiums and assume responsibilities as insurers in accordance with the contracts and pay the investments and yields under the contracts to the applicant or the insured. The aforesaid insurance applicant and insured shall be natural persons and may not be legal persons.

505. The investment-typed insurance can be classified into preset-yield investment-typed insurance (hereinafter referred to as "preset-yield products") and non-preset-yield investment-typed insurance (hereinafter referred to as "non-preset yield products"):

- A preset-yield insurance refers to an insurance for which a fixed or floating yield rate is agreed on in advance in the insurance contract. Through a preset-yield product, the insurer shall, upon the full performance of the insurance contract, pay to the insurance applicant or the insured both the investment in such insurance and the agreed yields on the utilization of such investment, or the amount of yield payable to the insurance applicant or the insured calculated according to the insurance contract where the insurance contract is rescinded or terminated.
- A non-preset-yield insurance refers to an insurance for which the insurance contract does not prescribe any investment yield rate. The insurer shall, upon the full performance of the insurance contract, or the rescission or termination thereof, pay to the insurance applicant or the insured the net sum of his/her investment in such product and the yield (or loss) payable on the utilization of such investment.

§2. Requirements of Offering Investment-Type Insurance

506. A property insurance company offering investment-type insurance shall meet the following requirements:

- the insurance company has been in operation for three consecutive full accounting years and it is profitable financially after offsetting its annual profits and losses in the past three accounting years;
- the company has a proper governance structure, well-developed internal governance rules and regulations, sound systems for business management, financial management, voucher and document management, computer and information management, cybersecurity, and information disclosure management, proper internal control framework and business operation procedures;
- the company is free from any administrative sanction or punishment for violation or offense in the past three years;

- the company is not under any investigation by competent regulation authorities in connection with any suspected violation or offense or undergoing rectification ordered by competent authorities;
- the solvency adequacy ratio of the company is above 150% for the past four consecutive quarters;
- the company has a separate management department for the utilization of insurance investments, well-developed fund utilization management rules and risk control systems; and
- other requirements as specified by the CBIRC.

507. The allowable quantity of investment-typed insurance offered by an insurance company is linked to the part of the solvency adequacy ratio of the company in excess of 150%. Such adequacy ratio excess shall be above the sum of 10% of the balance of the payable principle and interest of preset-yield products and 2.5% of the balance of the payable principle and interest of non-preset-yield products of the company.

Where the solvency adequacy ratio of the insurance company is lower than 50% at the end of the previous quarter, the insurance company shall promptly suspend the sale of investment-typed insurance and report such suspension and remedial measures to the CBIRC.

508. The sales volume of a specific investment-typed insurance may not exceed 30% of the total quantity of the investment-typed insurance offered by the insurance company. The total sales volume of all mature investment-typed insurance in a specific quarter of the year may not exceed 30% of the total quantity of the investment-typed insurance offered by the insurance company.

509. A property insurance company shall designate the period (indicating the starting and end time) and geographical scope of the sale of each type of its investment-typed insurance that it declares. Such period may not exceed two years as a general rule. Investment-typed insurance products may not be marketed in administrative divisions on or below the county level, with the exception of districts directly under the administration of cities.

510. A property insurance company may, according to the insurance responsibilities in connection with an investment-typed insurance product and the insured amount, appropriately identify the insurance premium rate, arrange relevant reinsurance matters and calculate and keep insurance liability reserve. Where insurance indemnity is due in connection with an investment-typed insurance product, the insurance company shall properly survey the insurance accident and assess the damages, and timely effect the payment of the insurance indemnity in accordance with the insurance terms and conditions.

§3. Contractual Terms of Investment-Type Insurance Contract

511. It is required by the regulatory authority that in developing investment-typed insurance products, a property insurance company shall properly coordinate its departments in charge of products, actuarial service, fund utilization, legal compliance, among others, so as to give full play to the roles of such departments. The terms and conditions of investment-typed insurance products declared by the property insurance company shall comply with the IL and applicable regulatory provisions of the CBIRC, and shall cover such matters as insurance responsibilities, exemption of responsibilities, insurance premiums, application for and payment of insurance indemnities.

512. The insurance terms and conditions of a preset-yield insurance shall include the method of identifying the yield rate of the product, the formula and method of calculating such yields, and the calculation and payment of yields upon the rescission or termination of the insurance contract, in addition to the matters in the above paragraph.

In addition to the matters included in the previous paragraph, the insurance terms and conditions of a non-preset-yield insurance shall include warning of the risks involved in the product, the method of calculating and disclosing the net asset value of the product, the purchasing cost of the product, the manager of the product, the collection and payment method of the service fee and custody fee payable to the product trustee, as well as the rate of such fees, the collection and payment methods of other fees and expenses related to the fund management and utilization of the product, the rate and calculation and collection method of the insurance premiums, the evaluation method of the fund accounts, the distribution principles of the yields on the product, the opening of individual accounts, the calculation method of the value of individual accounts and the procedure for the application and collection of the values of such individual accounts.

513. A property insurance company may, for the purpose of preventing and controlling risks, set the yield rate of a preset-yield product upon the maturity thereof in a prudent and appropriate manner.

The yield rate of a preset-yield insurance may not be one percentage point higher than the then-current bank interest rate on fixed-term deposits. The yield rate of a product with a maturity term of more than five years shall be calculated in light of the then-current bank interest rate on fixed-term deposit with a term of over five years. Furthermore, for the purpose of preventing risks and adapting to the development of the market, the CBIRC may set the maximum yield rates of the products declared by the insurance companies.

The insurance companies may not make any commitment to the insurance applicant or the insured on yields on non-preset-yield insurance, nor may it implicitly undertake to cover losses that the insurance applicant or the insured may suffer in connection with the non-preset-yield products.

§4. INSURER'S OBLIGATIONS AS TO THE MANAGEMENT OF INVESTMENT-TYPE INSURANCE BUSINESS

I. Examination and Approval of Investment-Type Insurance Business

514. Investment-typed insurance products shall be made and adjusted by the headquarters of insurance companies and reported to the CBIRC for examination and approval. When an insurance company reports an investment-typed insurance product to the CBIRC for examination and approval, it shall submit the following materials in addition to these required under the Administrative Measures for Insurance Clauses and Insurance Premium Rates of Property Insurance Companies:

- the clients' handbook;
- promotional materials;
- the proposed sales period and geographic areas; and
- an account of the cost of the product.

The cost account of a preset-yield insurance shall include: the insurance premium rates, the yield rate of the product upon the maturity thereof, as well as the ratio between such fees and expenses as the commission fee and management fee payable to the bank, as well as the breakeven point of the product deducted on the basis of the aforementioned factors.

The cost account of a preset-yield insurance product shall include:

- the classification, ratio and method of calculation and collection of insurance premium and management fee;
- overall business performance of the insurance company in the past three years;
- report on the sales of its investment-typed product(s), if any; and
- other materials as may be required by the CBIRC.

515. The client's handbook of a preset-yield insurance product shall include the following:

- a brief introduction to and main features of the product;
- insurance liability and insured amount;
- business processes and formalities, including reporting of insurance accident, claims, notification of the loss of the insurance contract, as well as the amendment, rescission or termination of the insurance contract;
- a profile of the property insurance company;
- customer service hotline number(s) and contact information of the insurance company;
- the calculation method and example of the yields on each insurance policy upon the expiration, rescission or termination of the insurance policy under different economic environment, especially in the case of unfavorable developments in the economic environment.

In addition to the information above, the client's handbook of a non-preset-yield insurance product shall also include the following:

- warning on the risks involved in the investment in the product as well as characteristics of such investment;
- investment object and scope;
- provisions concerning the disclosure of information on the fund account and individual account;
- application for the investment fund and individual account value; and
- other materials as may be required by the CBIRC.

The insurance company shall prepare a detailed and informative client's handbook and provide the same to the applicant or the insured along with the insurance policy.

Where the client's handbook includes information on the past performance of the insurance company, the insurance company shall make a special statement that its past performance is not necessarily indicative of its future performance; the performance of any other non-preset-yield product under the management of the company cannot be deemed as guarantee of the performance of the product.

II. Running of Investment-Type Insurance Business

516. A property insurance company shall, in accordance with applicable provisions of the CBIRC on financial and capital utilization, set up well-developed systems for the financial management, fund utilization and investment risk control in connection with its investment-typed insurance products, and set up a sound and professionalized investment management department and investment risk control department. Investment-typed insurance products shall be managed on the basis of separate accounts and financial accounting. Different types of investment-typed products shall be independent of each other in terms of accounts, and bookkeeping.

A property insurance company shall practice an asset custody system to the fund gained through investment-typed insurance products. Such asset custody system shall comply with applicable regulatory provisions of the CBIRC. The fund invested into investment-typed insurance products of a property insurance company that are sold via banks or in the form of direct sales shall be transferred to the special account of the headquarters of the insurance company within three working days.

The property insurance company shall open separate accounts for each type of non-preset-yield products, entrust properly qualified asset management companies to manage such products, and open a separate individual account for each applicant or insured.

Every working day, a property insurance company shall evaluate each fund account of its non-preset-yield products, calculate and collect relevant fees and expenses and timely transfer such fees and expenses, calculate the net investment yield and net asset value of such accounts.

In addition, on each working day, the property insurance company shall calculate the net asset value of each individual account, and timely disclose relevant investment information to the applicants and insured investing in non-preset-yield insurance products concerning their fund accounts and individual accounts. Furthermore, on each working day, the property insurance company shall disclose the net product value of its non-preset-yield products on the previous working day as well as the accrued net value thereof on its business premises, the business premises of its sales agencies and on the website of the insurance company.

The property insurance company shall, within twenty days after the end of each insurance policy year, send to the applicants or the insured the annual reports on their individual accounts, detailing such matters as the value of and movement of fund into and out of such accounts.

517. Where a non-preset-yield insurance product is under any of the following circumstances, a property insurance company concerned shall prepare an ad hoc report within two days after such circumstance arises and disclose the applicable of the following circumstances to the public:

- any change in the utilization strategy of the investment in such product;
- replacement of the manager and trustee of the fund invested in such product;
- deciding on matters concerning distribution of product yield;
- change in the rate and collection method of purchase or redemption fees; and
- any change in the calculation and collection rate and method of product management fee and custody fee.

The property insurance company shall, within fifteen days after the end of each quarter of the year, complete the quarterly report on its non-preset-yield products, which shall include a profile of the products, major financial indicators and performance in product net value, managers' report, investment portfolio report and information on changes in product shares. The financial data in the quarterly reports are not subject to auditing, except for where the CBIRC provides otherwise. Such unaudited financial data shall be indicated with the words "unaudited."

The property insurance company shall complete the formulation of the annual report on its non-preset-yield products prior to March 31 each year, which shall at least include the following: major reminders and product catalogue and profile, major financial indicators and product net value performances, information on product yield distribution, product managers' report, product trustees' report, auditing report, financial and accounting report, investment portfolio report, the number of product holders and makeup of such holders (the top ten holders), changes in product shares, disclosures on major issues and catalogue of reference documents, among others.

The ad hoc announcement, quarterly reports and annual reports on non-preset-yield products shall be released via at least one of the newspapers designated by the CBIRC for information disclosure.

518. A property insurance company shall establish a management system dedicated to the vouchers and other documents related to its investment-typed insurance products. The insurance policies of a property insurance company shall be printed by the headquarters of the insurance company according to a uniform format and shall be managed by specializing staff members and stored at proper place. The registration, issuance, use, cancelation upon verification and archiving of insurance policies shall be timely and accurate.

A property insurance company shall strengthen its comprehensive management of the clients of its investment-typed insurance products, establish a client information bank and fully use information of clients of the investment-typed insurance products in accordance with law. The insurance company shall bear the obligation of keeping confidential the information of the clients of its investment-typed insurance products, and may not transfer to any third party such information of the clients of its investment-typed insurance products.

519. A property insurance company may not entrust any entity that has not entered into a written sales agency agreement to sell its investment-typed insurance products. Where the property insurance company entrusts a bank to sell its investment-typed insurance products, it shall enter into a written sales agency agreement with the bank, in which the rate and payment method of the commission fee payable to the bank and other rights and obligations of both parties shall be specified. Where it entrusts a bank to sell its investment-typed insurance products, a property insurance company may not issue insurance policies unless and until it has verified the insurance information submitted by the sales agency and all payments have been made to the insurance company.

A property insurance company shall, prior to the end of the first month of each quarter of a year, consolidate all sales agency agreements that its headquarters sign in the previous quarter and report the same to the CBIRC for record-filing; the sales agency agreements signed by the branches of the insurance company shall be consolidated and reported to competent local insurance regulatory bureau for record-filing.

The rate of commission fee paid by the property insurance company to its sales agencies for its preset-yield insurance products may not exceed 0.8% in the case of products with a term of one year, or 0.5% in the case of products with a term of above one year.

520. Where a property insurance company directly sells its investment-typed insurance products, it shall form a team of marketing professionals, set up a management system for such team, and designate a department to train, assess and manage such marketing professionals.

Marketing personnel shall have proper professional ethical integrity, sufficient knowledge of the features of investment-typed insurance products and the business processes of the company, and be free of any records of malpractice such as violations of rules and regulations or fraud.

Where the property insurance company directly sells its investment-typed insurance products, it may not issue insurance policies against such products unless and until it has received the corresponding investment made in such products. Investment fund received outside the business premises of the insurance company shall be collected in the form of POS terminals or by bank transfer payments such as bank transfer checks instead of in cash.

521. A property insurance company shall set up an emergency response system and prepare settlement measures for the mass premature rescission or termination of insurance contracts on investment-typed insurance products.

Where on a working day, the balance of the amount refundable to the policyholders or the insured due to their application for the premature rescission or termination of the insurance contracts of a specific type of investment-typed insurance product and the income of the insurance company from such type of insurance product exceed 10% of the balance in the accounts of such type of products, this situation shall be deemed as mass premature rescission or termination of insurance contracts. In the case of a mass premature rescission or termination of insurance contracts, the property insurance company shall report to the CBIRC within two working days after such situation arises.

522. A property insurance company shall employ an independent accountant firm at the end of each year to audit the operational management and fund use of the investment-typed insurance products of the year. The audit report shall be submitted to the CBIRC by the end of April of the following year. The audit report shall include finance, portfolios and the calculation and allocation of investment yield and loss, calculation and provision of liability reserves and assessment of product management. Where it is necessary, the CBIRC may require the insurance company to employ an accounting firm to audit the operation and management of the investment-typed insurance products of the insurance company.

523. The property insurance companies offering investment-typed insurance products shall timely submit such documents and materials as the annual audit reports, sales agency agreement and statistics related to their investment-typed insurance products. Where a property insurance company fails to submit such documents and materials on time, it shall be punished in accordance with Article 171 of the IL.

Where the property insurance company compiles or submits any false report, statement, file or any other material, it shall be punished in accordance with Article 172 of the IL.

524. A property insurance company may not change its investment-typed insurance products or the geographical scope of the sales thereof without the approval by the CBIRC. During the sales of such products, the insurance company shall file their officially released client's handbooks and promotional materials to the CBIRC for the record. The form and contents of such client's handbooks and promotional materials shall be uniformly designed by the headquarters of the insurance company and may not be modified by any of its branches.

The property insurance companies shall strictly control the pricing risks of their investment-typed insurance products, pay close attention to the influence of changes in the economic and financial environment on the investment-typed insurance products, set up their respective emergence response system so as to effectively prevent and control such risks.

Part V. Basic Life Insurance

Chapter 1. Common Type Insurance

§1. Death Insurance

525. Death insurance contract is a kind of insurance contract which takes the insured's death as the condition for payment of insurance money. It can be further divided into term life insurance contract, the whole life insurance contract, the pure endowment insurance and the endowment insurance.

I. Term Life Insurance Contract

526. Term life insurance contract is an insurance policy which takes the insured's death as condition for payment of insurance money and the insurance period is a fixed period of time. Once the insured dies, the insurance money will be paid all at one time. If the insured is still alive after the expiration of the period of insurance, the insurer will not pay the insurance money and will not refund the premium paid by the applicant. Therefore, its premium is relatively lower than other life insurance.

527. Such insurance is generally taken out for those who are raised or supported by the applicant. In order to protect the personal safety of the personnel concerned, the IL makes restrictions on two aspects. One is the restriction on the scope of the insured. Article 33 of the IL provides that no insurance applicant shall take out any personal insurance in which insurance money shall be paid conditioned upon the death of the insured for a person without the civil conduct capacity, and no insurer shall underwrite such insurance. Of course, parents who take out personal insurance for their underage children shall not be subject to the preceding article. However, the total insurance money paid for the death of the insured shall not exceed the limit as prescribed by the insurance regulatory body under the State Council.

528. The other restriction is on the manner of insurance. Article 34(1) of the IL provides that where an insurance contract takes death as the condition for payment of insurance money, and the insured has not consented thereto and recognized the insured amount, the contract shall be null and void. But parents who take out personal insurance for their underage children shall not be subject to this article. Even Article 4 of the Notice of the CIRC on Regulating the Behavior of Life Insurance

Companies to Present Insurance also provides that if the life insurance presented takes death as the condition for payment of the insurance money, the insured's consent and recognition of the insured amount should be guaranteed. Besides, Article 34(2) of the IL provides that an insurance policy issued under a contract which takes death as the condition for payment of insurance money shall not be transferred or pledged without the written consent of the insured. The reason why the law makes such restriction is to prevent moral hazard.

529. The insured persons who are suitable for choosing term life insurance are mainly those who are engaged in relatively dangerous work in a short period of time and are in urgent need of protection, or those whose family is in poor financial condition, whose children are still young and whose family expenditure is mainly met by the economic income of the insured.

II. Whole Life Insurance

530. Whole life insurance contract is an insurance policy which takes the insured's death as condition for payment of insurance money and the insurance period is the insured's whole life. Under this contract, the insurer is responsible until the death of the insured. A distinctive feature of the whole life insurance contract is that the policy has cash value and it has a strong saving nature. Therefore, its premium is relatively higher than that of the term life insurance.

III. Pure Endowment Insurance Contract

531. Contrary to the death insurance contract, pure endowment insurance contract is a life insurance which takes the insured's survival within a certain period of time as the condition of payment of insurance money. If the insured dies within the insurance period, the insurance contract will be terminated and the premium paid by the applicant will not be returned. Pure endowment insurance is mainly to prevent the insured from living difficulties in the future, so that the elderly can enjoy their old age with this kind of insurance benefits, so most of the insured are the elderly.

IV. Endowment Insurance Contract

532. Endowment life insurance means that the insured shall be paid a certain amount of insurance money if he or she dies during a certain period of time after the contract becomes effective; if the insured still survives after the expiration of the period of insurance, the insurer shall also pay the agreed amount of insurance money.

533. In terms of the development of life insurance contract, it is a comprehensive life insurance contract on the basis of the development of both the death insurance contract and the pure endowment insurance contract insurance. It overcomes the disadvantage of the two kinds of insurance contract in satisfying the needs of dangerous groups. In pure endowment insurance contract, the applicant pays the premium in installments or in a lump sum, and the insurer pays the agreed insurance money to the beneficiary in installments or in a lump sum when the insured survives the agreed time limit or a certain age. However, if the insured dies before the expiration of the time limit, the insurance premium paid is in principle attributed to the insurer, and the insurer is not obliged to pay the insurance money and return the premium paid. For the insured who has died before the deadline, it can be said that both people and money are lost. In the pure life insurance contract (death insurance contract), the applicant pays the insurance premium in installments or in a lump sum to the insurer. When the insured dies, the insurer pays the agreed insurance money to the beneficiary or his/her inheritor. In the term life insurance contract, the insurer is not responsible for the payment of the insurance money if the insured still survives after the expiration of the term, which can be seen that though people are still alive they cannot obtain any benefit from the insurer to improve their lives.

In order to make up the abovementioned deficiency, the endowment life insurance contract has the opportunity to develop. No matter whether the insured dies during the duration of cover or still survives after the expiration of the period of insurance, the insurer has the obligation to pay the insurance amount. Therefore, in the case of death as an insurance accident, the endowment life insurance contract is designed to secure the livelihood of the beneficiary; in terms of survival as an insurance accident, it aims to save money to provide material security for the insured's later life. Whether the insured dies or survives, the insurer should pay the insurance money so as to satisfy the needs of people perfectly.

§2. Annuity Insurance

534. Annuity insurance is a kind of life insurance which takes the insured's survival as the condition for payment of insurance money. Under the annuity insurance contract, during the life of the insured, the insurer shall pay the insurance money to the insured regularly and termly within the agreed time limit according to the amount and manner agreed upon in the contract. Since such insurance usually pays a certain amount of money to the insured in an annual cycle, it is called annuity insurance. According to China's insurance practice, annuity insurance contracts can be divided into the following forms.

I. Pension Annuity Insurance Contract

535. The pension annuity insurance contract is a kind of life insurance contract aiming to provide security for the elderly. The conclusion of such a contract is subject to two conditions: first, the age agreed in the contract to pay the insurance money to the insured shall not be less than the age of the retirement specified by the state; second, the interval between two consecutive payments must not exceed one year.

II. Fixed-Benefit Annuity Insurance Contract

536. The fixed-benefit annuity insurance contract means that if the insured survives within the time limit agreed in the insurance contract, the insurer will pay the insurance money agreed according to the contract; if the insured dies within the agreed time limit or dies at the expiration of the period of insurance, the insurer will stop paying the insurance money.

III. Joint Annuity Insurance Contract

537. A joint annuity insurance contract is a life insurance contract where there are two or more insured and the annuity payment lasts until the last insured dies. Annuity insurance is an economic reserve for the insured who has a long life but lose the ability to work and then lose his income or exhaust his savings. If a person's life expectancy is the same as his estimated life expectancy, he would neither benefit nor suffer a loss from his annuity insurance. If his life expectancy exceeds the expectation, he will receive an additional payment. Under this insurance contract, the annuity paid by the insurer mainly comes from the insurance premium paid by the insured who has not lived to his life expectancy, so the annuity insurance is beneficial to the longevity.

IV. Variable Annuity Insurance Contract

538. The variable annuity insurance contract is an insurance contract which combines the characteristic of the annuity insurance and the variable insurance, and the cash value of the policy and the amount of the annuity payment change according to the investment performance. This kind of insurance is designed to cope with inflation and is an insurance product designed to secure the insured to maintain a stable purchasing power. Under this insurance contract, the insurance company will collect the premium paid by the insured into a special account which is mainly invested in publicly traded securities and the investment dividend will be distributed to the applicants, but the applicants have to bear the investment risk. The applicant, on the one hand, by purchasing such kind of insurance product, can obtain the guarantee; on the other hand, the high return can be obtained at the cost of high risk. In this sense, purchasing the variable annuity insurance is similar to investing in mutual fund.

V. Group Annuity Insurance Contract

539. A group annuity insurance contract is an annuity insurance contract concluded by a group and the insurer, and the premium is paid by the group and the insured jointly, or paid mainly by the group. Under such insurance contract, members of the group take the insurance certificate issued according to the insurance contract as the basis of receiving the annuity.

Chapter 2. Health Insurance

§1. Introduction

I. Definition

540. Health insurance means personal insurance in which the payment of insurance benefit is conditioned upon losses incurred for health reasons, including but not limited to disease insurance, medical insurance, disability income insurance, and health-care insurance. In fact, for a long time, most health insurance or disease insurance in China does not cover the disability or death caused by childbirth. Maternity insurance is usually included in social insurance. It is mainly operated as an additional type of health insurance in the commercial field.

541. Article 2(1) of the AMHI provides that the term of health insurance refers to the insurance whereby an insurance company pays insurance money for the losses caused by health reasons by means of sickness insurance, medical insurance, disability income insurance and care insurance, etc.

542. It can be considered that health insurance can guarantee not only the expenditure of corresponding medical expenses but also the expenditure of nursing expenses when disability is caused by illness or accidental injury, and even the living expenses of relatives when the insured dies from illness. Therefore, health insurance can also be said to be a comprehensive insurance. In insurance practice, sometimes it can also be used as an additional insurance of life insurance; that is, the applicant can add illness and childbirth liability when purchasing ordinary life insurance.

II. Classification of Health Insurance

543. According to the AMHI, health insurance can be divided into long-term health insurance and short-term health insurance according to the different insurance period. Long-term health insurance refers to the health insurance the insurance period of which is more than one year, or though less than one year contains a renewal warranty clause. The AMHI provides that life insurance companies and health insurance companies established legally may operate health insurance business after being approved by the CBIRC. Other insurance companies, approved by the CBIRC, may operate short-term health insurance business. According to the different conditions of paying insurance premium, health insurance can be divided into disease insurance, medical insurance, disability income insurance and care insurance.

544. Article 3(4) of the AMHI provides that the term of renewal warranty clause refers to the contractual stipulation that the insurance company must continue underwriting the insurance in accordance with the stipulated premium rate and original clauses after the insured submits the application of renewal upon the expiration of the preceding insurance period.

A. *Sickness Insurance*

545. Sickness insurance refers to the insurance that the occurrence of disease as stipulated in the insurance contract is the condition for payment of insurance premium. Whether it is physical disease or disease caused by an external bacterial infection, it needs to be brewed within the human body for a certain time, which is different from the accidental injury. Diseases usually have certain latency, which is different from the sudden and dramatic changes in accidental injuries. Generally speaking, health is the norm of life, so diseases in health insurance are limited to accidental occurrence. Therefore, the insured's aging and weakness caused by natural phenomena cannot be attributed to accidental reasons. This is different from whole life insurance.

B. *Medical Insurance*

546. Medical insurance takes the occurrence of medical behavior stipulated in the insurance contract as the condition of payment. The insurance money paid by the insurer generally includes hospitalization fee, examination fee, treatment fee, operation fee, nursing fee and medicine fee, etc. The ongoing reform of social medical system in China urges the need for commercial medical insurance. China's commercial medical insurance market is immature, the variety is too single, and there is great room for development in the future.

C. *Disability Income Insurance*

547. Disability income loss insurance includes not only the loss of workability caused by illness but also the loss of workability caused by accidental injury. It provides protection for the insured's income reduction or interruption within a certain period of time as agreed. The disability income insurance in China started very soon in insurance practice.

D. *Care Insurance*

548. Nursing needs are caused by dysfunction of daily living ability, but dysfunction of daily living ability may be caused by disease, accidental injury and natural aging. The AMHI does not take these factors into account, and does not make a distinction between medical insurance and nursing insurance. In this way, there may be many overlaps between health insurance and accident injury insurance in China. In other words, health insurance and accident injury insurance are compatible in terms of insurance payment conditions. It is undeniable that with the development of the universal two-child policy, the care insurance will become the focus of our society.

§2. Contents of the Health Insurance

I. Insurance Period

549. The insurance period of the health insurance is agreed by the applicant and the insurer. Generally, health insurance is a kind of short-term insurance whose insurance period is usually one year which starts at 0:00 from the commencement of the policy and ends at 24:00 on the expiring day. The insured and the insurer may also agree on the insurance period of more than one year. The modern health insurance shows a trend toward long-term insurance whose insurance period differs from five to ten years and even the whole life of the insured. In the case of life insurance plus health insurance, the insurance period of health insurance is the same as life insurance.

550. It should be noted that the health insurance has a "waiting period"; that is, the insurance contract stipulates that within a certain period (such as three months) from the date the applicant and the insurer enter into the insurance contract, the insurer does not assume any liability for the disease covered by the contract. The "waiting period" stipulated by the health insurance belongs to the period of insurance liability, but the insurer does not bear any responsibility for paying the insurance benefit within the "waiting period."

II. Liability

551. The insurer is responsible for the payment of insurance benefits for the insured's illness, childbirth, or disability or death due to illness and childbirth.

A. Disease

552. Disease refers to the physical and mental pain suffered by the insured due to his own body, or the defect on physical function. Disease is a health disorder. Health insurance covers diseases that are different from injuries which are caused by external reasons. The insurance contract may stipulate the scope or type of the "disease." If the contract has restrictions on the "disease," the insurer shall only assume the insurance liability arising from the "disease" stipulated in the insurance contract.

B. Childbirth

553. Childbirth refers to the phenomenon of women's production. Women should seek medical help when they are giving birth. Childbirth is not a disease. It is a physiological phenomenon of women's production. However, because childbirth can cause physical discomfort or suffering, and even can cause disability or death, health insurance takes it as a disease. The childbirth covered by health insurance is only limited to women and cannot be applied to men, so health insurance should clearly specify whether the scope of insurance coverage includes "birth-child," and take different premium rate according to the distinction between men and women, old and young.

C. Disability or Death Due to Illness or Childbirth

554. The insured's disability or death is due to illness or childbirth and is not caused by accidental injury. There are close relationships between the insured's disability or death and the risk of disease and childbirth covered by health insurance. Therefore, health insurance should provide coverage.

III. Exclusion

555. Health insurance covers the risk of disease or childbirth of the insured and the risk of disability or death caused by disease or childbirth, but not all the disease and the risk of disability or death caused by disease are insured by the insurer. Health insurance contract generally stipulates the liability exemption; that is, the insurer does not bear the obligation of insurance payment.

556. The liability exemptions of the health insurance contract can usually be classified into the following ones:

- an accident that has occurred at the time of the conclusion of the contract; for example, the insured is already sick or pregnant when entering into an insurance contract;
- the uncovered disease, such as the "disease" that the health insurance contract expressly stipulates that it does not bear the responsibility for payment and the insured's disability or death due to the disease;
- accidents caused by the insured intentionally, such as the insured's suicide or self-injury;
- accidents caused by abnormal medical treatment, such as disability or death caused by illegal abortion of the insured.

Chapter 3. Accidental Injury Insurance

§1. Introduction

I. Definition of the Accidental Injury Insurance

557. Accidental injury insurance means personal insurance in which the payment of insurance benefit is conditioned upon the occurrence of an accident resulting in the death or disability of the insured or the occurrence of any other accident as agreed upon in the insurance contract.

558. In accidental injury insurance, the insured's death or disability must be caused by accidental injury. If it is caused by illness, old age, childbirth, etc., the insurer will not be held responsible.

559. Accidental injury insurance is not directly related to human life. When formulating the insurance premium rates for accidental injury insurance, the life factors such as age and gender of the insured are usually not taken into consideration. And there is no restriction on the physical condition of the insurer. The nature of the occupation of the insured is the main factor in the calculation of the rate.

560. The items under accident insurance coverage are mainly basic insurance items and derivative insurance items. The basic insurance items include the following:

- Death benefit. When an accident causes the insured to die, the insurer pays the death benefit. There are two kinds of death that are legally effective: one is physical death, which is a confirmed death, the other is declared death, which is a death presumed in accordance with legal procedures.
- Disability benefit. The disability here includes two meanings: one is the permanent disability (or defect) of the human tissue, such as the limb separation, the other is the permanent loss of the normal function of the human organ, such as the loss of vision, hearing, smell, language function, etc. When an accident causes the insured to be physically disabled, the insurer pays disability benefit.

561. There are two main types of derivative insurance items: one is the funeral payment derived from death benefit and the living expenses for the survivor; the other is the medical payment and income loss payment derived from the disability payment.

II. Definition of Accidental Injury

562. Injury is the objective fact that an outside dangerous object destructively contacts with or acts on a person's body in some way. The causative, the injured object, and the fact of injury are the three elements that constitute the injury, and are indispensable. The causative is an object or substance that directly causes harm to a victim. It can be physical, chemical or biological. The injured object refers to the object harmed by the causative, that is the damage to a certain part or several certain parts of the human body, which can destruct the physical function of the human being rather than damage on psychology or on people's rights. The fact of injury refers to the objective fact that the destructive material contacts with or acts on the human body, which usually includes injury caused by burn, explosion, collision, fall, collapse, burial, overturning, electric shock, acute poisoning, radiation, etc.

563. The coverage of the accidental injury insurance does not include all kinds of injury, but casualties caused by accidental injuries. Accidental injury should consist of the following three elements: first, accidental injury is unintentional; that is, the accident is not the result of the will of the person. The victim is unintentional and cannot foresee the result of the accident and the result has violated the subjective wishes of the victim. For example, a pedestrian is injured by a flying object; the worker is accidentally electrocuted to death during the operation. Second, it is foreign; that is, the injury is caused by reasons other than the victim himself, not by the insured's own reasons. If the insured is killed or disabled due to illness, it is not an accidental injury. Finally, it is sudden; that is, the cause of the injury is sudden, rather than long-standing or long-term, and the victims are not able to prevent it when they are at risk.

§2. Classification of Accidental Injury Insurance

I. Classification by Subject-Matter

564. According to the subject matter of insurance, accidental injury insurance can be divided into two types: group accidental injury insurance and individual accidental injury insurance.

A. Group Accidental Injury Insurance

565. Group accidental injury insurance is the most important type of accidental injury insurance. It has the following characteristics:

> First, the applicant and the insured are not the same one. The applicant is an organization, and the insured is a member of the organization, such as school students, corporate employees, etc.
> Second, the insured's death is the condition for the payment of insurance benefit. Therefore, when the insurance contract is concluded, the applicant should ensure that the insured has consented and recognized the insured amount.
> Third, there is generally no upper limit for the sum insured, but there is the minimum sum.

Fourth, the insurance premium rate is low. Because the applicant is the organization, the insurer's management cost is reduced; as a consequence, the premium rate should also be reduced.
Fifth, usually, the insurance premium is paid-in insurance. The premium should be paid in a lump sum at the beginning, and the policy will be valid after the insurance premium is paid.

B. Individual Accidental Injury Insurance

566. Individual accidental injury insurance only provides coverage for one person. Motor vehicle driver and passenger accidental injury insurance, aviation accidental injury insurance, passenger accidental injury insurance and travel accidental injury insurance are the main types of individual accidental injury insurance.
It has the following four characteristics:

(1) most of them are voluntary insurance, but some are compulsory insurance;
(2) the insurance period of most insurance types is shorter;
(3) the underwriting conditions are relatively loose, and generally, there is no qualification of the insured. Anyone who is in good health and can work normally can be the subject of this kind of insurance;
(4) the insurance premium rate is low, and the coverage is relatively wide.

II. Classification by Implementation

A. Voluntary Accidental Injury Insurance

567. Voluntary accidental injury insurance is a variety of accidental injury insurance that the applicant chooses based upon his/her will and needs. For example, the safety insurance for primary and secondary school students and the accidental injury insurance for residential tourists in China are among the types of this insurance. Base on the parents' and passengers' consent, the insurance premium is collected by the school or hotel and then submitted to the insurance company.

B. Compulsory Accidental Injury Insurance

568. Compulsory accidental injury insurance is an accidental injury insurance that is stipulated by the government. For example, the Regulations on Compulsory Accidental Injury Insurance for Railway Passenger, the Regulations on Compulsory Accidental Injury Insurance for Ship Passenger and the Regulations on Compulsory Accidental Injury Insurance for Airplane Passenger issued by the Chinese government as early as 1951 stipulate that: where trains, ships and aircraft are taken in the country, passengers must pay the premium in term of the rules. The insurance benefit shall be paid by the PICC in accordance with the provisions of the above three regulations in the event of an accident.

III. Classification by Insurable Risk

A. *General Accident Insurance*

569. General accidental injury insurance covers various accidental injuries caused by ordinary risks. The insurance procedure is relatively simple. The insurance company prepares the terms in advance, and the insured only needs to make a decision of "yes" or "no." In practice, many specific types of insurance are such kind of insurance, such as the group accidental injury insurance and personal safety insurance currently existing in China.

B. *Special Accidental Injury Insurance*

570. Special accidental injury insurance covers accidental injury events that occur or are caused at specific times, locations, or specific reason. Because of the "three specifics," compared with general accidental injury insurance, the probability of insurable risk is greater, so it is called special accidental injury insurance, for example accidental injuries in swimming pools or playgrounds, in intense sports competitions or activities such as river rafting, mountain climbing, and skiing. In practice, most of them are taken by the applicant and the insurer based on mutual consent.

IV. Classification by Structure of Insurance

A. *Pure Accidental Injury Insurance*

571. The liability for pure accidental injury insurance is limited to accidental injuries. The group accidental injury insurance, road passenger accidental injury insurance, students' accidental injury insurance, driver accidental injury insurance, etc., which are currently operated in China, are all pure accidental injury insurance.

B. *Additional Accidental Injury Insurance*

572. Additional accidental injury insurance covers two situations: one is other insurance plus accidental injury insurance, and the other is accidental injury insurance with additional other kinds of insurance. For example, the life insurance currently operated in China is the basic insurance conditioned on the survival of the insured at the expiration of the insurance period or death within the insurance period, which can be added the accidental injury insurance that covering the disability of the insured by accidental injury. Another example is the accidental injury insurance for residential passengers. The insurance liability includes the death and disability caused by accidental injuries and the loss of passengers' carry-on luggage, which is the accidental injury insurance plus property insurance.

§3. Content of the Accidental Injury Insurance

I. Sum Insured

573. The calculation of the sum insured of the accidental injury insurance is the same as life insurance. Since the life and body of human being cannot be measured by money, the insured determine the sum insured according to his needs of protection and economic ability.

II. Calculation of the Premium Rate

574. The premium rate of the accidental injury insurance is based on the loss rate rather than the death rate and interest rate. When calculating the rate, in general, the insurer will not consider the age and gender of the insured. This is because the risk faced by the insured is closely related to the occupation, type of work or activities he takes part in. There is no great difference in the probability of the insureds if they are different in age and gender. Under the same conditions, the higher the risk of the insured's occupation, job type or activity, the more insurance premiums should be paid. Therefore, the underwriting conditions for accidental injuries are loose, the elderly can be insured, and the insured do not need to have a physical examination.

III. Liability

575. The insurance liability for accidental injury insurance overlaps the term insurance liability in life insurance. Both are responsible for deaths caused by accidental injuries; however, accidental injury insurance is not responsible for deaths caused by non-accidental injuries such as diseases which are insured by the term insurance. For disability caused by accidental injuries, accidental injury insurance will cover, but the term insurance will not.

In addition, there are three requirements of the insurance liability for accidental injury insurance:

(1) the insured suffers accidental injury within the insurance period;
(2) the insured dies or is disabled within the liability period;
(3) the accidental injury suffered by the insured is the direct or proximate cause of death or disability.

IV. Period of Insurance

576. The duration of the accidental injury insurance is relatively shorter and is inconsistent with the liability period which is generally one year, and the insurance period for some very short-term accidental injury insurance is usually only a few days or a few hours. However, the period of liability does not end with the end of the insurance period.

The period of liability is a concept specific to accidental injury insurance, which refers to a certain period starting from the date of the insured's accidental injury, usually 90 days, 180 days, 360 days or 13 weeks, 26 weeks, 52 weeks. Accidental injury insurance emphasizes that the insured's death or disability after injury must occur within the liability period. As long as the accidental injury suffered by the insured occurs within the duration of the insurance, and the consequences of death and disability are caused within a certain period of time from the date of the accidental injury, the insurer shall bear the obligation to pay the insurance benefit, including the medical expenses and income loss.

V. Compensation

577. In accidental injury insurance, the method of fixed compensation shall be used, which means the insurer will pay the insurance benefit according to the amount agreed in the insurance contract, regardless of the actual loss of the insured. Generally, the insured amount of death and disability are listed in the contract separately. When the insured dies due to accidental injury, the death benefit will be paid totally and the policy is terminated at the same time. When the insured is disabled due to accidental injury, the disability benefit will be paid proportionally according to the degree of disability, but the total amount of compensation does not exceed the sum insured. When the insured suffers accidental injury more than one time within the insurance period, the insurer will pay the insurance benefit according to the insurance contract for the disability or death caused by each accidental injury, but the total amount of the payment does not exceed the sum insured.

VI. Exclusions

578. If the injury suffered by the insured belongs to the liability exemptions as stipulated in the accidental injury insurance contract, the insurer shall not bear the insurance liability.

The exclusions of the accidental injury insurance generally include the following situations:

- the disability or death is caused by the insured's intentional suicide, self-injury or criminal acts;
- the injuries are caused by the insured's unnecessary risk-taking behavior;

- the insured has a disease, or the insured is disabled or dead because of the disease, unless the injury insurance covers the risk of disability or death caused by disease;
- the insured is disabled or killed because of war or military action;
- medical expenses incurred by accidental injury, unless the injury insurance covers the risk of medical payment.

Chapter 4. Participating Insurance

§1. INTRODUCTION

I. Definition

579. Participating insurance contract refers to a new type of life insurance in which the policyholder can also share the insurer's operating surplus on a regular basis, in addition to the fixed insurance benefit. The policyholder here refers to the person who enjoys the benefits of the insurance product and the right to share the dividend in accordance with the participating insurance contract. There must be a separate account for the participating insurance and the account is settled independently. This kind of insurance product can give the policyholders a chance to enjoy the results of the insurer's operation, so it is warmly welcomed as soon as it enters into the insurance market.

II. Characteristics

580. Policyholders share dividends at a fixed rate. According to the participating insurance contract, the insured cannot only obtain various guarantees of the contract, which means in the event of an insurance accident, the insurer should bear the liability for compensation, but also can share part of the surplus generated by the participating insurance business operated by the insurer in the form of dividends every year. The dividend that the insurer allocates to the customer each year is not arbitrary, but is clearly stipulated by the insurance regulatory authority. At present, the insurance company should allocate at least 70% of the annual distributable surplus to the customer as a dividend every year to ensure that the customer has the right to share the operating results of the insurance company.

581. Dividend insurance contract has certain risks. No insurance company in the world can promise that its annual business operations can keep profitable, nor can it promise that the annual operating surplus can be maintained at a high level. The operating status of an insurance company is affected by various factors such as the social and economic environment, its own business philosophy, risk estimating level, cost and expenditure status, and investment income. In the year when the insurance company is in good operating condition, the customer can get more dividends; but in the year of poor conditions, the dividends received by customers are correspondingly reduced and may be zero. Therefore, dividend insurance is not an investment means of no risk. The client himself has to bear some risks. When entering into an insurance contract, the insurer is obliged to clearly explain this to the client. The client should also think twice and be cautious.

582. The insurance benefit of the participating insurance contract includes dividend. The difference between a participating insurance contract and an ordinary life insurance contract is that when the insured dies, the insurer only pays the beneficiary the death benefit agreed upon in the contract, and when the insured lives to a certain age or time limit, the insurer only pays the insured the survival benefit or annuity stipulated in the contract. The insurer of the participating insurance contract shall pay the abovementioned insurance benefit to the beneficiary, and shall also pay the cumulative dividends and interest that have not yet been received. When the policyholder of the dividend insurance contract applies for surrender, the insurer shall also refund the cumulative dividend and interest.

III. Principle of Dividend Distribution

583. Dividend distribution is distributing the surplus of the dividend accounts to policyholders. Normally, the insurer will not allocate all the surplus, but decide how much of the total surplus should continue to be retained at the end of each year, and how much should be allocated to policyholders. Part of the surplus allocated to policyholders is called the current distributable surplus. In order to protect the rights of the insured and the insurer, the insurance regulatory authority of each country clearly stipulates the dividend ratio of the participating insurance. The CBIRC also clearly stipulates that life insurance companies must allocate at least 70% of the distributable surplus of the current year to the customers. In addition to the dividend ratio, there are three principles of dividend distribution needed to be followed.

A. Principle of Efficiency

584. The principle of efficiency requires that the surplus distribution should take into account the interests of both the policyholder and the insurer. It should pay attention to the reasonable expectation of the policyholders, arose the enthusiasm of the policyholders to insure, and consider the impact of the dividend distribution on the future dividend level, investment strategy and the solvency of the insurance company in the future.

B. Principle of Fairness

585. The principle of fairness must run through the entire insurance period, with a fair distribution of surplus between different types of policies and different policyholders. The insurer must adhere to the principle of good faith, distinguish the participating insurance account from other insurance accounts, and allocate the surplus based on the contribution of each policy to the surplus. The greater the contribution, the more dividends are distributed.

C. Principle of Simplicity

586. The principle of simplicity requires that the insurance company's dividend distribution policy should have a certain continuity, with a relatively moderate level throughout the entire policy period. The way dividends are distributed should be simple and easy, so that the applicant can better understand.

§2. CONTENTS OF THE PARTICIPATING INSURANCE

I. Source of the Dividend

587. The dividends of the participating insurance are mainly derived from the difference between the predetermined interest rate, the predetermined mortality rate and the predetermined expense rate assumed in the policy pricing, and the actual rate of return on investment, the actual mortality rate and the actual expense rate, which is commonly referred to as the mortality margin, interest margin and expense margin.

A. Mortality Margin

588. The mortality margin is the benefit of a surplus derived from the difference between the pure premium received at the predetermined mortality rate and the actual mortality cost when the actual mortality rate is lower than the predetermined mortality rate.

Death benefit = (predetermined mortality rate – actual mortality rate) × risk insured amount.

The risk insured amount is the balance of the insured amount minus the liability reserve. In a life insurance policy, such as the whole life insurance and the endowment insurance, the liability reserve increases with the increase of the insurance period. Therefore, the risk insured amount decreases with the increase of the insurance period, and approaches zero at the expiration of the period. Therefore, the mortality margin has a decreasing trend in each insurance period, and is zero at maturity. Insurance companies use the "experience life table" in insurance pricing. Whether it is the experience life table issued by the state or the life table compiled by the insurance company according to its practice, the conservative principle is adopted, so that the insurance company actually bears less compensation than assumed, which results in a mortality margin. Therefore, in general, insurance companies can obtain a more stable mortality margin.

B. Expense Margin

589. The expense margin is the benefit derived from the actual operating expense rate being lower than the expected operating expense rate.

Expense margin = (predetermined expense rate – actual expense rate) × insurance premium.

In the initial stage of the insurance, insurance companies have to pay a large amount of fees, such as agent commission, medical examination fees, publicity expenses, and the cost of printing insurance certificates and so on, which will result in an expense loss, but the insurance company will optimize management, streamline the process, improve the economic efficiency and other methods to control the cost, so that the actual cost is less than expected, resulting in an expense margin.

C. *Interest Margin*

590. The interest margin is the benefit derived from the actual rate of return on investment being higher than the predetermined interest rate.

Profit margin = (actual rate of return on investment – predetermined interest rate) × liability reserve

In order to ensure the long-term effectiveness of the life insurance policy, the actuary sets a predetermined interest rate in term of insurance regulations, company policies and experience at the time of calculating the premium rate. The conservative principle is also adopted when determining the predetermined interest rate; that is, if the actual rate of return on investment is greater than the predetermined interest rate, the interest margin is generated.

II. Dividend Distribution

A. *Distributing Objects*

591. Different participating insurances have different dividend distribution objects. In general, the dividends of the individual participating insurance are distributed to the policyholders; the dividends of the group annuity insurance are separately sent to the group payment portion and the individual payment portion of the insured's personal account. In practice, there is also group dividend insurance that is fully paid by the enterprise and the dividends are distributed to the enterprise totally which is agreed in the policy. It should be noted that the policyholder can submit a written request to the insurer within a certain period before the end of the fiscal year to ask for the dividends generated by the group payment portion of the current fiscal year.

B. *Distributing Date*

592. According to the nature of different participating insurance, the insurer makes different provisions on the distributing date of the dividend. Some participating insurance clause stipulates that the dividends are accounted in the fiscal year and are distributed on the day which is corresponding to the day when the policy is valid. Some stipulate that the dividends are accounted and distributed on the fiscal year, but the date of distribution has no relationship with the attachment day. And some stipulate that the dividends are accounted in the fiscal year, but they are not distributed year by year. The dividends of the previous years are respectively accumulated in the form of compound interest from the attachment day and then the insurer pays all the dividends to the policyholder in a lump sum at the termination of the insurance contract. If the dividend is not distributed on time at the distributing day, the insurance company shall pay the interest from the original date of distribution to the actual date of distribution.

III. Mode of Dividend Distribution

593. There are two modes to distribute the dividends: one is the reversionary dividend, and the other is the cash dividend. After the end of each fiscal year, the insurance company will allocate the distributable surplus in the previous fiscal year to the policyholders in a certain proportion by means of reversionary dividend or cash dividend.

A. Reversionary Dividend

594. Reversionary dividend, also known as "British dividend," refers to the dividends that are distributed each year in the form of increasing the insured amount throughout the insurance period. The policyholder can only draw the dividends at maturity.

This mode is composed of three parts: annual dividend, special reversionary dividend and terminal dividend. The annual dividend means that the dividends are added to the insurance amount in a certain proportion by the compound interest method each year. The special reversionary dividend means that the dividends are added to the insurance amount at one time in some special cases, such as the change of the government tax policy. The terminal dividend is generally a certain proportion of the distributed dividends or the total insured amount, and the surplus generated during part of the policy period is deferred to the end of the policy period for distribution, which reduces the uncertainty of the source of dividends during the policy period, and stabilizes the annual dividend level.

The reversionary dividend gives insurance companies the flexibility to smooth the dividend distribution, maintain a stable annual dividend, and make ultimate adjustment with a terminal dividend. Since there is no cash dividend outflow and the dividend distribution is deferred, insurance company's investable assets are increased, so that they can increase the proportion of investment in long-term assets, thereby increasing the return on investment and the dividend income of policyholders.

The only way for the policyholder to choose the dividend is to increase the insured amount of the policy, and the policyholder has less flexibility in choosing a dividend. Under the reversionary dividend, after the insurance company distributes the dividend to the policyholder, they will balance the dividend of the current year with the terminal dividend, and increase the stability of the dividend level. Because there are two kinds of dividend—reversionary dividend and terminal dividend—it is not easy for policyholders to understand the meaning and relationship between the two.

B. Cash Dividend

595. The cash dividend, also known as "American dividend," means that the insurer distributes the surplus directly to the policyholders by cash. The dividend distribution between policies varies with product, age of the insured, gender, and policy period, which reflects the contribution rate of policyholders to the participating accounts. The principle of contribution to the distribution of surplus under the cash dividend reflects the principle of fairness in dividend distribution among different policyholders. The cash dividend is commonly used by insurance companies in North America. At present, most domestic insurance companies in China use this approach.

For policyholders, cash dividends are more controllable and can be transferred at any time to meet a variety of needs. For insurance companies, the cash dividends increase the company's cash flow expenses while reducing the liabilities at the same time and thus reducing the pressure on insurance companies to pay.

The cash dividend is more transparent. The insurance company has to allocate most of the surplus under market pressure to maintain a high dividend rate to attract policyholders. This part of the assets cannot be effectively utilized, so the investable assets of insurance companies are decreased. In addition, the annual dividends will exert a greater pressure on the cash flow of insurance companies. To ensure the liquidity of assets, insurance companies will reduce the proportion of investment in long-term assets, which affects the total investment income to a certain extent. Therefore, policyholders will finally get a lower dividend.

IV. Mode of Drawing

596. Cash dividends are collected in the form of cash dividend option, dividend accumulation, premium reduction dividend option, and paid-up additional insurance dividend option.

A. Cash Dividend Option

597. Cash dividend option means that the policyholder will receive the dividend in cash. It is the most popular and most used dividend option, and also the easiest and most direct way to receive dividends. Most dividend insurance products on the market currently offer this dividend option.

B. Dividend Accumulation Option

598. Dividend accumulation option means that the dividends are kept in insurance companies and earn interest by means of compound interest according to the company's annual dividend accumulation interest rate. Then the dividends are paid at the termination of the contract or when the policyholders apply. There are two specific ways: first, after the dividend is distributed, the dividends are accumulated according to the dividend accumulation interest rate announced by the insurance company; second, dividends are accumulated at the agreed dividend accumulation interest rate when insured.

C. Premium Reduction Dividend Option

599. Premium reduction dividend option refers to the way in which policyholders choose to pay premiums for renewals. Compared with the payment of the insurance premium after the receipt of the cash dividend, this option simplifies the procedure of receiving the insurance premium and paying the renewal. If there are remaining after the premium is paid, policyholder can choose other dividend option.

D. Paid-Up Additional Insurance Dividend Option

600. Paid-up additional insurance dividend option refers to the way in which the insurance company takes the annual dividend as the insurance premium to purchase the same insurance as the original one. This option is similar to the traditional life insurance with increased insured amount. The difference is that the increasing range of the insured amount changes with the change of the dividend, so it is not fixed. At present, not all participating insurances in China provide this option. It should be noted that the liability of the paid-up additional insurance is the same as the original policy.

Chapter 5. Universal Life Insurance

§1. INTRODUCTION

I. Definition

601. Universal insurance is a life insurance product that has the protection function of insurance and set up separate policy accounts. Universal insurance has both insurance and savings investment functions. In terms of investment income, it provides the lowest return guarantee for the policy accounts. The so-called universal of universal life insurance does not mean that the product can meet all the people's needs in protection and income expectation, but means that it allows the adjustment on the insured amount, insurance premium and payment period according to the protection needs and financial status of different stages of life. Therefore, the applicant can choose a moderate ratio of protection and investment.

II. The Operating Mechanism of Universal Life Insurance

602. Since the universal insurance has both the protection and investment functions, each premium paid by the policyholder enters into the universal account after deducting the initial fee, and then calculates the death risk premium (protection cost) according to the age, sex and net amount at risk. And the death risk premium is deducted at the beginning of each period (usually one month as a cycle). The death risk premium is used to purchase the corresponding personal security, usually with a natural rate. After the initial fee, death risk premium and other expenses (such as policy management fee) are deducted, the remaining premium forms the account value, and then is operated by the insurance company in investment.

603. The beginning-of-period value of the insurance policy account bears interest at the new investment rate and is accumulated to the end, becoming the end-of-period value of the insurance policy account. In the second cycle of the policy, policyholders can pay premiums based on their own circumstances. If the first premium is sufficient to cover the fee of the second cycle and the death risk premium, the policyholders need not pay the premium during the second cycle. If the value of the previous account is not enough, the policy will be invalid due to insufficient premium payment. The second premium paid by the policyholder will enter into the universal account after deducting the initial fee. The death risk premium and fee of the current period will also be deducted from the balance of the previous period's account value and the current premium. The balance is the value of the account at the beginning of the second cycle. This part of the balance is accrued to the end of the period by the new investment rate and becomes the balance of the account value at the ending of the second cycle. This process is repeated, and once the balance in the policy account is not enough for payment of the current risk premium and other fees, and there is no new premium payment, the policy will be invalid.

604. Policyholders can also pay additional premiums or draw the account value partially as needed. The additional insurance premium will participate in the above account operation after deducting the initial fee, and the insurance company can charge a service fee at a certain percentage when the policyholders draw part of the account value. If the policyholder surrenders in the middle, the insurance company may refund the remaining portion (the cash value) after deducting the surrender fee according to a certain percentage of the account value.

III. Characteristics

A. High Transparency

605. The Measures for the Administration of the Disclosure of Information on New-Type Personal Insurance Products issued by the CBIRC provide that information on universal life insurance may be disclosed in forms including but not limited to:

– explanations and introductions on media or company websites;
– explanations and introductions at product presentation meetings;
– explanations and introductions by salespersons;
– follow-ups by customer service staff; and
– reports and materials sent on a regular basis.

606. The policy benefits of universal life insurance at the end of a year shall be illustrated in tables, which shall, at a minimum, include:

– premiums paid regularly or in a lump sum, top-up premiums, and accumulative premiums;
– charges, among which the initial charges, policy overhead, risk premium, and other major charges shall be listed item by item;
– the value in the universal life insurance policy account; and
– balance of the policy account, death benefit, and cash value of the insurance policy at the end of a year under different assumed crediting interest rates.

607. An insurance company shall, once a month at a minimum, publish the daily crediting interest rate and the annualized crediting interest rate of the month on its website and shall agree in an insurance contract that one policy status report at a minimum shall be provided to the insurance applicant every year.

B. Flexible Function

608. The flexibility of universal insurance is mainly reflected in the following three aspects.

First, the payment is flexible. As long as the policy account value is sufficient to cover the cost of protection and various fees stipulated by the insurance company, the applicant can arrange the time and amount of payment according to his financial situation. Even if the renewal premium is not paid temporarily, the policy will not be void. At the same time, the applicant can also pay additional premiums based on his investment needs. Normally, the insurance company will set a minimum and maximum limit on the premiums paid.

Second, the amount of insurance premium can be adjusted. Within the scope stipulated by the insurance company, the basic insurance amount of the universal life insurance can be adjusted according to the insurance needs of the insured at different life stages under the premise of the unchanged premium paid, so as to meet the demand for protection and investment at all stages of life.

Third, the drawing of the policy account value is convenient. The applicant may draw part of the value of the policy account from time to time as a child's education fund, marriage fund, venture capital, medical reserve or pension reserve for himself or other members of the family. Insurance companies generally only limit the minimum amount of a single drawing and the minimum amount of the remaining policy account value, and there is no provision for the number of drawing.

C. Minimum Guaranteed Interest

609. The insurance company provides a minimum guaranteed interest rate for the universal life insurance policy, and the applicant can share the return on investment with the insurance company above the minimum guaranteed interest. When the actual rate of return of the account is lower than the minimum guaranteed interest rate, the settlement rate of the universal life insurance shall be the minimum guaranteed interest rate. The Notice of the CIRC on Relevant Matters concerning the Policy Reform of Premium Rates of Ordinary Personal Insurance stipulates that the minimum guaranteed interest rate for universal life insurance shall not be higher than 2.5%. The minimum guaranteed interest rates set by insurance companies are not the same, and the final return depends on the level of capital utilization and comprehensive management capabilities. It is worth noting that the minimum guaranteed interest rate of the universal life insurance is only for the funds in the investment account, and not for all the insurance premiums.

§2. Products of Universal Insurance

I. Universal Insurance Policy Account

610. The insurance company should set up a universal insurance policy account for universal life insurance. The policy account can be a separate account or part of the company's ordinary account. It can provide information such as asset value, account value and settlement interest, and meet the insurance company's requirements for management and interest rate settlement of the policy account.

First, the policy of universal life insurance should provide a minimum guaranteed interest rate, which must not be negative. When the actual rate of return on investment of the policy account is lower than the minimum guaranteed interest rate, the insurance company shall settle on the minimum guaranteed interest rate. In general, the insurance company shall not promise a fixed minimum guaranteed interest rate throughout the insurance period, but will stipulate the applicable period of the minimum guaranteed interest rate. The existence of the minimum guaranteed interest rate limits the asset allocation of the insurance company to a certain extent, thus affecting the potential return level of the product. *The Interim Measures for the Administration of the Utilization of Insurance Funds* issued by the CBIRC provide that the utilization of insurance funds shall be limited to the following forms:

- making bank deposits;
- purchasing and selling negotiable securities, including bonds, stocks, shares of securities investment funds, etc.;
- investing in the real estate; and
- other fund utilization forms as prescribed by the State Council.

Second, the insurance company should set up a smooth reserve for the policy account to smooth the settlement rate for different settlement periods. The smooth reserve cannot be negative and can only be derived from the accumulation of the difference between the actual return on investment and the settlement interest. When the actual return on investment is less than the minimum guaranteed interest rate, the insurance company can make up the difference by reducing the smooth reserve; when it cannot be replenished, the insurance company should make up the difference by adding capital into the policy account. In other cases, the insurance company cannot add capital to the policy account in any form. The assets of the policy account cannot be less than liabilities.

Finally, the insurance company can use different settlement rates and different minimum guaranteed interest rates for the following different situations in the policy account: (1) different universal life insurance products; (2) different groups of universal life insurance customers; (3) different time for sale of universal life insurance products.

If different settlement rates or different minimum guaranteed rates are used, the insurance company shall establish a corresponding sub-policy account. When the insurance company adopts different settlement rates or different minimum guaranteed rates in the same policy account, the corresponding operation method should be complete and reasonable and obey the principles of fairness and consistency.

II. Liability

611. As a new type of life insurance, universal life insurance mainly provides death insurance liability. In addition, it can also attach major diseases, accidental injuries, hospitalization, premium exemption and other liabilities.

III. Insured Amount

A. Calculation of the Insured Amount

612. There are two modes to calculate the death benefit. In mode A, the death benefit is fixed, and the death risk insurance amount is adjusted every period, so that the sum of the death risk insurance amount and the investment account value becomes a balanced death benefit. Thus, if the value of the account increases, the death risk insurance amount will be reduced in equal amounts. Conversely, if the value of the account is reduced, the death risk insurance amount will increase in equal amount. The death risk insurance amount is equal to the death benefit minus the investment account value. This approach is similar to other traditional policies with cash value payments.

In mode B, the death benefit is defined as the sum of the death risk insurance amount and the account value. Thus, if the value of the account is increased, the death benefit will increase in equal amount; if the value of the account is reduced, the death benefit will decrease in equal amount. In this way, the death benefit provided by the insurance company is equal to the sum of the insurance amount and the investment account value at any time.

In mode A, in order to avoid exceeding the prescribed insured amount due to the high value of the account, some insurance companies have set a minimum death risk insurance amount, thereby increasing the total death benefit. According to the stipulation of the CBIRC, the personal death risk insurance amount of the individual universal life insurance at the time of issuance of the policy shall not be less than 5% of the account value, and the death risk insurance amount of the universal life insurance with the annuity option and the group universal life insurance can be zero.

B. Calculation of the Survival Benefit

613. For the survival insurance liability, the insurance company generally pays the policy account value. For example, a certain universal life insurance clause stipulates: "If the insured survives until the insurance period expires, the insurer will pay the full survival benefit in terms of the policy account value at maturity and then the contract is terminated."

C. Adjustment of the Insured Amount

614. During the validity of the universal life insurance policy, the applicant can apply for increasing or decreasing the agreed insured amount according to the different needs of the various stages of life. After the insurance company has approved the application, the increased or decreased insured amount comes into effect from the next settlement date. The insurance company generally stipulates the upper and lower limits of the adjustment of the insured amount, and the applicant can make adjustments within the interval.

Generally, for the increased or decreased insured amount, insurance companies will stipulate some restrictions. For example, some insurance companies require that the applicant may apply for increasing or decreasing the insured amount one year after the contract comes into effect, and can only adjust once a year.

It is important to note that after the change in the insured amount, the risk premium will change accordingly. If the insured commits suicide within two years from the effective date of the new insured amount, the insurance company will not assume the obligation to pay the increased insured amount.

IV. Premium Payment

615. The applicant of universal life insurance can pay the premium flexibly. Insurance companies usually stipulate the maximum and minimum limits for each payment, and the insured can pay premium at any time and there is no special requirement on the amount. Most insurance companies only require that the first premium must be enough to cover the fee of the first month and the death risk premium, but in fact most of the applicants pay the first premium far higher than the minimum amount specified. Since the universal life insurance policy cannot force the insured to pay the fixed premium, the insurance companies usually send a premium reminder to the applicants according to the target premium selected by the policy plan to remind them of the payment.

616. From the mode of payment, the premium payment of universal life insurance is divided into two types: payment on a regular basis and payment in a lump sum, which can be chosen freely by the applicant when insured. In the mode of payment in a lump sum, the applicant can also pay additional premium as needed. In the mode of payment on a regular basis, the premium can usually be divided into basic premium and additional premium. The applicant can also pay top-up premium as needed. The above three kinds of premium will enter into the investment account after deducting the initial charges and are used to accumulate the value of the policy account. The mode of payment on a regular basis includes payment annually, semi-annually, quarterly and monthly.

A. Basic Premium and Additional Premium

617. The basic premium and the additional premium are the premiums payable by the applicant to the insurance company at the attachment of the contract or during the validity of the insurance contract according to the mode of payment, payment amount and payment period as stated in the application form or endorsement. The basic premium shall not be higher than the insured amount divided by 20, and shall not be higher than RMB 6,000. The insured amount here refers to the death insured amount agreed at the time the policy is issued. If the insurance company sells multiple universal life insurance policies of the same product to the same applicant and the same insured, the sum of the basic premium of all valid policies shall not exceed RMB 6,000. Therefore, when the insurance company stipulates that the minimum basic premium of a universal life insurance product is higher than RMB 3,000, the same applicant can only buy one piece of this kind of product for the same insured. The additional premium is the difference between the payment on a regular basis and the basic premium. The additional premium is different from the basic premium in the initial charges. The mode of premium payment of the universal life insurance is more flexible and insurance companies usually stipulate the minimum amount of the first premium.

B. Top-Up Premium

618. After the applicant pays the premium payable in the current period in accordance with the universal life insurance contract, he or she can pay the top-up premium at any time with the consent of the insurance company, but some insurance companies will stipulate the basic conditions for the payment of top-up premium.

C. Continuity Bonus

619. Although the premium payment of universal life insurance is flexible, the insurance company still hopes that the applicant can pay the premium on time. Therefore, in order to encourage the applicant to continue to pay the premium, the insurance company offers a continuity bonus. The so-called continuity bonus is offered by the insurance company on the condition that the policy is valid continuously or the premium is paid continuously and the requirements of the contract must be satisfied. The insurance company shall clearly state the conditions and amount of the continuity bonus in the insurance contract and product manual. The continuity bonus generally goes directly to the investment account without deducting any fees. When the continuous payment of premium is taken as a reward, the top-up premium does not enjoy a continuity bonus. The Notice of the CBIRC on Several Issues Concerning the Measures for the Administration of Insurance Clauses and Insurance Premium Rates of Personal Insurance Companies provides that universal insurance may provide a continuity bonus but shall satisfy the following requirements:

– if the bonus is paid at a certain percentage of the account value, cumulative premiums paid, or premium paid in a lump sum, the first payment of the bonus shall be made five years after the insurance policy takes effect;
– if the bonus is paid at a certain percentage of the premium paid for the current period, the bonus may be paid since the insurance applicant pays the second installment of premiums, but may not exceed 2% of the premium paid for the current installment. If no premium is paid for an installment, no bonus shall be paid for that year.

V. Fee Collection

A. *Initial Charges*

620. The initial charges are the fees deducted before the insurance premium enters into the policy account. The initial charges are deducted from the premium paid by the applicant and cannot be deducted in the form of a reduction in the value of the investment account. The following are the regulatory requirements for initial charges.

1. Payment on a Regular Basis

621. The ratio of the initial charges of the basic premium shall not be higher than the upper limit shown in the table below. If the applicant postpones the premium payment, the upper limit of the initial charges of the basic premium shall be based on the upper limit of the original policy year of the insurance premium. The upper limit of the initial charges for additional premium is 5%, and for top-up premium it is 5%:

Policy Year	*Upper Limit of the Initial Charges (in %)*
the first year	50
the second year	25
the third year	15
the fourth and fifth year	10
later years	5

2. Payment in a Lump Sum

622. The ratio of the initial charges for the universal life insurance whose premium is paid in a lump sum shall not be higher than the upper limit listed in the table below. The upper limit of the ratio of initial charges for the top-up premium is 5%:

Premium	*Upper Limit of the Initial Charges (in %)*
≤50,000	10
>50,000	5

B. Death Risk Premium

623. The death risk premium refers to the guaranteed cost of the death risk insured amount. The death risk premium is calculated by the insurance company based on the insured's gender, age, physical health condition, death risk insured amount and other underwriting factors, and is charged by deducting the value of the investment account. Insurance companies can also charge the risk premium of other insurance liabilities by deducting the value of the investment account. Death risk premiums are prepaid and generally are charged once a month, and the settlement date of each month is the deduction date. At 0:00 on the settlement date, the insurance company usually charges the death risk premium corresponding to the period from the deduction day to the day before the settlement day of next month.

C. Policy Overhead

624. The policy overhead refers to the administrative fee charged to maintain the insurance contract. The policy overhead is a fixed amount which is not related to the value of the investment account and may differ from that of the first year and the renewal year of the policy. The insurance company cannot charge the policy overhead in the form of a certain proportion of the investment account value.

D. Service Charge

625. The service charge is charged by the insurance companies when they provide service such as account conversion, partial drawing and so on and is charged to pay the relevant management fees. The service charge is generally a certain percentage of the value of the drawn account, and is deducted when the above service is offered.

E. Surrender Charge

626. The surrender charge is charged when the policy is surrendered in the middle or partially drawn, and is used to cover the cost of the policy that has not been amortized. This charge is generally charged on a certain percentage of the value of the policy account or the account value of the partial drawing according to the number of years the policy has passed.

1. Payment on a Regular Basis

627. For the universal life insurance whose premium is paid on a regular basis, the surrender charge shall not be higher than the ratio of the value of the policy account or the policy account value of the partial drawing:

Policy Year	Upper Limit of the Surrender Charge (in %)
the first year	10
the second year	8
the third year	6
the fourth year	4
the fifth year	2
the sixth year and later	0

2. Payment in a Lump Sum

628. For the universal insurance whose premium is paid in a lump sum, the surrender charge shall not be higher than the following proportion of the value of the policy account or the policy account value of the partial drawing:

Policy Year	Initial Charge≤0 (in %)	Initial charge>0 (in %)
the first year	10	10
the second year	9	8
the third year	8	6
the fourth year	7	4
the fifth year	6	2
the sixth year	5	0
the seventh year	4	0
the eighth year	3	0
the ninth year	2	0
the tenth year	1	0
later years	0	0

VI. Surrender at the Cooling-Off Period

629. Usually, within ten days from the receipt of the insurance contract and signing the return receipt by the applicant, if the applicant does not agree that the insurance contract is in line with his own needs, he may cancel the insurance contract in writing and the insurance company will refund the entire insurance premium without interest. Some insurance companies will deduct some cost.

It should be noted that the ten days of the "cooling-off period" refer to ten natural days. Generally speaking, if the applicant surrenders within ten days, the insurance company has the responsibility to postpone the surrender time in case of holiday. *The Notice of the CIRC on Further Regulating the Sales Behavior of Commercial*

Banks' Agency Insurance Business stipulates that, if the insurance products sold by commercial banks are insured for more than one year, fifteen natural days shall be agreed in the contract as the cooling-off period. And the rights of the applicant during the cooling-off period should be stated in the contract. The cooling-off period begins from the date the insured receives the insurance policy and signs it in writing.

Part VI. Extended Life Insurance

Chapter 1. Investment-Linked Life Insurance

§1. Introduction

I. Definition

630. Investment-linked life insurance means a life insurance product with the function of insurance protection and with certain asset values in at least one investment account. It has the function of insurance protection, investment and financial management, but does not guarantee the minimum yield.

Part of the premium paid by the applicant is used for the insurance coverage of the insured, which is equivalent to life insurance in the traditional sense. Once the insured has an insurance accident within the insurance period, the insurance company will pay the insurance money in terms of the contract. The rest of the premium is transferred to the investment account opened by the insurance company by means of purchasing the investment unit. The account is operated by professional investors and the investment income is enjoyed by the applicant, but the investment risk is borne by the applicant.

Investment-linked insurance is "unbundled insurance." All insurance premiums are clearly communicated; that is, customers can clearly understand the death cost and management cost of the product. While traditional insurance and participating insurance are "bundled insurance," it is often difficult for customers to accurately understand how insurance companies charge death costs, management costs or sales costs.

II. Characteristics

A. Insurance Protection, Investment and Financial Management Functions

631. Investment-linked insurance sets up two types of accounts: insurance account and investment account, with dual functions of protection and investment.

As an independent account, the investment account does not have a debtor–creditor relationship with other assets or other accounts managed by the insurance company, nor does it bear joint and several liability. It is the basis for determining the value of a policy account. Different investment accounts can choose different investment strategies and portfolios. The applicant may choose to allocate the premium into one or more investment accounts, and the distribution ratio is determined by the applicant based on his/her aim of the return on investment and risk preference. After receiving the premium, the insurance company deducts the relative initial charges and then transfers the premium to different investment accounts by the ratio agreed in the contract to purchase the investment unit of the corresponding investment account. The applicant can adjust the distribution ratio of premiums among different investment accounts, and can also convert assets between different investment accounts.

B. Independent Investment Account and Expert Financial Management

632. Different from the participating insurance and universal life insurance whose investment income depends on the company's overall investment income, the funds of the investment account under investment-linked insurance are operated separately from other funds of the insurance company and are operated by professional investors. The investment income is enjoyed by the applicant, and at the same time, the investment risk is borne by them. In order to clarify the value of the investment account under each specific policy, the insurance company divides the investment account funds into a number of equal investment units, converts the funds included in the investment account into a number of investment units, which is directly associated with the securities fund, and determines the price of the investment unit based on the actual investment income and expenses. Taking advantage of the scale effect of the funds and the advantages of expert financial management of the insurance company, investment-linked insurance adopts a stable and flexible investment approach in order to maximize the interests of the customer.

C. The Amount of Insurance Money Is Not Fixed

633. In contrast to traditional life insurance with a fixed interest rate, the investment income of the investment-linked insurance is not capped, and the bottom is not guaranteed. Therefore, the return on earnings and the risk of loss is the highest among all life insurances.

The amount of insurance money of traditional life insurance is fixed and guaranteed, but that of the investment-linked insurance is floating with the insurance company's investment income, so it is considered to offset the adverse effects of inflation on life insurance effectively. The death or disability benefit of an investment-linked insurance policy consists of two parts: the first part is the minimum death benefit agreed upon by the policy, which is fixed; the second part is the variable death benefit, which varies with the investment income. The insurance company generally pays insurance money based on the greater amount of the sum insured and the investment account value or the sum of the two.

The value of the investment account varies with the return on investment and is 100% owned by the policyholders. Correspondingly, the risk of the investment account is also entirely borne by them.

Investment accounts under investment-linked insurance do not guarantee the minimum return on investment. Investment gains or losses and asset profits and losses are all included in the investment account, and the policy benefits are directly linked. If the actual investment income is high, the insurance benefit or the cash value of the policy is high and vice versa.

D. Clear Fee Collection and Transparent Account Management

634. Compared with traditional products and participating insurance, the proportion of all fees charged by investment-linked insurance and the method of deduction are clearly stated and reasonably disclosed. The applicant can check the status of the personal investment account, have an annual exclusive financial report, and the income is more transparent. The insurance company will regularly announce the investment income related to the investment account. When signing an insurance contract, the insurance company shall explain the initial charges and various fees charged for the investment account management. The selection of the investment account and the deduction of various fees shall be confirmed by the applicant. The insurance company evaluates the value of the investment account assets regularly and publishes the investment unit price on the insurance company's website or the public media approved by the insurance regulatory authority once a week at a minimum, usually daily. And the insurance company should announce the investment account information on the company's website and the public media approved by the CBIRC every half year and send the policy status report to the applicant every year according to the contract.

E. Flexible Premium Payment and Freedom of Investment Choice

635. The applicant can choose to pay the premium in a lump sum or on a regular basis to determine the investment plan according to his/her own financial situation. If they choose to pay the premium on a regular basis, the insurance company shall provide additional premiums in addition to the basic premium to increase the applicant's investable amount. During the validity period of the insurance contract, the applicant may also pay top-up premium to increase the value of the policy account, or draw part of the money from the account on the condition that the minimum premium of the corresponding insured amount is satisfied. Insurance companies generally offer different investment strategies and investment portfolios for the applicant to meet the market demand that differs in risk preference and income pursuit. The applicant can choose an investment account based on his/her risk tolerance and determine the proportion of assets allocated between different investment accounts.

F. Profit Mainly Comes from Expense Margin

636. For investment-linked insurance, only the following fees can be charged: initial charges, buy-and-sell spread, death risk premium, policy overhead, asset overhead, service fee and surrender fee. Unlike traditional life insurance whose profit comes from the "three margins," the investment-linked insurance does not have the "interest margin" because the investment income is all enjoyed by the applicant. Investment-linked insurance generally focuses on investment, and the death risk premium is relatively low, so the "death margin" is not obvious. Its profit mainly comes from the expense margin. Among the seven charges, the expense margin derived from the investment unit's buy-and-sell spread and the asset overhead is the main source of profit for this insurance.

G. High Professional Requirements for Sales Personnel

637. Investment-linked insurance is an "open-end fund" in insurance, involving a lot of complex investment knowledge. Therefore, it must rely on insurance sales personnel with high quality, high education, excellent knowledge and integrity to describe the investment function of the insurance objectively, and introduce the investment risks, investment channels and other financial management knowledge in detail.

H. Risk Assessment of the Applicant

638. The insurance policy is added to the applicant's risk assessment, and the criteria and categories of the applicant's risk appetite are determined by this, and the accounts with different risk levels of the investment-linked insurance are matched with them as the basis for account selection.

If the applicant refuses to accept the risk tolerance survey explicitly, each life insurance company shall provide the necessary reminder to the applicant, reveal the risks that may be faced in purchasing the investment-linked insurance, and require the person to copy the following contents and sign, that is, "I have read the insurance clause, product brochures and insurance tips, understand the product characteristics of investment-linked insurance, cost deduction and uncertainty of investment returns, voluntarily give up the risk tolerance survey, and are willing to bear the relevant risks." The insurance company will keep it properly.

§2. STRUCTURE OF INVESTMENT-LINKED LIFE INSURANCE

639. The typical investment-linked insurance structure is that each insurance premium received enters into the investment account after deducting the initial charges and the buy-and-sell spread. The assets in the investment account are divided into investment units of equal value, and each fund entered is used to purchase a certain amount of investment units. The buying and selling price of the investment unit is different. When the buying price is higher than the selling price, the difference is used as the fee charged by the insurance company to make up for the transaction costs incurred due to the sale of the asset. Besides the initial charges and the buy-and-sell spread, the insurance company may also charge the death risk premium and policy overhead from the investment account on a regular basis. When providing account conversion, partial drawing and other services, the insurance company can charge a handling fee, and if the policy is surrendered midway, the surrender fee may be charged.

I. Investment Account and Policy Account

640. The investment account of investment-linked insurance is the capital account opened for investment-linked insurance products by insurance companies for the separate management of assets and the investment risk is entirely borne by the policyholder. It is the independent account provided by the insurance company for premium investment.

641. The policy account of the investment-linked insurance is an account set up by the insurance company for the purpose of performing the insurance liability and clarifying the rights of the applicant or the insured to record the investment account selected by the applicant and the number of investment units held in each investment account.

II. Liability

642. Investment-linked insurance, as a life insurance product, must include one or more insurance liabilities. According to the Actuarial Measures on Investment-Linked Insurance (AMILI), investment-linked insurance can provide insurance liabilities other than death insurance liability. In general, besides basic insurance liability such as death benefit and survival benefit, it will also provide coverage for accidental death, accidental disability and so on, and provide other forms of protection through additional insurance.

III. Insured Amount

A. Determination of the Insured Amount

1. Determination of the Death Benefit

643. There are two ways to determine the amount of death benefit. Mode A refers to the larger of the insured amount agreed by the contract and the value of the policy account. The death benefit in this way is unchanged in the former period of the policy year. When the policy account value exceeds the insured amount, the death benefit will change with the fluctuation of the investment account value.

The advantage of this mode is that the insured's death protection will not be less than the predetermined amount, and at the same time reduce the applicant's insurance protection cost. As the age of the insured increases, the expected mortality rate increases, and the cost of insurance protection increases accordingly, especially in the high age group. In this way, as the value of the policy account increases, the death risk amount will decrease, and the insurance protection cost calculated according to the death risk amount will decrease accordingly, so as to prevent the insured from paying too much when it is necessary to support the elderly. The AMILI stipulates that the death risk amount of personal investment-linked insurance at the time of the issuance of the policy shall not be less than 5% of the value of the policy account, and the death risk amount refers to the effective insured amount minus the policy account value.

644. Mode B refers to the sum of the insured amount and the value of its policy account. The death benefit amount in this way fluctuates with the value of the policy account, but the risk amount (the difference between the death benefit and the investment account value) remains unchanged.

The advantage of this method is that it is easy for customers to understand, but when the insured is in a high age group, he or she needs to pay a higher insurance cost. At this time, the applicant can apply for a reduction in the insured amount. Otherwise, there may be insufficient investment income to pay the cost of insurance protection, which results in a decrease in the value of the policy account.

2. Determination of the Survival Benefit

645. For life insurance liability, the insurance company generally pays the value of the policy account. For example, the clause of an investment-linked insurance product stipulates that: "During the insurance period of this contract and the contract is valid, if the insured will survive at 0:00 on the first anniversary day of the insurance policy after the age of 80, we will pay the maturity insurance money according to the value of the policy account and the validity of this contract is terminated at the same time."

B. Adjustment of the Insured Amount

646. Some investment-linked insurance products allow the policyholder to change the insured to meet the holder's protective needs in different life stage, but the application for increasing the insured amount is generally required to provide insurable guarantees.

IV. Premium Payment

A. *Mode of Premium Payment*

1. Premium Payment in a Lump Sum

647. The applicant of the investment-linked insurance must pay the premium at one time when signing the contract. The amount of the premium paid can be determined by the applicant under the conditions stipulated by the insurance company. For example, the clause of an investment-linked insurance product stipulates that: "In this contract, the amount of premiums paid is determined by you, but not less than RMB 3,000, and must be paid in full at one time." There is no concept of basic premiums and additional premiums under this mode.

2. Premium Payment on a Regular Basis

648. The premium payment on a regular basis means that the applicant pays the premium regularly in accordance with the contract. It is composed of the basic premium and the additional premium, just like the universal life insurance. The insurer can collect a higher initial charge for basic premiums but a lower initial charge for additional premiums. The main purpose of dividing the premiums paid regularly into basic premiums and additional premiums is to prevent the insurance company from charging the applicant an excessive initial charge.

As for the basic insurance premiums for investment-linked insurance, the ARILI provides that the basic insurance premium shall not be higher than the insured amount divided by 20 and shall not exceed RMB 6,000. The insured amount here refers to the death insured amount at the time of issuance of the policy; if the insurance company sells multiple investment-linked policies with the same product to the same applicant and the same insured, the sum of the basic insurance premiums of all valid policies shall not exceed RMB 6,000.

B. *Flexible Payment Mechanism*

649. At present, most of the investment-linked insurances have introduced the flexible payment mechanism. The so-called flexible payment is mainly reflected in three aspects:

(1) Premium adjustment. Under the regular payment mode, the applicant can apply for an increase or decrease in the amount of premiums paid in each period within the validity of the contract, so that the applicant may have greater financial flexibility.
(2) Additional premiums. Under the regular payment mode, the insurance company allows the applicant to add premiums at any time in addition to the agreed premiums to increase the value of the policy account.

(3) Premium deferred period. On the basis of the regular payment mode, the premium deferred period can be agreed, which allows the applicant to postpone the payment within the agreed time limit. The insurance company maintains the validity of the policy by deducting the investment unit in the applicant's policy account to pay the risk premium and the policy overhead.

However, the emergence of the premium deferred period may face the following two situations. First, if the premium deferred period precedes the grace period, then the insurance contract is suspended at the expiration of the grace period. Second, if the premium deferred period is later than the grace period, the insurance contract may be suspended when the value of the policy account is insufficient to cover the protection cost and policy overheads.

C. Continuity Bonus

650. Like the universal life insurance, in order to avoid the policy failure caused by its flexible payment mode and encourage the applicant to pay the premium continually, the insurance company will provide a continuity bonus, and should clearly indicate the condition and amount of the bonus in the insurance contract and product manual.

The AMILI stipulates that the investment-linked insurance can provide a continuity bonus which is a reward for a continuing effective policy or for a continuous payment of the premium, and the insurance company should clearly indicate the conditions and amount of the payment of the continuity bonus in the contract and the product manual.

651. The Notice of the CBIRC on Several Issues concerning the Measures for the Administration of Insurance Clauses and Insurance Premium Rates of Personal Insurance Companies stipulates that investment-linked insurance may provide a continuity bonus but shall satisfy the following requirements:

- if the bonus is paid at a certain percentage of the account value, cumulative premiums paid, or premium paid in a lump sum, the first payment of the bonus shall be made five years after the insurance policy takes effect;
- if the bonus is paid at a certain percentage of the premium paid for the current period, the bonus may be paid since the insurance applicant pays the second installment of premiums, but may not exceed 2% of the premium paid for the current installment. If no premium is paid for an installment, no bonus shall be paid for that year.

D. Premium Allocation

652. After receiving each premium, the insurance company will deduct the initial charges at first, and the remaining are allocated to each investment account by the distribution ratio agreed upon in the contract to be used to purchase the investment unit of the investment account. Different investment accounts are distinguished and named in terms of the investment direction, investment scope and investment risk. Each investment-linked insurance product will be linked to several investment accounts (a product should be linked to at least one investment account in accordance with the requirements of the CBIRC) which is chosen by the applicant freely when insured. Generally, the accounts can be divided into five types: index type, radical type, hybrid type, security type and currency type.

653. The investment unit is the basic measuring unit of the assets in the investment account, and the assets allocated to the investment account are divided into equal units, each of which is called an investment unit. The investment unit price refers to the price of each investment unit. The investment unit price of investment-linked insurance is divided into the purchasing price and the selling price. The purchasing price of the investment unit is the price at which the funds are transferred into investment units when they enter into the account. The selling price of the investment unit is the price at which the investment units in the investment account are cashed out when the funds are withdrawn from the investment account.

654. The amount of premiums paid by the insured each time to the investment account is transferred into the number of investment units according to the purchasing price of the investment unit on the next asset assessment date of the date of receipt of the premium.

V. Fee Collection

655. Compared with traditional life insurance and participating insurance, investment-linked insurance is quite transparent in the collection of fees. The fees deducted by insurance company should specify the nature of the fees and how they are used. Only the following fees can be charged by the investment-linked insurance.

A. Initial Charges

656. The initial fee refers to the expenses deducted before the insurance premium enters into the investment account. It is generally used for commissions, investment account opening and other aspects of the insurance business. The initial charges of investment-linked insurance may not be deducted in the form of a reduction in the value of the policy account. In terms of the mode of payment and the type of applicant, the proportion of initial charge collection has different maximum limits. The following are the regulatory requirements for the initial charges of the AMILI.

1. Regular Payment

657. The ratio of the initial charges of the basic premium shall not be higher than the upper limit listed in the table:

Policy Year	*Upper Limit of the Initial Charges (in %)*
1st year	50
2nd year	25
3rd year	15
4th, 5th year	10
later years	5

The upper limit of the ratio of initial charges for additional premiums is 5%, and that of the top-up premiums is also 5%.

2. Payment in a Lump Sum

658. The ratio of the initial charges must not be higher than the upper limit listed in the table:

Premium	*Upper Limit of the Initial Charges (in %)*
≤50,000	10
>50,000	5

The upper limit of the ratio of initial charges for top-up premium is 5%, and the upper limit of the ratio of initial charges for the group investment-linked insurance premium is also 5%.

B. Bid-Ask Spread

659. The bid-ask spread is the difference between the prices at which the applicant buys and sells the investment unit. Since the premium is transferred into the investment unit by the purchasing price and the investment units realizes the cash by the selling price, the insurance company actually charges a difference between the two prices to cover the expenses incurred as a result of asset purchasing and selling. The AMILI provides that the difference between the purchasing and selling price of investment-linked insurance shall not be higher than 2%.

C. Death Risk Premium

660. The death risk premium refers to the guarantee cost of the death risk insured amount. The AMILI provides that the risk premiums shall be collected by deducting the number of investment units, the calculation method of which is multiplying the death risk insured amount by the death risk premium rate. The deducted number of the investment units is derived from the risk premium divided by the current selling price of the investment unit. The insurance company shall indicate the highest level of death risk premium rate in the insurance contract, which shall be expressed as a certain percentage of the experience life table of China's life insurance industry. Death premium for non-standard insurance contract shall be determined by the insurance company in accordance with the generally accepted actuarial principles. An insurance company may collect risk premium for other insurance liabilities by deducting the number of investment units.

D. Policy Overhead

661. The policy overhead refers to the administrative fee charged from the applicant or the insured for maintaining the insurance contract, which is generally used for daily management of the policy, printing the policy status reports, etc.

The policy overhead should be a fixed amount that is not related to the value of the policy account and may differ at the first year and the renewal year of the policy. The insurance company may not collect the policy overhead in the form of a certain proportion of the value of the policy account. The insurance company deducts the policy overhead from the account by deducting the number of investment units. The number of investment units deducted shall be calculated according to the current selling price of the investment unit divided by the policy overhead.

For group investment-linked insurance, the insurance company may charge a policy overhead in the form of a fixed amount for each insured on the basis of the policy overhead charged from the insured.

E. Asset Management Fee

662. Asset management fees refer to the fees charged by a certain proportion of the net asset value of the account and is generally used for account asset transactions and other expenses. The net asset value of the account, after deducting the asset management fee that the insurance company should collect in the current period, shall be equal to the ending account value (account value = total assets – total liabilities).

The AMILI stipulates that the upper limit of the annual percentage of asset management fee for investment-linked insurance is 2%. If the insurance company entrusts the account assets to a third party, the sum of the asset management fees collected by the insurance company and the third party shall not exceed 2%. In practice, the proportion of collection by each insurance company is different, and the proportion of collection of different investment accounts is also different.

663. The asset management fee is deducted when assessing the investment account; that is, it is deducted before the investment unit is priced. The net asset value of the previous asset assessment date deducts the asset management fee that the insurance company should collect in the current period, that is the investment account value of the current asset assessment date. The calculation formula of asset management fee for each period is as follows:

- asset management fee of the investment account = the net value of investment account at the previous asset assessment date math-figure the ratio of asset management fee collection monthly math-figure the number of days since the last assessment math-figure the number of days in the current month;
- asset management fee of the investment account = the net value of investment account at the previous asset assessment date math-figure the ratio of asset management fee collection yearly math-figure the number of days since the last assessment math-figure 365;
- asset management fee of the investment account = the net value of the investment account math-figure the number of days since the last assessment math-figure the ratio of asset management fee collection math-figure 365.

F. Service Charge

664. The service charge is the fee that the insurance company can collect when providing the service such as account conversion to pay the relevant management fees. The charge can be determined by a certain percentage of the account transfer value each time, or can be charged at a fixed amount each time, generally deducted from the account transfer value.

G. Surrender Fee

665. The surrender fee refers to the fee charged by the insurance company when the policy is surrendered or partially drawn to cover the obtaining cost of the policy that has not been amortized. The surrender fee charged by the insurance company is generally a certain proportion of the account value or the corresponding account value when partially drawing, and the upper limit of the proportion needs to be met. The upper limit provides as follows:

Policy Year	Payment on a Regular Basis (in %)	Payment in a Lump Sum	
		Initial Charges≤0 (in %)	Initial Charges>0 (in %)
1st year	10	10	10
2nd year	8	9	8
3rd year	6	8	6

Policy Year	Payment on a Regular Basis (in %)	Payment in a Lump Sum	
		Initial Charges≤0 (in %)	Initial Charges>0 (in %)
4th year	4	7	4
5th year	2	6	2
6th year	0	5	0
7th year		4	
8th year		3	
9th year		2	
10th year		1	
Later years		0	

VI. Refund at Cooling-Off Period

666. Just like the life insurance product of more than one year, there is also a cooling-off period clause in the investment-linked insurance. The cooling-off period is usually ten days from the effective date of the insurance contract.

667. Generally speaking, if there is a holiday, the insurance company has the responsibility to delay the surrender time for the customer when the applicant requests surrender within ten days.

Where the duration of an insurance product sold by a commercial bank in its bank assurance business exceeds one year, there shall be a cooling-off period of fifteen natural days in the contract, and the policyholder's rights during the cooling-off period shall be stated in the contract. The cooling-off period shall be calculated from the day when the insurance applicant receives the insurance policy and signs for it.

668. During the cooling-off period, the applicant may file a surrender in writing and return the relevant documents of the insurance contract to the insurance company. The insurance company will rescind the contract at 0:00 or 24:00 of the day when they receive the written notice of surrender and the relevant documents of the contract from the applicant. The insurance company does not assume the insurance liability from the beginning, and refund different amount according to different circumstances:

- if the applicant chooses to invest after the cooling-off period, the premium has not been transferred to the policy account, and the insurance company refunds the full premium paid with no interest;
- if the applicant chooses to invest immediately after the insurance contract takes into effect, and the assets value of the independent account changes, the insurance company may only deduct the reduced value of the applicant's assets and the expenses of realizing the assets, and shall not deduct the commission and expense incurred in selling the insurance policy.

§3. Investment Account of the Investment-Linked Life Insurance

I. Opening, Modification and Management of the Investment Accounts

A. Opening of the Investment Account

669. Investment-linked insurance products can be set up with one or more investment accounts for the applicant to choose. It is a special account provided by insurance companies for premium investment. The assets are managed separately, and the profits and losses of investment and asset are all included in the investment account. Different investment accounts have different investment strategies and portfolios for the applicant to choose. The investment risk of each investment account is completely borne by the applicant. Therefore, the applicant can choose the appropriate investment account and the proportion of premium distribution in terms of his/her risk tolerance, but the insurance company generally stipulates the minimum premium distribution ratio and the highest number of the investment account. In addition, the applicant can also adjust the distribution of premiums among different investment accounts.

B. Modification of the Investment Accounts

670. When relevant laws, regulations and policies change, the existing investment portfolios do not comply with them, or when the investment environment changes, the existing investment channels no longer adapt to the needs of the market, or when new investment channels emerge, under the premise of protecting the interests of the applicant completely, and approved by the CBIRC, the insurance company may set up new investment accounts, or combine, divide, close existing investment accounts, or combine and disintegrate the investment units in the investment account under this contract, or stop the transfer of the investment account after the implementation of the prescribed procedures in accordance with relevant regulations. But when combining and disintegrating the investment units in the investment account, the insurance company should guarantee that the value of each investment account remains unchanged.

C. Management of Investment Accounts

671. The insurance company may exercise the management right over the assets of the investment account in accordance with the relevant laws and regulations of the state and the relevant regulations formulated by the insurance regulatory authority. The assets of the investment account are audited annually by an independent accounting firm recognized by the insurance regulatory authority.

The insurance company has the right to determine its investment portfolio according to the investment objectives and strategies of various investment accounts. In addition, it has the right to modify the stipulation about the investment portfolio with the approval of the insurance regulatory authority and prior written notice to the applicant.

The insurance company has the right to entrust all or part of the investment rights and management of the investment account to other suitable financial institutions, subject to the relevant laws, provisions, regulations and rules.

II. Classification of Investment Accounts

672. At present, the insurance companies in China that invest in investment-linked insurance products have set up independent investment accounts, some of which only link one investment account, and some link multiple investment accounts. The clause in the contract of each insurance company will indicate the investment objectives, investment scope, investment strategy and investment risk of the provided account. The name of the investment account opened by the insurance company is diverse, but through different asset allocation mode, the investment accounts with different characteristics are generally built based on the difference in the risk tolerance of the applicant and on the expected risk-return status of different assets.

III. Investment Scope of the Investment Account

673. An insurance company shall, according to the characteristics of insurance businesses and funds, set up "general accounts" and "independent accounts" to conduct the separate account management of asset allocation. General accounts are the capital accounts for which an insurance company assumes part or all investment risks. The capital of an insurance company shall be managed by reference to the general accounts. Independent accounts are the capital accounts which are independent from the general accounts and all the investment returns from which are directly enjoyed by the insurance applicants or beneficiaries. The investment accounts of the investment-linked insurance are in the category of "independent accounts." The investment scope of the independent account assets is the following five categories of assets, and the investment proportion of each asset is agreed by the insurance company and the applicant or the beneficiary through written contract.

IV. Evaluation of the Investment Account

674. In accordance with relevant regulations, an insurance company should evaluate the value of its investment account once a week at a minimum. But currently, most insurance companies in the market are evaluating the value of the account on a daily basis. If the insurance company provides multiple investment accounts, each account should be valued.

When an insurance company evaluates the value of an investment account, it should judge whether the investment account is in an expansion phase or a contraction phase. In the long-term, when the purchasing amount of the investment unit is greater than the redemption amount of the investment unit, the investment account is in the expansion stage: conversely, when the purchasing amount of the investment unit is less than the redemption amount of the investment unit, the investment account is in a contraction stage.

In addition, when evaluating an investment account, all assets and liabilities in the investment account should be assessed. The calculation formula is shown in the table as follows:

	Expansion Phase	*Contraction Phase*
Total assets of the account	value of all investment assets calculated at the *purchasing* price of the account assets + assumed transaction costs and tax incurred when all investment assets are purchased on the account evaluation date	value of all investment assets calculated at the *selling* price of the account assets – assumed transaction costs and tax incurred when all investment assets are purchased on the account evaluation date
Total liabilities of the account	Payables for purchased assets Payable for tax Payable for asset management fee Other liabilities	
Account value	account value = total assets of the account – total liabilities of the account	

675. The AMILI provides that the asset value of each investment account shall not be less than its corresponding unit reserve amount, and when the asset value of the investment account is higher than the corresponding unit reserve amount, the excess shall not exceed 2% of the asset value of the investment account or RMB 5 million.

V. Pricing of the Investment Unit

676. Pricing of the investment unit refers to the process in which an insurance company evaluates the value of an investment account and determines the price of the investment unit. The purpose of evaluating the value of the investment account is to determine the price of the investment unit.

A. *Pricing Principles*

677. The pricing of investment units should be fair to each applicant; that is, in the transaction of any investment unit, the interests of the applicant who does not participate in the transaction are not affected.

B. *Pricing Method*

678. There are two ways to determine the price of an investment unit:

(1) The single pricing method; that is, the insurance company determines the price of a single investment unit on each asset evaluation date based on the average market price of the assets in the investment account, which has the advantage of being easy for the insurance company to operate and easy for the applicant to understand.
(2) Double pricing method; that is, when evaluating the value of an investment account, it is necessary to determine first whether the investment account is in an expansion phase or a contraction phase, and then determine the investment account asset value to determine the purchasing price and the selling price of the investment unit. This method is fairer in principle, but it is more complicated to explain to the applicant. According to the requirements of the CBIRC, the pricing of investment units should be based on the double pricing method.

C. *Pricing Frequency*

679. Consistent with the assessment of the account value, the pricing should be once in a week at a minimum in practice, but most insurance companies exercise the pricing on a daily basis. The more the pricing, the higher the requirements asked for the insurance company's internal operating system.

D. *Calculation Formula*

680. The formula for calculating the price of an investment unit is as follows:

– Selling price of the investment unit = investment account value ÷ the number of the investment unit;
– Purchase price of the investment unit = selling price of the investment unit x (1 + buy-and-sell spread);
– Investment account = total assets of the investment account – total liabilities of the investment account.

The number of investment units refers to the total number of investment units of an investment account assessed by the insurance company on the asset assessment date, which is equal to the sum of the investment units of this investment account held by all the applicants.

681. The purchasing price and the selling price of the investment unit are for the applicant. The purchasing price of the investment unit refers to the price when the applicant purchases the investment unit from the insurance company. The selling price of the investment unit refers to the price when the applicant sells the investment unit to the insurance company. The insurance company shall indicate the purchasing price and the selling price of the investment unit in a reasonable RMB currency unit. The minimum unit shall retain at least four decimal places after the decimal point.

It is important to note that for the applicant's request to buy or sell an investment unit, the insurance company should use the unit price of the next asset assessment date as the transaction price of the investment unit. Otherwise, it must be reported to the CBIRC for approval.

§4. Policy Account of the Investment-Linked Life Insurance

I. Opening of the Policy Account

682. The policy account is a personal account opened by the insurance company for each applicant in order to fulfill the insurance liability of the investment-linked insurance contract and clarify the rights of the applicant, to record the investment account selected by the applicant and the number of the investment unit held in each investment account. Generally, the policy account is opened after the insurance contract takes effect or at the first asset evaluation day after the expiration of the cooling-off period.

II. Evaluation of the Policy Account Value

A. Number of the Investment Units in the Policy Account

683. The initial number of the investment unit in the policy account is equal to the amount of premiums allocated to the investment account divided by the purchasing price of the investment unit in this account.

The number of investment units in each investment account in the policy account will increase or decrease with the payment of insurance premiums, the collection of various fees, the transfer of all or part of the policy account value, or the collection of part of the policy account value.

B. Calculation of the Policy Account Value

684. On any asset valuation day, the policy account value is equal to the sum of the figure derived from multiplying the number of investment units in each investment account held in the policy account and the selling price of the investment unit of the corresponding investment account on the asset valuation day.

685. If the applicant only holds the investment units of one investment account, on any asset valuation date, the policy account value is equal to the figure derived from multiplying the number of investment units in the policy account and the selling price of the investment unit in the investment account on the asset valuation date. The formula is as follows:

policy account value = the number of the investment units × the selling price of the investment unit.

686. If the applicant holds the investment unit of more than one investment accounts, the investment unit value in each investment account in the policy account is first calculated according to the above formula, and the sum is the policy account value.

III. Investment Option of the Policy Account

687. The investment options of the policy account include the option of investment account and investment ratio and the transfer of the investment account.

A. Option of Investment Account and Investment Ratio

688. The applicant can choose the proportion of the premium in each investment account when insuring. If the applicant does not choose an investment account, the insurance company has the right to transfer all the premiums to be allocated to the designated investment account. During the validity period of the insurance contract, the insurance company may allow the applicant to change the investment ratio of the investment account, but the changed investment ratio is only applicable to future premiums.

B. Transfer of the Investment Accounts

689. After the insurance contract takes effect, the applicant can apply in writing for transferring all or part of the policy account value from one investment account to other investment accounts. The number of investment units in each investment account in the policy account is adjusted accordingly.

The value of the policy account to be transferred will be transferred at the price of the investment unit on the next asset evaluation day from the day the insurance company receives the transfer application, and the transfer of the investment account will be traded at the same investment unit price. This price can be the purchasing price of the investment unit and can also be the selling price of the investment unit. The insurance company may charge a service fee for the transfer of the assets between different investment accounts, or may not charge the fee. Different insurance companies have different restrictions on the time interval and amount of asset transfer.

IV. Collection of the Policy Account Value

690. The value of the policy account is all owned by the applicant. The applicant may notify the insurance company in writing at any time, and provide corresponding certificates and materials to receive the value of the policy account in part or in full, but the drawing amount must meet the requirements of the insurance company. The fee for partial drawing and the surrender fee of whole drawing must be paid as required. The difference between the policy account value and the surrender fee is the cash value. The policy account value and cash value should be listed on the policy benefit illustration form. After the value of the policy account is partially drawn, the number of investment units in the policy account is reduced accordingly.

Chapter 2. Variable Annuity Insurance

§1. Introduction

I. Definition

691. The term "variable annuity insurance" refers to personal insurance where the insurance benefits are linked to the unit price of an underlying investment in the investment account, and a guaranteed minimum benefit is provided according to the insurance contract.

II. Characteristics

692. Variable annuity insurance combines the characteristics of investment-linked insurance and traditional annuity products. On the one hand, it can share the investment income brought by the rise of the capital market; on the other hand, it can protect the applicant from the losses caused by the fluctuation of the capital market by guaranteeing the minimum policy benefits, so as to guarantee the future annuity payment level or other insurance benefits satisfying the agreed standard. From the perspective of the applicant, the main features are as follows:

- the investment income belongs to the applicant who can share the income from the rise of the capital market;
- the transparency of the operation of the investment account is high, and the price of the investment account is published regularly, which is convenient for inquiry;
- the investment account of the variable annuity product is opened and accounted independently, so the interests of the applicant are better protected;
- it provides a guaranteed minimum benefit to protect the applicant from large investment losses;
- the applicant has an annuity option and can choose the mode of annuity collection as needed;
- tax incentives are available in some countries and regions.

The above characteristics of the variable annuity are very attractive to the people who are pursuing old-age security, and are favored by the market. However, insurance companies that operate the variable annuity business also bear higher risks than general life insurance products, including the pricing risk of guaranteed policy benefits, market volatility risk, interest rate risk, mortality rate risk and hedging risk.

III. Differences Between Variable Annuity Insurance and Other Financial Products

A. Differences Between Variable Annuity and Traditional Annuity

693. Investment account settings. The variable annuity opens an independent investment account, the assets of which are separated from other assets of the insurance company. But the traditional annuity assets are not distinguished from the ordinary assets of the insurance company.

Annuity benefits. The policy value of the variable annuity is that the future annuity payment fluctuates with the performance of the investment account. The applicant not only has the possibility of sharing the investment income of the capital market but also needs to face the investment losses that may be suffered, so it is changeable. While when the traditional annuity policy is signed, the future annuity benefits have been determined.

Mode of operation. The investment unit price and investment account information of the variable annuity are published regularly, which is easy for inquiry, while that of the traditional annuity does not need to be published.

Investment account selection. The applicant who buys the variable annuities can choose the investment ratio of each account according to the capital market situation and personal needs, and has some control over the investment process, while the traditional annuity applicant does not participate in the investment process at all.

B. Differences Between Variable Annuity Insurance and Other Life Insurance

694. Compared with other life insurance, variable annuities differ in terms of payment mode, account opening, account transparency and source of income.

Payment mode. The payment mode for variable annuity products is similar to traditional life insurance products and is a fixed payment. If the policy is void due to the failure to pay the premium in time, it can also be reinstated according to the reinstatement clause.

Account opening. Variable annuity insurance divides the premium into ordinary accounts and independent investment accounts. Independent investment accounts operate in the same way as the investment-linked insurance.

Account transparency. The operation of investment account in the variable annuity insurance is transparent and the proportions of various fees are listed separately. The structure of the premium is clear, the price of the investment unit is published regularly, and the annual investment report is sent to the customer on a regular basis.

Source of income. The source of income of variable annuity insurance and investment-linked insurance is the same, all from investment account income. The difference is that investment-linked insurance generally has no guaranteed minimum benefit, while universal life insurance and variable annuity insurance generally have the guaranteed minimum benefit.

C. Differences Between Variable Annuity Insurance and Fund

695. The income of the variable annuity depends on the investment income of the selected portfolio, and its capital generally invests in domestic and foreign stocks, bonds, currency, etc., which is no different from the investment fund, but the variable annuity has the characteristics that the fund investment does not have.

It can resist the financial risks brought by longevity. In the payment period, the variable annuity can provide a continuous cash flow covering a specific time period, which can range from the retirement of the annuity receiver to his death or other time period of his choice. There is also variable annuity insurance designed to guarantee that the annuity that can be received each year from the second year of the insurance is not less than the annuity received in the first policy year. These securities can help annuity receiver withstand the financial risks of longevity.

It can resist the financial risks brought by death. If the insured dies shortly after the beginning of the payment period, many products will provide a "guarantee period" to ensure that the annuity receiver can receive the annuity within that period. If the insured dies before the date of payment, a one-time death benefit can be obtained, which is not less than the premium already paid or the value of the investment account.

Other insurance products can be attached. The most common is the addition of high death insurance. There is also a "locked death benefit," which means locking the value of the investment account as a death benefit at a certain high-yield time, as well as many additional options such as "guaranteed minimum benefit clause" and "long-term care insurance." Of course, these additional insurances require additional premium payment.

§2. Variable Annuity Insurance Products

I. Operational Principle of the Variable Annuity Insurance

696. The operational principle of China's variable annuity insurance is the same as that of international practice. It is generally divided into two stages: the annuity accumulative period and the annuity payment period. During the accumulative period, the applicant pays the premium in a lump sum or on a regular basis (most of the existing products in China are paid in a lump sum), and the premium enters the investment account of the variable annuity after deducting the initial charges, the bid-ask spread and other related fees, and is operated by professional investors to increase the assets of the investment account on the basis of providing the guaranteed minimum benefit. The investment account is divided into several units of equal value, and the applicant obtains the number of investment units of the corresponding investment account of the insurance company after paying the premium. The policy value shall be calculated as per the number of investment units multiplied by the price of the investment unit at the time. After the accumulative period, the annuity payment period begins. During the annuity payment period, the annuity receiver can receive an annuity according to the agreed standards and time limit, or exercise the annuity option according to the agreement to convert the insurance proceeds at maturity into the annuities.

697. Unlike the general investment-linked insurance, variable annuity insurance can provide a guaranteed minimum benefit, that is, to provide the applicant with a guaranteed minimum benefit, such as the guaranteed minimum death benefit, the guaranteed minimum maturity benefit, the guaranteed minimum accumulative benefit, the guaranteed annuity payment, the guaranteed minimum surrender benefit when the policy value decreases caused by the fall of price of the asset in the investment account. In order to provide the guaranteed minimum benefit, the insurance company must adopt a certain management mode to manage the variable annuity investment and collect the charges of the guaranteed benefit from the applicant.

II. Fee Collection

A. *Initial Charge*

698. The initial charge is the fee deducted before the premium enters the investment account, which is collected at a certain percentage of the premium income.

B. *Buy-and-Sell Spread*

699. The buy-and-sell spread is the difference between the price at which an applicant buys and sells the investment unit, which is expressed as a percentage of the price of the investment unit.

C. *Risk Premium*

700. The risk premium, also known as the risk protection cost, is deducted according to the risk protection amount selected by the applicant. At present, most of the variable annuity products in China are paid in a lump sum, and the risk protection provided by them is different.

D. *Policy Overhead*

701. The policy overhead is charged for maintaining the insurance contract from the applicant, which is expressed as a fixed amount that has no relationship with the value of the policy account. China's current variable annuity insurance products do not charge the policy overhead.

E. Asset Management Fee

702. The asset management fee is charged by a certain percentage of the net asset value of the account; that is, the annual asset management fee shall be calculated as per the net value of the investment account multiplied by the asset management fee ratio, and will be deducted from the net asset value of the investment account when the value of the investment account is evaluated on each price evaluation day. The asset management fee for existing products in China is 1% at a minimum, and 2% at a maximum.

F. Service Fee

703. The service fee is charged by the insurance company when providing services like account conversion and partial collection to pay the relevant management fees. Since most of the products in China now only have one investment account and do not support partial collection, most products are not charged a service fee.

G. Surrender Fee

704. The surrender fee is charged by the insurance company when the policy is surrendered or partially collected to make up the unamortized policy cost, which is expressed as a certain percentage of the account value at the time of surrender. This charge decreases gradually as the cost of the policy is amortized over time, and the range and period of it are determined by the form of the annuity.

H. Guaranteed Benefit Expense

705. The guaranteed benefit expense is charged by the insurance company for providing the guaranteed minimum benefit. It can be collected in a manner of deducting the number of investment units by a certain percentage of the policy account value or the guaranteed minimum benefit.

III. Guaranteed Benefit of Variable Annuity Insurance

A. Guaranteed Minimum Death Benefit

706. Guaranteed minimum death benefit means that when the insured dies, the beneficiary may receive a minimum death benefit if the account value is lower than the minimum death benefit as agreed on in the insurance policy, or may receive the account value if the account value is higher than the minimum death benefit.

B. Guaranteed Minimum Income Benefit

707. Guaranteed minimum income benefit means that a minimum annuity payment standard is set when an insurance policy is signed and issued.

C. Guaranteed Minimum Accumulation Benefit

708. Guaranteed minimum accumulation benefit means that on a current asset appraisal day during the accumulation period of variable annuity insurance, if the unit price of investment is lower than the agreed proportion of the highest historical unit price of investment, the account value shall be calculated as per such a proportion of the highest historical unit price of investment; or if the unit price of investment is higher than the agreed proportion of the highest historical unit price of investment, the account value shall be calculated as per the unit price of investment. The term "highest historical unit price of investment" refers to the highest historical unit price of investment since the opening of the account.

D. Guaranteed Minimum Maturity Benefit

709. Guaranteed minimum maturity benefit means that at the expiry of the insurance period, the beneficiary may receive a minimum maturity benefit if the account value is lower than the minimum maturity benefit as agreed on in the insurance policy; or may receive the account value if the account value is higher than the minimum maturity benefit.

IV. Management Model of China's Variable Annuity Insurance

710. Article 11 of the Interim Measures for the Administration of Variable Annuity Insurance provides that an insurance company providing variable annuity insurance shall adopt a management model recognized by the CBIRC, unless it only provides the guaranteed minimum death benefit. The management models recognized by the CBIRC include the internal portfolio hedging model and the constant proportion portfolio insurance model.

A. Internal Portfolio Hedging Model

711. Variable annuity insurance provides the guaranteed minimum benefit for the insured, which is equivalent to the insurance company selling a European put option. Insurance companies can buy the same option from outside, such as investment banks, reinsurance companies, etc. to hedge risks. On the one hand, this practice is limited by the development of the capital market; for example, currently, hedging operation can be made in the foreign exchange field in China, while hedging operation in other areas can be more limited. On the other hand, the hedging operation has counterparty risk; the expected cost is much higher and the feasibility is much lower.

The first variable annuity insurance in China adopts an internal portfolio hedging model to achieve the guaranteed minimum benefit, that is under the principle of matching management of assets and liabilities, managing guaranteed minimum policy benefits in the form of internal option simulation. This product offers a 100% guarantee on the annuity at maturity. The internal portfolio of the product is divided into treasury bond and investment account. As a risk-free asset, treasury bonds also generate a coupon to hedge the downside risk of the investment account while guaranteeing the value at maturity. The investment account falls, and the proportion of treasury bond in the portfolio is increased to hedge the downside risk. The investment account rises, and the proportion of investment accounts in the portfolio is increased to enjoy the market's rising income. The advantage of this hedging model is that it can adapt to the ever-changing market situation, and dynamically and quickly adjust the ratio of treasury bond to investment account. This dynamic ratio adjustment introduces advanced hedging technology and rich experience, and relies on a professional hedging service platform.

B. Constant Proportion Portfolio Insurance Model

712. In the constant proportion portfolio insurance model, the investment proportion between risky assets and risk-free assets in the investment account is dynamically adjusted according to the investment multiplier, floor and other parameters to manage the guaranteed minimum policy benefits. Its aim is to maximize revenue under the premise of maximizing the protection of the principal, that is fixing the investment floor. The account rises, the insured shares the proceeds, and if the account falls sharply and the investment floor is broken, it is necessary to buy the risk-free assets to lock up the gains.

§3. Risk and Management of Variable Annuity Insurance

I. Risk of Variable Annuity Insurance

713. For the applicant, on the one hand, the guaranteed minimum benefit can be obtained; on the other hand, the benefits brought by the rise of the securities market can be shared. Different from the investment-linked insurance, the applicant no longer bears all the investment risks, and the insurance company bears the guaranteed minimum benefit, so part of the investment risks is borne by the insurance company.

The products of variable annuity insurance are complex, technical and risky. The main risks are summarized in the following four categories.

A. Investment Risk

714. Investment risk is the risk of using the funds in the investment account. When the account value is higher than the guaranteed minimum benefit, all the investment risks of the investment account are borne by the policyholder. The investment risks are mainly stock market risk, bond market risk and currency market risk. When the investment account unit price is close to or below the guaranteed minimum benefit, all account assets will be converted into risk-free assets. When the account value is lower than the guaranteed minimum benefit, the main risk of the investment account is borne by the insurance company.

B. Product Designing Risk

715. Product designing risk is the product pricing risk, which mainly includes interest rate risk, mortality rate risk, expense rate risk and commitment risk.

The interest rate risk means that variable annuity insurance assumes the insurance liability for customers for decades and fluctuations of the interest rate will generate the impact of different degree on cash flow, asset and liability structure, product quality, and the behavior of applicant and debtor.

For the mortality rate risk, the payment of variable annuity insurance is based on the insured's living conditions, so estimating the mortality rate incorrectly will cause risks to the insurance company, that is collect excessive or too low fees, resulting in low competitiveness or loss. The determination of mortality rate determines the quality of the product.

For the expense rate risk, since the variable annuity insurance provides the guaranteed minimum benefit, it will charge an additional management fee besides the account management fee of investment-linked insurance. Therefore, the higher the guaranteed benefit, the higher the management fee charged.

The commitment risk is charged due to the promise of providing the guaranteed minimum benefit, so the actuary must estimate the costs and risks that these commitments and customer choices bring to the company.

C. Sales Risk

716. Variable annuity insurance products are complex and professional, and require a high degree of depth and breadth of knowledge of the sales man. Therefore, misleading risks are prone to occur in the sales process of variable annuity insurance.

D. Behavioral Risk of Policyholder

717. The behavior of the policyholder, including partial collection, surrender, and conversion of the maturity insurance proceeds into annuities, will affect the cost of guarantee. Insurance companies need to design the product cautiously and monitor the investment progress closely.

II. Risk Management of Variable Annuity Insurance

718. The risk of variable annuity insurance is high and the development of its product is not mature. Therefore, the following aspects are regulated in the Interim Measures for the Administration of Variable Annuity Insurance to control the risk.

A. Standardized Management Mode

719. The core risk of variable annuity insurance is to provide the guaranteed minimum policy benefits, which is borne by the insurance company. Therefore, the Interim Measures explicitly require the insurance company to adopt the corresponding management model to mitigate risks, and specify two management modes: first, internal portfolio hedging model; that is, an insurance company shall, under the principle of matching management of assets and liabilities, manage guaranteed minimum policy benefits in the form of internal option simulation; second, constant proportion portfolio insurance model; that is, the investment proportion between risky assets and risk-free assets in the investment account is dynamically adjusted according to the investment multiplier, floor and other parameters to manage the guaranteed minimum policy benefits.

B. Standardized Reserve Drawing

720. Reserve is the core to ensure that insurance companies assess risks cautiously, fully price the risks, and ensure adequate solvency, and are the focus of national regulation.

For the guaranteed benefit reserve, *the Interim Measures* learn the content of the latest version of the variable annuity insurance reserve assessment guide in U.S., introducing the Monte Carlo stochastic simulation method for the first time, requiring insurance companies to adopt a variety of different scenarios (at least thousand scenarios) where there may generate a fund gap to draw the reasonable reserves. Each scenario must also be tested to meet certain criteria.

In addition, *the Interim Measures* also attached a set of security locks, which adopts the traditional static actuarial appraisal method to assess under the assumption that the capital market fell by 30%. Compared with the stochastic simulation results mentioned above, the larger is chosen, which guarantees the conservativeness and prudence of the reserve drawing.

C. Pilot Company Qualification Control

721. In the pilot notice of variable annuity insurance, the pilot company is required to meet the following conditions:

- the investment-linked insurance business has been operated for three years;
- there is no record of major administrative punishment in the last year;
- the solvency is in the adequate category II at the end of the latest two quarters before the application is submitted at the end of the previous year;
- an information system supporting the management model of variable annuity insurance has been established.

Through the above provisions, it is necessary to ensure that the company has the management experience in investment insurance product, and has sufficient solvency. At the same time, each qualified company can only pilot one product to encourage the company to do work better.

D. Restriction on Pilot Sales Area

722. The pilot of variable annuity insurance is planned to adopt a regional restriction method. Based on the comprehensive consideration of a variety of aspects such as insurance consumer maturity, economic development, past market regulation, etc., the planned pilot areas are limited to Beijing, Shanghai, Guangzhou, Shenzhen and Xiamen.

E. Limitation of the Total Sales Volume

723. On the basis of restricting the sales area, it is proposed to control the total volume of sales simultaneously and directly link it to the actual capital under solvency to ensure that the risk is within the company's tolerance.

The pilot notice requirement for variable annuity insurance requires that the insurance company should apply for the sales amount of the variable annuity insurance pilot, and the sales amount shall not exceed the less one between four times the actual capital and RMB 8 billion under the solvency at the end of the recent quarter.

F. Management of the Sales Channel and Sales Force

724. The first is the restrictions on sales channels, which bans the insurance companies from selling through bank savings counters and telemarketing channels. The second is to establish a risk assessment system to measure the risk tolerance of customers. The third is the restrictions on the qualification of sales personnel, such as experience in life insurance product sales more than one year, no major violations and fraud, forty hours of special training and exams, etc. The fourth is to strengthen the sales management responsibility of the insurance company.

G. Customer Qualification Selection

725. In general, variable annuity insurance is suitable for insurance consumers with low-risk tolerance but expecting certain investment returns. At the same time, the insurance consumers must have some knowledge of insurance and investment.

The pilot notice of variable annuity insurance clearly requires that insurance companies should ensure that the variable annuity insurance is sold to insurance consumers with corresponding risk tolerance through the "risk tolerance questionnaire."

H. Pricing Restrictions on Guaranteed Benefits

726. From a technical perspective, the pricing of guaranteed benefits depends on the economic environment and stochastic simulation. At the same time, a large number of economic and actuarial parameters need to be determined. There is no direct restriction on pricing in the pilot notice, but the insurance company is required to price the guaranteed minimum policy benefit under the principle of fairness and reasonableness, so that the pricing level cannot only cover the cost of providing the guaranteed minimum policy benefit but also obtain a reasonable profit margin to ensure the company's stable and sustainable operation.

I. Guaranteed Solvency

727. A good level of solvency can guarantee the stability of the pilot company's operations and improve its ability to withstand risks, ultimately ensuring that the insurance company can fulfill its commitment of providing the guaranteed minimum benefits for insurance consumers.

The guaranteed solvency is regulated in the following three aspects:

(1) there are also clear restrictions on the solvency level of insurance companies in the conditions for pilot application;
(2) the sales volume must not be higher than four times the actual capital under the solvency at the end of the recent quarter;
(3) for the reserve, it is required to draw the guaranteed benefit reserve and a strict drawing method is established, which ensures a solid foundation for solvency supervision.

Part VII. Social Insurance

Chapter 1. Basic Pension Insurance

§1. Introduction

728. The objects of setting up the basic pension insurance system are to adhere to and improve the pattern that combines social pooling with individual accounts, consolidate and expand the financing channel that comprises individual contributions, collective allowance and government subsidies, improve the benefit payment policy that combines basic pension and individual account pension, promote the incentive mechanism for systems such as more pension for longer-term contributions and more pension for more contributions, establish a normal adjustment mechanism for basic pension, improve the service network and elevate the management level to provide the insured residents with convenient and fast services. At the end of the "12th Five-Year Plan," the systems of New Rural Pension Insurance and the Urban Resident Pension Insurance will be largely implemented nationwide in a combined way and will be aligned with the basic pension system for employees. By 2020, China will have established a fair, unified and standardized pension system for urban and rural residents, which, in combination with social relief, social welfare and other social security systems, will give full play to the active role of the traditional security methods such as family support to better safeguard the basic livelihood of the elderly in urban and rural areas.

729. The Social Insurance Law (SIL) and the Opinions of the State Council on the Establishment of a Unified Basic Pension System for Urban and Rural Residents (hereinafter in this chapter referred to as "the Opinions") provide the basic legal framework for the basic pension insurance.

730. Urban and rural residents that are neither staff of state organs and institutions nor covered by the basic pension system for employees with an age of 16 or above (excluding students) may participate in the pension insurance for urban and rural residents at their registered domiciles.

§2. Basic Pension Insurance Fund

I. Fund Composition

731. In general, by Article 11(2) of the SIL, the basic pension insurance fund shall consist of contributions from the employers and employees and government subsidies.

In detail, the urban and rural residents' pension fund consists of individual contribution, collective allowance and government subsidies.

A. Individual Contribution

732. Any urban and rural resident's pension fund participator shall pay the pension insurance premium in accordance with rules. Currently, the premium may be paid under twelve annual standards: (RMB) 100, 200, 300, 400, 500, 600, 700, 800, 900, 1,000, 1,500 and 2,000. Provincial people's governments or those in autonomous regions or municipalities directly under the Central Government may create any additional standard according to the practical situation to the extent that the highest standards for payment shall not exceed the local flexible employees' annual payment for basic pension insurance for employees, and shall submit the addition to the Ministry of Human Resources and Social Security for record. The Ministry of Human Resources and Social Security shall, in concert with the Ministry of Finance, adjust the standards for payment in due time on the basis of the income growth of urban and rural residents and other information. The insured may choose the standards for payment by himself, and will gain more if he pays more.

B. Collective Allowance

733. Any qualified village collective economic organization shall provide the insured with subsidies for payment based on the standards determined in a democratic way at village meeting convened by villagers' committee and qualified communities are encouraged to include the collective allowance into the fundraising scope for community dedication programs. Other socioeconomic organizations, public charity organizations and individuals are encouraged to provide endowment to the insured for payment. The amount of subsidies and endowment shall not exceed the highest standards for payment provided by local authority.

C. Government Subsidies

734. Governments shall pay basic pension in full to the insured eligible for receiving the urban and rural residents' pension insurance benefits, among which, Central Government shall provide the full subsidies to central and western regions on the basis of the standards for basic pension determined by Central Government, and shall provide 50% subsidies to eastern region.

Local people's governments shall provide subsidies to the insured for payment. The subsidy for those choosing the minimum standard is no less than RMB 30 per capita per year; for anyone choosing a higher standard for payment, corresponding subsidies may be raised properly; for anyone choosing a standard of RMB 500 or more for payment, corresponding subsidies shall be no less than RMB 60 per capita per year, and specific standards and measures shall be determined by provincial people's governments or those in autonomous regions or municipalities directly under the Central Government. For the group who has difficulty in payment, such as the severely disabled person, local people's governments shall pay, on their behalf, part or all of the pension insurance premium at the minimum standard.

II. Fund Management and Operation

735. Article 9 of the Opinions provides that the fund for New Rural Pension Insurance and the fund for Urban Resident Pension Insurance shall be consolidated into the pension fund for urban and rural residents, and the financial and accounting system and various business management rules and regulations relevant to the pension fund for urban and rural residents shall be perfected. The pension fund for urban and rural residents shall be incorporated into the fiscal special account of social security fund, and shall be divided into two items as receipt and payment for management through separate recording and independent accounting. No area, department, unit or individual may misappropriate or make a fraudulent application and claim for the fund. All parts of the country shall, on the basis of consolidation of the pension system for urban and rural residents, gradually push forward the provincial administration for pension fund for urban and rural residents. The pension fund for urban and rural residents shall be put into investment or operation under the uniform national provisions to preserve or increase its value.

III. Fund Supervision

736. Article 10 of the Opinions provides that the departments of human resources and social security at all levels shall, in concert with relevant departments, earnestly perform their supervision and administration responsibilities, establish and perfect internal control system and fund audit and supervision system to supervise and examine the fundraising, delivery, transfer, distribution, deposit and management, shall disclose information in accordance with relevant provisions and accept social supervision. Financial departments and auditing departments shall supervise the receipt and payment, management and investment and operation of the fund in accordance with their respective responsibilities. For illegal and undisciplined acts, such as making a fraudulent application and claim, unwarranted diversion of resources and corruption and waste, relevant departments shall handle them seriously in accordance with the relevant state laws and regulations. Effective ways of social supervision with villager (resident) representatives' participation shall be actively explored to make the fund use open and transparent to the public and enable the system to run in the sunshine.

737. Regarding the investment of pension insurance fund, Articles 12, 52 and 57 of the Administrative Measures for Investment with Basic Pension Insurance Fund further provide that:

- The state shall supervise and control the investment with the endowment funds in a strict manner. The investment with the endowment funds shall be in strict compliance with relevant laws and regulations, and it is strictly prohibited to engage in insider trading, carry out transactions by using undisclosed information, manipulate markets and commit other unlawful acts, as well as damage the endowment funds and interests of others, and obtain illegitimate interests through affiliated transactions and by other means. No organization or individual may embezzle, misappropriate and divert the endowment funds invested and operated.
- The Ministry of Human Resources and Social Security and the Ministry of Finance shall, in accordance with the law, supervise the investment management business of the endowment funds conducted by the trustees, custody institutions, investment management institutions and the relevant entities, and strengthen the investment risk prevention. The PBC, the CSRC and the CBIRC shall, in accordance with their respective duties, supervise the operating activities of the custody institutions and investment management institutions. The departments involved shall intensify communications and information sharing in the course of supervision.
- Information on the operation of the investment with the pension insurance funds shall be regularly announced to the public via the press, websites and other media, so as to guarantee the public's right to know and accept the public supervision. Any organization or individual has the right to report or complain about any act in violation of laws and regulations, and the competent department concerned shall investigate and handle the report or complaint carefully.

§3. Basic Pension Insurance Account

738. Article 11(1) of the SIL provides that the basic pension insurance shall be a combination of social pooling and individual account.

Article 12 of the SIL further provides that an employer shall make basic pension insurance contributions at the state-fixed rate of the employees' payroll, and the contributions shall be deposited into the basic pension insurance pooling fund. An employee shall make basic pension insurance contributions at the state-fixed rate for his/her wage, and the contributions shall be deposited into his/her individual account. A member of the basic pension insurance as proprietor of privately or individually owned business with no hired labor, part-time worker who is not covered by the basic pension insurance system through his/her employer, or any other person in employment of flexible forms shall make basic pension insurance contributions as set by the state; and the contributions shall be divided and deposited separately into the pooling fund and an individual account.

739. Article 5 of the Opinions provides that the state establishes the individual accounts for lifelong recording of pension insurance for the insured, so that all the individual contribution, subsidies provided by local people's governments for the insured, collective allowance and the subsidies provided by other socioeconomic organizations, public charity organizations and individuals can be recorded in the individual account. The deposit in the individual account bears interests pursuant to national provisions.

Advance withdrawal from an individual account shall not be allowed. The interest rate of an individual account shall be no less than that for a fixed-term bank account, and interests accrued are not subject to taxation. The balances in the individual account are hereditary upon the death of the account bearer.

§4. Basic Pension Insurance Benefits

740. By Article 15 of the SIL and Article 6 of the Opinions, the urban and rural residents' pension insurance benefits, consisting of the basic pension and the individual account pension, are paid throughout life.

I. Basic Pension

741. The Central Government determines the minimum standards for basic pension, establishes a normal adjustment mechanism for the minimum standards for the basic pension, and adjusts the minimum standards for nationwide basic pension in due time in accordance with the economic development and price changes. Local people's governments may properly raise the standards for basic pension in accordance with the actual situation; the basic pension paid to the one who has paid for long time may be added, where appropriate, with the extra and additional expenses arising therefrom borne by local people's governments. Specific measures shall be determined by provincial people's governments and those in autonomous regions or municipalities directly under the Central Government, and shall be submitted to the Ministry of Human Resource and Social Security for record.

II. Individual Account Pension

742. The current monthly calculation and distribution standard for the individual account pension is the amount reached by dividing the total deposit in the individual account by 139 (the same as the calculation and distribution coefficient for the individual account pension in respect of the basic pension insurance for employees). The individual account balance may be inherited in accordance with the law in case of death of the insured.

§5. CONDITIONS FOR RECEIVING THE PENSION INSURANCE BENEFITS

743. By Article 16 of the SIL and Article 7 of the Opinions, any individual who has been included in the pension insurance system for urban and rural residents, reached the age of 60, accumulatively paid the insurance for fifteen years but has not received any basic pension stipulated by the state may get the pension for urban and rural residents on a monthly basis.

Article 17 of the SIL provides that when a member of the basic pension insurance dies from illnesses or causes not related to work, the next of kins of the member are entitled to receive funeral subsidies and bereavement allowances; when a member becomes completely unfit for work due to illnesses or causes not related to work before reaching the legal retirement age, the member is entitled to illness and disability allowances. The expenses required shall be covered from the basic pension insurance fund.

744. Article 7 of the Opinions further provides that where any individual who can enjoy the pension benefit for urban and rural residents has died, the pension payment shall be stopped from the next month after his/her death. If the condition permits, local people's governments may seek for the establishment of a system of funeral subsidies in accordance with their practical situations. Social insurance agencies shall check the name list of the persons that can receive the pension every year. The villagers' (residents') committee shall assist the social insurance agencies in carrying out relevant work, release to the public the qualification for receiving pension for the insured living in the administrative village (community), and verify the pension payment records for urban and rural individuals with those for employees to ensure there is no repetition, omission or false.

§6. TRANSFER OF PENSION AND CONVERGENCE OF SYSTEMS

745. Article 19 of the SIL provides that the basic pension insurance relationship of a member who has worked across different pooling districts shall transfer together with the member, and the member's lengths of contribution payment shall be cumulative. When the member reaches the legal retirement age, his/her basic pension shall be calculated in segregation corresponding to the phases of contribution payment, yet the pension shall be paid in integration as an aggregate. The concrete approach shall be regulated by the State Council.

746. Article 8 of the Opinions further provides that where a person participating in pension insurance for urban and rural residents transfers its household register and it is accordingly required to transfer its pension record to another area, he or she may apply such transfer in the area of destination, transfer all the amount saved in its individual account on a lump-sum basis, and continue to participate in and pay the premium according to the provisions of the area of destination, with the payment years calculated accumulatively; where the person has received the pension benefits for urban and rural residents according to the provisions, his/her pension record shall not be transferred no matter whether the household register is transferred or not. For the linkup among pension insurance system for urban and rural residents and other social security systems (including the basic pension system for employees, the system of veteran benefit and placement, the system of subsistence allowances for both urban and rural residents, the rural system of five guarantees) as well as the reward and assistance system for some rural families that comply with family planning regulations, relevant provisions shall apply.

Chapter 2. Basic Medical Insurance

§1. Introduction

747. Article 23 of the SIL provides that employees shall participate in basic medical insurance schemes. Basic medical insurance contributions shall be paid by both employers and employees in accordance with the relevant national regulations. Individual industrial or commercial households with no employees, part-time employees who do not make social insurance contributions with their employers and other laborers in flexible employment may participate in basic medical schemes and pay contributions themselves in accordance with the relevant national regulations.

748. Articles 24 and 25 of the SIL provide that the state shall establish and improve the basic medical insurance system for rural and urban residents. A combination of individual contribution and governmental subsidies shall apply to basic medical insurance for urban residents. Measures for the new-type cooperative medical system for rural areas shall be formulated by the State Council. The government shall grant subsidies to individuals who are entitled to the minimum living guarantee, the disabled who lose working ability and minors or the elderly at or above the age of 60 as per their individual contributions.

§2. Legal Framework

749. Article 27 of the SIL provides that if the accumulated contribution period of a participant to an employees' basic medical insurance reaches the number of years as required by the relevant national regulations when he or she reaches the statutory retirement age, the individual will not pay basic medical insurance contributions after his/her retirement and shall begin to be entitled to basic medical insurance benefits. If such a period fails to reach the number of years as required by the relevant national regulations, the individual may continue paying contributions until his/her contribution period reaches the number of years as required by the relevant national regulations.

750. Medical expenses which meet the basic medicine directory, clinical service items and medical service facility standards and those incurred in emergent treatment shall be reimbursed by the basic medical insurance fund in accordance with the national regulations.

Medical expenses which need to be reimbursed by the basic medical insurance fund shall be settled directly by social insurance agencies with medical institutions and medicine operating entities. Social insurance administrative departments and health administrative departments shall establish a settlement system for cross-regional medical expenses to facilitate the receipt of basic medical insurance benefits.

751. By Article 30 of the SIL, the following medical expenses shall not be reimbursed by the basic medical insurance fund:

- those to be reimbursed by the work-related injury insurance fund;
- those to be borne by a third party;
- those to be borne by public health departments; or
- those incurred in overseas medical institutions.

If a third party refuses to pay medical expenses for which it is obligated to pay in accordance with the law or if it is impossible to determine the third party, the medical expenses shall be reimbursed by the basic medical insurance fund in advance; thereafter, the fund is entitled to claim for payment from the third party.

752. Based on the demand for social insurance service, social insurance agencies may enter into service agreements with medical institutions or medicine operating entities to regulate medical services. Medical institutions shall provide participants in a basic medical insurance scheme with reasonable and necessary medical service.

753. If an individual has been employed in different regions, his/her basic medical insurance relation shall be changed as per his/her work location, and the contribution period shall be accumulated.

Chapter 3. Work-Related Injury Insurance

§1. Introduction

754. The basic purpose of the work-related injury insurance is to guarantee the availability of medical treatment and economic compensation to employees who suffer from work-related accidental injuries or occupational diseases, facilitate the prevention of work-related injuries and professional rehabilitation, and spread work-related injury risks assumed by employers.

755. Enterprises, public institutions, social bodies, privately owned non-enterprise entities, foundations, law firms, accounting firms, and other organizations as well as individual business operators with hired workers ("employers") within the territory of China shall participate in work-related injury insurance and pay work-related injury insurance premiums for all of their staff members or hired workers ("employees") in accordance with the provisions hereof. The employees of public institutions, social bodies, privately owned non-enterprise entities, foundations, law firms, accounting firms, and other organizations and the hired workers of individual business operators within the territory of China shall have the right to enjoy the benefits of work-related injury insurance in accordance with the provisions hereof.

An employer shall make known within itself the relevant details of its participation in work-related injury insurance. An employer and its employees shall abide by the laws and regulations regarding safe production and the prevention and treatment of occupational diseases, implement rules and standards for safety and sanitation, prevent the occurrence of work-related injury accidents and avoid and reduce occupational diseases. Where an employee suffers from work-related injury, the employer shall adopt measures to ensure that such employee receives timely medical treatments.

756. The SIL and the Work-Related Injury Insurance Regulations (WRIIR) provide the basic legal framework of the work-related injury insurance.

§2. Work-Related Injury Insurance Fund

757. Work-related injury insurance fund consists of work-related injury insurance premiums paid by employers, interests on work-related injury insurance funds and other funds included in the work-related injury insurance fund in accordance with the law.

758. Employers shall pay work-related injury insurance premiums on time. Employees need not pay work-related injury insurance premiums themselves. The amount of work-related injury insurance premium payable by an employer shall be the total payroll of its employees multiplied by its premium rate. For any industry in which it is difficult to pay work-related injury insurance premiums on the basis of the gross amount of wages, specific methods for paying such premiums shall be specified by the administrative department of social insurance of the State Council.

759. Work-related injury insurance funds shall be deposited into a financial account dedicated for social security funds and shall be used for the payment of benefits of work-related injury insurance, the fees for the work capability assessment, the publicity and training with respect to work-related injury prevention and other expenses prescribed herein and the payment of other expenses required by laws or regulations to be used for work-related injury insurance.

No entity or individual may use the work-related injury insurance funds for investment and operation, construction or reconstruction of offices or distribution of bonuses, or appropriate such funds for other purposes.

760. A certain percentage of the work-related injury insurance funds shall be maintained as reserves for the payment of work-related injury insurance benefits in the event of major accidents in integrally planned regions. Where the reserves are insufficient for such payment, the people's governments of such regions shall make an advance payment. The specific ratio of reserves to the total amount of funds and the procedures for the use of reserves shall be specified by the people's governments of provinces, autonomous regions or municipalities directly under the Central Government.

§3. Determination of Work-Related Injuries

761. Under any of the following circumstances, an employee shall be determined as suffering a work-related injury:

- where he is injured in an accident at work during working hours in the workplace;
- where he is injured in an accident while engaging in preparatory or winding-up work related to his work before or after working hours in the workplace;
- where he is injured by violence or in any other accident in connection with the performance of his duties during working hours in the workplace;
- where he suffers from an occupational disease;
- where, during a work-related travel, he is injured in connection with his work or his whereabouts become unknown after an accident;
- where he is injured in a traffic accident for which he is not principally responsible or in a city rail transit, passenger ferry and train accident while going to or returning from work; or
- other circumstances specified in laws and administrative regulations in which it is determined that he suffers a work-related injury.

762. Under any of the following circumstances, an employee shall be deemed as suffering a work-related injury:

(1) where he dies immediately or within forty-eight hours after emergency treatment for a disease suddenly arising during working hours in the workplace;
(2) where he is injured in emergency rescue and disaster relief efforts and any other act to protect the interests of the state or the public interest; or
(3) where he is injured and disabled in war or on duty while in military service and has obtained a certificate for injured and disabled soldiers, and suffers from a relapse of the old injury while being employed by the employer.

Where an employee falls under the circumstances of Item (1) or (2) of the preceding paragraph, he shall be entitled to work-related injury insurance benefits in accordance with the relevant provisions hereof. Where an employee falls under the circumstance of Item (3) of the preceding paragraph, he shall be entitled to work-related injury insurance benefits other than the lump-sum disability allowance in accordance with the relevant provisions hereof.

763. Under any of the following circumstances, an employee shall not be determined or deemed as suffering a work-related injury:

- where he commits a crime willfully;
- where he is intoxicated, or taking addictive drugs; or
- where he inflicts harm on himself or commits suicide.

764. Where an employee is injured in an accident or is diagnosed or deemed after authentication as having an occupational disease pursuant to the provisions of the Prevention and Treatment of Occupational Diseases Law, his employer shall file an application for determination of work-related injuries to the administrative department of social insurance of an integrally planned region within thirty days of the date of occurrence of the accidental injury or the date of diagnosis or authentication of the occupational disease. Under special circumstances, the time limit for application may, subject to the consent of the administrative department of social insurance, be extended as appropriate.

Where the employer fails to file an application for determination of work-related injuries pursuant to the preceding paragraph, the employee with the work-related injury, his immediate family members or the trade union may directly file an application for determination of work-related injury to the administrative department of social insurance of an integrally planned region where the employer is located within one year of the date of occurrence of the accidental injury or the date of diagnosis or authentication of the occupational disease.

Matters related to the work-related injury which are required under the preceding paragraph to be ascertained by the administrative department of social insurance at the provincial level shall be handled in accordance with the principle of territory-based jurisdiction by the administrative department of social insurance of a city divided into districts where the employer is located. Where the employer fails to file an application for determination of work-related injuries within the time limit prescribed in the preceding paragraph, the relevant expenses incurred during the time limit such as the work-related injury benefits which comply with the provisions hereof shall be borne by the employer.

765. To file an application for the determination of work-related injuries, the following materials shall be submitted:

- an application for determination of work-related injuries;
- evidence materials for any labor relationship with the employer (including the de facto labor relationship); and
- a certificate of medical diagnosis or a certificate of diagnosis of occupational disease (or a letter of authentication of diagnosis of occupational disease).

The application for determination of work-related injuries shall include the basic details of the accident such as the time and place of its occurrence, the cause of the accident and the degree of injury suffered by the employee.

Where materials provided by the applicant for the determination of work-related injuries are incomplete, the administrative department of social insurance shall inform the applicant of all materials that need to be supplemented in a written notice. After the applicant has supplemented the materials as required by the written notice, the administrative department of social insurance shall accept the application.

766. After the administrative department of social insurance has accepted an application for determination of work-related injuries, it may, in light of the requirements of the examination and verification of the application, investigate for the purpose of verification the accident and injury and the employer, the employee, the relevant trade union, the relevant medical institution and other relevant departments shall provide assistance. The authentication of diagnosis of occupational disease and diagnosis dispute shall be handled in accordance with the relevant provisions of the Prevention and Treatment of Occupational Diseases Law. Where a certificate of diagnosis of occupational diseases or a letter of authentication of diagnosis of occupational diseases is obtained in accordance with the law, the administrative department of social insurance shall not carry out further investigations for verification purposes.

Where an injury is considered as a work-related one by the employee or his immediate family members but not by the employer, the burden of proof shall be borne by the employer.

767. The administrative department of social insurance shall make a decision on the determination of work-related injuries within sixty days of the date of acceptance of the application for determination of work-related injuries and shall send a written notice to the employee who applies for determination of work-related injuries or his immediate family members and his employer.

With respect to any application for determination of work-related injuries involving clear facts and definite obligations and rights, the administrative department of social insurance shall make a decision on the determination of work-related injuries within fifteen days of the date of acceptance of any such application.

Where a decision on the determination of work-related injuries relies on the conclusion of a judicial authority or relevant competent administrative authority, the time limit for making the decision on determination of work-related injuries shall be suspended during the period in which the judicial authority or relevant competent administrative authority does not reach a conclusion.

Any staff member of the administrative department of social insurance who has interest in the applicant applying for determination of work-related injuries shall withdraw from the case.

§4. Work Capability Assessment

768. Where an employee suffers a work-related injury, and is disabled after the injury is in a stable condition upon treatment or his work capability is affected, the employee shall go through a work capability assessment.

A work capability assessment is an assessment of the degree of impairment in work function and self-care ability.

Impairment in work function is classified into ten disability grades, with the grade one being the most severe disability and the grade ten being the mildest disability.

Impairment in self-care ability is classified into three grades: total self-care disability, substantial self-care disability and partial self-care disability.

769. An application for work capability assessment shall be filed by an employer, an employee with a work-related injury or his immediate family members to the work capability assessment committee of a city divided into districts, and the decision on determination of work-related injuries and information relevant to the medical treatment of the work-related injury of the employee shall be provided.

770. After the work capability assessment committee of a city divided into districts has received an application for work capability assessment, it shall select three or five relevant medical and health experts at random from its expert pool to form an expert panel to issue an assessment opinion. The work capability assessment committee of the city divided into districts shall reach a work capability assessment conclusion with respect to the employee with a work-related injury on the basis of the assessment opinion of the expert panel. Where necessary, it may entrust a qualified medical institution to assist in the relevant diagnosis.

The work capability assessment committee of the city divided into districts shall reach a work capability assessment conclusion within sixty days of the date of receipt of the application for work capability assessment. The time limit for reaching a work capability assessment conclusion may be extended for a period of thirty days where necessary. The work capability assessment conclusion shall be served in a timely manner upon the entity or individual who applies for the assessment.

771. Where any entity or individual who applies for a work capability assessment is dissatisfied with the assessment conclusion of the work capability assessment committee of a city divided into districts, the entity or individual may, within fifteen days of the date of receipt of the assessment conclusion, apply to the work capability assessment committee of the province, autonomous region or municipality directly under the Central Government for reassessment. The work capability assessment conclusion of the work capability assessment committee of the province, autonomous region or municipality directly under the Central Government shall be final.

772. A work capability assessment shall be conducted in an objective and impartial manner. Where any member of the work capability assessment committee or expert who participates in the assessment is related to the parties concerned, he shall withdraw from the assessment.

Where, within one year after a work capability assessment conclusion is reached, the employee with a work-related injury or his immediate family members, his employer or the agency believes that there is a change in his disability, he may apply for a work capability reexamination and assessment.

§5. Work-Related Injury Insurance Benefits

773. Article 38 of the SIL provides that the following expenses related to work-related injury are payable from the work-related injury fund in accordance with national provisions:

- medical expenses for work injury and rehabilitation expenses;
- food allowances during hospitalization;
- transportation, accommodation and food expenses incurred for medical services outside the pooling district;
- expenses for provision and installation of disability aid equipment;
- the expenses of personal care as set by the working fitness assessment committee for people who need personal care in life;
- lump-sum disability subsidies, and disability allowances payable monthly to disabled employees of degrees one through to four;
- lump-sum medical subsidies payable to employees upon termination or rescinding of labor contracts;
- funeral expenses, pension allowances for dependents and subsidies for work-related deaths paid to the survivors when employees die from work-related causes; and
- expenses incurred for working fitness assessments.

The WRIIR explains in very details how those expenses are calculated and paid, which will be introduced as follows.

I. Medical Expenses and Other Related Expenses

774. Any employee who receives treatment for work-related accidental injury or occupational disease shall be entitled to work-related injury medical benefits.

An employee shall seek medical treatment for a work-related injury at a medical institution which has entered into a service agreement. In the case of an emergency, the employee may first seek emergency treatment at the nearest medical institution.

Where expenses required for treating the work-related injury fall within the catalogue of treatments, the catalogue of pharmaceuticals and hospitalization service standard for work-related injury insurance, they shall be paid from work-related injury insurance funds. The catalogue of treatments, the catalogue of pharmaceuticals and hospitalization service standard for work-related injury insurance shall be prescribed by the administrative department of social insurance of the State Council in conjunction with the administrative department of public health, the pharmaceutical regulatory department and other departments of the State Council.

Food allowance for an employee who is hospitalized for the treatment of a work-related injury and travel and food and boarding expenses required for the employee with the work-related injury to seek medical treatment outside an integrally planned region with the referral certificate of a medical institution and the consent of the handling agency shall be paid from work-related injury insurance funds and the specific standards for such payment shall be specified by the people's governments of the integrally planned region.

An employee with a work-related injury shall not be entitled to work-related injury medical benefits for treatment of a disease not arising from work-related injury, and such matter shall be handled in accordance with measures for basic medical insurance.

Where expenses incurred for the rehabilitative treatment of an employee with a work-related injury at a medical institution that has entered into a service agreement satisfy the applicable provisions, they shall be paid from work-related injury insurance funds.

Where administrative review or administrative litigation occurs after the administrative department of social insurance makes a decision on the determination of work-related injuries, the payments of medical expenses to the employee with a work-related injury for medical treatment of the work-related injury shall not be stopped during the period of administrative review or administrative litigation.

An employee with a work-related injury may, due to daily life or employment needs and subject to the confirmation of the work capability assessment committee, wear artificial limbs, orthosis, artificial eyes and false teeth or equip himself with an aiding device such as a wheelchair, and the necessary costs shall be paid from work-related injury insurance funds at a rate specified by the state.

II. Benefits During the Suspension-of-Work-with-Pay Period

775. Where an employee needs to suspend his work in order to receive medical treatment for a work-related accidental injury or an occupational disease, his original wage and welfare benefits shall remain unchanged and payable monthly by his employer during the suspension-of-work-with-pay period.

The suspension-of-work-with-pay period shall normally not exceed twelve months. Where the injury is severe or the circumstances involved are exceptional, such period may, subject to confirmation by the work capability assessment committee of a city divided into districts, be extended as appropriate. However, such extension shall not exceed twelve months. After the disability grade of the employee with a work-related injury is assessed, the original benefits shall be terminated, and the employee shall be entitled to disability benefits in accordance with the relevant provision of the laws and regulations. Where the employee with a work-related injury still needs medical treatment after the end of the suspension-of-work-with-pay period, the employee shall continue to enjoy work-related injury medical benefits.

Where an employee with a work-related injury and self-care disability needs nurse care during the suspension-of-work-with-pay period, his employer shall be responsible for nurse care.

III. Expenses Incurred for Daily Life Care

776. Where an employee with a work-related injury has been assessed with respect to his disability grade and confirmed by the work capability assessment committee as requiring daily life care, expenses incurred for daily life care shall be paid monthly from work-related injury insurance funds.

Expenses incurred for daily life care shall be paid according to the three different grades of self-care disability, namely total self-care disability, substantial self-care disability and partial self-care disability, and the rates shall be 50%, 40% or 30% of the average monthly wage of employees in an integrally planned region in the preceding year, respectively.

IV. Disability Allowance and Disability Subsidy

777. The disability allowance and disability subsidy that an employee with a work-related disability may enjoy depend upon the grade of disability:

(1) Grade 1-4
- The labor relationship shall remain unchanged, and the employee shall withdraw from his post and enjoy the following benefits.
- A disability allowance paid from the work-related injury insurance funds according to the disability grade in a lump sum at any of the following rates: for grade one disability, the employee's wages for twenty-seven months; for grade two disability, the employee's wages for twenty-five months; for grade three disability, the employee's wages for twenty-three months; and for grade four disability, the employee's wages for twenty-one months.
- A monthly disability subsidy paid from the work-related injury insurance funds at any of the following rates: for grade one disability, 90% of the employee's wage; for grade two disability, 85% of the employee's wage; for grade three disability, 80% of the employee's wage; and for grade four disability, 75% of the employee's wage. Where the actual amount of the disability subsidy is lower than the local minimum wage standard, the difference shall be paid from the work-related injury insurance funds.
- The disability subsidy shall be terminated after the employee reaches the retirement age and go through retirement formalities and the employee

shall then be entitled to basic endowment insurance benefits in accordance with the relevant provisions of the state. Where the basic endowment insurance benefits are lower than the disability subsidy, the difference shall be paid from the work-related injury insurance funds.

- Where an employee with a work-related disability is assessed as having a disability between grade one and grade four, the employer and the employee shall base on the disability subsidy to pay the basic medical care insurance premium.

(2) Grade 5-6

- A disability allowance paid from work-related injury insurance funds in accordance with the disability grade in a lump sum at any of the following rates: for grade five disability, the employee's wages for eighteen months; and for grade six disability, the employee's wages for sixteen months.
- His labor relationship with the employer shall remain unchanged and the employer shall arrange appropriate work for the employee. Where it is difficult to arrange any work for the employee, the employer shall pay a monthly disability subsidy to the employee at any of the following rates: for grade five disability, 70% of the employee's wage and for grade six disability, 60% of the employee's wage, and the employer shall also pay as required on behalf of the employee all the social insurance premiums payable by the employee. Where the actual amount of the disability subsidy is lower than the local minimum wage standard, the difference shall be made up by the employer.
- Upon the request of an employee with a work-related injury, the labor relationship between the employee and the employer may be dissolved or terminated, the work-related injury medical allowance shall be paid to the employee in a lump sum from the work-related injury insurance funds and the employer shall pay to the employee a disability employment allowance in a lump sum. Specific standards for the lump-sum work-related injury medical allowance and the lump-sum disability employment allowance shall be specified by the people's governments of provinces, autonomous regions and municipalities directly under the Central Government.

(3) Grade 7-10

- A disability allowance paid from work-related injury insurance funds according to the disability grade in a lump sum at any of the following rates: for grade seven disability, the employee's wages for thirteen months; for grade eight disability, the employee's wages for eleven months; for grade nine disability, the employee's wages for nine months; and for grade ten disability, the employee's wages for seven months; and
- Upon termination of the labor or employment contract after the expiration of the term thereof, or upon dissolution of the labor or employment contract at the request of the employee, the work-related injury medical allowance shall be paid to the employee in a lump sum from the work-related injury insurance funds and the employer shall pay to the employee a disability employment allowance in a lump sum. Specific standards for the lump-sum work-related injury medical allowance and lump-sum disability employment allowance

shall be specified by the people's governments of provinces, autonomous regions and municipalities directly under the Central Government.

V. Funeral Allowance, Bereavement Payment and Other Benefits

778. Where an employee dies as a result of his work, the immediate family members of the employee shall receive a funeral allowance, a bereavement payment to dependent family members and a lump-sum work-related death allowance from work-related injury insurance funds in accordance with the following provisions:

(1) The funeral allowance shall be six months' average monthly wage of an employee in the integrally planned region in the preceding year.
(2) A bereavement payment to dependent family members shall be made at a certain percentage of the employee's wage to each of the family members of the employee who, before the employee's death, is dependent on the employee as the primary source of income and who has no work capability. Rates for such payment are as follows: 40% per month for the spouse, 30% for each of other family members per month, an additional 10% plus the aforementioned rate for each widowed elder or orphan per month. The sum of the bereavement payment to all dependent family members so determined shall not be higher than the wage of the employee before his work-related death. The specific scope of dependent family members shall be specified by the administrative department of social insurance of the State Council.
(3) The rate for the lump-sum work-related death allowance shall be twenty times the average per capita disposable income of national urban residents for the previous year.
(4) Where a disabled employee dies as a result of the work-related injury during the suspension-of-work-with-pay period, the immediate family members of the employee shall be entitled to the benefits specified above.
(5) Where an employee with a disability between grade one and grade four dies after the suspension-of-work-with-pay period, the immediate family members of the employee shall be entitled to the benefits specified in Items (1) and (2) above.

VI. The Cessation of Enjoyment of Work-Related Injury Insurance Benefits

779. By Article 43 of the SIL and Article 42 of the WRIIR, under any of the following circumstances, an employee with a work-related injury shall cease enjoying work-related injury insurance benefits:

- where he has lost eligibility to receive the benefits;
- where he refuses to undergo a work capability assessment;
- where he refuses to receive medical treatment.

In addition, by Article 40 of the SIL, when work-injured employees meet the conditions for receiving basic old-age pensions, payment of disability allowances shall cease, and the employees shall instead receive basic old-age pensions. If basic old-age pensions are less than disability allowances, the differentials shall be made up from the work injury insurance fund.

VII. Repayment of Work-Related Injury Insurance Benefits

780. The law provides two situations in which the work-related injury insurance benefits paid may be recoverable.

By Article 41 of the SIL, when a work injury accident occurs while the employer does not make work injury contributions as required by law, work injury benefits shall be paid by the employer. If the employer refuses to pay, interim payment shall be arranged from the work injury insurance fund. Interim payment for work injury benefits paid from the work injury fund shall be paid off by the employer. When the employer refuses to pay off, the social insurance agency may demand repayment.

By Article 42 of the SIL, when a work injury accident is caused by a third party, and the third party refuses to pay medical expenses for work injury treatment or the third party cannot be identified, interim payment for the expenses shall be arranged from the work injury insurance fund. The work injury insurance fund has the right to demand repayment from the third party after providing the interim payment.

VIII. Miscellaneous

781. Where, during a business travel, an employee's whereabouts become unknown after an accident or in the course of emergency rescue or disaster relief, his wage shall continue to be paid for three months from the month in which the accident occurred and be terminated on the fourth month, and thereafter the dependent family members of the employee shall be paid a bereavement payment to dependent family members on a monthly basis from work-related injury insurance funds. Where the family members have living difficulties, 50% of the lump-sum work-related death allowance may be paid in advance.

782. Where an employee is dispatched to work abroad and is required to participate in local work-related injury insurance in accordance with the laws of the destination country or region, the employee shall participate in local work-related injury insurance and his work-related injury insurance relationship in China shall be suspended. Where the employee cannot participate in local work-related injury insurance, his work-related injury insurance relationship in China shall not be suspended.

§6. SUPERVISION AND ADMINISTRATION

783. The administrative departments of social insurance shall supervise and inspect the collection of work-related injury insurance premiums and the receipt and payment of work-related injury insurance funds in accordance with the law. Financial departments and audit departments shall supervise the receipt, payment and management of work-related injury insurance funds in accordance with the law.

Every organization or individual has the right to report illegal acts relating to work-related injury insurance. The administrative departments of social insurance shall investigate such report in a timely manner, handle it in accordance with the relevant provisions, and maintain the confidentiality of the informant.

Trade unions shall safeguard the lawful rights and interests of employees with a work-related injury and conduct supervision over the work-related injury insurance work of employers in accordance with the law.

Disputes arising between employees and employers with respect to work-related injuries shall be handled in accordance with the relevant provisions for the settlement of labor disputes.

Under any of the following circumstances, the relevant entity or individual may either apply for administrative review in accordance with the law or institute an administrative action with a people's court in accordance with the law:

- the employee who applies for determination of work-related injuries, his immediate family member or his employer is dissatisfied with the decision not to accept the application for the determination of work-related injuries;
- the employee who applies for determination of work-related injuries, his immediate family member or his employer is dissatisfied with the conclusion of the determination of work-related injuries;
- the employer is dissatisfied with its premium rate determined by the handling agency;
- the medical institution or the aiding device supply institution that has entered into a service agreement deems that the handling agency fails to comply with the relevant agreement or provisions; or
- the employee with a work-related injury or his immediate family members are dissatisfied with the work-related injury insurance benefits verified by the handling agency.

Chapter 4. Unemployment Insurance

§1. Introduction

784. The ultimate purpose of unemployment insurance is two-sided: to guarantee basic livings of the unemployed during the unemployment period and promote their reemployment.

785. Article 44 of the SIL provides that each employee shall enroll in the unemployment insurance system, and the employer and employee shall jointly make unemployment insurance contributions as set by the state. More specifically, Article 2 of the Unemployment Insurance Regulations (UIR) states that enterprises and institutions in cities and towns, namely enterprise with foreign investment, privately owned enterprise in cities and towns as well as other enterprises in cities and towns, as well as their staff and workers shall pay unemployment insurance premium in accordance with the UIR. The unemployed of enterprises and institutions in cities and towns may enjoy the benefits of unemployment insurance in accordance with the UIR.

The people's governments of provinces, autonomous regions and municipalities directly under the Central Government, in accordance with the actual local situations, may determine whether the UIR applies to social organizations and their full-time staff, private non-enterprise units and their staff and workers, or individual industrial and commercial businesses in cities and towns with employees that are located within their respective administrative areas.

786. The administrative department of labor security under the State Council is in charge of unemployment insurance work throughout the country. The administrative departments of labor security under the people's governments at or above the county level are in charge of unemployment insurance work within their respective administrative areas. Social insurance agencies engaging in unemployment insurance business established by administrative departments of labor security in accordance with provisions of the State Council will undertake concretely the unemployment insurance work.

§2. Unemployment Insurance Funds

787. By Article 5 of the UIR, unemployment insurance funds include the following items: (1) unemployment insurance premium paid by enterprises and institutions in cities and towns as well as their staff and workers; (2) interest of unemployment insurance fund; (3) financial subsidies; (4) other funds incorporated into unemployment insurance funds in accordance with the law.

788. Enterprises and institutions in cities and towns shall pay unemployment insurance premium at a rate of 2% on the basis of their total amount of salaries. Staff and workers in enterprises and institutions in cities and towns shall pay unemployment insurance premium at a rate of 1% on the basis of their own salaries. Farmer workers employed by enterprises and institutions in cities and towns on the basis of contract do not pay unemployment insurance premium themselves.

Unemployment insurance funds shall be used for the following expenditure: (1) unemployment insurance compensation; (2) medical subvention during the period of receiving unemployment insurance compensation; (3) funeral allowance for the unemployed died during the period of receiving unemployment insurance compensation and pension for spouse and direct relatives supported by the dead person; (4) subsidy for accepting job training and job seeking during the period of receiving unemployment insurance compensation. Measures and Schemes for such subsidy are to be stipulated by people's governments of provinces, autonomous regions and municipalities directly under the Central Government; (5) other expenses relating to unemployment insurance stipulated or approved by the State Council.

789. Unemployment insurance funds must be deposited into special accounts of social security funds opened by financial departments in state-owned commercial banks. They shall be managed in a way of separate channeled receipts and expenditures and supervised by financial departments in accordance with the law. Unemployment insurance funds deposited into banks and used to buy national debts in accordance with the state provisions are accounted interests respectively according to the deposit rates of resident deposits during the same period and interests of national debt. The interests are merged into unemployment insurance funds. Unemployment insurance funds shall be used for their specific purposes, and may not be misused for other purposes or used to balance financial expenses and receipts.

§3. Unemployment Insurance Benefits

790. By Article 45 of the SIL and Article 14 of the UIR, qualifications for the unemployed who may receive unemployment insurance compensation are as follows:

- have participated in the unemployment insurance scheme, the unit to which they belong and they themselves have performed the obligation of paying premium not less than one year;
- have suspended employment undue to their own willingness;
- have undergone unemployment registration and have requested new jobs.

The unemployed are entitled to receive other unemployment insurance benefits during the period of receiving unemployment insurance compensation.

791. By Article 51 of the SIL and Article 15 of the UIR, where any one of the following circumstances occur during the period of receiving unemployment insurance compensation, the unemployed shall stop receiving unemployment insurance compensation and shall be deprived of other unemployment insurance benefits:

- reemployment;
- performance of military service;

- emigration to foreign countries;
- enjoyment of basic pension benefits;
- imprisonment and reeducation through labor;
- refusal of reemployment recommended by departments and agencies designated by local people's governments without any rational reasons;
- other circumstances stipulated by laws and administrative regulations.

792. Enterprises and institutions in cities and towns shall promptly issue certificates of termination or dissolution of employment relation for the unemployed, inform persons concerned of the rights to enjoy unemployment insurance benefits and submit name lists of the unemployed to social insurance agencies for the record within seven days of the termination and dissolution of the employment relationship.

After unemployment, staff and workers of enterprises and institutions in cities and towns shall promptly undergo registration with designated social insurance agencies on the basis of the certificates of termination and dissolution of employment relation issued by their work units.

Unemployment insurance compensation is to be accounted from the registration day and is paid monthly by social insurance agencies.

Social insurance agencies shall issue documents to the unemployed on the basis of which they receive unemployment insurance compensation from the designated bank.

793. If the accumulative time period in which the units to which the unemployed belong before their unemployment and the unemployed themselves pay premiums is not less than one year but not more than five years, the maximum period of receiving unemployment insurance compensation is twelve months; if the accumulative time period of paying premiums is not less than five years but not more than ten years, the maximum period of receiving unemployment insurance compensation is eighteen months; if the time period of paying premiums is not less than ten years, the maximum period of receiving unemployment insurance compensation is twenty-four months; if anyone is re-unemployed after reemployment, the time period of paying premiums shall be recalculated. The time period of receiving unemployment insurance compensation may be calculated together with the previous period in which he should have received but have not received unemployment insurance compensation, but the maximum time period may not be longer than twenty-four months.

794. The standard for unemployment insurance compensation is to be set by the people's governments of provinces, autonomous regions and municipalities directly under the Central Government at a level which is lower than the minimal local wage standard but higher than the minimal living security standard for urban residents.

795. For the duration of receiving unemployment benefits, unemployed persons shall be entitled to basic medical insurance benefits if they are members of the basic medical insurance for employees. Basic medical insurance contributions due from unemployed persons shall be paid from the unemployment insurance fund. Unemployed persons are not liable for basic medical insurance contributions.

The unemployed who receive medical treatment during the period of receiving unemployment insurance compensation may apply for medical subvention from social insurance agencies. The standard for medical subvention is to be set by the people's governments of province, autonomous region or municipality directly under the Central Government.

If the unemployed die during the period of receiving unemployment insurance compensation, their family dependents are to be paid one-off funeral allowance and pension with reference to local regulations on employed staff and workers.

When a person dies and concurrently qualifies for a funeral subsidy under the basic old-age insurance, a funeral subsidy under work injury insurance, and a funeral subsidy under unemployment insurance, the survivors can only choose one of the three.

796. If a former worker employed by a unit on the basis of contract has been working continuously for not less than one year, and the unit has paid unemployment insurance premium, where no contract is renewed when the employment contract is expired or the contract is terminated in advance, the social insurance agency shall pay one-off living subsidy to the former worker according to the length of his working period. Measures and standards for such subsidy are to be stipulated by the people's governments of provinces, autonomous regions and municipalities directly under the Central Government.

797. If the unemployed are qualified for minimal living ensuring standard for urban residents, they are entitled to enjoy the benefit of the minimal living ensuring standard for urban residents.

798. The unemployment insurance relationship of a member who has worked across different pooling districts shall transfer together with the member, and the member's lengths of contribution payment shall be cumulative.

§4. Administration and Supervision

799. By Article 24 of the UIR, in the administration of social insurance, the administrative department of labor security shall perform the following duties:

- implement and enforce laws and regulations on unemployment insurance;
- guide the work of social insurance agencies;
- conduct supervision and inspection on collection of unemployment insurance premium and payment of unemployment insurance compensation.

800. By Article 25 of the UIR, when undertaking concretely the work of social insurance, social insurance agencies shall perform the following duties:

- being responsible for registration, investigation and statistics of the unemployed;

- being responsible for administration of unemployment insurance funds in accordance with the provisions;
- checking and determining unemployment insurance benefits, and issuing documents for the unemployed by which they receive unemployment insurance compensation and or other subsidies from designated banks;
- appropriating subsidiary fees for vocational training and job seeking for the unemployed;
- offering free consultation service to the unemployed;
- other duties stipulated by the state to perform.

801. By Articles 26 and 27 of the UIR, financial departments and auditing departments shall supervise the collection, payment and administration of unemployment insurance funds in accordance with the law. Outlays for social insurance agencies shall be listed in budget and appropriated from government finance.

Chapter 5. Maternity Insurance

§1. Introduction

802. Maternity insurance is a social insurance system that is provided by the state and society in a timely manner when the labor force is temporarily interrupted due to childbirth through national legislation. The maternity insurance benefits in China mainly include two items. One is maternity allowance, and the other is medical treatment for maternity. Its purpose is to help working women recover their workability and return to work by providing maternity allowances, medical services and maternity leave to working women.

§2. Legal Framework

803. Employees shall participate in maternity insurance schemes. Maternity insurance contributions shall be paid by employers rather than employees in accordance with the relevant laws and regulations.

If an employer has paid maternity insurance contributions for its employees, the employees shall be entitled to maternity insurance benefits and their unemployed spouses shall be entitled to maternity medical benefits in accordance with national regulations. Such benefits shall be reimbursed by maternity insurance fund. Maternity benefits shall include maternity-related medical fees and maternity allowance.

804. By Article 55 of the SIL, maternity-related medical fees include:

- medical expenses for maternity;
- medical expenses for family plan; and
- other expenses as set forth by laws and regulations.

805. By Article 56 of the SIL, in any of the following circumstances, an employee may be entitled to maternity allowance in accordance with the relevant regulations of the state:

- a female employee is taking maternity leave;
- an employee is taking leave for sterilizing operation; or
- other circumstances as specified in laws and regulations.

Maternity allowance shall be calculated and paid based on an employer's average monthly wage in the previous year.

806. It should be noted that since March 25, 2019, the State Council started to implement the merger of maternity insurance and basic pension insurance, which has been done by the end of 2019. The maternity insurance fund is merged into the basic pension insurance fund, and it is collected at a uniform level.

Chapter 6. Social Insurance Fund

§1. Constitution

807. Social insurance funds include basic pension insurance fund, basic medical insurance fund, work-related injury insurance fund, unemployment insurance fund and maternity insurance fund, which shall be deposited in a special account. Accounts shall be separately established and calculated in accordance with the national accounting system for each social insurance fund. The use of the social insurance fund shall be for the insurance purpose only. No organization or individual may embezzle or appropriate the social insurance fund. The national pooling fund shall be gradually established for basic pension insurance, and provincial pooling funds shall be gradually established for other social insurance. The specific schedules and steps will be determined by the State Council.

§2. Management

808. Budget shall be made to keep the balance between revenue and expenditure of the social insurance fund. The people's governments at or above the country level shall provide necessary subsidies to social insurance fund that is inadequate to pay social insurance benefits.

809. In the premise of security, investment and operation of social insurance fund shall comply with the regulations of the State Council to guarantee the maintenance and increase of its value. The social insurance fund may not be invested or operated in violation of the relevant regulations, be used in construction or renovation of offices and reimbursement of human resources costs, operating costs, management costs or be appropriated for other purposes in violation of laws or administrative rules.

810. Social insurance agencies shall regularly publish information on participation in social insurance schemes and the revenue, expenditure, balance and profit of social insurance fund.

811. The state shall establish a national social security fund, which consists of the funds allocated from the national budget and those raised through other channels approved by the State Council, to complement and adjust the expenditure of the social insurance fund. The national social security fund management agency shall be responsible for the management and operation of the national social security fund and guarantee the maintenance and increase of its value in addition to security. Information on the revenue and expenditure, management, investment and operation of the national social security fund shall be published on a regular basis. The financial department, social insurance administrative department and audit agency under the State Council shall supervise the revenue and expenditure, management, investment and operation of the national social security fund.

Chapter 7. Social Insurance Organization and Management System

§1. Social Insurance Agency

812. Social insurance agencies shall be established in all regions providing for pooling funds. Social insurance agencies may, in accordance with the needs in work, establish branches and service networks in their respective regions following the approval of the local social insurance administrative departments and administrative departments for establishment of governmental agencies. The human resources costs and the basic operation and management costs of social insurance agencies are guaranteed by the financial department at the same level in accordance with the relevant state regulations.

Social insurance agencies shall establish and improve the business, finance, security and risk management systems. Social insurance agencies shall pay social insurance benefits in full and on time.

813. Social insurance agencies may collect information necessary for their work by providing social insurance services, collecting statistics and undertaking investigations. The relevant entities and individuals shall provide such information in a faithful and timely manner.

Social insurance agencies shall establish files for employers in a timely manner, record social insurance information of participants and contributions completely and correctly, and properly maintain original certificates of registration and applications and the accounting documents of payment and settlement.

Social insurance agencies shall record contributions made by individuals and their employers, social insurance benefits and individuals' other rights and interests in a complete, correct and timely way. They shall also deliver free of charge records of individual rights and interests regularly to social insurance participants.

814. Employers and individuals are entitled to inquire and verify their records of contributions and social insurance benefits, and require social insurance agencies to provide consultancy or other services relating to social insurance.

The national social insurance information system shall, in accordance with the national uniform planning, be jointly established by the people's governments at or above the county level which shall be responsible for information at their corresponding levels.

§2. Social Insurance Supervision

815. The standing committees of the people's congresses at all levels shall review and deliberate on the special work report made by government at the same level on the revenue and expenditure, administration, investment and operation of the social insurance fund as well as the supervision and inspection thereof, organize inspection on the enforcement of this law, and exercise their supervisory power in accordance with the law.

816. Social insurance administrative departments under the people's governments at or above the county level shall strengthen their supervision and inspection of employers and individuals' compliance with SIL and regulations. Where the social insurance administrative department investigates, the employer(s) or individual(s) under investigation shall provide accurate information and shall not refuse to cooperate, provide false statements or conceal information.

817. Financial authorities and audit agencies shall, according to their respective duties and responsibilities, supervise the revenue and expenditure, management, investment and operation of the social insurance fund.

818. Social insurance administrative departments shall supervise and inspect the revenue and expenditure, management, investment and operation of the social insurance fund. If they become aware of problems pursuant to such supervision and inspection, the administrative departments shall offer proposals for rectification, make a decision to resolve the problems or make suggestions to resolve the same to other relevant departments. The inspection results of the social insurance fund shall be disclosed to the public on a regular basis.

Social insurance administrative departments are entitled to take the following measures when conducting supervision and inspection of the social insurance fund:

- to review, record and duplicate materials relating to the revenue and expenditure, management, investment and operation of the social insurance fund and seal and keep those that might be transferred, concealed or destroyed;
- to inquire into the entities and individuals involved in the investigation and require them to provide explanations and relevant certification for issues relating to the investigated matters; and
- to prohibit any entities or individuals from concealing, transferring, embezzling or appropriating the social insurance fund and order them to rectify such acts.

819. The people's governments in regions providing for pooling funds shall establish supervisory committees on social insurance which consist of representatives of employers, social insurance participants and trade unions, legal experts and economic experts to gather and analyze information on the revenue, expenditure, management, investment and operation of social insurance fund, give advice and opinions on social insurance and conduct supervision as a non-governmental entity.

Social insurance agencies shall report information on the revenue, expenditure, management, investment and operation of social insurance fund to supervisory committees on social insurance on a regular basis. Supervisory committees on social insurance may retain accounting firms to conduct annual and special audit of the revenue, expenditure, management, investment and operation of social insurance fund, and the audit results shall be disclosed to the public.

Where they are aware of problems in the revenue, expenditure, management, investment and operation of the social insurance fund, social insurance agencies shall have the right to give advice on rectifications. Where social insurance agencies and their staff violate the relevant laws, the committees may advise the relevant departments to deal with such violations in accordance with the law.

Social insurance administrative departments and other relevant administrative departments, social insurance agencies and contribution collection agencies as well as their personnel shall keep confidential information on employers and individuals in accordance with the law and shall not divulge such information in any manner.

820. Any organization or individual has the right to report acts (or lodge a complaint) which violate the SIL and regulations.

Social insurance administrative departments, health administrative departments, social insurance agencies, social insurance contribution collection agencies, fiscal departments and audit authorities shall handle the reports or complaints within their jurisdiction. Any reports or complaints not within their jurisdiction shall be forwarded to the competent departments or authorities with a written notice, and the competent departments or authorities shall handle these reports or complaints in a timely manner and may not shift their responsibilities to others.

821. Where an employer or individual believes that an act of a social insurance agency has infringed upon its/his rights and interests, it/he may apply for an administrative review or initiate administrative litigation.

Where a social insurance agency fails to handle social insurance registration, verify social insurance contribution, pay social insurance benefits or facilitate formalities for the removal and continuity of social insurance relations in accordance with law, or infringes upon other social insurance interests, an employer or individual shall be entitled to apply for administrative review or institute an administrative lawsuit.

Individuals who have social insurance disputes with their employers may apply for mediation or arbitration or institute a lawsuit. Where employers infringe upon individuals' social insurance interests, the individuals may also require social insurance administrative departments or social insurance contribution collection agencies to resolve such problems.

Part VIII. Insurance Intermediaries

Chapter 1. Insurance Agent

§1. Introduction

I. Definition

822. To better understand the insurance agent, let us first look at the definition of the agent. The legal effect of the agent's behavior in the name of the principal interacting with the third party to the extent as authorized by the principal is directly attributable to the principal. Therefore, we define insurance agent as the agent which handles the insurance-related business on behalf of the client within the scope of authorization and collects the corresponding commission. It is the intermediary that enables the insurer and the insured to enter into an insurance agreement, and both the insurer and the insured have the right to appoint their own agent.

In a broad sense, insurance agents include insurance agents and insurance brokers. Insurance agents and insurance brokers are agents, but their principals are different. The insurance agent is the agent of the insurer, and the insurance broker is the agent of the applicant or policyholder. A narrowly defined insurance agent refers only to an agent entrusted by the insurer.

Article 125 of the IL defines the insurance agent specifically: the insurance agent shall be institutions or individuals who charge commissions to insurers and operate insurance business on behalf of the insurers to the extent as authorized by insurers.

II. Classification of Insurance Agent

823. According to the special laws and departmental regulations, insurance agents are divided into full-time insurance agencies, concurrent-business insurance agencies and individual insurance agents. The main basis for this classification is the business form of insurance agents in the industry and market.

A. *Full-Time Insurance Agency*

824. A full-time insurance agency refers to an insurance agency that specializes in insurance agency business. According to the Provisions on the Supervision and Administration of Full-Time Insurance Agencies (hereinafter referred to as the

"Agencies' Provisions"), it means institutions which engage in the insurance business on behalf of insurance companies as authorized by insurance companies and collect commissions from insurance companies, including full-time corporate insurance agents and their branch offices.

B. *Concurrent-Business Insurance Agency*

825. Concurrent-business insurance agents shall refer to the entities which are entrusted by the insurers to handle insurance business on behalf of the latter at the time of engaging in their own business. At present, there are mainly four kinds of concurrent-business insurance agency in China.

The financial institution concurrent-business agency uses the characteristics of the banking, postal savings institutions, credit unions, securities and other financial institutions of contacting with all walks of life to handle insurance business for customers in their counters.

The industry concurrent-business agency makes use of a certain industry's special demand for insurance and the convenience of the business handling to operate the insurance business for insurer, such as travel agency operates the customer travel insurance, railway department operates the cargo insurance, airline operates the aviation accident insurance, car dealers sell motor vehicle insurance, etc.

The enterprise concurrent-business agency, the competent department of the enterprise, is entrusted by the insurer to concurrently carry out the insurance business of the subordinate enterprise or the insurance business of the internal employees, such as the enterprise agent carrying out various life insurance business, family property insurance, etc.

The social group concurrent-business agency is the agent of the insurance business through the special functions of certain community organizations. In China, there have been concurrent agency forms such as the maternal and child health insurance operated by the Family Planning Association, and the life insurance or property insurance operated by the Association of Individual Workers.

C. *Individual Insurance Agent*

826. According to Article 117 of the IL, an individual insurance agent shall be an individual who charges commissions to insurers and operates insurance business on behalf of insurers to the extent as authorized by insurers.

Broadly speaking, insurance marketers and agent practitioners who sign agency agreements with insurance companies and full-time and concurrent-business insurance agencies can be regarded as individual agents, while narrow-defined individual insurance agents refer to the individuals who are approved by the industry regulator and register in the industrial and commercial sector, in the form of individual proprietorship or partnership. In the more mature insurance agency market, there are many professional insurance consultants or financial planners, that is individual insurance agents in the form of individual organizations. For example, the organization forms of insurance agents, brokers and notaries in Taiwan can be divided into two categories: individual form and company form. Anyone with a qualification can apply to start a business in their own form. In the case of a company application, more than one qualified person should be employed for the signing and the registration is required. In order to adapt to the development of the insurance market, China has been exploring the form of individual insurance agents.

III. Obligations of Insurance Agent

827. The insurance agency relationship involves three parties. As an agent, its agency behavior directly affects the insurer, the insured and its own interests. In order to prevent agents from using the information asymmetry between the insurer and the insured to seek private benefits and suppress their moral hazard, it is necessary to clarify the scope of the insurance agent's obligations.

A. *Obligations to Be Performed in Accordance with the Insurance Agency Contract*

828. The insurance agent contract stipulates the scope of the agent's basic obligations, and the agent should complete the entrusted matters in accordance with the instructions of the client in a diligent and careful manner. It includes three levels of meaning: diligence and attention, personal execution, and completion of entrusted matters. "Diligence and attention" require the agent to maintain the client's interests diligently, prudently, and responsibly in the performance of the contract in accordance with the standards of a good agent. For example, the proposal made by the agent should be in the best interests of the client, making a claim at a reasonable speed to avoid unnecessary delays causing damage to the client. "Personal execution" is the implicit meaning of diligence and attention. The agent is entrusted based on the personal trust of the principal. Without the permission of the principal, the agent must handle the matter "on his own" and may not entrust others. "Completion of the entrusted matters" means that the agent must strictly obey the instructions of the principal, which is the basis of the insurance agency relationship. If the principal's instructions are ambiguous, the agent should try to clarify the principal's true intentions, and must explain his instructions in a reasonable manner in any case.

829. The specific content of the agent's basic obligations can be refined into the following.

First, obligation to make a contract explanation. Based on the preexisting nature of the insurance policy and the professionalism of the insurance clause, the insurance agent should clearly explain the insurance clause, especially the liability exemption clause and the main rights restriction clause for the insured, and should bring them to the full attention of the insured. In some areas, this obligation is imposed on insurance agent practitioners in the form of regulations of regulatory department and industry association.

Second, obligation to disclose the matter they know or ought to know. In the process of contracting, the insured party shall inform the insurer of the condition of the insured or the subject-matter insured, so that the insurer can determine whether to insure and the rate of the insurance premium. The agent shall inform the insurer of what he knows or ought to know, and if the agent knows but fails to inform the insurer, it shall be deemed that the insurer is aware of it and shall not refuse to assume the insurance liability on this ground.

Third, obligation to notify the danger in a timely manner. The agent is obliged to notify the insurer of the increase of danger before the occurrence of the insurance accident and the relevant circumstances of the insurance accident, so that the insurer can take corresponding measures in time to reduce losses.

Fourth, obligation to transfer documents in a timely manner. The agent shall promptly forward the relevant documents, especially the insurance policy. The delivery time of the insurance policy determines the time for the conclusion of the contract and its validity, thereby determining the time when the insurance liability begins.

Fifth, obligation to collect insurance premiums. The agent is entrusted by the insurer to collect insurance premiums within the authorization, and is obliged to transfer all the money collected to the insurer to realize the main rights of the insurer in the insurance contract.

B. Obligations to Be Performed in Accordance with the Principle of Good Faith

830. The inherent nature of insurance agents seeking to maximize their own interests is the root cause of many insurance disputes. To solve this problem, it is not enough to stipulate the agent's obligations to the insurer in the agency contract; we also need to resort to the principle of good faith to protect the interests of policyholders. Because, in a sense, the applicant is also the principal of the insurance agent, they entrust the insurance agent to handle the insurance application. Therefore, in accordance with the principle of good faith, the insurance agent should not only faithfully handle the insurance for the insured at any time but should also give the insured an objective, independent and best advice based on their interests. An insurance agent must serve the principal in good faith, avoiding the acts that conflict with the interests of the principal, because a person in a position of trust cannot have the right to seek personal gain and should avoid to allow themselves in a situation where their own interests and obligations conflict. The principle of good faith requires an insurance agent to perform the following obligations to the insured in the agency activity:

> First, obligation of truthful disclosure. The insurance agent shall disclose the relevant circumstances that affect the insured's determination of entering into the insurance contract, such as the credibility of the insurer, the business situation, the pros and cons and risk of the insurance provided, and other professional and technical information, and sincerely take the insured's interests into consideration to help them make objective and rational choices.

Second, obligation of confidentiality. During the conclusion of the insurance contract, the insured shall, in order to perform the obligation of truthful disclosure, inform the agent of his own property and personal health status that the outsider is not aware of, and the agent is obliged to keep it confidential which is the basic requirement of the principle of good faith. Similarly, professional ethics also requires agents not to disclose the commercial secrets of the insurer that they inevitably know in their business to avoid causing losses to the insurer.

Third, obligation of notification. During the performance of the insurance contract, the insurer's operating conditions may change for some reason. If the change will affect the realization of the insured's insurance contract, the agent has a notification obligation because the agent knows the situation of the insurer more conveniently and comprehensively than the insured.

C. *Obligations to Be Performed in Accordance with the Implied Principle*

831. In the practice of insurance agency, in order to fulfill the purpose of the insurance contract satisfactorily, in addition to the obligations expressly stated in the agency contract, the agent shall voluntarily perform certain obligations in accordance with the statutory implied terms and the practices of the insurance industry. The implied obligations of the agent include two categories: one is that the agent may contract within the scope of the authorization. It is the statutory obligation of the agent to replace the insurer to conclude the insurance contract with the insured. The agent should imply that he has a real and legal insurance agency right, that is the responsibility of contracting within the scope of the authorization. The agent's failure to act as agent, termination of agency or surpassing agency authority is the performance of the agent's breach of implied obligation. Another type of implied obligation is that after an insured event occurs, the agent assists the insured in making a claim under the insurance contract. If the insurance contract does not stipulate that the agent shall handle the claim for the client, there is currently a dispute as to whether the obligation is recognized as an implied term of the insurance contract. According to the characteristics of the insurance agent, as a participant in the insurance legal relationship, the agent often has a large amount of original materials, and often keeps the documents that prove the claim in practice, so it is obliged to help the insured to resolve the claim dispute after the insurance accident occurs.

§2. Establishment of the Full-Time Corporate Insurance Agent

I. Formation of the Full-Time Corporate Insurance Agent

832. Article 5 of the Agencies' Provisions provides that except as otherwise specified by the CBIRC, a full-time insurance agency shall adopt either of the following forms of organization: limited liability company and joint-stock limited company.

According to *the Agencies' Provisions*, a full-time corporate insurance agent to be formed within the territory of the PRC shall satisfy the qualification requirements prescribed by the CBIRC and obtain an insurance agency business permit (hereinafter referred to as the "permit"). The name of a full-time insurance agency shall include the words "insurance agency" or "insurance sales," and its trade name shall not be the same as that of any existing insurance intermediary institution, except as otherwise specified by the CBIRC. According to *the Agencies' Provisions*, for the formation of a full-time corporate insurance agent, the following conditions shall be met:

- its shareholders or promoters are of good credit standing and have no record of any major violation of laws in the last three years;
- its registered capital reaches the minimum amount specified in the CL and *the Agencies' Provisions*. The minimum registered capital of a full-time corporate insurance agent to be formed shall be RMB 50 million, except as otherwise specified by the CBIRC. The registered capital of a full-time corporate insurance agent must be paid-in monetary capital.

833. According to the CL, the bylaw of a full-time corporate insurance agent should include: the name and domicile of the company; business scope of the company; registered capital of the company; names of shareholders; forms, amount and date of capital contributions made by shareholders; the organizations of the company and its formation, their functions and rules of procedure; legal representative of the company; other matters deemed necessary by shareholders.

834. The proposed chairman of the board of directors or executive director and senior executives of a full-time insurance agency shall meet the following conditions and be subject to the confirmation of the CBIRC:

- having an educational background of junior college or above;
- having two years or more of economic work experience;
- having the management capability required for performing his/her duties and being familiar with ILs and administrative regulations and the relevant provisions issued by the CBIRC;
- being honest and trustworthy and having good conduct;
- one with ten years or more of financial work experience may be exempt from the condition in Item (1) of the preceding paragraph.

835. Other requirements include having a sound organizational structure and adequate and effective management rules; having business, financial, and other computer software and hardware facilities suitable for its business development and other conditions as set out in laws, administrative regulations, and the provisions issued by the CBIRC.

836. It also provides that an entity or individual prohibited by any law or administrative regulation from investing in enterprises may not be a promoter or a shareholder of a full-time corporate insurance agent. Where any employee of an insurance company invests in a full-time corporate insurance agent, the employee shall inform the insurance company in writing of the investment; and where a director or senior executive of an insurance company or an insurance intermediary institution invests in a full-time corporate insurance agent, such investment shall be subject to the consent of the shareholders' meeting in accordance with the relevant provisions of the CL.

II. Approval of the Formation of a Full-Time Corporate Insurance Agent

837. To apply for the formation of a full-time corporate insurance agent, all the shareholders or all the promoters shall designate a representative or jointly authorize an agent to handle matters related to the application with the CBIRC. According to the regulations of the CBIRC, the formation and approval of the business scope of the full-time insurance agency in the province, autonomous region or municipality directly under the Central Government are accepted and approved by the local insurance regulatory bureau; the formation and approval of the business area which is not limited to the province, autonomous region or municipality directly under the Central Government where the registered place is located shall be carried out in accordance with the approval procedures of the insurance brokerage institution, and shall be accepted by the local insurance regulatory bureau and conducted for preliminary examination, and then shall be approved by the CBIRC.

838. After receiving an application for formation of a full-time corporate insurance agent, the CBIRC may alert the applicant to risks and conduct interviews on issues related to the formation to learn the market development strategy, business development plan, development of internal control rules, personnel structure, and other relevant matters of the company to be formed. The CBIRC may, as actually needed, organize an on-site check.

After approving the formation of a full-time corporate insurance agent according to the law, the CBIRC shall issue a permit to the applicant. Only after receiving the permit may the applicant engage in the insurance agency business.

839. Under any of the following circumstances, a full-time insurance agency shall report it to the CBIRC in writing within five days of occurrence thereof:

- modification of the name of the agency or any branch office thereof;
- modification of the domicile of the agency or the business premises of any branch office thereof;
- modification of the name of any promoter or principal shareholder of the agency;
- modification of any principal shareholder of the agency;
- modification of the registered capital of the agency;
- material modification of the equity structure of the agency;
- modification of the form of organization of the agency;
- division or combination of the agency;
- amendment of the company bylaws;
- formation or abolition of any branch office of the agency.

840. Where any modification of a full-time corporate insurance agent involves any matter recorded in the permit, it shall surrender the original permit, obtain a new one, and issue an announcement in accordance with the relevant provisions of *the Measures for the Administration of Insurance Permits.*

841. The permit of a full-time corporate insurance agent shall be valid for three years, and a full-time corporate insurance agent shall apply to the CBIRC for renewal thirty days before its permit expires. Where a full-time corporate insurance agent applies for renewal of its permit, the CBIRC shall, before the expiration of the permit, comprehensively review and assess the full-time corporate insurance agent's operations in the last three years and make a decision to approve or disapprove the renewal. In the case of disapproval, it shall provide a written explanation of the reasons for the disapproval. The full-time corporate insurance agent shall surrender the original permit to the CBIRC within ten days of receiving the decision, or in the case of approval, obtain a new permit.

The branch offices of a full-time corporate insurance agent shall include branches and business departments. To form a branch office, a full-time corporate insurance agent shall meet the following conditions:

- its internal control rules are adequate and effective;
- its registered capital satisfies the requirements of *the Agencies' Provisions*;
- its existing organizational structure is in normal operation, and it has committed no major violation of laws in the last year;
- the proposed primary person in charge satisfies the office qualifications as set out in *the Agencies' Provisions*;
- the branch office to be formed has business premises satisfying the prescribed requirements and other facilities related to its operations.

§3. Supervision on the Full-Time Corporate Insurance Agent

I. Operation Rules

842. The purpose of the operation rules is to regulate the operation of the insurance agency so that it can develop in a healthy and orderly manner to ensure the stable operation of the insurance company, and ultimately fully protect the interests of the insured. According to *the Agencies' Provisions*, the operating rules of insurance agencies mainly have the following contents.

A. Business Territory

843. According to *the Agencies' Provisions,* a full-time insurance agency may engage in the following insurance agency business:

- selling insurance products as an agent. A full-time corporate insurance agent can promote insurance products to institutions and individuals through various channels to attract insurance business. Their insurance products cover property insurance and life insurance. Compared with other forms of insurance agents, the full-time corporate insurance agents are more professional and regulated in this business;
- collecting insurance premiums as an agent. The collection of insurance premiums is an important business of insurance agents. However, in the course of business operations, insurance agents are not allowed to issue insurance policies directly. At the same time, insurance premiums must be paid to insurance companies in time according to insurance agency contracts;
- conducting damage survey and claim settlement for the relevant insurance business as an agent. When a customer comes into danger, the insurance agent uses its advantage of being familiar with the customer's situation to assist the insurance company in the investigation and settlement of the loss.

B. Branch Office

844. To engage in the insurance agency business in a province, autonomous region, or municipality directly under the Central Government other than its place of registration, a full-time corporate insurance agent shall form branch offices. The business territory of a branch office of a full-time corporate insurance agent shall not be beyond the province, autonomous region, or municipality directly under the Central Government where it is located.

C. Account

845. A full-time insurance agency shall establish special account books to record the revenues and expenditures in the insurance agency business. A full-time insurance agency which collects insurance premiums as an agent shall open an independent premium agent account to conduct settlement.

D. Business Archive

846. A full-time insurance agency shall establish complete and standardized business archives, including the following at a minimum:

- basic information on the insurance policies sold as an agent, including but not limited to the names of insurers, insurance applicants, and the insured, the names of products, insured amounts, premiums, and methods of payment;
- information on the collection of insurance premiums as an agent and delivery of collected premiums to insurance companies represented;
- information on the amounts of insurance agency commissions and the collection thereof;

– other important business information.

The records of a full-time insurance agency shall be true and complete.

E. Client Notification Letter

847. A full-time insurance agency shall clearly alert an insurance applicant to the clauses in the insurance contract regarding the liability exemptions or exceptions, surrender, deduction of other expenses, cash value, and cooling-off period, among others. Besides, a full-time insurance agency shall prepare a standard client notification letter and present it to clients in conducting business. The client notification letter shall, at a minimum, include the basic information on the full-time insurance agency and the insurance company represented, such as the names, business premises, scope of business, and contact methods thereof. If there is any affiliation between the full-time insurance agency or its director or senior executive and the insurance company represented or the relevant insurance intermediary institution, it shall be explained in the client notification letter.

F. Agency Contract

848. To engage in the insurance agency business, a full-time insurance agency shall enter into a written agency contract with an insurance company represented, agreeing on the rights and obligations of both parties and other relevant matters. An agency contract may not violate laws, administrative regulations, and the provisions issued by the CBIRC. A full-time insurance agency shall properly manage and use the various documents and materials provided by the insurance companies represented; and submit the remaining documents and materials to the insurance companies represented within thirty days after the end of the agency relationship.

G. Professional Liability Insurance and Bond

849. A full-time corporate insurance agent shall take out professional liability insurance or deposit a bond within twenty days of obtaining a permit. A full-time corporate insurance agent shall, within ten days of taking out professional liability insurance or deposit a bond, submit to the CBIRC a photocopy of the professional liability insurance policy or a photocopy of the bond deposit agreement and a photocopy of the original voucher of deposit of the bond.

850. A full-time corporate insurance agent which takes out professional liability insurance shall ensure the continuing validity of the insurance. The compensation limit for each accident under the professional liability insurance policy owned by a full-time corporate insurance agent shall not be less than RMB 1 million, and the cumulative compensation limit under a one-year policy shall not be less than RMB 5 million and not be less than two times the full-time insurance agency's operating revenue in the prior year. If the cumulative compensation limit under professional liability insurance reaches RMB 50 million, further increase in the compensation limit under professional liability insurance is not required.

851. A full-time corporate insurance agent that deposits a bond shall deposit the bond at 5% of its registered capital; if it increases its registered capital, it shall increase the amount of the bond accordingly; but if the amount of the bond deposited reaches RMB 1 million, further increase in the bond is not required. The bond of a full-time corporate insurance agent shall be deposited in the form of bank deposit or any other form recognized by the CBIRC. If the bond is deposited in the form of bank deposit, it shall be deposited in a special account in a commercial bank. Under any of the following circumstances, a full-time corporate insurance agent may use the bond:

- its registered capital is reduced;
- its permit is canceled;
- it takes out professional liability insurance meeting the prescribed conditions;
- other circumstances as set out by the CBIRC.

Within five days of using the bond, a full-time corporate insurance agent shall report it to the CBIRC in writing.

H. Practitioner

852. Insurance agency practitioner means an employee of a full-time insurance agency who engages in the sale of insurance products, damage survey, claim settlement, or other relevant business. The practitioners of a full-time insurance agency shall meet the conditions as set out by the CBIRC.

A full-time insurance agency shall provide its practitioners with training on IL and insurance business and education on professional ethics. The prejob training received by an insurance agency practitioner shall not be less than eight hours, and an insurance agency practitioner shall receive on-the-job training and education every year for not less than thirty-six hours accumulatively, including not less than twelve hours of training on legal knowledge and education on professional ethics.

I. Forbidden Conduct

853. No full-time corporate insurance agent may forge, alter, lease out, lend, or transfer its permit.

The insurance agency business conducted by a full-time insurance agency shall not exceed the scope of business and the business territory of the insurance company represented, except insurance agency business involving coinsurance outside its business territory, insurance underwritten outside its business territory, or master policies as otherwise specified by the CBIRC.

In conducting the insurance agency business, a full-time insurance agency and its practitioners may not deceive insurance applicants, the insured, beneficiaries, or insurance companies by the following means:

- concealing or fabricating any important information related to the insurance contract;
- conducting any misleading sale;
- forging or modifying without permission the insurance contract, selling false insurance documents, or providing false certifications to the parties to the insurance contract;
- obstructing an insurance applicant from performing or inducing any insurance applicant not to perform the obligation of telling the truth;
- fraudulently obtaining commissions by fabricating any insurance agency business or surrender;
- conducting any false claim settlement;
- fraudulently obtaining a claim payment by colluding with any insurance applicant, insured, or beneficiary;
- otherwise deceiving an insurance applicant, insured, beneficiary, or insurance company.

854. In conducting the insurance agency business, a full-time insurance agency and its practitioners may not be:

- forcing or inducing an insurance applicant to enter into or restricting an insurance applicant from entering into an insurance contract or restricting the normal operations of any other insurance intermediary institution, by taking advantage of administrative power, shareholder privileges, or professional advantage or by any other improper means;
- misappropriating, intercepting, or encroaching on insurance premiums, surrendering values, or claiming payments;
- providing or promising to provide any insurance company or employee thereof, insurance applicant, insured, or beneficiary with any benefit not under the contract;
- seeking improper benefits for any other institution or individual by taking advantage of its business;
- divulging any trade secret or individual privacy of an insurance applicant, insured, beneficiary, or insurance company known in its operations.

855. A full-time insurance agency may not damage the goodwill of competitors by fabrication or spreading false facts, nor disrupt the insurance market order by false advertisements, false publicity, or any other act of unfair competition. A full-time insurance agency may not conduct insurance agency transactions with any institution or individual which illegally engages in the insurance business or insurance intermediary business. A full-time insurance agency may not withhold commissions from the insurance premiums collected. A full-time insurance agency may not enter into insurance contracts on behalf of insurance applicants. A full-time insurance agency may not recruit practitioners on condition of their payment of fees or purchase of insurance products, may not promise unreasonably high returns, and may not use the number of directly or indirectly recruited persons or sale performance as the main basis for computing the remuneration of practitioners.

II. Market Exit

856. The CBIRC shall not grant the renewal of the permit of a full-time corporate insurance agent which falls under any of the following circumstances:

- failing to file a renewal application before the expiration of its permit;
- no longer meeting any company formation condition;
- being unable to conduct normal operations for internal mismanagement;
- failing to effectively address issues related to its major violation of laws;
- failing to pay the regulatory fees as required.

857. Where the permit of a full-time corporate insurance agent expires and the CBIRC does not grant renewal of the permit or the permit is retracted, canceled, or revoked according to the law, liquidation shall be organized or the insurance agency business shall be settled according to the law, and a liquidation or settlement report shall be submitted to the CBIRC.

Where a full-time corporate insurance agent is dissolved, a liquidation group shall be formed according to the law to conduct liquidation, and within ten days of appearance of the cause of dissolution, a written report shall be submitted to the CBIRC. After the end of liquidation, the full-time corporate insurance agent shall submit a liquidation report to the CBIRC.

858. Where a full-time corporate insurance agent is dissolved, if it is discovered in the process of liquidation that the full-time corporate insurance agent is unable to repay its due debts and its assets are not enough to repay all its debts or it is evidently insolvent, a bankruptcy application shall be filed according to the law, and the liquidation of its property and the disposition of its claims and debts shall be governed by the statutory procedures for bankruptcy.

Where the business license of a full-time corporate insurance agent is revoked or a full-time corporate insurance agent is abolished, ordered to close, or legally declared bankrupt by a people's court, a liquidation group shall be formed according to the law to conduct liquidation under the statutory procedure and submit a liquidation report to the CBIRC.

859. The CBIRC shall nullify the permit of a full-time corporate insurance agent which exits the market under any of the following circumstances, and issue an announcement of it:

- its permit expires, and according to the law, the CBIRC does not grant renewal of its permit;
- its permit is retracted, canceled, or revoked according to the law;

- it is dissolved, its business license is revoked, or it is abolished, ordered to close, or declared bankrupt according to the law;
- other circumstances as set out in laws and administrative regulations.

A full-time corporate insurance agent whose permit is nullified shall surrender the original permit in a timely manner.

III. Supervisory Inspection

860. A full-time insurance agency shall, according to the relevant provisions issued by the CBIRC, submit the relevant reports, statements, documents, and materials in a timely, accurate, and complete manner, and submit the relevant electronic texts as required by the CBIRC. The statements, reports, and materials submitted by a full-time insurance agency shall bear the signature of the legal representative or the primary person in charge or a person authorized by him or her and the seal of the agency.

861. A full-time insurance agency shall properly preserve its business archives, account books, business ledgers, original vouchers of the commission revenue, and other relevant materials for not less than five years if the duration of insurance is not more than one year and for not less than ten years if the duration of insurance is longer than one year, starting from the day when the insurance contract is terminated.

A full-time insurance agency shall, according to the relevant provisions, pay the regulatory fees into an account designated by the CBIRC. A full-time corporate insurance agent shall, within three months after the end of each accounting year, engage an accounting firm to audit its financial condition including but not limited to its assets, liabilities, and profits, and submit the relevant audit report to the CBIRC. The CBIRC may, as needed, require a full-time corporate insurance agent to submit a specific external audit report.

862. The CBIRC may, as needed in supervision, hold regulatory interviews with the chairman of the board of directors or executive director and the senior executives of a full-time insurance agency, requiring them to provide explanations on the major issues in operation. The CBIRC shall conduct an on-site inspection of a full-time insurance agency according to the law, including but not limited to the following:

- whether the formation or modification of the agency has been approved or whether the obligation to report the same has been performed according to the law;
- whether its capital is true and adequate;
- whether the set-aside and use of the bond is in compliance with the relevant provisions;
- whether it complies with the provisions on professional liability insurance;
- whether its operations are lawful;

- whether it is in good financial condition;
- whether the reports, statements, and materials submitted to the CBIRC are timely, complete, and true;
- whether its internal control rules are adequate and effectively implemented;
- whether the appointment of its chairman of the board of directors or executive director and senior executives complies with the relevant provisions;
- whether it has effectively performed the duty of managing its practitioners;
- whether its announcements are published in a timely and true manner;
- whether its computer equipment and information systems are in good operating condition.

863. Where a full-time insurance agency is under investigation by the CBIRC for any of the following reasons, the CBIRC shall have the authority to order it to stop part or all of its business during the period of investigation:

- it is suspected of any serious violation of IL or administrative regulation;
- there is any major risk in its operations;
- it is unable to conduct normal operations.

864. A full-time insurance agency shall, according to the following requirements, cooperate with the CBIRC in an on-site inspection, and may not refuse or obstruct the supervisory inspection legally conducted by the CBIRC:

- it shall provide the relevant documents and materials as required, and may not delay the provision of or displace or conceal them;
- its relevant managers, financial staff members, and practitioners shall appear on the site to provide explanations and answer questions as required.

A full-time insurance agency which falls under any of the following circumstances may be placed by the CBIRC under priority inspection:

- there are any abnormal changes in its operations or financial condition;
- it fails to submit reports and statements on time or provides any false reports, statements, documents, and materials;
- it is suspected of any major violation of laws or has received any administrative punishment by the CBIRC;
- other circumstances under which the CBIRC deems priority inspection necessary.

865. In the process of an on-site inspection, the CBIRC may engage an accounting firm and other private intermediary institutions to provide the relevant services, and if so, shall enter into written engagement agreements with them. The CBIRC shall inform the inspected full-time insurance agency of the engagement.

866. A full-time insurance agency which believes that an inspector has violated any law or administrative regulation or the relevant provisions issued by the CBIRC may report it or submit a complaint to the CBIRC. A full-time insurance agency shall have the right to apply for administrative reconsideration or institute administrative litigation against the administrative disposition measure taken by the CBIRC.

IV. Legal Liability

867. Any illegal operation of the insurance agency business without a permit shall be banned by the CBIRC, and the CBIRC shall confiscate any illegal income and impose a fine of not less than the amount nor more than five times the amount of the illegal income on the violator or if there is no illegal income or the amount of illegal income is less than RMB 50,000, impose a fine of not less than RMB 50,000 nor more than RMB 300,000 on the violator.

868. Where an administrative licensing applicant conceals relevant information or provides false materials in the application for the formation of a full-time corporate insurance agent or for any other administrative licensing, the CBIRC shall reject or disapprove its application and issue a warning to it, and the applicant may not apply for the administrative licensing again within one year.

869. Where a licensee forms a full-time corporate insurance agent or passes administrative licensing from the CBIRC by fraud, bribery, or any other improper means, the CBIRC shall revoke the administrative licensing according to the law, and issue a warning to and impose a fine of RMB 10,000 on the licensee; and the applicant may not apply for the administrative licensing again within three years.

870. Where a full-time insurance agency fails to submit a report as required on the occurrence of any matter about its modification, using of bond and dissolving, the CBIRC shall order it to take corrective action, issue a warning to it, and impose a fine of not more than RMB 10,000 on it if there is no illegal income or impose a fine of not more than three times the amount of illegal income but not exceeding RMB 30,000 on it if there is any illegal income; and for the directly liable supervising executive or any other liable person of the agency, issue a warning to and impose a fine of not more than RMB 10,000 on him or her.

871. Where a full-time insurance agency appoints any person not satisfying the office qualifications, the CBIRC shall order it to take corrective action and impose a fine of not less than RMB 20,000 nor more than RMB 100,000 on it; and for the directly liable supervising executive or any other liable person of the agency, issue a warning to and impose a fine of not less than RMB 10,000 nor more than RMB 50,000 on him or her.

872. Where a full-time insurance agency employs any person not meeting the prescribed conditions, the CBIRC shall order it to take corrective action, and issue a warning to and impose a fine of not more than RMB 10,000 on it; and for the directly liable supervising executive or any other liable person of the agency, issue a warning to and impose a fine of not more than RMB 10,000 on him or her.

873. Where a full-time corporate insurance agent leases out, lends, or transfers its permit, the CBIRC shall order it to take corrective action and impose a fine of not less than RMB 10,000 nor more than RMB 100,000 on it; if the circumstances are serious, order it to suspend business for an overhaul or revoke its permit; and for the directly liable supervising executive or any other liable person of the company, issue a warning to and impose a fine of not less than RMB 10,000 nor more than RMB 50,000 on him or her.

874. For a full-time insurance agency falling under any of the following circumstances, the CBIRC shall order it to take corrective action, issue a warning to it, and impose a fine of not more than RMB 10,000 on it if there is no illegal income or impose a fine of not more than three times the amount of illegal income but not exceeding RMB 30,000 on it if there is any illegal income:

- conducting business beyond the approved scope of business or business territory;
- conducting business beyond the scope of business or business territory of the insurance company represented;
- conducting insurance agency transactions with any entity or individual which illegally engages in the insurance business or insurance intermediary business;
- failing to manage and use as required the various documents and materials delivered to it by insurance companies.

For a full-time insurance agency falling under any of the following circumstances, the CBIRC shall order it to take corrective action and impose a fine of not less than RMB 20,000 nor more than RMB 100,000 on it; if the circumstances are serious, order it to suspend business for an overhaul or revoke its permit; and for the directly liable supervising executive or any other liable person of the agency, issue a warning to and impose a fine of not less than RMB 10,000 nor more than RMB 100,000 on him or her:

- failing to deposit a bond as required or using the bond in violation of the relevant provisions;
- failing to take out the professional liability insurance as required or failing to maintain the continuing validity of the professional liability insurance;
- failing to establish as required the special account books to record its business revenues and expenditures.

875. Where a full-time insurance agency fails to prepare or present a client notification letter as required, the CBIRC shall order it to take corrective action, and issue a warning to and impose a fine of not more than RMB 10,000 on it; and for the directly liable supervising executive or any other liable person of the agency, issue a warning to and impose a fine of not more than RMB 10,000 on him or her.

876. Where a full-time insurance agency or any of its practitioners seeks any illegal benefits by taking advantage of executing any insurance agency business in the process of conducting the insurance agency business, the CBIRC shall issue a warning to and impose a fine of not more than RMB 10,000 on the agency or practitioner.

877. Where a full-time insurance agency fails to submit or preserve the relevant reports, statements, documents, or materials under *the Agencies' Provisions* or fails to provide the relevant information or materials as required, the CBIRC shall order it to take corrective action during a specified period; and if it fails to do so, impose a fine of not less than RMB 10,000 nor more than RMB 100,000 on it; and for the directly liable supervising executive or any other liable person of the agency, issue a warning to and impose a fine of not less than RMB 10,000 nor more than RMB 50,000 on him or her.

878. For a full-time insurance agency falling under any of the following circumstances, the CBIRC shall order it to take corrective action and impose a fine of not less than RMB 100,000 nor more than RMB 500,000 on it; and if the circumstances are serious, may restrict its scope of business, order it to stop accepting new business, or revoke its permit; and for the directly liable supervising executive or any other liable person of the agency, issue a warning to and impose a fine of not less than RMB 50,000 nor more than RMB 100,000 on him or her:

- preparing or providing any false reports, statements, documents, or materials;
- refusing or obstructing any legally conducted supervisory inspection.

879. For a full-time insurance agency falling under any of the following circumstances, the CBIRC shall order it to take corrective action, issue a warning to it, and impose a fine of not more than RMB 10,000 on it if there is no illegal income or impose a fine of not more than three times the amount of illegal income but not exceeding RMB 30,000 on it if there is any illegal income; and for the directly liable supervising executive or any other liable person of the agency, issue a warning to and impose a fine of not more than RMB 10,000 on him or her:

- failing to pay the regulatory fees as required;
- failing to put its permit or a photocopy thereof (bearing the official seal of the corporate body owning it) and its business license at its domicile or business premises as required;
- failing to surrender its permit as required;
- failing to undergo the modification registration of its permit as required or failing to apply for the renewal of its permit during the prescribed time limit;
- failing to manage its business archives as required;
- failing to use as required an independent account to collect insurance premiums as an agent;
- the actual term of office of its temporary person in charge exceeding the prescribed period;
- failing to issue announcements as required;
- withholding commissions from the insurance premiums collected as an agent;
- entering into insurance contracts on behalf of insurance applicants.

880. Where any provision of Articles 165–170 of the IL is violated, if the circumstances of the violation are serious, the CBIRC may disqualify the directly liable supervising executive and other directly liable persons of the violator from holding the corresponding offices.

For a violation of any law or administrative regulation with serious circumstances, the CBIRC may prohibit the relevant liable persons from access to the insurance sector for a certain period or even for life.

881. Where it is discovered after a director, senior executive, or practitioner of a full-time insurance agency resigns that such a person violated the insurance regulatory provisions during his/her former service in the agency, the person shall be held liable according to the law.

882. Where the CBIRC discovers that a full-time insurance agency is suspected of tax evasion, illegal fundraising, pyramid sales, or money laundering, among others, which falls under the jurisdiction of any other authority, it shall report or transfer it to the other authority. Where a violator of *the Agencies' Provisions* is suspected of a crime, the CBIRC shall report or transfer it to the judicial authority.

Chapter 2. Insurance Broker

§1. Introduction

I. Definition

883. Article 118 of the IL provides that insurance brokers shall be institutions which, based on the interests of insurance applicants, provide intermediary services for insurance applicants and insurers to enter into insurance contracts, and charge commissions according to the law. Article 6 of *the Provisions on the Supervision and Administration of Insurance Brokers* (hereinafter referred to as "*the Brokers' Provisions*") provides that except as otherwise specified by the CBIRC an insurance broker shall adopt the forms of organization of limited liability company or joint-stock limited company.

II. Rights and Obligations

884. In the event that an insurance broker enters into an insurance contract and provides intermediary services for the insured and the insurer, it shall bear the corresponding obligations but at the same time is entitled some rights. National laws and regulations and insurance practices stipulate the basic rights and obligations of insurance brokers.

885. The basic rights of insurance brokers include the following.

First, the right to request a commission. In the insurance market, insurance brokers are entrusted by the insured to handle insurance procedures. After completing the insurance formalities and delivering the insurance premiums, the insurer shall draw a certain percentage (i.e., commission) from the insurance premiums to the insurance broker as remuneration;

Second, the right to lien on policy. Once the insurance broker accepts the entrustment to complete the insurance application, the insurance broker must deliver the insurance premium to the insurer regardless of whether the insured has delivered the premium to the insurance broker. In order to prevent the insured from paying the insurance premiums, the insurance broker shall have a lien on the insurance policy before receiving the insurance premium.

886. The basic obligations of an insurance broker include the following.

First, providing insurance information to facilitate the conclusion of an insurance contract. When an insurance broker provides an intermediary service, it shall truthfully inform the client (i.e., the policyholder) of all the relevant information on insurance contract and the insurance that he knows or ought to know. Insurance brokers should also carefully and conscientiously discuss with insurance customers to determine the insurance premiums and insured amount and should try to find the best insurance conditions for their clients through their knowledge and experience to promote the conclusion of insurance contracts.

Second, supervising the performance of insurance contracts. First, when an insurance broker receives an insurance policy, he must carefully check the content to see whether it meets the insurance requirements. Second, the insurance customer should be informed of the coverage and conditions of the insurance that should be observed. Finally, the insurance broker is obliged to notify the insurer when changes in circumstances may affect the client's insurance requirements.

Third, assisting the claim. In the event of an accident covered by an insurance contract, the insurance broker is usually notified first, and the insurance broker subsequently informs the insurer and immediately begins to investigate the claim. After a detailed assessment of the accident, the insurance broker shall finish some necessary claim documents and submit them to the insurer. Insurance brokers should use their knowledge and experience to obtain the maximum amount of compensation for the insured under legal conditions.

Fourth, responsibility for damage. Once the insured has suffered losses or bore unreasonable expenses due to the fault of insurance broker, the insurance contract was not able to protect the interests of the insured; as a consequence, when an accident under cover occurred, the insurer refuses to pay compensation or pay less than expected, or the insured has to pay higher insurance premiums than normal; as a result, the insurance broker shall bear the corresponding liability for the damage of the insured. Article 128 of the IL stipulates that an insurance broker which, for its fault, causes any loss to an insurance applicant or insured shall assume compensatory liability.

III. Insurance Brokerage Contract

A. Characteristics of Insurance Brokerage Contracts

887. In order to safeguard the rights and obligations of both parties better and reduce insurance brokerage disputes, insurance brokers should take the form of contracts to serve the customer. The contractual behavior of an insurance broker is determined by the nature of the civil legal behavior of the insurance broker. Since the behavior of the insurance broker has the characteristics of intermediary, agency and consultation, it has the general characteristics of the intermediary contract, the entrustment contract and the consulting contract.

1. Intermediary Contract

888. Intermediary act is that the intermediary reports the opportunity or provides the media service of entering into contract for the client. Since the insurance brokers who, based on the entrustment of the insured and the interests of the insured, enter into insurance contracts for the insured, they provide intermediary services and receive commissions according to law. The contract signed by the insured and the insurance broker at the time of entrustment is an intermediary contract. The intermediary behavior of an insurance broker has both the general attributes of the intermediary contract and its special characteristics. In the insurance intermediary behavior, the commission of the intermediary is obtained from the insurer rather than from the principal because the insurance broker introduces businesses for the insurer. The purpose of the insurance brokerage contract is to provide the client with the opportunity to contract with the insurer according to their request, that is to match their contract; therefore, as the intermediary, the insurance broker cannot participate in the negotiation of the contract in his own name.

2. Entrustment Contract

889. The entrustment is the act of the consignor and the consignee agreeing that the consignee will handle the consignor's affairs. Since the insurance broker can apply for insurance and handle the claim for the insured or the beneficiary, the insurance broker at this time is actually the consignee of the consignor, and the contractual behavior at this time is the entrustment contract act. In the entrustment contract of an insurance broker, the consignee is an insurance broker, and the consignor is the applicant, the insured, and the beneficiary. The insurance entrustment contract is an agreement that the insurance broker, in the name of the consignor, handles the insurance affairs according to the entrustment of the consignor. In the application of the law, the insurance entrustment contract shall be in accordance with the relevant law of the agency contract and the broker. The characteristics of the insurance entrustment contract are as follows. The first is the agency nature. This is the most important feature of the contract. The agency is embodied as follows: the scope of the entrusted transaction and the authority of the agent are clearly agreed with the consignor; the agent must act in the name of the consignor; the agent independently performs the meaning representation within the scope of the consignor's authorization; the consequences of all agency acts are borne by the consignor. The second is intervention. The insurance entrustment contract is different from the insurance intermediary contract. The agent directly intervenes in the specific negotiation of the contract according to the authorization, and the insurance broker even independently completes the negotiation, conclusion and claim of the insurance contract in the name of the consignor.

3. Consulting Contract

890. Consulting is the act of feasibility argumentation, prediction, special investigation, analysis and evaluation on specific projects. An insurance consulting contract is a contract in which an insurance broker provides a demonstration, forecast or investigation report on a specific insurance project according to the requirements of the client, and the client pays the consulting fee, for example, providing disaster prevention, loss prevention or risk assessment and risk management consulting services for policyholders; formulating insurance plans for policyholders for the purpose of entering into insurance contracts; and providing consulting services of claim for insured or beneficiary. In order to standardize such consultations to protect the legitimate rights and interests of the parties, insurance brokers should sign a consulting contract with the client before providing consulting services.

B. Insurance Brokerage Contract Term

891. The rights and obligations of both parties to the insurance brokerage contract are reflected in the terms of the contract. The basic terms of the insurance brokerage contract include: the name of the project; the content, methods and requirements of the insurance brokerage service; related confidential matters and credit matters; the time limit, place and method of performance; the commission or consulting fee standard and its payment method; the liability for breach of contract and the default method of calculating the amount of damages; the solution to the dispute and so on.

§2. ESTABLISHMENT OF THE INSURANCE BROKER

892. According to *the Brokers' Provisions*, except as otherwise specified by the CBIRC, an insurance broker shall adopt the forms of organization of limited liability company or joint-stock limited company. To engage in insurance brokerage business within the territory of China, an insurance brokerage shall satisfy the requirements prescribed by the CBIRC and obtain an insurance brokerage business permit.

893. According to the CL, the limited liability company and the joint-stock limited company are all enterprise legal persons. A joint-stock limited company means that its capitals are divided into equal shares and the shareholder shall be liable for the company to the extent of the shares it has subscribed to. The company shall bear the liabilities for its debts with all its property. To establish a joint-stock limited company, there shall not be less than 2 but not more than 200 promoters, of whom half or more shall have a domicile within the territory of China. A joint-stock limited company has the superiority of its ability to pool capital. However, an insurance broker is a technical service organization and its most important resources are all kinds of professional and technical personnel. The role of various physical assets in its management is not very prominent. Therefore, insurance brokers can choose the form of a limited liability company. A limited liability company shall be established by no more than fifty shareholders that make capital contributions. The shareholder shall be liable for the company to the extent of the capital contributions it has paid, and the company is responsible for its liabilities for all its assets. The CL allows the establishment of a one-person company. The shareholders of a one-person limited liability company can be either natural persons or legal persons, but a natural person can only set up one one-person limited company. The company-based insurance brokerage company is generally in the form of a limited liability company, which is also the organization form of insurance brokers recognized by all countries.

894. According to *the Brokers' Provisions*, the minimum registered capital of an insurance brokerage company whose business area is not limited to the province, autonomous region, municipality directly under the Central Government or city under separate state planning where industrial and commercial registration formalities are undergone shall be RMB 50 million. The minimum registered capital of an insurance brokerage company whose business area is the province, autonomous region, municipality directly under the Central Government or city under separate state planning where industrial and commercial registration formalities are undergone shall be RMB 10 million. The registered capital of an insurance brokerage company must be paid-in monetary capital.

895. The name of an insurance broker shall include the words "insurance brokerage." The identifier of an insurance broker shall not be the same as that of an existing professional insurance intermediary institution, except when an insurance broker has the same actual controller as the professional insurance intermediary institution.

896. To apply for engaging in insurance brokerage business, an insurance brokerage company shall, after obtaining a business license, submit the application materials in a timely manner in accordance with the requirements of the CBIRC and disclose the relevant information. The CBIRC and its local office shall implement administrative licensing according to their statutory duties and procedures.

897. After receiving an application for engaging in insurance brokerage business, the CBIRC and its local office shall, by interview, correspondence, on-site acceptance and other means, understand and examine the business records of the applicant's shareholders and the applicant's market development strategy, business development plan, internal control system building, personnel structure, information system configuration, operation and other relevant matters, and conduct risk testing and warning.

898. The CBIRC and its local office making a decision of approving an insurance brokerage company to engage in the insurance brokering business shall issue a permit to the applicant. Only after obtaining a permit may an applicant engage in the insurance brokerage business, and an applicant shall register the relevant information in the regulatory information system as set forth by the CBIRC in a timely manner. Where the CBIRC and its local office decides to disapprove the application, a written decision shall be made and the reasons shall be explained. An applicant shall, within fifteen days of the date of receiving a written decision of the CBIRC and its local office, report to the administrative department for industry and commerce where the industrial and commercial registration formalities are undergone. A company that survives shall not engage in insurance brokerage business, handle the industrial and commercial modification registration of its name, business scope and bylaws, among others, according to the law, and ensure that there is no such word as "insurance brokerage" in its name.

899. An insurance brokerage company whose business area is not limited to the province, autonomous region, municipality directly under the Central Government or city under separate state planning where industrial and commercial registration formalities are undergone may carry out insurance brokerage activities within the territory of China. Where an insurance brokerage company whose business area is limited to the province, autonomous region, municipality directly under the Central Government or city under separate state planning where industrial and commercial registration formalities are undergone dispatches insurance brokerage practitioners to a place other than the industrial and commercial registration places to provide services for insurance business whose insurance applicants and insured are natural persons shall form a local branch. To form a branch, a provincial branch company shall be formed first and be designated to handle the matters concerning the application for administrative licensing, regulatory report and submission of statements, among others, and to be responsible for managing other branches. The branches of an insurance brokerage company shall include branch companies and business departments.

900. To form a new branch to carry out insurance brokerage business, an insurance brokerage company shall meet the following conditions:

- the insurance brokerage company and its branch have not been subject to criminal punishment or major administrative punishment in the most recent year;
- the insurance brokerage company and its branch are not under investigation by the relevant department for being suspected of involvement in any violation of law or crime;
- the insurance brokerage company and its branch have not caused any mass visits and complaints involving thirty or more persons or abnormal centralized surrender of policies involving hundred or more persons in the most recent year;
- a branch formed in the most recent two years did not exit market after operation for less than one year;
- it has sound branch management system;
- a newly formed branch has qualified business premise, business financial information system, and other facilities matching the business operation;
- the primary person in charge of a newly formed branch satisfies the office qualifications as set forth in *the Brokers' Provisions*;
- other conditions as prescribed by the CBIRC.

901. An insurance brokerage company that is determined by a relevant entity of the state as an object subject to joint punishment for serious dishonesty and shall be subject to corresponding penalties in the insurance field, or has other bad records of serious dishonesty within the most recent five years shall not form any new branch to carry out insurance brokerage business.

902. A branch of an insurance brokerage company shall, within fifteen days of the registration date recorded in the business license, report to the local office of the CBIRC in writing, register the relevant information in the regulatory information system as required by the CBIRC, make public disclosure in accordance with the relevant provisions, and submit the application materials or reporting materials on application for the confirmation of satisfaction of office qualifications of the primary person in charge.

903. An insurance broker falling under one of the following circumstances shall, within five days of occurrence of such circumstance, report through the regulatory information system as required by the CBIRC, and make public disclosure in accordance with the relevant provisions:

- changing the name, domicile or business premise;
- changing the shareholders, registered capital or organizational form;
- changing the shareholder's name, designation, or amount of contribution;
- amending the bylaws;
- making equity investment, and forming an overseas insurance institution and non-business institution;
- division, merger and dissolution of the insurance broker, and termination of insurance brokerage business activities by a branch;
- changing the primary person in charge of a branch other than provincial branch company;
- being subject to administrative punishment or criminal punishment or under investigation for being suspected of involvement in any violation of law or crime;
- other reporting matters as prescribed by the CBIRC.

904. An insurance broker falling under the relevant circumstances as prescribed in the preceding paragraph shall comply with the relevant provisions issued by the CBIRC. An insurance brokerage company that makes any change involving any matter recorded in the permit shall handle registration of change in the permit according to *the Measures for the Administration of Insurance Permits* and other relevant provisions, surrender the original permit, obtain a new one, and make an announcement.

§3. Supervision on the Insurance Broker

I. Market Access

A. Business Permit

905. To carry out insurance brokerage business, an insurance brokerage company shall meet the following conditions:

- its shareholders satisfy the requirements of *the Brokers' Provisions* and make contribution with self-owned, true and legal funds, other than bank loans or any other form of non-self-owned capital;
- its registered capital satisfies the requirements of *the Brokers' Provisions* and is under custody according to the relevant provisions issued by the CBIRC;

- the business scope recorded in its business license complies with the relevant provisions issued by the CBIRC;
- its bylaws comply with the relevant provisions;
- its name satisfies the requirements of *the Brokers' Provisions*;
- its senior executives meet the office qualifications as set forth in *the Brokers' Provisions*;
- it has a governance structure and internal control system in compliance with the provisions issued by the CBIRC, and scientific and reasonable business model;
- it has a fixed domicile suitable for its scale of business;
- it has business and financial information management systems in compliance with the provisions issued by the CBIRC;
- other conditions as set forth in laws, administrative regulations, and the provisions issued by the CBIRC.

906. An entity or individual falling under one of the following circumstances shall not become a shareholder of any insurance brokerage company:

- the entity or individual has been subject to criminal punishment or major administrative punishment in the most recent five years;
- the entity or individual is under investigation by the relevant department for being suspected of involvement in any serious violation of law or crime;
- the entity or individual is determined by a relevant entity of the state as an object subject to joint punishment for serious dishonesty and shall be subject to corresponding penalties in the insurance field, or has other bad records of serious dishonesty within the most recent five years;
- the entity or individual cannot invest in any enterprise according to the laws and administrative regulations;
- other circumstances under which the entity or individual is inappropriate to become a shareholder of the insurance brokerage company as recognized by the CBIRC under the principle of prudential regulation.

907. Where an employee of an insurance company or a practitioner of a professional insurance intermediary institution makes investment in an insurance brokerage company, a written certification showing that his/her employer is aware of the investment shall be provided; and where a director, supervisor or senior executive of an insurance company or professional insurance intermediary institution makes investment in an insurance brokerage company, the consent of the shareholders' meeting or the general meeting of shareholders shall be obtained according to the relevant provisions.

B. Office Qualifications

908. The "senior executive" of an insurance broker means the following persons:

– the general manager and deputy general manager of an insurance brokerage company;
– the primary person in charge of a provincial branch;
– other persons who exercise important functions and powers over the business operation and management of the company.

A senior executive of an insurance broker shall, before taking office, obtain the office qualifications confirmed by the local office of the CBIRC. A senior executive of an insurance broker shall meet the following conditions:

– he or she has an educational background of junior college or above;
– he or she has three or more years of financial work experience or five or more years of economic work experience;
– he or she has the business operation management capability required for performing duties and is familiar with the ILs and administrative regulations and the relevant provisions issued by the CBIRC;
– he or she is honest and trustworthy and has good conduct.

A person with ten years or more of financial work experience may be exempted from the restriction of the first item. A primary person in charge of a branch other than provincial branch company appointed by an insurance broker shall meet the conditions as prescribed in the preceding two items.

909. A person falling under one of the following circumstances shall not serve as senior executive of any insurance broker or primary person in charge of any branch other than provincial branch company:

– he or she serves as director, supervisor, or senior executive of an insurance company or insurance intermediary institution whose permit has been revoked for violation of laws and is personally or directly liable as a leader for the revocation of permit, and three years have not elapsed since the date of revocation of permit;
– he or she is director, supervisor, or senior executive of a financial institution who has been disqualified for taking office by the financial regulatory authority for his/her violation of laws or discipline, and five years have not elapsed since the date of disqualification;
– he or she is prohibited from access to the financial industry during a certain period as decided by the financial regulatory authority, and the period has not expired;
– two years have not elapsed since a warning is granted or a fine is imposed by the financial regulatory authority;
– he or she is under investigation by the judicial authority, the discipline inspection and supervision department, or the financial regulatory authority;
– he or she is determined by a relevant entity of the state as an object subject to joint punishment for serious dishonesty and shall be subject to corresponding penalties in the insurance field, or has other bad records of serious dishonesty within the most recent five years;

– other circumstances as set forth in laws, administrative regulations, and the provisions issued by the CBIRC.

910. Senior executives of an insurance broker and primary persons in charge of a branch other than provincial branch company shall not concurrently serve as primary persons in charge of two or more branches. A senior executive of an insurance broker or a primary person in charge of a branch other than provincial branch company concurrently taking other business management offices shall have the necessary time to perform the duties.

911. Without approval of the shareholders' meeting or general meeting of shareholders, a senior executive of an insurance broker or a primary person in charge of a branch other than provincial branch company shall not concurrently take any office in any institution having conflict of interest with the insurance broker.

912. An insurance broker applying to the local office of the CBIRC for confirmation of satisfaction of office qualifications for senior executives shall faithfully enter the application form and submit the relevant materials. The local office of the CBIRC may investigate or interview the proposed senior executives of an insurance broker.

913. The senior executives of an insurance broker shall pass the examinations on ILs and regulations and relevant knowledge as recognized by the CBIRC. A senior executive of an insurance broker that is transferred to or concurrently holds another post in the same institution is not required to be subject to confirmation of satisfaction of office qualifications.

914. Where a senior executive of an insurance broker or a primary person in charge of a branch office other than provincial branch company is prosecuted for any suspected crime, the insurance broker shall, within five days of the date when he or she is prosecuted, register the relevant information in the regulatory information system as prescribed by the CBIRC.

915. A senior executive of an insurance broker or a primary person in charge of a branch office other than provincial branch company that falls under one of the following circumstances and has been appointed by the insurance broker shall be removed from office, and where he or she is confirmed to satisfy the office qualifications, his/her office qualifications shall be automatically invalidated:

– after being confirmed to satisfy office qualifications, he or she is not appointed for over two months;
– he or she leaves the insurance broker;
– the CBIRC imposes the administrative punishment of prohibition from access to the insurance industry on him or her;
– it has not been five years since he or she finished serving a criminal sentence for corruption, acceptance of bribes, embezzlement of property, appropriation of

property or disturbance of the socialist market order; or it has not been five years since he or she finished serving a criminal sentence with deprival of political rights for any crime;
- it has not been three years since the completion of the bankruptcy liquidation of a company or enterprise in which he or she serves as director or factory director or manager, and he or she was personally liable for the bankruptcy liquidation of the company or enterprise;
- it has not been three years since a company or enterprise in which he or she serves as legal representative forfeited its business license if the company or enterprise forfeited its business license for any violation of law and was ordered to close down, and he or she was personally liable for the forfeiture and closedown;
- he or she has a relatively large amount of personal debts which have not been paid off upon maturity.

916. An insurance broker falling under one of the following circumstances may appoint a temporary person in charge for a maximum of three months, and shall not continuously appoint the temporary person in charge for the same position:

- the original person in charge resigns or is removed from office;
- the original person in charge is unable to normally perform his/her duties for any illness, accident, or other reason;
- any other special circumstances as recognized by the CBIRC.

The temporary person in charge shall have the capability appropriate for performing his/her duties and satisfy the relevant requirements of *the Brokers' Provisions*. To appoint a temporary person in charge, an insurance broker shall, within five days of the date of making a decision, register relevant information in the regulatory information system as prescribed by the CBIRC.

C. Practitioner

917. An insurance broker shall employ insurance brokerage practitioners with good moral character. An insurance broker shall not employ any insurance brokerage practitioner falling under any of the following circumstances:

- it has not been five years since he or she finished serving a criminal sentence for corruption, bribery, embezzlement of property, appropriation of property or disturbance of the socialist market economic order;
- he or she has been prohibited from access to the financial industry during a certain period as decided by the financial regulatory authority, and the period has not expired;
- he or she is determined by a relevant entity of the state as an object subject to joint punishment for serious dishonesty and shall be subject to corresponding penalties in the insurance field, or has other bad records of serious dishonesty within the most recent five years;

– other circumstances as prescribed by laws, administrative regulations, and the provisions issued by the CBIRC.

918. An insurance brokerage practitioner shall have the professional capability required for engaging in insurance brokerage business. An insurance broker shall strengthen the pre-post training and follow-up education for insurance brokerage practitioners, which shall at least include business knowledge, legal knowledge and professional ethics. An insurance broker may entrust the self-regulation organizations or other institutions of the insurance intermediary industry to organize training. An insurance broker shall establish complete archives on the training of insurance brokerage practitioners. An insurance broker shall conduct practicing registration for its insurance brokerage practitioners in accordance with the relevant provisions. Practicing registration shall only be conducted for insurance brokerage practitioners through one insurance broker. Where an insurance brokerage practitioner alters his/her insurance broker, the new insurance broker shall conduct practicing registration for him or her, and the original insurance broker shall cancel the practicing registration in a timely manner.

II. Operation Rules

A. Business Territory

919. An insurance broker may engage in the following business, in whole or in part:

– drafting insurance application proposals, selecting insurance companies, and handling the insurance application formalities for insurance applicants;
– assisting the insured or beneficiaries in claiming compensation;
– reinsurance brokerage business;
– providing clients with disaster or loss prevention or risk assessment or management consulting services;
– other businesses relevant to insurance brokerage as prescribed by the CBIRC.

The insurance brokerage business carried out by an insurance broker shall not exceed the business scope and the business area of the underwriting insurance company, except insurance brokerage business involving coinsurance outside its business territory, insurance underwritten outside its business territory, or master policies as otherwise specified by the CBIRC.

B. Account

920. An insurance broker shall establish special account books to record the revenues and expenditures of the insurance brokerage business. An insurance broker shall open an independent account special for clients' funds, only in which may the following funds be deposited:

– the premiums paid to insurance companies by insurance applicants;
– the surrender values and insurance premiums collected on behalf of insurance applicants, the insured, and beneficiaries.

An insurance broker shall open an independent account to collect commissions and open and use other bank accounts in compliance with the provisions issued by the CBIRC.

C. Business Archive

921. An insurance broker shall establish complete and standardized business archives, including the following at a minimum:

– basic information on the insurance policies signed through the institution, including the designations or names of insurers, insurance applicants, and the insured, number of insurance policies, names of products, insured amounts, insurance premiums, methods of payment, date of purchasing insurance policies and insurance period, among others;
– the amount of commissions and collection methods corresponding to the insurance contracts, etc.;
– the information on payment of insurance premiums to insurance companies and information on the collection and payment of insurance premiums or surrender values on behalf of insurance applicants, the insured, or beneficiaries;
– the names of the practitioners providing brokerage services for the signing of the insurance contracts, the amount of remunerations and the accounts for collecting remunerations, among others;
– other business information as prescribed by the CBIRC.

The records of an insurance broker shall be true and complete.

D. Reinsurance Brokerage Business

922. An insurance broker shall carry out reinsurance brokerage business in accordance with the provisions issued by the CBIRC. To engage in reinsurance brokerage business, an insurance broker shall set up a special department to isolate the business flow, financial management, risk control and other respects from other insurance brokerage businesses. To engage in reinsurance brokerage business, an insurance broker shall establish complete and regulated business archives, including the following at a minimum:

– the confirmation letter on reinsurance arrangements;
– the ceded proportion that the reinsurer accepts.

An insurance broker shall respectively establish account books for reinsurance brokerage business and other insurance brokerage businesses to record its business income and expenditure.

E. Entrustment Contract

923. An insurance broker shall provide insurance companies with true and complete information on the purchase of insurance policies, and shall, according to the law, agree with insurance companies on the confidentiality, reasonable use and other matters of the information on purchase of insurance policies.

To engage in the insurance brokerage business, an insurance broker shall enter into entrustment contracts with clients, and agree on the rights and obligations of both parties and other relevant matters according to the law. An entrustment contract shall not violate laws, administrative regulations or relevant provisions issued by the CBIRC.

An insurance broker carrying out insurance brokerage business involving the payment of insurance premium or commissions to insurance companies shall agree with the insurance companies on the insurance premiums to be paid upon agreement with the insurance companies, the time limit for paying commissions, the liability for liquidated damages and other matters.

F. Client Notification Letter

924. In the process of carrying out business, an insurance broker shall develop and produce a standard client notification letter. A client notification letter shall, at a minimum, include the following items:

- its name, business premise, scope of business and contact methods;
- the methods for an insurance broker to obtain remunerations, including whether it has collected commissions from an insurance company;
- whether there is any affiliation relationship between the insurance broker and its senior executive and an insurance company or insurance intermediary institution related to its brokerage business;
- the channels of filing complaints and the methods of settling disputes.

An insurance broker shall properly preserve its business archives, account books, business ledgers, client notification letter, original vouchers of the commission revenue and other relevant materials for not less than five years if the duration of insurance is not more than one year and for not less than ten years if the duration of insurance is longer than one year, starting from the day when the insurance contract is terminated.

G. Professional Liability Insurance Policies or Deposit Margin

925. An insurance brokerage company shall, within twenty days of obtaining a permit, purchase professional liability insurance policies or deposit margin. An insurance brokerage company shall, within ten days of purchasing a professional liability insurance policy or depositing margin, submit a photocopy of the professional liability insurance policy or a photocopy of the margin deposit agreement and a photocopy of the original voucher of deposit of the margin to the local office of the CBIRC, and register relevant information in the regulatory information system prescribed by the CBIRC.

926. An insurance brokerage company that purchases professional liability insurance policy shall ensure the continuing validity of the insurance. The compensation limit for each accident under the professional liability insurance policy purchased by an insurance brokerage company shall not be less than RMB 1 million, and the cumulative compensation limit under a one-year policy shall not be less than RMB 10 million and not be less than two times the insurance broker's operating revenue in the previous year.

927. An insurance brokerage company depositing margin shall deposit the margin at 5% of its registered capital, and an insurance brokerage company increasing registered capital shall increase the amount of margin accordingly. An insurance brokerage company shall deposit margin in full. The margin of an insurance brokerage company shall be deposited in commercial banks in the form of bank deposit or be deposited in any other form recognized by the CBIRC.

928. Under any of the following circumstances, an insurance brokerage company may use the margin:

- its registered capital is reduced;
- its permit is canceled;
- it purchases qualified professional liability insurance policies;
- other circumstances as prescribed by the CBIRC.

Within five days after using the margin, an insurance brokerage company shall report to the CBIRC in writing.

H. Forbidden Conduct

929. An insurance broker shall not entrust any individual that has not undergone the formalities of practicing registration with the institution to carry out insurance brokerage business. An insurance broker shall conduct administration of practicing registration information on insurance brokerage practitioners, and register the personal information, scope of authorization and other matters, acceptance of punishment, and termination of employment relationships in a timely manner, to ensure the authenticity, accuracy and integrity of the practicing registration information.

An insurance broker and its practitioners shall not commit any of the following acts in the handling of insurance business:

- cheating the insurer, insurance applicant, insured or beneficiary;
- concealing important information on the insurance contract;
- obstructing an insurance applicant from faithfully performing or inducing any insurance applicant not to perform the obligation of notification;
- providing or promising to provide any insurance applicant, insured or beneficiary with any benefit not under the contract;
- forcing or inducing an insurance applicant to enter into or restrict an insurance applicant from entering into an insurance contract, by taking advantage of administrative power, post or profession or by any other improper means;
- forging or modifying without permission the insurance contract, or providing false certifications to the parties to the insurance contract;
- misappropriating, withholding or embezzling insurance premiums or insurance benefits;
- seeking improper benefits for any other institution or individual by taking advantage of its business;
- fraudulently obtaining insurance benefits by colluding with any insurance applicant, insured, or beneficiary;
- disclosing any trade secret of an insurer, insurance applicant or insured known in the process of business activities.

930. An insurance broker and its practitioners shall not demand or accept any remuneration or other property not under the contract from any insurance company or any employee thereof or seek any other illegal benefits by taking advantage of executing any insurance brokerage business in the process of carrying out insurance brokerage business. An insurance broker shall not damage the goodwill of competitors by fabrication or spreading false facts, nor disrupt the insurance market order by false advertisements, false publicity, or any other act of unfair competition. An insurance broker shall not carry out insurance brokerage business with any institution or individual which illegally engages in insurance business or insurance intermediary business. An insurance broker shall not recruit practitioners on condition of their payment of fees or purchase of insurance products, promise unreasonably high returns, or use the number of directly or indirectly recruited persons or sale performance as the main basis for computing the remuneration of practitioners.

III. Market Exit

931. The validity period of a permit of an insurance brokerage company for carrying out the insurance brokerage business shall be three years. An insurance brokerage company shall, thirty days before the expiry of the permit, apply to the local office of the CBIRC for renewal of the permit as required. Where an insurance brokerage company applies for renewal of its permit, the local office of the CBIRC shall, before expiry of the permit, comprehensively review and assess the insurance broker's operations in the previous three years and make a decision of approving or disapproving the renewal. In the case of disapproval, it shall provide a written explanation of the reasons for the disapproval. Where an insurance brokerage company fails to meet the conditions for engaging in the insurance brokerage business as prescribed in Article 7 of *the Brokers' Provisions* or fails to meet the conditions for continuing the insurance brokerage business licensing as prescribed in the laws and administrative regulations or as prescribed by the CBIRC, the local office of the CBIRC shall not extend the validity period of the permit. An insurance brokerage company shall, within ten days of the date of disapproving the renewal of the validity period of a permit, surrender the original permit to the local office of the CBIRC, and shall obtain a new permit within ten days of the date of receiving a decision, where renewal of the validity period is approved.

932. An insurance brokerage company shall, when withdrawing from the insurance brokerage market, abide by the laws, administrative regulations and other relevant provisions. Where an insurance brokerage company falls under one of the following circumstances, the local office of the CBIRC shall cancel its permit according to the law, and issue an announcement:

- the permit is not renewed upon expiry;
- the permit is retracted, canceled, or revoked according to the law;
- it is terminated according to the law due to dissolution or being declared bankrupt in accordance with the law or any other reason;
- other circumstances as set forth in laws and administrative regulations.

933. An insurance brokerage company whose permit is canceled shall surrender the original permit in a timely manner; and where a permit is unable to be surrendered, the local office of the CBIRC shall explain it in the announcement. An insurance brokerage company whose permit is canceled shall terminate its insurance brokerage business activities, and shall, within fifteen days of the date of cancelation of the permit, submit a written report to the administrative department for industry and commerce in the place where industrial and commercial registration is handled. If the company survives, it shall not engage in the insurance brokerage business, and shall modify its industrial and commercial registration of the name, business scope, bylaws and other matters according to the law, to ensure that there is no "insurance brokerage" in its name.

934. Under one of the following circumstances, an insurance broker shall cancel the practicing registration of an insurance brokerage practitioner within five days:

- an insurance brokerage practitioner is subject to any administrative punishment of prohibition from access to the insurance industry;
- an insurance brokerage practitioner terminates practice for other reasons;
- an insurance broker stops engaging in the insurance brokerage business for close-down, dissolution or other reasons;
- other circumstances as prescribed by laws, administrative regulations, and the provisions issued by the CBIRC.

An insurance broker terminating the insurance brokerage business shall appropriately handle the debtor-creditor relationship and shall not impair the lawful rights and interests of any insurance applicant, insured or beneficiary.

IV. Supervision and Inspection

935. The local offices of the CBIRC shall, under the territorial principle, take charge of the supervision and administration of insurance brokers within their jurisdictions. The local offices of the CBIRC shall pay attention to the supervision of the acts of insurance brokers within their respective jurisdictions, conduct on-site inspection and off-site supervision according to the law, impose administrative penalties and take other regulatory measures.

936. The CBIRC and its local offices may, according to the needs of supervision, hold regulatory interviews with the senior executives and relevant personnel of insurance brokers, requiring them to provide explanations on the major issues in the operation activities. The CBIRC and its local offices may, according to the supervision needs, designate supervisors to attend the shareholders' meetings, general meetings of shareholders or meetings of the board of directors of the insurance brokerage companies.

937. Where a branch of an insurance brokerage company has chaos in business operation and management and has seriously violated the laws and regulations, the insurance brokerage company shall, in accordance with the regulatory requirements of the CBIRC and its local office, take measures such as taking corrective action with a specified time limit, suspending operation and cancelation against the branch.

938. The CBIRC and its local offices shall conduct on-site inspection of insurance brokers according to the law, which shall mainly include the following contents:

- whether the business licensing and relevant matters are approved according to the law and the notification obligations are performed;
- whether its capital is true and adequate;
- whether the margin complies with the relevant provisions;
- whether the professional liability insurance complies with the provisions;
- whether its operations are lawful;
- whether it is in good financial condition;
- whether the reports, statements, and materials submitted to the CBIRC and its local offices are timely, complete and authentic;
- whether its internal control rules comply with the relevant provisions issued by the CBIRC;
- whether senior executives and primary person in charge of a branch other than provincial branch company are employed in compliance with the provisions;
- whether it has effectively performed the duty of managing its practitioners;
- whether the external announcements are issued in a timely and authentic manner;

– whether the business and financial information management systems comply with the relevant provisions issued by the CBIRC;
– other matters as prescribed by the CBIRC.

939. The CBIRC and its local offices shall perform their duties according to the law, and the entities and individuals under inspection and investigation shall cooperate therewith. In the process of an on-site inspection, the CBIRC and its local office may engage an accounting firm and other private intermediary institutions to provide the relevant services, and, if so, shall enter into written engagement agreements with them. The CBIRC and its local office shall inform the inspected insurance broker under inspection of the entrustment.

V. Legal Liability

940. Any illegal operation of the insurance brokerage business without a permit shall be banned by the CBIRC, and the CBIRC and its local office shall confiscate any illegal income and impose a fine of not less than the amount nor more than five times the amount of the illegal income on the violator or if there is no illegal income or the amount of illegal income is less than RMB 50,000, impose a fine of not less than RMB 50,000 nor more than RMB 300,000 on the violator.

941. Where an administrative licensing applicant conceals relevant information or provides false materials in the application for a permit for insurance brokerage business or for any other administrative licensing, the CBIRC and its local office shall reject or disapprove its application and issue a warning to it, and the applicant shall not apply for the administrative licensing again within one year.

942. Where an insurance broker appoints any person not satisfying the office qualifications, the CBIRC and its local office shall order it to take corrective action and impose a fine of not less than RMB 20,000 nor more than RMB 100,000 on it; and shall issue a warning to and impose a fine of not less than RMB 10,000 nor more than RMB 100,000 on the directly liable person in charge or other directly liable persons of the institution, and revoke his/her office qualifications under serious circumstances. An insurance broker failing to employ any primary person in charge of a branch other than provincial branch company as required or failing to appoint a temporary person in charge as required shall be ordered to take corrective action, be given a warning and be fined not more than RMB 10,000 by the CBIRC and its local office, and the directly liable person in charge and other directly liable persons of the institution shall be given a warning and be fined not more than RMB 10,000.

943. An insurance broker failing to employ any insurance brokerage practitioner as required or conduct practicing registration or management as required shall be ordered to take corrective action, be given a warning and be fined not more than RMB 10,000 by the CBIRC and its local office, and the directly liable person in charge and other directly liable persons of the institution shall be given a warning and be fined not more than RMB 10,000.

944. Where an insurance broker leases, lends, or transfers its permit, the CBIRC and its local office shall order it to take corrective action and impose a fine of not less than RMB 10,000 nor more than RMB 100,000 on it; if the circumstances are serious, order it to suspend business for an overhaul or revoke its permit; and issue a warning to the directly liable person in charge or any other directly liable person of the institution and impose a fine of not less than RMB 10,000 nor more than RMB 100,000 thereupon, and revoke his/her office qualifications under serious circumstances.

945. Where an insurance broker falls under any of the following circumstances in the process of using a permit, the CBIRC and its local office shall order it to take corrective action, issue a warning to it, and impose a fine of not more than RMB 10,000 on it if there is no illegal income or impose a fine of not more than three times the amount of illegal income but not exceeding RMB 30,000 on it if there is any illegal income; and issue a warning to the directly liable person in charge or any other directly liable person of the institution and impose a fine of not more than RMB 10,000 thereupon:

- failing to put its permit or photocopy thereof at its domicile or business premise as required;
- failing to undergo the modification registration of its permit as required;
- failing to surrender its permit as required;
- failing to issue announcements as required.

946. Where an insurance broker falls under one of the following circumstances, the CBIRC and its local office shall order it to take corrective action and impose a fine of not less than RMB 20,000 nor more than RMB 100,000 on it; if the circumstances are serious, order it to suspend business for an overhaul or revoke its permit; and issue a warning to the directly liable person in charge or other directly liable persons of the institution and impose a fine of not less than RMB 10,000 nor more than RMB 100,000 thereupon, and revoke his/her office qualifications under serious circumstances:

- failing to deposit margin or purchase professional liability insurance policy as required;
- failing to establish the special account books to record its business revenues and expenditures as required.

947. Where an insurance broker conducts business beyond the prescribed scope of business and carries out business activities beyond the operating area, or conducts insurance brokerage transactions with an entity or individual which illegally engages in insurance business or insurance intermediary business, the CBIRC and its local office shall order it to take corrective action, issue a warning to it, and impose a fine of not more than RMB 10,000 on it if there is no illegal income or impose a fine of not more than RMB 30,000 on it if there is any illegal income; and issue a warning to the directly liable person in charge or other directly liable persons of the institution, give a warning thereto and impose a fine of not more than RMB 10,000 thereupon.

948. Where an insurance broker fails to submit or preserve the reports, statements, documents or materials under *the Brokers' Provisions* or fails to provide the relevant information or materials as required, the CBIRC and its local office shall order it to take corrective action during a specified period; if insurance broker fails to do so, impose a fine of not less than RMB 10,000 nor more than RMB 100,000 on it; and issue a warning to the directly liable person in charge or other directly liable persons of the institution and impose a fine of not less than RMB 10,000 nor more than RMB 50,000 thereupon, and revoke his/her office qualifications under serious circumstances.

949. Where an insurance broker falls under any of the following circumstances, the CBIRC and its local office shall order it to take corrective action and impose a fine of not less than RMB 100,000 nor more than RMB 500,000 on it; and if the circumstances are serious, may restrict its scope of business, order it to stop accepting new business, or revoke its permit; and issue a warning to the directly liable person in charge or other directly liable persons of the institution and impose a fine of not less than RMB 10,000 nor more than RMB 100,000 on him or her, and revoke his/her office qualifications under serious circumstances:

- preparing or providing any false reports, statements, documents, or materials;
- refusing or obstructing any legally conducted supervisory inspection.

950. Where an insurance broker falls under any of the following circumstances, the CBIRC and its local office shall order it to take corrective action, issue a warning to it, and impose a fine of not more than RMB 10,000 on it if there is no illegal income or impose a fine of not more than three times the amount of illegal income but not exceeding RMB 30,000 on it if there is any illegal income; and issue a warning to the directly liable person in charge or any other directly liable person of the institution and impose a fine of not more than RMB 10,000 thereupon:

- failing to conduct custody of registered capital as required;
- failing to form a branch to carry out insurance brokerage business as required;
- failing to carry out internet insurance brokerage business as required;
- failing to carry out reinsurance brokerage business as required;
- failing to create or manage business archives as required;
- failing to use bank accounts as required;
- failing to use the margin in violation of *the Broker Provisions*;
- failing to pay the regulatory fees as required.

951. For a violation of any law or administrative regulation with serious circumstance, the CBIRC and its local offices may prohibit the relevant liable persons from access to the insurance sector for a certain period or even for life. Where it is discovered after a senior executive of an insurance broker, or a primary person in charge or practitioner of a branch other than provincial branch company resigns that such a person violated the relevant provisions issued by the CBIRC and its local offices during his/her former service in the insurance broker, the person shall be held liable according to the law.

Chapter 3. Insurance Adjuster

§1. Introduction

I. Definition

952. The insurance adjuster is one of the main bodies of the insurance intermediary. Together with the insurance agent and the insurance broker, it constitutes the three pillars of the insurance intermediary market and serves as a bridge between the insurer and the insured.

953. An insurance adjuster is an insurance intermediary service agency that accepts the entrustment of the insurer or the insured or other principals to provide assessment, identification or survey, loss assessment, adjustment, and issuance of an assessment report for the subject matter of the principal. But *the Provisions on the Supervision and Administration of Insurance Adjusters* (hereinafter in this chapter referred to as *the "Adjusters' Provisions"*) give a more standardized definition: the insurance adjustment means the appraisal, survey, identification, loss assessment, claim settlement and relevant risk assessment conducted in respect of the subject matters of insurance or insurance accidents by appraisal institutions and their appraisal professionals on a commission basis. And the insurance adjuster means appraisal institutions specialized in the aforesaid business, including insurance adjustment institutions and their branches.

This definition points out the business scope of the insurance adjuster, that is the appraisal, survey, identification, loss assessment, claim settlement and risk assessment of the subject-matter insured, which has an essential difference from the insurance agent and broker. The insurance adjuster's business emphasizes more on professionalism and impartiality. In addition, this definition points out the status of the insurance adjuster. That is, it serves the insurance parties—the insurer and the insured, the intermediate position between the insurer and the insured, indicating that the insurance adjuster is an integral part of the insurance intermediary.

II. Characteristics of the Insurance Adjuster

A. *Independence*

954. According to *the Adjusters' Provisions*, the insurance adjustment institutions include insurance adjustment companies and insurance adjustment partnerships. And entity or individual who is not allowed to invest in any enterprise according to the laws and administrative regulations shall not become a shareholder or partner of any insurance adjuster. It is known that the insurance adjuster is a modern enterprise established on the principle of "clear property rights, clear rights and obligation, separation of government and enterprise, and scientific management," but not a government department, and is economically independent from the insurer or the insured, without any investment relationship. There is no indirect or direct affiliation in personnel. Their behavior is not dependent on the government, any insurance company or policyholder, so they have their own independence.

B. Impartiality

955. Article 6 of *the Adjusters' Provisions* provides that insurance adjusters and their practitioners shall comply with the laws, administrative regulations, and the relevant provisions issued by the CBIRC, and follow the principles of independence, objectiveness and impartiality, which reflects the impartiality of the insurance adjuster. The insurance adjuster only conducts surveys, loss assessment, appraisal and issues the reports on the entrusted subject matter in accordance with the requirements of the client. When operating a business, the insurance adjuster does not represent the insured or the insurer, but rather considers the reasonable and legitimate rights of both the parties on a fair, just and open basis based on the insurance terms through their professional knowledge. They try to coordinate the relationship between the parties to enable the underwriting and claim settlement of the subject-matter insured to be recognized by them. Therefore, the insurance adjuster should not favor any party when conducting business operations, but should stand in the intervening position to coordinate the relationship between the insurer and the insured in an impartial manner, and he must not falsify and accept bribes and even collude with one party to deceive another party.

C. Extensiveness

956. The insurance adjustment covers the entire process from the beginning to the end of the insurance business. That is, from the process of insurance business, it includes underwriting adjustment and claims adjustment; from the category of insurance business, it includes enterprise property insurance adjustment, machine damage insurance adjustment, construction and installation engineering insurance adjustment, motor vehicle insurance adjustment, liability insurance adjustment, cargo transportation insurance adjustment, ship insurance adjustment, aircraft insurance adjustment, etc.; from the perspective of the characteristics of subject-matter insured, it also involves knowledge of various disciplines such as physics, chemistry, biology, mechanical engineering, electronics, law and so on. It can be seen that the insurance adjustment business is comprehensive and has a wide range.

D. Technicality

957. The insurance adjustment business has a high technical content. First, the insurance adjuster is required to master the insurance knowledge; second, they should have a good knowledge of the legal expertise related to the insurance business. In addition, due to the nature of the subject-matter insured and the physical, chemical or biological processes involved in natural disasters or accidents, insurance adjuster must understand the relevant engineering and technical issues, the consequences that various adjustment subject matters may suffer under various disasters, the methods to recover them, the calculation of losses and the prevention of disasters. Therefore, insurance adjuster must have professional technical knowledge, insurance knowledge and legal knowledge.

E. Regulatory

958. The insurance adjustment agency shall be established and operated according to law, and may only engage in insurance adjustment business within the scope permitted by law. As far as the insurance adjustment is concerned, when the insurance adjuster appraises the subject-matter insured before or after underwriting, all the conclusions are not fabricated, but are based on relevant laws or regulations. There should be law to rely on and basis for speculation. The appraisal report and certificate issued by the insurance adjuster to the client after the completion of adjustment have legal effects.

III. Functions of the Insurance Adjuster

959. Function refers to an inherent feature of an objective thing or phenomenon, which is determined by the nature and content of the thing. The function of the insurance adjuster refers to the inherent feature of the insurance adjuster, which is determined by the nature and content of the insurance adjuster. It is generally believed that the insurance assessor has four functions.

A. Appraisal Function

960. The appraisal function of the insurance adjuster includes the survey function, the identification function, the loss assessment function, the adjustment function and so on. The appraisal function is a key function of the insurance adjuster, which enables the claims to be settled quickly, accurately and scientifically.

B. Notarization Function

961. The reason why the insurance adjuster has a notarization function is that: first, the insurance adjuster has a wealth of insurance adjustment knowledge and skills, and is authoritative on the issue of whether the insurance adjustment is accurate or not; second, the insurance adjuster is a third party other than the parties to the insurance contract. It neither biases the insurer nor favors the insured, but appraises the subject-matter insured in the middle position, so that a fair adjustment can be made.

C. Intermediary Functions

962. The intermediary function of the insurance adjuster is that, first, the insurance adjuster can be entrusted by the insurer or the insured; second, the insurance adjuster engages in the insurance adjustment as a third party other than the insurance parties for whom he provides intermediary services.

D. Adjusting Function

963. The signing and implementation of the insurance contract lead to the emergence of the insurance legal relationship. The insurance adjuster can adjust the insurance legal relationship between the legal persons, natural persons and legal persons within a certain range. For example, a reasonable and notarized adjustment conclusion is often recognized by both the insurer and the insured, and can effectively adjust the legal relationship between them.

§2. Establishment of the Insurance Adjuster

964. The signing and implementation of the insurance contract lead to the emergence of the insurance legal relationship. The insurance adjuster can adjust the insurance legal relationship between the legal persons, natural persons and legal persons within a certain range. For example, a reasonable and notarized adjustment conclusion is often recognized by both the insurer and the insured, and can effectively adjust the legal relationship between them. To form an insurance adjuster, the applicant shall apply to the administrative department for industry and commerce for registration. The registered capital of an insurance adjuster shall be the amount of subscribed capital contribution registered with the enterprise registration authority.

965. The name of an insurance adjuster shall include the words "insurance adjustment." The name of an insurance adjuster shall not be the same as that of an existing professional insurance intermediary institution, except when an insurance adjuster has the same actual controller as the professional insurance intermediary institution. To engage in insurance adjustment business, an insurance adjustment institution shall, within thirty days from the date of obtaining the business license, undergo the recordation formalities with the CBIRC through the regulatory information system prescribed by the CBIRC, and concurrently submit paper materials as required.

I. Business Scope

966. Insurance adjustment institutions shall be classified into national insurance adjustment institutions and regional insurance adjustment institutions. A national insurance adjustment institution may carry out business within the territory of China (excluding Hong Kong SAR, Macao SAR and Taiwan), and form branches outside the territory of the province, autonomous region, municipality directly under the Central Government or city under separate state planning where its industrial and commercial registration is conducted. A regional insurance adjustment institution may only carry out business and form branches in the province, autonomous region, municipality directly under the Central Government or city under separate state planning where its industrial and commercial registration is conducted, unless otherwise prescribed by the CBIRC.

967. Where an insurance adjustment institution adopts the corporate form, it shall undergo the business recordation formalities with the CBIRC if it is a national institution, or undergo the business recordation formalities with the local office of the CBIRC at the place where its industrial and commercial registration is conducted if it is a regional institution. An insurance adjustment institution adopting the form of partnership shall undergo the business recordation formalities with the CBIRC.

II. Requirements on Form and Shareholder or Partner

968. According to *the Adjusters' Provisions*, the insurance adjusters shall, in accordance with the law, adopt the partnership or corporate form, employ insurance adjustment practitioners to carry out the insurance adjustment business. An insurance adjuster in the form of partnership shall have two or more accredited adjustment practitioners, and two-thirds or more of its partners shall be the accredited adjustment practitioners who have three or more years of work experience and have not been subject to the punishment of suspension of practice in the last three years. An insurance adjuster in the corporate form shall have eight or more accredited adjustment practitioners and two or more shareholders, and two-thirds or more of its shareholders shall be the accredited adjustment practitioners who have three or more years of work experience and have not been subject to the punishment of suspension of practice in the last three years. Where an insurance adjuster has two partners or shareholders, the two partners or shareholders shall be the accredited adjustment practitioners who have three or more years of work experience and have not been subject to punishment of suspension of practice in the last three years.

969. An entity or individual falling under any of the following circumstances shall not become a shareholder or partner of any insurance adjuster:

- the entity or individual has been subject to criminal punishment or major administrative punishment in the last five years;
- the entity or individual is under investigation by the relevant department for being suspected of involvement in any serious violation or crime;
- the entity or individual is determined by the relevant entity of the state as an object subject to joint punishment for serious dishonesty and shall be subject to corresponding penalties in the insurance field, or has other bad records of serious dishonesty within the last five years;

- the entity or individual is not allowed to invest in any enterprise according to the laws and administrative regulations;
- other circumstances under which the entity or individual is inappropriate to become a shareholder or partner of an insurance adjuster as determined by the CBIRC under the principle of prudential regulation.

Where an employee of an insurance company or a practitioner of a professional insurance intermediary institution makes investment in an insurance adjuster, a written certificate showing that his/her employer is aware of the investment shall be provided. Where a director, supervisor or senior executive of an insurance company or professional insurance intermediary institution makes investment in an insurance adjuster, the consent of the shareholders' meeting or the general meeting of shareholders of the company or institution shall be obtained according to the relevant provisions.

III. Condition

970. To carry out insurance adjustment business, an insurance adjustment institution shall meet the following conditions:

- its shareholders or partners satisfy the requirements of *the Adjusters' Provisions* and make capital contribution with self-owned, true and legal funds, other than bank loans or any other form of non-self-owned capital;
- according to the business development plan, it has the working capital required for routine business operation and assumption of risks. A national institution shall have working capital of RMB 2 million or more and a regional institution shall have working capital of RMB 1 million or more;
- the custody of its working capital complies with the relevant provisions issued by the CBIRC;
- the business scope recorded in the business license does not exceed the scope as prescribed in of *the Adjusters' Provisions*;
- its bylaws or partnership agreements comply with the relevant provisions;
- its enterprise name satisfies the requirements of *the Adjusters' Provisions*;
- its board chairman, executive director and senior executives meet the conditions set forth in *the Adjusters' Provisions*;
- it has a governance structure and internal control system in compliance with the provisions issued by the CBIRC, and scientific, reasonable and feasible business model;
- it has a fixed domicile suitable for its business scale;
- it has business and financial information management systems in compliance with the provisions issued by the CBIRC;
- it meets other conditions as prescribed by laws, administrative regulations, and the provisions issued by the CBIRC.

IV. Branch

971. An insurance adjustment institution that forms a branch in a province, autonomous region, municipality directly under the Central Government or city under separate state planning other than the place where its industrial and commercial registration is conducted shall designate a branch as a provincial branch to be responsible for handling the formation and recordation of the branches within its jurisdiction, submitting regulatory reports and statements and other relevant matters, and be responsible for managing other branches. The branches of an insurance adjustment institution shall include branch offices and business departments.

972. To form a new branch to carry out insurance adjustment business, an insurance adjustment institution shall meet the following conditions:

- the insurance adjustment institution and its branch have not received criminal punishment or major administrative punishment in the last year;
- the insurance adjustment institution and its branch are not under investigation by the relevant department for being suspected of involvement in any violation of law or crime;
- a branch formed in the last two years did not exit market after operation for less than one year;
- it has a sound branch management system;
- a newly formed branch has qualified business premises, business financial information system, and other facilities matching the business operation;
- it meets other conditions as prescribed by the CBIRC.

An insurance adjustment institution that is determined by a relevant entity of the state as an object subject to joint punishment for serious dishonesty and shall be subject to corresponding penalties in the insurance field or has other bad records of serious dishonesty in the last five years shall not form any new branch to carry out insurance adjustment business. A branch of an insurance adjustment institution shall, within ten days from the date of obtaining a business license for branch, undergo the recordation formalities with the local office of the CBIRC through the regulatory information system prescribed by the CBIRC and concurrently submit paper materials as required.

§3. Supervision on the Insurance Adjuster

I. Operation Rules

973. An insurance adjuster shall, in accordance with laws, administrative regulations, and the relevant provisions issued by the CBIRC, and under the principles of specifying responsibilities, strengthening balance, and strengthening risk management, establish sound corporate governance structure and rules; and clarify the management and control responsibilities, build a compliance system, focus on self-restraint, strengthen internal accountability, and ensure steady operation.

974. For accepted insurance adjustment business, an insurance adjuster shall designate two insurance adjustment practitioners at a minimum to undertake the insurance adjustment business. Insurance adjustment practitioners shall, in an appropriate manner, select appraisal methods. The insurance adjuster shall conduct internal examination of the adjustment report.

975. An insurance adjustment report shall be signed by at least two insurance adjustment practitioners who undertake the business, and the seal of the insurance adjustment institution shall be affixed thereto. An insurance adjuster and its practitioners shall lawfully assume liability for the adjustment reports they issue. An insurance adjustment institution shall put its recordation form and business license in a conspicuous place of its domicile or business premises. A branch of an insurance adjustment institution shall put the recordation form to which the official seal of the institution to which it is subordinate is affixed and the business license in a conspicuous position of its business premises.

A. Business Territory

976. An insurance adjuster may engage in the following business, in whole or in part:

- the pre-underwriting and post-underwriting inspection, valuation, and risk assessment of the subject matters of insurance;
- the post-claim survey, inspection, loss assessment, and claim settlement in respect of the subject matters of insurance as well as the disposition of their residual value;
- risk management consulting;
- other business as prescribed by the CBIRC.

B. Account

977. An insurance adjuster shall establish special account books to record the revenues and expenditures of the insurance adjustment business. An insurance adjuster shall open an independent account specially for capital to collect remunerations for insurance adjustment business. An insurance adjuster shall open and use other bank accounts in compliance with the provisions issued by the CBIRC.

C. Adjustment Archive

978. An insurance adjuster shall establish complete and standardized adjustment archives, which shall include the following at a minimum:

- the main information on its insurance adjustment business, including but not limited to the names of the clients and other parties, the subject matters of insurance, the types of accident, and the assessed value of loss;
- the remuneration for the adjustment business and the collection thereof;
- other business information as prescribed by the CBIRC.

The adjustment archives of an insurance adjuster shall be authentic and complete.

D. Entrustment Contract

979. To engage in the insurance adjustment business, an insurance adjuster shall enter into entrustment contracts with clients to agree on the rights and obligations of both parties and other relevant matters such as confidentiality and reasonable use of adjustment information according to the law. An entrustment contract shall not violate laws, administrative regulations or relevant provisions issued by the CBIRC.

Where a client rejects to provide or fails to faithfully provide the ownership certificate, financial accounting information and other materials required for carrying out adjustment business, an insurance adjuster shall have the right to reject its requirements of performing a contract according to the law. When a client requests issuance of a false adjustment report or falls under any other circumstance of illegally intervening in the adjustment results, the insurance adjuster shall have the right to terminate the contract.

E. Notification Letter

980. An insurance adjuster shall develop a standard client notification letter and present it to clients when carrying out business. A client notification letter shall, at a minimum, include the name, recordation information, business premises, scope of business, contact information, complaint channels, dispute settlement methods and other basic matters of the insurance adjuster.

F. Occupational Risk Fund and Professional Liability Insurance

981. An insurance adjuster shall, within twenty days from the date when the recordation is announced and based on business needs, establish an occupational risk fund, or purchase the professional liability insurance, and improve the risk prevention procedures. An insurance adjuster shall, within ten days from the date of establishing an occupational risk fund or purchasing the professional liability insurance, submit the photocopy of the deposit agreement on the occupational risk fund, the photocopy of the original voucher of deposit of the occupational risk fund or the photocopy of the professional liability insurance policy to the local office of the CBIRC, and register the relevant information in the regulatory information system as prescribed by the CBIRC.

982. An insurance adjuster that establishes an occupational risk fund shall pay 5% of its main business income in the last year into the fund, and accordingly increase the amount of the occupational risk fund, if the annual main business income is increased; and it is not required to increase the occupational risk fund, if the deposit amount of the occupational risk fund reaches RMB 1 million. An insurance adjuster shall deposit occupational risk fund in full in the first quarter each year. The occupational risk fund of an insurance adjuster shall be deposited in a special account opened with a commercial bank in the form of bank deposit or be deposited in any other form recognized by the CBIRC. To use the occupational risk fund, an insurance adjuster must comply with the relevant provisions of the CBIRC.

983. An insurance adjuster that purchases professional liability insurance shall ensure the continuous validity of the insurance. The limit of liability for each accident under the professional liability insurance purchased by an insurance adjuster shall not be less than RMB 1 million, and the cumulative one-year limit of liability shall not be less than RMB 10 million and not be less than the insurance adjuster's main business income in the last year.

G. Forbidden Conduct

984. During the process of carrying out the insurance adjustment business, an insurance adjuster shall not be:

- seeking illicit benefits by taking advantage of its business;
- permitting another institution to carry out business in its name, or carrying out business by illegally using the name of another institution;
- soliciting business by illicit means such as maliciously beating down prices, offering kickbacks, conducting false publicity or disparaging or defaming any other adjustment institution;
- accepting any business to which it is an interested party;
- accepting the authorization of both parties to the conflict of interest respectively and conducting appraisal of the same appraisal object;
- issuing any false adjustment report or any adjustment report with material omission;
- retaining or designating a person who does not comply with the provisions to carry out adjustment business;
- committing any other violation of law or administrative regulation;
- concealing or fabricating any important information related to the insurance contract;
- fraudulently obtaining insurance benefits by colluding with any client or relevant party;
- disclosing any trade secret or individual privacy of a client or relevant party known in its operation;
- falsely issuing invoices or exaggerating the amount of adjustment remuneration.

II. Market Exit

985. Under any of the following circumstances, an insurance adjuster shall, within five days, cancel the practicing registration of an insurance adjustment practitioner:

- an insurance adjustment practitioner is subject to administrative punishment of suspension of practice;
- an insurance adjustment practitioner terminates practice for other reasons;
- an insurance adjuster stops engaging in the insurance adjustment business for closedown, dissolution or other reasons;
- other circumstances as prescribed by laws, administrative regulations, and the provisions issued by the CBIRC.

986. Insurance adjustment institutions shall implement the annual reporting system. An insurance adjustment institution shall, before January 31 of each year, submit the report for the last year to the CBIRC and its local office. For insurance adjustment institutions which fail to submit their annual reports on schedule, the CBIRC and its local offices shall disclose their abnormal operation information to the public. For an insurance adjustment institution whose annual reporting matters fail to satisfy the regulatory requirements, the CBIRC and its local offices shall take corresponding regulatory measures.

987. Where a branch of an insurance adjustment institution has chaos in business operation and management and has any major violation of laws and regulations, the insurance adjustment institution shall, in accordance with the regulatory requirements of the CBIRC and its local office, take measures such as making rectification within a prescribed time limit, suspending business and cancelation against the branch. An insurance adjuster terminating the insurance adjustment business shall appropriately handle the debtor-creditor relationship and shall not impair the lawful rights and interests of any client or any other relevant parties.

III. Supervision on the Practitioner

988. An insurance adjuster shall employ insurance adjustment practitioners of good character. An insurance adjuster shall not employ any person falling under any of the following circumstances:

- he or she is given a criminal punishment due to intentional crime or due to criminal negligence in appraisal, finance, accounting and auditing activities, and it has not been five years since the date of completion of the execution of the sentence;
- he or she has been prohibited from entering the financial and asset appraisal industry during a certain period as decided by the regulatory authority, and the period has not expired;

- he or she is determined by a relevant entity of the state as an object subject to joint punishment for serious dishonesty and shall be subject to corresponding penalties in the insurance field, or has other bad records of serious dishonesty in the last five years;
- other circumstances as prescribed by laws, administrative regulations, and the provisions issued by the CBIRC.

989. An insurance adjustment practitioner shall have the professional capability required for engaging in insurance adjustment business. An insurance adjuster shall strengthen the pre-post training and follow-up education for insurance adjustment practitioners. The training shall at least include professional knowledge, legal knowledge and professional ethics. An insurance adjuster may entrust a self-regulatory organization in the insurance intermediary industry or any other institution with the training. An insurance adjuster shall establish complete archives on the training of insurance adjustment practitioners.

990. An insurance adjustment practitioner carrying out the insurance adjustment business shall join an insurance adjuster. An insurance adjuster shall conduct practicing registration for its insurance adjustment practitioners in accordance with the relevant provisions. An insurance adjustment practitioner may only carry out business in one insurance adjuster, and may only conduct practicing registration through one insurance adjuster. Where an insurance adjustment practitioner changes his/her insurance adjuster, the new insurance adjuster shall conduct practicing registration for him or her, and the original insurance adjuster shall cancel the practicing registration in a timely manner.

991. An insurance adjustment practitioner shall enjoy the following rights:

- requiring the client to provide the relevant ownership certificate, financial accounting information and other materials, and necessary assistance required for the implementation of fair appraisal procedures;
- consulting documents, certificates and materials required for conducting business from the relevant state authorities or any other organization in accordance with the law;
- rejecting illegal intervention in the adjustment acts and adjustment results of the client or any other organization or individual;
- signing adjustment reports in accordance with the law;
- other rights as prescribed by laws and administrative regulations.

992. An insurance adjustment practitioner shall perform the following obligations:

- being honest and trustworthy, and legally conducting business in an independent, objective and impartial manner;
- abiding by the appraisal standards, performing the investigation functions, conducting independent analysis and estimates, and carrying out business in a diligent and prudential manner;

- completing required continuing education, and maintaining and improving professional capability;
- checking and verifying the authenticity, accuracy and integrity of relevant documents, certificates and materials used in adjustment activities;
- keeping confidential state secrets, trade secrets and personal privacy to which he or she has access in the adjustment activities;
- disqualifying himself or herself if he or she is an interested person with respect to the client or any other relevant party or the adjustment object;
- accepting the self-regulation of the self-regulatory organization in the insurance intermediary industry, and performing the obligations prescribed by the bylaws;
- performing other obligations prescribed by laws and administrative regulations.

993. During the process of carrying out the adjustment business, an insurance adjustment practitioner shall not commit any of the following conduct:

- accepting authorization in private to engage in business and collect fees;
- engaging in business for two or more insurance adjusters concurrently;
- soliciting business by illicit means such as fraud, inducement or coercion, or disparaging or defaming any other adjustment practitioner;
- permitting any other person to conduct business in his/her own name, or conducting business by illegally using any other person's name;
- signing any adjustment report on the business which he or she has not undertaken;
- demanding, accepting or demanding or accepting in any disguised form remuneration and property other than those agreed upon in contracts, or seeking other illicit benefits;
- signing any false adjustment report or any adjustment report with major omissions;
- committing any other conduct in violation of any law or administrative regulation.

IV. Supervision on Senior Executives

994. For the purposes of *the Adjusters' Provisions*, "senior executives" of an insurance adjuster mean the following persons:

- the general manager and deputy general manager of an insurance adjustment company;
- the executive partner of an insurance adjustment partnership;
- the primary person in charge of a branch;
- executives who have the same function and power as the aforesaid personnel.

995. The board chairman or executive director or senior executive of an insurance adjuster shall meet the following conditions:

- he or she has an educational background of junior college or above;

- he or she has three or more years of financial work experience, has three or more years of experience in the relevant work of asset appraisal, or has five or more years of experience in economic work;
- he or she has the management capability required for performing his/her duties and is familiar with ILs and administrative regulations and the relevant provisions issued by the CBIRC;
- he or she is honest and trustworthy and has good character.

996. A person with ten years or more of financial or asset appraisal work experience may be exempted from the restriction of the first item in terms of educational background. A person who falls under any of the circumstances shall not serve as the board chairman, executive director or senior executive of an insurance adjuster:

- he or she is a director, supervisor, or senior executive of an insurance company or professional insurance intermediary institution whose permit has been revoked for violation of law and is personally liable or directly liable as a leader for the revocation of permit, and it has not been three years since the date of revocation of permit;
- he or she is a director, supervisor, or senior executive of a financial institution who has been disqualified for taking office by the financial regulatory authority for his/her violation of law or discipline, and it has not been five years since the date of disqualification;
- he or she is prohibited from entering the financial industry during a certain period as decided by the financial regulatory authority, and the period has not expired;
- he or she is a professional of an asset appraisal institution or verification institution whose practicing qualification has been revoked for his/her violation of law or discipline, and it has not been five years since the date of revocation;
- it has not been two years since the person was given a warning or fined by the financial regulatory authority;
- he or she is under investigation by the judicial authority, the disciplinary inspection and supervision department, or the financial regulatory authority;
- he or she is determined by a relevant entity of the state as an object subject to joint punishment for serious dishonesty and shall be subject to corresponding penalties in the insurance field, or has other bad records of serious dishonesty in the last five years;
- he or she is a partner who has debts of a partnership that have not been paid off;
- other circumstances as prescribed by laws, administrative regulations, and the provisions issued by the CBIRC.

997. An insurance adjuster shall establish employment relationships with its senior executives by entering into written labor contracts with them. The board chairman or executive director or senior executive of an insurance adjuster shall not concurrently serve as the primary person in charge of two or more branches. Without approval of the shareholders' meeting or meeting of partners, a director or senior executive of an insurance adjuster shall not hold a concurrent post in an institution which has any conflict of interest with him or her. A partner of an insurance adjuster shall not, independently or in cooperation with others, carry out any business in competition with the insurance adjuster. To appoint the board chairman, executive director or senior executive, an insurance adjuster shall, within five days from the date of making a decision, faithfully submit the reporting materials as required and register the relevant information in the regulatory information system as prescribed by the CBIRC. The local offices of the CBIRC may investigate or interview the board chairman, executive directors and senior executives employed by an insurance adjuster. The local offices of the CBIRC may require an insurance adjuster to replace its board chairman, executive director or senior executive who fails to meet the office qualifications. Where the board chairman, executive director or senior executive of an insurance adjuster is prosecuted for any suspected crime, the insurance adjuster shall register the relevant information in the regulatory information system as prescribed by the CBIRC respectively within five days after the prosecution is instituted and within five days after the case is closed. Where a director, executive director or senior executive of an insurance adjuster is suspected of involvement in any serious violation of law or crime and is under formal investigation by an administrative authority or judicial authority, the insurance adjuster shall suspend the office of the relevant person, and register the relevant information in the regulatory information system as prescribed by the CBIRC.

998. Under any of the following circumstances, an insurance adjuster may appoint a temporary person in charge for a maximum of three months, and shall not continuously appoint the temporary person in charge for the same position:

- the original person in charge resigns or is removed from office;
- the original person in charge is unable to normally perform his/her functions for any illness, accident, or other reason;
- any other special circumstance as recognized by the CBIRC.

999. The temporary person in charge shall have the capability appropriate for performing his/her duties and satisfy the relevant requirements set forth in *the Adjusters' Provisions*. To appoint a temporary person in charge, an insurance adjuster shall, within five days from the date of making a decision, register relevant information in the regulatory information system as prescribed by the CBIRC.

V. Supervision and Inspection

1000. The local offices of the CBIRC shall, under the territorial principle, take charge of the supervision and administration of insurance adjusters and their insurance adjustment business activities within their jurisdictions. The local offices of the CBIRC shall pay attention to the supervision and administration of the acts of insurance adjusters within their respective jurisdictions, conduct on-site inspection and off-site supervision and administration according to the law, impose administrative penalties and take other regulatory measures.

1001. The CBIRC and its local offices may, according to the supervision and administration needs, hold regulatory talks with the board chairman, executive directors and senior executives of an insurance adjuster, requiring them to provide explanations on the major issues in business operations. The CBIRC and its local offices may, according to the supervision needs, designate supervisors to attend the general meetings of shareholders, meetings of partners, or meetings of the board of directors of the insurance adjusters as non-voting delegates.

1002. The CBIRC and its local offices shall conduct on-site inspection of insurance adjusters according to the law, which shall mainly include the following contents:

- whether recordation has been conducted or the reporting obligations have been fulfilled as required;
- whether the occupational risk fund or the professional liability insurance complies with the provisions;
- whether its business operations are lawful;
- whether it is in good financial condition;
- whether the reports, statements, documents and materials are submitted to the CBIRC and its local offices in a timely, complete and authentic manner;
- whether its internal control rules comply with the relevant provisions issued by the CBIRC;
- whether the formation, management and control of branches comply with the provisions;
- whether the appointment of the board chairman, executive directors and senior executives complies with the relevant provisions;
- whether it has effectively performed the duty of managing its practitioners;
- whether the business and financial information management systems comply with the relevant provisions issued by the CBIRC;
- whether the conditions as prescribed in Article 15 of *the Assets Appraisal Law* are continuously met;
- other matters as prescribed by the CBIRC.

1003. An insurance adjuster shall, according to the following requirements, cooperate with the on-site inspection by the CBIRC and its local offices, and shall not refuse or obstruct the supervision and inspection legally conducted by the CBIRC and its local offices:

- it shall provide the relevant documents and materials as required, and shall not fabricate, displace or conceal them, or delay the provision thereof;
- its relevant managers, financial personnel, and practitioners shall appear on the site to provide explanations and answer questions as required.

1004. In the process of an on-site inspection, the CBIRC and its local office may engage an accounting firm and other private intermediary institutions to provide the relevant services, and if so, shall enter into written entrustment agreements with them. The CBIRC and its local office shall inform the insurance adjuster under inspection of the entrustment.

VI. Legal Liability

1005. Where an insurance adjustment institution fails to undergo recordation formalities with the CBIRC or its local office in accordance with *the Adjusters' Provisions* or fails to meet the conditions as prescribed in *the Adjusters' Provisions*, the CBIRC and its local office shall order it to take corrective action, and order it to suspend business and may impose thereupon a fine of not less than RMB 10,000 but not more than RMB 50,000, if it refuses to take corrective action. Where an insurance adjustment institution forms a branch and fails to undergo the recordation formalities according to *the Adjusters' Provisions*, the local office of the CBIRC shall order it to take corrective action, give it a warning, and impose thereupon a fine of not more than RMB 10,000 if there is no illegal income or impose thereupon a fine of not more than three times the amount of illegal income but not exceeding RMB 30,000 if there is any illegal income.

1006. Where an insurance adjustment institution carries out adjustment business in violation of *the Adjusters' Provisions*, the CBIRC and its local office shall order it to take corrective action, give it a warning, and impose thereupon a fine of not more than RMB 10,000 if there is no illegal income or impose thereupon a fine of not more than three times the amount of illegal income but not exceeding RMB 30,000 if there is any illegal income.

1007. Where an insurance adjuster conceals relevant information, provides false materials and undergoes the recordation formalities by deception, bribery or other illicit means, the CBIRC and its local office shall cancel its recordation, give it a warning, and impose thereupon a fine of not more than RMB 10,000 if there is no illegal income or impose thereupon a fine of not more than three times the amount of illegal income but not exceeding RMB 30,000 if there is any illegal income. Where an insurance adjuster employs an unqualified chairman, executive director or senior executive, the CBIRC and its local office shall order it to take corrective action, give it a warning and impose thereupon a fine of not more than RMB 10,000. Where an insurance adjuster fails to conduct practicing registration and management of insurance adjustment practitioners as required, the CBIRC and its local office shall order it to take corrective action, give it a warning and impose thereupon a fine of not more than RMB 10,000.

1008. Where an insurance adjuster falls under any of the following circumstances, the CBIRC and its local office shall order it to take corrective action, give it a warning and impose thereupon a fine of not more than RMB 10,000:

- failing to establish the occupational risk fund as required or purchase the professional liability insurance as required;
- using the occupational risk fund in violation of the relevant provisions or failing to maintain the validity and continuity of the professional liability insurance;
- failing to establish as required the special account books to record its business revenues and expenditures.

1009. Where an insurance adjuster carries out business activities beyond the recorded business scope or conducts insurance adjustment business with any institution or individual which illegally engages in the insurance business or insurance intermediary business, the CBIRC and its local office shall order it to take corrective action, give it a warning, and impose thereupon a fine of not more than RMB 10,000 if there is no illegal income or impose thereupon a fine of not more than three times the amount of illegal income but not exceeding RMB 30,000 if there is any illegal income.

1010. Where an insurance adjuster violates *the Adjusters' Provisions* and falls under any of the following circumstances, the CBIRC and its local office shall give it a warning, and may order it to suspend business for not less than one month but not more than six months, confiscate its illegal income and impose thereupon a fine of not less than one time the amount of illegal income but not more than five times the amount of illegal income, if there is any illegal income. If the circumstances are serious, the administrative department for industry and commerce shall revoke its business license. If any crime is constituted, it shall be held criminally liable in accordance with the law:

- seeking illicit benefits by taking advantage of its business;
- permitting another institution to carry out business in its name, or carrying out business by illegally using the name of another institution;
- soliciting business by illicit means such as maliciously beating down prices, offering kickbacks, conducting false publicity or disparaging or defaming any other adjustment institution;
- accepting any business to which it is an interested party;
- accepting the authorization of both parties to the conflict of interest respectively and conducting appraisal of the same appraisal object;
- issuing any adjustment report with material omission;
- failing to preserve any adjustment archives within the prescribed time limit;
- retaining or designating a person who does not comply with the provisions of *the Asset Appraisal Law* to carry out adjustment business;
- neglecting to manage its adjustment practitioners, which has caused adverse consequences.

1011. Where an insurance adjuster issues a false adjustment report, the CBIRC and its local office shall order it to suspend business for not less than six months but not more than one year, confiscate its illegal income and impose thereupon a fine of not less than one time the amount of illegal income but not more than five times the amount of illegal income, if there is any illegal income. If the circumstances are serious, the administrative department for industry and commerce shall revoke its business license. If a crime is constituted, it shall be held criminally liable in accordance with the law.

1012. Where an insurance adjuster falls under any of the following circumstances, the CBIRC and its local office shall order it to take corrective action, give it a warning and impose thereupon a fine of not more than RMB 10,000:

- failing to submit the relevant reports, statements, documents, or materials as required;
- developing or providing any false reports, statements, documents, or materials;
- refusing or obstructing any legal supervision and inspection.

1013. Where an insurance adjuster falls under any of the circumstances, the CBIRC and its local offices shall order it to take corrective action, give it a warning, and impose thereupon a fine of not more than RMB 10,000 if there is no illegal income or impose thereupon a fine of not more than three times the amount of illegal income but not exceeding RMB 30,000 if there is any illegal income:

- failing to place its working capital under custody as required;
- failing to form a branch to carry out insurance adjustment business in accordance with the relevant provisions;
- failing to appoint a temporary person in charge in accordance with the relevant provisions;
- failing to put its recordation form at its domicile or business premises as required;
- failing to maintain or manage business archives as required;
- failing to use bank accounts in accordance with the relevant provisions;
- failing to collect remunerations in accordance with the relevant provisions;
- failing to carry out the adjustment work according to the statutory requirements;
- failing to disclose information as required;
- failing to pay the regulatory fees as required.

1014. Where an insurance adjustment practitioner has a relationship of interest with the client or other relevant parties or adjustment objects and fails to disqualify himself or herself according to the law, the CBIRC and its local office shall order him or her to take corrective action, give him or her a warning, and impose thereupon a fine of not more than RMB 10,000 if there is no illegal income or impose thereupon a fine of not more than three times the amount of illegal income but not exceeding RMB 30,000 if there is any illegal income.

1015. Where an insurance adjustment practitioner violates *the Adjusters' Provisions* and falls under any of the following circumstances, the CBIRC and its local office shall give him or her a warning, and may order him or her to suspend practice for not less than six months but not more than one year; confiscate his/her illegal income, if there is any illegal income; and order him or her to suspend practice for not less than one year but not more than five years if the circumstances are serious. If a crime is constituted, he or she shall be held criminally liable in accordance with the law.

- accepting authorization in private to engage in business or collect fees;
- engaging in business for two or more insurance adjusters concurrently;
- soliciting business by such improper means as fraud, inducement or coercion, or disparaging or defaming any other adjustment practitioner;

- permitting any other person to conduct business in his/her own name, or conducting business by illegally using any other person's name;
- signing any adjustment report on business not undertaken by him or her or any adjustment report with major omissions;
- demanding, accepting or demanding or accepting in any disguised form remuneration and property other than those agreed upon in contracts, or seeking other illicit benefits.

1016. Where an insurance adjustment practitioner signs a false adjustment report, the CBIRC and its local office shall order him or her to suspend practice for not less than two years but not more than five years; confiscate his/her illegal income, if there is any illegal income; and order him or her to suspend practice for not less than five years but not more than ten years if the circumstances are serious. If a crime is constituted, he or she shall be held criminally liable in accordance with the law and be prohibited from engaging in adjustment business for life.

1017. Where an insurance adjuster or an insurance adjustment practitioner is subject to punishment other than that of being ordered to suspend business or practice three times accumulatively within one year due to violation of provisions, the CBIRC and its local office may order the violator to suspend business or practice for not less than one year but not more than five years.

1018. Where an insurance adjustment practitioner violates the relevant provisions and causes loss to the client or any other relevant party, the insurance adjuster where he or she works shall assume the liability for compensation in accordance with the law. After performing the liability for compensation, an insurance adjuster may recover the indemnity from an insurance adjustment practitioner with intent or gross negligence.

1019. The CBIRC and its local offices shall impose administrative punishments on the insurance adjusters and their practitioners for their illegal acts according to the law, inform the self-regulatory organizations in the insurance intermediary industry of the punishments in a timely manner, and disclose them to the public in accordance with the law.

Part IX. Reinsurance

Chapter 1. Introduction

§1. Brief History of Development of Reinsurance Market in China

1020. The history of the development of reinsurance market in China is relatively short. In nearly ten years after the recovery of insurance business from 1979, China only has one insurance company, namely PICC, and there was no reinsurance market during that period. In March 1988 and April 1991 respectively, Ping An Insurance Company and CPIC were established in Shenzhen and Shanghai, and China began to implement the statutory reinsurance system, namely 30% of each insurance business of the insurance company shall be ceded to PICC. In 1993, two more insurance companies were granted to operate the reinsurance business. The reinsurance market was preliminarily established.

1021. In February 1996, PICC was restructured and part of it became PICC Reinsurance Company Limited, which was the first company specializing in reinsurance business.

In October 2003, the world's largest reinsurance company Munich Re opened its branch in Beijing, which was the first foreign reinsurance company being allowed to operate in China as regards life and non-life reinsurance business.

At the end of 2003, China Reinsurance (Group) Corporation was established. It is China's sole state-owned reinsurance group; it has always been the main channel of reinsurance in China. It was cofounded by the Ministry of Finance of China and the Central Huijin Investment Company Limited with a registered capital of RMB 42,479,808,085. The Ministry of Finance and the Central Huijin Investment Co., Ltd. hold 12.72% and 71.56% of the shares, respectively. It is now Asia's largest and the world's eighth-largest reinsurer in terms of reinsurance premium income.

1022. In 2014, *the Several Opinions of the State Council on Accelerating the Development of the Modern Insurance Service Industry* issued by the State Council expressly indicated that the modern insurance service industry must accelerate the development of reinsurance market; increase reinsurance market players; develop the regional reinsurance centers; increase reinsurance products and technological innovation; increase the supportability of reinsurance on agriculture, traffic, energy, chemical, water conservancy, subway, aerospace, nuclear power and other national key projects of large risk and special risk; enhance the ability of reinsurance to diversify natural disaster risks; strengthen the reinsurance support for China's overseas enterprises; and enhance China's reinsurance market's pricing power and the right to speak around the world.

In 2016, the *China's Insurance Industry Development 13th Five-Year Plan* further expressed that the development goal regarding reinsurance is to improve and perfect the reinsurance market system; appropriately increase the reinsurance market players; develop the regional reinsurance center; enhance China's reinsurance market's pricing power and the right to speak around the world; increase the supportability of reinsurance on agriculture, traffic, energy, chemical, water conservancy, aerospace, nuclear power and other national key projects. Reinsurance is supposed to play a leading role in the insurance market innovation; the authorities should encourage reinsurance companies and insurance companies to carry out further cooperation regarding product development, service network and data sharing, etc. The authorities should also support the reinsurance companies to participate in infrastructure construction such as industry data platform, disaster management and risk management service system, and promote the analysis of industry data. The reinsurance registration system should be improved; to prevent financial risks from being transmitted cross-border through reinsurance business, more research resources should be devoted to formulate the offshore reinsurance margin system.

Nowadays, China has become the third-largest insurance market in the world and the regulators have already further released the reinsurance policies; it is therefore suggested that China's reinsurance market has stepped into the fast track and it is estimated that the scale of China's domestic reinsurance market in 2020 will reach RMB 330 billion.

§2. Definition, Nature and Types of Reinsurance

1023. It is well established that in insurance, the matching of exposure and protection to assure both solvency and profitability is fundamental. Reinsurance-of-whatever type is a principal means to this end, as *the Management Rules for Reinsurance of Property Insurance Companies* issued by the CBIRC provide: "Reinsurance is an important means for a property insurance company to manage and control risks and an important part of the company's business strategies, and plays an irreplaceable role in terms of transferring risks, stabilizing business operations, improving technologies and enhancing underwriting abilities."

1024. By Article 28 of the IL, "reinsurance" means that the insurer transfers a portion of its insured business to another insurer in the form of a ceded policy. Noticeably, the insurer is not entitled to cede 100% of its insured business to reinsurer under Chinese law, as provided by Article 11 of *the Provisions on the Administration of the Reinsurance Business* (hereinafter referred to as *the "Reinsurance Provisions"*): "with the exception of aviation and aerospace insurance, nuclear insurance, oil insurance and credit insurance, direct insurance companies carrying on treaty reinsurance and facultative reinsurance shall observe the following stipulations: (a) the business of each risk unit ceded to the same reinsurance ceded company shall not exceed the insured amount or 80% of the liability of the direct insurance business; and (b) the insured amount or limit of liability ceded to related enterprises in each facultative reinsurance shall not exceed the insured amount or 20% of the limit of liability of the direct insurance business."

1025. Reinsurance contract is regarded as a kind of liability insurance under Chinese law. The subject matter of reinsurance is the indemnity or payment liability of the insurer of direct insurance.

1026. In addition to the IL, the most important law regarding reinsurance in China is *the Reinsurance Provisions*. Article 4 expressly states that when carrying on reinsurance business, insurers, insurance association, insurance brokers and other insurance institutions that are located in China (excluding Hong Kong SAR, Macao SAR and Taiwan) shall abide by these Provisions.

1027. In accordance with Article 2 of *the Reinsurance Provisions*, there are four basic types of reinsurance:

(a) According to the different ways of transfer of insurance liability:
  - treaty reinsurance, which refers to the business act of an insurance company, which concludes a contract with other insurance companies beforehand, stipulating to reinsure the insurance business undertaken by it to other insurance companies within a certain period;
  - facultative reinsurance, which refers to the business act of an insurance company, which temporarily stipulates with other insurance companies to reinsure the insurance business undertaken by it to other insurance companies.

(b) According to the different ways of apportion of insurance liability:
  - proportional reinsurance, in which the reinsurer shares a pro rata portion of the losses and premiums of the insurer;
  - non-proportional reinsurance, in which the insurer is indemnified by the reinsurer for the amount of loss in excess of a specified retention, subject to a specified limit.

1028. Reinsurance contract and original insurance contract are two independent contracts. The rights and obligations under the two contracts are also independent. Thus, in the light of privity of contract, by Article 29 of the IL, the reinsurer may not request payment of premiums from the applicant of the original insurance contract; the insured or beneficiary of the original insurance contract may not submit any claim against the reinsurer for payment of indemnities or insurance benefits; the reinsurance cedent may not refuse to perform or delay the performance of its responsibilities under the original insurance policy on the grounds that the reinsurer has not performed its reinsurance responsibilities.

Chapter 2. Formation of Reinsurance Contract

1029. Formation of reinsurance contract follows the basic pattern of formation of contract, namely offer and acceptance. However, formation of facultative reinsurance contract and reinsurance treaty may vary to a certain extent.

§1. Formation of Facultative Reinsurance Contract

1030. In 2016, based on the best market practice, the CIA published a practical guidance on formation of facultative property reinsurance contract, the essence of which could be summarized as follows:

(1) The reinsurance ceding party, when arranging the facultative reinsurance business, shall finish the reinsurance arrangement before the attachment of insurance policy or cover note. In principle, if the reinsurance ceding party indeed has the need of reinsurance and the business is in accordance with the conditions for the arrangement of reinsurance treaty, the priority shall be given to the treaty arrangement.
(2) The offer shall be given at least five working days in advance by the reinsurance ceding party to the ceded party. The contents of the offer shall generally include the conditions of reinsurance, the commissions, the ceding portion, the valid term of the offer, the risk information, etc.
(3) The reinsurance ceded party, after receiving the offer, shall generally provide substantial response or feedback within three working days.
(4) On the basis of contractual certainty principle, the parties to the reinsurance contract shall check all the business conditions as to the formation of reinsurance contract, including basic risk information (risk covered, exemptions, the term of reinsurance, the limit of liability, deductibles, etc.), ceding portion, commissions, brokerage (if any), applicable law and dispute resolution, etc.
(5) There are two scenarios which are useful references and can be altered according to the factual background of the particular case.
    - *Scenario One*: the reinsurance ceding party or reinsurance broker sends the offer to the designated reinsurance ceded party. All the business terms of the offer have been clearly expressed. The facultative reinsurance contract concludes provided that the reinsurance ceded party's acceptance mirrors the offer.
        - Offer:
          "With reference to the captioned account, we are very glad to invite you to write a line for it subject to the slip attached.
          The brief info of the account is shown as follows:
          Ceding company: XXX
          Type: PAR/BI
          Interest: XXXX
          Period: 2016.01.01—2016.12.31
          TSI: PAR: RMB XXXXX
          BI: RMB XXXX

Loss record for the past 2 years: Clean
Ceding share: 5% of 100%
Total deduction: XX% (tax included)
We hope you could reply to it as soon as possible.
Should you have any enquiry please do not hesitate to contact us."

- *Acceptance*
  "With captioned account, we would like to participate 5% of 100%, subject to the terms and conditions of the offer."

- *Scenario Two*: the reinsurance ceding party or reinsurance broker sends the offer to the designated reinsurance ceded party, the latter accepts with the attachment of intention to participate, conditions precedent to the formation of reinsurance contract and warranty clauses. The facultative reinsurance contract concludes provided that the reinsurance ceding party or reinsurance broker gives the final confirmation to the intention to participate, conditions precedent to the formation of reinsurance contract and warranty clauses.
  - *Offer*
    "With reference to the captioned account, we are very glad to invite you to write a line for it subject to the slip attached.
    The brief info of the account is shown as follows:
    Ceding company: XXX
    Type: PAR/BI
    Interest: XXXX
    Period: 2016.01.01—2016.12.31
    TSI: PAR: RMB XXXXX
    BI: RMB XXXX
    Loss record for the past 2 years: Clean
    Total deduction: XX% (tax included)
    We hope you could reply to it as soon as possible.
    Should you have any enquiry please do not hesitate to contact us."
  - *Intention to participate*
    "With captioned account, we'd like to participate X% of 100%, subject to the following conditions and terms:
    1. No loss until binding our share;
    2. Total Deduction XX % (tax included);
    3. Other terms and conditions as slip and original policy;
    4. The quotation is valid for XX working days;
    5. No binding until ceding company confirm our offer;
    6. PPW 120 days.

  Waiting for your confirmation."
  - *Confirmation*
    "We are pleased to confirm your XX% of 100% share for captioned, subject to the following conditions and terms:
    1. No loss until binding XXX's share (2016. X.X);
    2. Total Deduction XX% (tax included);
    3. Other terms and conditions as slip and original policy;
    4. PPW 120 days.

Final slip will be provided soon."

(6) The formation of facultative reinsurance contract shall be subject to the written or electronic confirmations of the parties to the reinsurance business.

(7) Upon the formation of the facultative reinsurance contract or original policy, the ceding party shall, in accordance with the final insurance and reinsurance conditions, issue the official reinsurance policy (including the slip and other business conditions regulating the rights and obligations of parties to the reinsurance contract) and bills (hard or electronic copy) to the ceded party, and require the latter to sign a copy. The official facultative reinsurance contract shall be signed and stamped by the authorized representatives of each party.

§2. Formation of Reinsurance Treaty

1031. In terms of formation of reinsurance treaty, section 2 of *the Management Rules for Reinsurance of Property Insurance Companies* issued by the CBIRC provides a useful guidance as follows:

(1) An insurance company shall formulate reinsurance treaties based on an overall consideration of its business composition, risk profile, aggregate liability, capital funds, net assets, market strategies, and other factors.

(2) An insurance company shall attach great importance to the formulation of clauses of reinsurance treaties and consult and reach an agreement with the reinsurer on main clauses before the reinsurance treaty officially comes into force. The property insurance company shall enter the reinsurance treaty business information into its business and financial systems no later than ten working days after confirmation of the treaty. Unless the property insurance company and the reinsurer have agreed in writing on an extension, both parties shall finish signing the official reinsurance treaty within three months after the reinsurance treaty officially comes into force.

(3) The final treaty conditions shall be determined by both parties to reinsurance upon consultations under the principle of free will; however, the treaty conditions shall not violate the laws, regulations and regulatory provisions of the countries or regions where both parties to reinsurance are located.

(4) In the formulation of a proportional treaty, particular attention shall be paid to the reinsurance scope, treaty type, treaty term, underwriting ability, limit per accident (both parties to reinsurance shall decide whether to include such a clause according to the actual circumstances), reinsurance commission fee, accounting clauses, exceptions, errors and omissions, treaty statements, treaty amendment and termination, the handling of unearned premiums and undue liability, scope of territory, jurisdiction of courts, and arbitration.

(5) In the formulation of a non-proportional treaty, particular attention shall be paid to the reinsurance scope, treaty term, starting point for compensation, and the maximum underlying retention on the basis of the insured amount or liability limit, the maximum limit of protective liability, the stratification of liability limit, premium rate, liability recovery times, treaty type (such as risk

excess, accident excess, and excess of loss ratio), definition for each accident in excess of compensation, exceptions, scope of territory, jurisdiction of courts, and arbitration.

(6) A property insurance company shall select qualified reinsurers to actively make reinsurance arrangements after determining the conditions of its own reinsurance treaty. When making arrangements on the proportional reinsurance treaty, the property insurance company shall effectively avoid the passive retention of treaty liability that shall be otherwise ceded as caused by incomplete reinsurance. Incomplete reinsurance means that the sum of the received shares as confirmed by the reinsurers is less than the maximum share of the treaty that shall be ceded.

(7) In uncompleted reinsurance, the automatic treaty underwriting ability of the property insurance company shall be the maximum treaty underwriting ability multiplied by the reinsurance completion proportion. The underwriting ability for the part that has not been ceded in the treaty shall not be regarded as the effective treaty underwriting ability of the property insurance company.

Chapter 3. Obligations of the Insurer (Reinsured)

§1. Obligation to Pay Reinsurance Premium

1032. The obligation to pay reinsurance premium is probably the most fundamental obligation on the part of the insurer.

The ways of performing and the legal consequences of non-performing of the obligation may refer to stipulations regulating the relationships between the applicant and insurer in Part II, Chapter 4, §1.

§2. Obligation to Disclose

1033. By Article 5 of *the Reinsurance Provisions*, when carrying on reinsurance business, the insurer, insurance associations and insurance broker shall observe the principle of prudence and the duty of utmost good faith.

The most important aspect of duty of utmost good faith is the duty to disclose. By Article 29(2) of the IL, at the request of the reinsurer, the reinsurance cedent shall disclose to the reinsurer in writing the liability borne by the reinsurance cedent and other circumstances of the original insurance policy. Article 15 of *the Reinsurance Provisions* also provides that the reinsurance cedent shall disclose to the reinsurer in writing the material information which has an impact upon the pricing of reinsurance and reinsurance conditions. It is suggested that those circumstances or information mainly include the material circumstances relating to the original insurance, such as the conditions of the applicant, insured and beneficiary, the subject matter of insurance, the insured value, the insured amount, the premium, the insurance period, the risks and exclusions, the payment of indemnities or insurance benefits, etc.

§3. Obligation to Keep Confidentiality

1034. By Article 6 of *the Reinsurance Provisions*, the reinsurance ceding company has the obligation to keep confidentiality regarding the business secrets known in the course of carrying on reinsurance business.

§4. Obligation to Provide Material Information after the Conclusion of Reinsurance Contract

1035. By Article 15 of *the Reinsurance Provisions*, after the conclusion of reinsurance contract, the reinsurance cedent shall promptly provide the information which has a significant impact upon the establishment of reinsurer's reserve and advance payment to the reinsurer, such as major claims information and claims reserve, etc.

§5. OBLIGATION TO ACCEPT THE ACCOUNT CHECK

1036. The reinsurance contract usually provides that the insurer has the obligation to accept the account check in relation to the ceding business conducted by the reinsurer at any time during the usual office hour and at any place, the costs and expenses of checking shall be borne by the insurer.

Chapter 4. Obligations of the Reinsurer

§1. Obligation to Pay Indemnities

1037. Upon the occurrence of insured event, in the light of contractual privity, the insurer of the original insurance contract shall pay the indemnities to the insured or beneficiary in the first place, then it can require the reinsurer to pay indemnities in accordance with the reinsurance contract.

§2. Obligation to Pay Commissions

1038. The reinsurance contract usually provides that the reinsurer shall pay certain amount of commissions to the insurer (reinsured). In proportional reinsurance business, the commissions may consist of ceding commissions and pure benefit commissions.

Both kinds of commissions are the remunerations paid by the reinsurer to the insurer. However, the pure benefit commissions are based upon the profits obtained under the reinsurance contract. From the perspective of the insurer, it is a kind of profit allocation made by the reinsurer.

§3. Obligation to Keep Confidentiality

1039. By Article 6 of *the Reinsurance Provisions*, the reinsurance ceded company also has the obligation to keep confidentiality regarding the business secrets known in the course of carrying on reinsurance business.

Chapter 5. Typical Clauses in Reinsurance Contract

1040. In order to enhance business efficiency, reinsurance companies usually prepare a full set of standard clauses to deal with different reinsurance business. Although details may vary, generally, a typical reinsurance contract may contain the following common clauses:

(1) *The parties to the reinsurance contract:* this clause usually stipulates the name, address and contact details of the reinsured and reinsurer.
(2) *The duration of the reinsurance contract:* this clause usually stipulates the policy term of the reinsurance contract: the term of non-proportional reinsurance contract is usually one year; the term of proportional reinsurance contract is usually irregular.
(3) *The business clause:* this clause usually stipulates the type of reinsurance contract, the type of business (marine reinsurance, fire reinsurance, etc.), the geographical area (global, national or regional, etc.).
(4) *Exemptions:* this clause usually stipulates the risks and liabilities which will not be borne by the reinsurer.
(5) *Follow the fortune clause:* this clause usually stipulates that a claim settlement decision made by the ceding company shall automatically apply to the reinsurer under the premise that the ceding company determines a loss with due diligence according to insurance clauses. The reinsurer's compensation liability shall be limited to the scope of insurance liability prescribed in the original insurance policy and the reinsurance contract, excluding the bad debt, bankruptcy, and other financial risks of the ceding company as well as ex gratia compensation (voluntary compensation made by the ceding company though aware that it has no actual compensation liability) without the approval of the reinsurance company. This clause usually finds its place in facultative proportional reinsurance. Article 20 of *the Reinsurance Provisions* expressly provides that the reinsurer shall observe the principle of "follow the fortune" when handling the reinsurance claim, unless otherwise agreed or the payment is ex gratia. After receiving and reviewing the claim documents, if there is no doubt, the reinsurer shall usually confirm the claim in five working days and sign the claim payment and recovery bill in a timely manner.
(6) *Errors and omissions clause:* this clause usually states if the errors, omissions or delays are caused by the negligence of the reinsured, the reinsured shall promptly notify the reinsurer and correct the mistake in a timely manner.
(7) *Reinsurance premium clause:* this clause usually stipulates the basis and method of calculation of the reinsurance premium, and the taxes and other expenses that are payable by the reinsurer to reinsured.
(8) *Reinsurance commission clause:* this clause usually stipulates the method of calculating and paying the commission to the reinsured by the reinsurer.
(9) *Reinsurance claim clause:* this clause usually stipulates that after paying the insured under the original insurance contract, the insurer (reinsured) shall notify the reinsurer in a timely manner. In the event of heavy losses, the direct insurer may require the reinsurer to make a cash payment.

(10) *Accounting clause:* this clause usually stipulates the issues regarding the preparation, delivery and financial settlement of reinsurance accounts.

(11) *Dispute resolution clause:* it is common to choose arbitration as a mechanism to resolve the dispute. If it is so chosen, the clause shall stipulate the scope, seat, institution, procedure and legal effect of arbitration. As reinsurance business is usually international, the applicable law shall usually be chosen by the parties in the clause too. If the parties choose litigation as a mechanism to resolve the dispute and the dispute is domestic, by Article 26 of *the Civil Procedure Law*, a lawsuit brought on reinsurance contract dispute shall be under the jurisdiction of the people's court of the place where the defendant has its domicile.

(12) *Termination clause:* this clause usually stipulates the procedure and method to terminate the reinsurance contract.

Chapter 6. Reinsurance Claims

1041. As to the management of claims, it is established that both parties to reinsurance shall conduct claim management strictly in accordance with the agreed reinsurance conditions, and no party shall for any reason refuse or delay the fulfillment of responsibilities such as issuing loss advice, providing claim materials and refunding indemnity.

1042. In proportional reinsurance, the ceding company shall calculate the refunded payment on reinsurance ceded according to the reinsurance proportion confirmed by both parties to reinsurance, and shall not readjust the reinsurance plan, including the reinsurance proportion at the time of payment refund, except for correcting any reinsurance error or omission.

In non-proportional reinsurance, if any accident or catastrophe lasts for a period exceeding the time prescribed in the treaty for an accident or catastrophe, the ceding company shall, when calculating the payment refund amount, select the proper accident or catastrophe time slot according to treaty clauses, and the insurance losses that occurred at a time outside the selected time slot shall not be included in the reinsurance treaty for refund.

1043. In facultative reinsurance business, if there is any special clause in the contract (such as the claims control clause or claims cooperation clause), the ceding company shall, despite the size of losses in a claim, immediately notify the reinsurer of the claim according to the provisions of the reinsurance contract after learning the occurrence of the claim, notify the reinsurer of the claim settlement process in a timely manner, provide the relevant claim materials, and cooperate with the reinsurer in carrying out on-site investigations according to the provisions of the reinsurance contract. The ceding company shall actively communicate and reach a consensus with the reinsurer on the claim settlement plan in the claim settlement process, and avoid difficulties in indemnity refund after the close of a case as caused by the inconsistent claim settlement opinions of both parties to reinsurance.

1044. For an insurance accident with the possibility to recover compensation, the ceding company shall actively recover compensation from the liable party and notify the reinsurer of the recovery progress in a timely manner. The ceding company shall, after a successful recovery, refund the recovered compensation which belongs to the reinsurer in a timely manner.

Selected Bibliography

Fan, J. & Wang, J. & Zhang, L., *Insurance Law*, Beijing: Law Press, 2017.

Li, Y., *Insurance Law*, Beijing: Law Press, 2019.

Taiwan Insurance Institute, *English-Chinese Dictionary of Insurance*, Beijing: Law Press, 2014.

SPC's Civil Adjudication Tribunal No. 2, *Guidance on the Trial of Insurance Cases*, Beijing: Law Press, 2015.

SPC's Civil Adjudication Tribunal No. 2, *Interpretation and Application of Judicial Interpretation II of the Insurance Law*, Beijing: People's Court Press, 2013.

SPC's Civil Adjudication Tribunal No. 2, *Interpretation and Application of Judicial Interpretation III of the Insurance Law*, Beijing: People's Court Press, 2015.

SPC's Civil Adjudication Tribunal No. 2, *Interpretation and Application of Judicial Interpretation IV of the Insurance Law*, Beijing: People's Court Press, 2018.

SPC's Draft Group of Judicial Interpretation of Insurance Law, *Interpretation and Application of the Articles of Chapter of Insurance Contract in the Insurance Law*, Beijing: China Legal Publishing House, 2010.

Wang, J., *Collection of Judicial Rules in the Insurance Cases*, Beijing: Law Press, 2016.

Zhu, N., *Property and Liability Insurance*, Beijing: Renmin University Press, 2016.

Zou, H., *Insurance Law*, Beijing: Social Sciences Academic Press, 2017.

Selected Bibliography

Index

The numbers here refer to paragraph numbers.

www.ingramcontent.com/pod-product-compliance
Ingram Content Group UK Ltd.
Pitfield, Milton Keynes, MK11 3LW, UK
UKHW020131290926
15471UKWH00003B/410

9 789403 533230